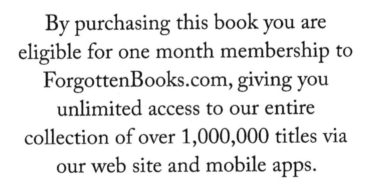

ISBN 978-0-260-04646-8
PIBN 10924302

FRONT PANEL.

BACK PANEL.

BARCLAY BROS.,

OWNERS OF

Dark and Light Granite Quarries.

SPECIALTIES :

Vaults and Large Monuments.

Pneumatic Surfacing Machine.

Pneumatic Tools.

Column Cutting Machinery and

Polishing Mill.

SIDE PANEL.

SIDE PANEL.

ROBERT BURNS MONUMENT,

Unveiled at Barre, Vt., July 21, 1899.

Monument and Statue cut entirely from Barre Granite.

Designed by William Barclay, and executed by
Barclay Bros., in their own sheds at Barre, Vt.

Bottom base of Monument, 8 feet square.

Total Height, 27 feet 10 inches.

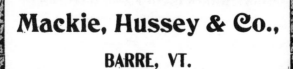

CROSS BROS.,
NORTHFIELD, VT.

MANUFACTURERS OF

Mausoleums, Tombs,

AND

Large * Monumental * Work

— FROM BARRE OR OTHER GRANITES.

A LOW-PRICED MAUSOLEUM.

The accompanying cut illustrates a low-priced Mausoleum which we recently erected in the cemetery at Worcester, Mass. It contains twelve catacombs and plenty of room in the vestibule. The floor is of mosaic, the face plates and door polished marble with standard bronze fittings. Two stained glass windows with bronze grill, sash and also bronze gate. The roof is all in one piece and absolutely water proof, a modern up-to-date mausoleum for a very little money. Would be pleased to correspond with any who have a prospective client. Our plant is second to none in the trade and we have every convenience known to the trade for producing work of a higher grade and we respectfully solicit a share of your patronage.

CROSS BROTHERS,   **NORTHFIELD, VT.**

GRANITE

ENTERED AT THE BOSTON POST OFFICE AS SECOND-CLASS MAIL MATTER.

Vol. X.   BOSTON, MASS., JANUARY 1, 1900.   No. 1

A. M. HUNT, EDITOR.

Published Monthly in the Interests of the Producer
Manufacturer, and Retailer of Granite as used
for Monumental or Building Purposes.

Terms of Subscription

To ANY PART OF THE UNITED STATES OR CANADA:
One copy, one year   -   -   -   - $1.00, in advance.
One copy, six months   -   -   -   75 cents, in advance.
ADVERTISING RATES FURNISHED UPON APPLICATION.

A. M. HUNT & CO., Publishers,
131 DEVONSHIRE STREET,   -   -   BOSTON, MASS.

Editorials

HAPPY New Year to all advertisers and subscribers prospective or present; the past year has
been one of remarkable prosper-
ity to the granite business. Not only has it been
marked with an increasing demand for monumental
work in granite, but monuments have averaged larger
and more elaborate than ever before. Carved work
has been the feature which shows the greatest amount
of improvement. This has been brought about by the
general use of pneumatic tools, and no shed is considered complete without a pneumatic tool equipment.
There never has been the demand for monuments at
this season or any other season of the year that there
is at the present time. This has been brought about
to some extent by the demands of the cutters for
shorter hours and more pay, which possibly means an
advance in price after March or May 1st, and retail
dealers are taking advantage of the present prices and
placing orders, as it is generally believed that there
will be an increase in prices. Even if the cutters had

not made their demand an increase in price would
naturally follow on account of the increased cost of
material which is used in the cutting, polishing and
boxing of granite work. We drew the attention of
the trade to the state of affairs in our August issue as
follows: "We do not wish to unnecessarily alarm the
trade, but we should certainly advise the retail monumental dealer, if possible, to close all contracts at the
earliest moment, so as to secure the benefit of present
prices as, in our opinion, if prosperity continues, there
will be a change in the price demanded for monumental work by the manufacturers, made necessary by
the demands of the cutters and the increase in price of
material which is used in the cutting, polishing,
quarrying and boxing of granite. Of course it is impossible to state at the present time just what the
cutters will demand, but we claim that it is always well
to be on the safe side, and we believe the safe side for
the retail dealer is to place all contracts possible and
have them completed between now and March 1,
1900." A large number of dealers have taken advantage of the warning and are ordering their monumental work ahead of the usual time. This, together
with the prosperous times all over the country, served
to place the manufacturers in a position where it has
been necessary, in many cases, to refuse orders. Following are some of the demands of the granite cutters:
"Aside from the eight-hour day and $3 for minimum
rate, there shall be a pay day ever Friday, and workmen shall be paid in full up to the last previous week.
All over-time shall be paid for once and one-third. All
granite cutters working outside and exposed to the
weather shall receive twenty-five cents per day extra."

Another matter of importance in the past year has
been the endeavor to form a syndicate of the quarries
at Barre, Vt., and Quincy, Mass. As has been stated
in previous issue, the Barre attempt failed on account
of the lack of funds to carry out the options at the
time they expired. The Quincy syndicate is still in
prospect and according to the latest news nothing
definite has been done, although it is said that some
money has recently been paid to the quarry owners in
order to renew the expiring options. The matter of
forming the combination, which means the payment
of the necessary money to the quarry owners, has been
delayed so long that, as one of the quarry owners
state, "We have lost faith in it." The only cloud in the
atmosphere is the prospect of trouble with the cutters
when the present bill of prices expire. This, you will

recall, was the state of affairs one year ago. At that
time the difficulty was settled without a strike and we
have faith to believe that this will be the final result
this year. Settlement of the matter for the manufacturers has been left to the New England Granite
Manufacturers' Association, which association represents all other associations. Among the retail dealers,
reports from all over the country show that prosperity
rules and this has been further proved by the number
of orders placed at the manufacturing centres. The
number of failures among retail dealers reported for
the past twelve months is 24, as against 23 reported
for 1898. They are divided as follows: Connecticut,
one; California, two; Illinois, three; Kentucky, one;
Maine, two; Missouri, two; Minnesota, one; New
Hampshire, three; New York, five; Pennsylvania,
four; and one quarry owner and wholesale dealer at
Barre, Vt. From our own standpoint we have had a
remarkably successful year. One year ago we en-
larged our publication to the present size and changed
the number of issues from two a month to one. We
have been very much gratified by its success in the
new form. Subscriptions have more than doubled in
number, and we shall endeavor during the coming year
to add new features, thus giving additional value.

HERE is a question which we would like
to ask in connection with the demand of
the workmen that eight hours shall constitute a day's work, etc. As we understand it, this demand is a national one and is embodied in the constitution of the Granite Cutters'
National Union; in fact, the members of the local
union say that they cannot settle this matter themselves, but settlement will have to be made with their
headquarters. In the circular recently issued by the
secretary of the Granite Cutters' National Union and
sent to all manufacturers is the following: "It will
suffice at the present time to again call attention of
employers that all agreements which have been entered into by our union or any of its branches and in
conflict with said eight hour day, $3 minimum rate
shall terminate on or before May 1, 1900, at which
date, at the latest, said minimum goes into full effect."
The present bill of prices expires at Quincy, Mass., on
March 1st, and at Barre, Vt., on the same date. This
being the case, will these two points be allowed to
make a settlement at that date, or can an agreement
be entered into so that they can work under the old
bill of prices until May 1st, when it is evident that all
bills now in force expire. It would be manifestly unfair for the manufacturers at these two points to be
obliged to work under any advance, if advance was
granted, for two months before other points found it
necessary under the existing bill to make a settlement. We should consider this a very important matter and worthy of some attention from the manufacturers. Another matter of vital importance to
manufacturers and we should also say to the workmen,
and should be absolutely insisted upon, is the time for
which the bill which may be settled upon should run.
Ever since our connection with the business there has
always been prospects of trouble ahead. It interferes
with the year's business, as manufacturers are unable
to make prices, and therefore a great many orders are

cancelled on this account. Five years should be the
shortest time for the bill to run. If the present demands of the workmen are conceded, there are prospects of another competitor from across the water, as
the demands of the workmen and the increased price
of material brings the cost of producing a monument
fully up to the fifty per cent duties which were placed
upon imported granite, thus doing away with the
work put in upon the tariff question.

Stone Workers and Their Unions.

It is not out of place at this time to give the retail
dealers a general idea as to the different classes of
workmen in the granite industry. There are three
general classes of workmen employed in stone working: quarrymen who quarry the stone and receive on
an average 16 cents per hour; paving cutters who are
paid by the thousand for the number of square blocks
cut, with which we all are familiar, used mainly in
paving streets; and granite cutters, or stone cutters as
they are commonly called.

The quarrymen and paving cutters have a union of
their own, known as the Stone Workers' Union in
this section of the granite industry, and it was with this
Stone Workers' Union that the trouble of last summer
with the Rockport Granite Company on Cape Ann occurred. That was amicably adjusted.

The stone cutters are most skilled workmen; it re-
quiring a period of apprenticeship of three years to begin to be a stone cutter, and then the trade is in its in-
fancy, as far as being mastered is concerned. A first
class stone cutter is expected to cut from diagrams
furnished by the foreman, any class of work
from "rock-faced ashler" to the finest "bush-ham-
mered" work of 12 cuts. Each man is timed upon his
work, and the man who does the most work in the
best manner in a given time is the one longest in the
employ of the company.

One can readily see that this class of work necessarily commands a higher rate of compensation than
that of the quarryman or paving cutter, aside from the
fact that the union of the stone cutters, known as the
Granite Cutters' National Union, is one of the oldest
in the country. Its branches are scattered throughout the United States. Its chief officer consists of a
secretary, Mr. James Duncan, whose headquarters are
located at 200 Summer street, Boston, and there the
organ of the stone cutters is published monthly. In
this Granite Cutters' Journal is always found a list of
the yards in different places employing union men,
statements as to where it is advisable for stone cutters
to keep away from, list of members of the order in
good standing travelling with a clear card, and lists of
members who are travelling without clear cards.

In every union yard in the United States is a member of the local branch of the order, known as the
"shop steward," whose duty is to approach every
new man employed as a stone cutter and inquire for
his card. If he has it, well and good; if not, and he
can give no satisfactory account of its whereabouts
his case is investigated and if he has a clear record he
is taken into the union at a normal fee. But in case
his record is unclean, a fine, graded to the enormity
of his offence to the union is imposed, and this must

1. METHOD OF TRANSPORTATION.   3. THE SHAMROCK.   5. POSTOFFICE.
2. COTTAGE AND QUARRY VIEW.   4. THE ABERDEEN.   6. QUARRY VIEW.

teresting island along the whole Maine coast, if you did but know its history.

Now and then there is the desultory click of a hammer, but for the most part silence reigns supreme. There are two or three families there this summer and a small amount of stone is being cut for a public building in New York, but on the crest of the hill stands the old Shamrock House and clustering round its base are a score of smaller buildings, weather-beaten and slowly going to pieces. The grass grows lush in front of the company store and the bell in the cupola hangs silent.

On the side where schooners once waited their turn for a load of stone the lobster buoys wash back and forth with the tide, and the old wharf where the vessels berthed is rotten and gone. Back a few rods from the million dollars—a record which has never been equalled on the Atlantic seaboard.

From its quarries came the stone that built the treasury building at Washington and the massive postoffice in New York city. The stone was not only quarried here but was finished, ready for the builder, in the cutting sheds that once filled every available foot of space on the island.

So cramped for room were they in those early days that many of the workmen had to sleep on the mainland three miles away, and row back and forth to their work. The place grew up almost by magic and its population went in a twinkling when work ceased.

That was more than twenty years ago and save for the wear and tear of time things are just as they were left. Frank A. Crockett, who is keeper of the islands for Thomas Dwyer of New York, lives there the year round and for nine years now he has been monarch of all he surveys. It's a lonesome place to be in with the evidences of old-time hustle on every side, next to nothing being done at present. But the keeper has grown used to it and goes about his work every day as regularly as though the thousands were marching into the cutting sheds and the quarries and the clink of the hammer was to be heard, clicking out its olden chorus of cherry music.

The Dix Island Granite Company was a tripartite affair and the shares were owned by Beals, Learned and Dixon.

These three men were interesting figures in the industrial life of Maine at that time. Horace Beals was the prime mover and he was a man of intense energy and wonderful resources. He came to Maine from Connecticut. He had seen hard luck in the state of wooden nutmegs, but it did not discourage him in the least. He was in the granite business there and had quite extensive works at Millstone Point, but they were not always the bright and shining financial success that he could have wished.

He failed once or twice, but this was something which Beals allowed was good for a man. He used to say that a man never knew what there was in him till he had been on his business uppers two or three times. He said that if a man began making money the first thing he was likely to get it into his noddle that it always grew that way and he'd be worse off than ever when he found that it didn't.

(To be Continued.)

Monthly Trade Record.

This department is compiled and edited by the United Mercantile Agency. Subscribers, in accordance with the terms of their contracts are entitled to receive further information relative to the parties hereafter mentioned, upon application to the main office. As the names of many business men who are good will appear herein, subscribers can readily see the importance of making inquiries if interested, previous to taking any action.

ARKANSAS.
Clarksville, *M—Sharyer, S. C., 76.
Imboden, *M—Imboden Marble Works, 76.
DELAWARE.
Wilmington, *M—Davidson, Wm., 105.
GEORGIA.
Dalton—Dalton Marble Works, 50.
Fairburn, *M—Warlick, J. F., 76.
ILLINOIS.
Decatur, *M—Brown & Son, 46.
Fulton, *M—Doran, M. R., 50.
Quincy, *M—Daugherty & Co., 30.
INDIANA.
Alexandria, *M—Brenneman, J. F., 98 $1,000.
Lafayette, *M—Vitts, Jacob J., reported in December issue as 89 should have been 14.
Lebanon, *M—Dooley, Holmes & Co., succeed S. W. Dooley & Co.
Sullivan, *M—Sullivan Marble & Granite Works, 76.
IOWA.
...tionville, *M—Burkhead & Maynard, 76.
. Bluffs, *M—Lewis & Stadler, 64.
.llo, *M—Bateman & Mellholen, 64, J. E. ...n 58.

KENTUCKY.
Cynthiana, *M—Garnett, C. Marble Co., Clark Garnett 93 $500.
MAINE.
Bangor, *M—Fogg, Ambrose, 50-46.
MARYLAND.
Baltimore, *M—Johnson, William H., 78.
MASSACHUSETTS.
Holyoke, *M—Ryan, T. F., 86.
Quincy, GZ—Bizzozero, Ernest, 93 $500.
Worcester, *M—Evans & Co., Arthur M. Evans, 78.
MICHIGAN.
Marine City, *M—Thatcher, E. B., 50.
Standish, *M—Griege, C. C., 76.
MISSOURI.
Hamilton, *M—Moore & Stockton 64, G. W. Moore 58.
MONTANA.
Bozeman, *M—Scott & Nelson 64, W. N. Scott 58.
NEBRASKA.
Brokenbow, *M—Glaze, I. D., 76.
NEW JERSEY.
Hoboken, *M—Riley Bros., 14 $2,781.
Jersey City, *M—Kidder, George R., 14 $1,015.
NEW YORK.
Bath, *M—Wilson, J. B. & Co., 64, J. B. Wilson 58.
Fredonia, *M—Forbes & Cardot, 76.
Mount Vernon, *M—Caterson, Robert, 50.
Oswego, *M—Fisher, C. W., 50.
Sandy Creek, *M—Sherman & Reed succeed Sherman & Hollis.
Wolcott, *M—Lawrence, J. E., 70.
OHIO.
Cleveland, *M—Sears Monumental Works, 50, and T. Fred Smith, 105.
Clyde, *M—Hughes Marble & Granite Works, 70.
Hillsboro, *M—Harsha Monument Co., 50.
Montpelier, *M—Weaver, W. O., deed $1,000.
Warsaw, *M—Lowery, J. M., 76.
PENNSYLVANIA.
Butler, *M—Renno, F. M., 20.
Chester, *M—Rawnsley & Oglesby 64, P. P. Oglesby 58.
Lancaster, *M—Flick & Killinger 64.
RHODE ISLAND.
Westerly, GZ—Keleher & Flynn 64, Maurice Flynn 58.
TENNESSEE.
Knoxville, *M—Carpenter, H., 76.
Knoxville, *M—Collins, John, 76.
VERMONT.
Barre, GZ—Abbiati, E., 76.
Barre, GZ—Bianchi, L. & Co., 76.
Barre, GZ—Cavana & Co., 76.
Barre, GZ—Comolli & Co., 76.
Barre, GZ—Fontana & Bro., 76.
East Barre, GZ—Gibson & Zepf, 76.
Hardwick, GZ—Arnold Bros. succeed Arnold & Wiles.
Hardwick, GQ—Webber, H. E., 76.
North Derby, *M—Moir & Frost, 76.
WEST VIRGINIA.
Huntington, *M—Mitchell, M. V. & Son, 86 to F. F. Swanson.
WISCONSIN.
Oshkosh, *M—Heim, Charles, 50.
Plymouth, *M—Nickel & Kegler 64, G. Kegler 58.

Quincy Notes

Among the retail dealers recently visiting Quincy were the following: A. R. Baxter, secretary; Alexander McDonald, Trenton, N. J.; J. M. Miller, Iowa City, Ia.; Mr. O'Brien, of O'Brien & Davine, Westfield, Mass. and Charles F. Pool, Waverly, New York.

Quincy granite manufacturers have been patient waiters for the frequently promised boom in their particular industry, but it was not until this year that they have experienced anything like the good old times the pioneers in the granite business were wont to talk about. The volume of business done in Quincy this year has been immense. True it is that but few of what might be termed large and costly monuments have been cut, but there has been a raft of medium sized work turned out, and today most of the firms are nearly as busy as they were in the height of the season. The early months of the year gave promise of a good volume of business if the labor trouble that was then threatening could be averted. The first of March, however, found the manufacturers and cutters still at loggerheads over the bill of prices, the principal bone of contention being the minimum price that should be paid for a day's work. An agreement not having been reached by the first of the month the cutters went out. Both parties realized that a long struggle meant the ruination of the year's business, and efforts were made to reach some form of an agreement. Frequent meetings of the two committees were held, the state board of arbitration being present at some of them. The small committees were unable to reach an agreement and then both committees were increased to seventeen members each, and on the night of March 11 these two committees got down to business, and when the meeting adjourned, during the early morning hours of the following day, an agreement had been reached, and on the following Tuesday work was resumed in the yards, although in some cases with a reduced force, owing to the enforcement of the weekly payment law and the increased minimum price per hour.

From that time on to the present time business has been booming. The weekly payment clause has worked fairly well, although it has been somewhat of a hardship upon some of the smaller manufacturers. It is, of course, difficult to get at just the amount of finished work shipped during the year, for at the railroad terminals in making up the tonnage each month no distinction is made between rough and finished stock. It can, however, be estimated fairly accurate; for, as a rule, the larger part of the rough stock shipped is sent from the Quincy Quarry Railroad and comparatively little from the West Quincy or Quincy Adams terminal. The amount of granite shipped from each terminal is published every month in Granite, and from these figures we find that up to the first of December there was shipped from the three terminals above mentioned 245,800,647 pounds, two-thirds of which was finished stock. This does not include the amount transported in teams or by water, of which there is a considerable amount, and of which no estimate can be obtained.

The figures for the month of December cannot be given at this writing, but based upon the amount shipped the first half of the month, it is estimated that the December shipments will be fully 18,300,000 pounds, which will swell the total shipments for the year to 264,100,347. This is an increase of 49,817,400 pounds over the previous year. The following tables give the shipments from each of the terminals for each month during the years 1898 and 1899:

GRANITE SHIPMENTS FOR 1899.

Month.	Quincy Adams.	West Quincy.	Quarry Railroad.
January,	1,523,531	4,586,160	13,336,170
February,	1,095,600	2,333,960	5,683,800
March,	5,083,890	6,489,040	12,792,190
April,	5,631,448	3,744,420	6,230,340
May,	10,023,556	5,123,805	12,729,560
June,	9,181,839	5,242,260	13,562,850
July,	5,842,890	4,989,990	12,165,300
August,	6,376,753	4,263,430	14,890,930
September,	4,289,763	6,031,890	13,576,540
October,	4,884,064	11,041,780	9,610,075
November,	4,701,443	9,713,320	9,028,060
*December,	4,300,000	4,500,000	9,500,000
Totals,	62,934,477	68,060,055	133,105,815

*Approximate.

GRANITE SHIPMENTS FOR 1898.

Month.	Quincy Adams.	West Quincy.	Quarry Railroad.
January,	1,434,497	2,737,845	5,974,332
February,	1,615,090	1,804,930	6,736,780
March,	3,225,770	3,716,600	9,183,714
April,	4,717,307	4,665,150	8,999,590
May,	8,022,645	6,001,990	7,019,900
June,	3,861,880	2,901,220	6,166,210
July,	3,413,202	3,339,795	9,445,440
August,	6,059,531	3,703,040	11,461,470
September,	6,490,923	4,827,800	13,579,950

BEATTIE . QUINCY .

A SUGGESTION FOR CARVING.

October,	5,211,228	5,711,500	14,805,228
November,	4,295,618	6,907,285	10,805,650
*December,	5,200,000	4,000,000	9,000,000
Totals,	53,547,691	50,317,155	113,178,264

*Approximate.

During the early part of the year a scheme was started to consolidate all of the quarries throughout the city, and in this matter readers of GRANITE have been kept well informed of the situation. The plan has as yet not reached maturity, and the time it will have reached that stage and be successfully launched, is as much a matter of doubt now as it has been for some months past. At times during these months it has looked as though the bubble would burst. Then it would look as though the scheme was an assured fact. The general impression among granite men at this writing is that it will go through all right, the belief being based upon the fact that too much money has already been expended in developing the scheme to have it fail. Representatives of the bankers, who are supposed to be furnishing a large part of the money, have been in town this month and have made a thorough inspection of the quarries, which it is prepared to unite; and rumor says that they were very much pleased with them, and that they would make a favorable report to their superiors. Mr. Swithin, who is engineering the scheme, says that the syndicate is sure to go through and that it will be only a matter of short time before everything will be transferred, and that the delay is caused by one of the New York men being away. Just what effect this syndicate, when formed, will have upon the granite business in Quincy is a matter of speculation.

In common with other granite centres throughout New England the Quincy Granite Manufacturers' Association received their notice from the Cutters' Union December 1, that after March 1, 1900, the minimum price per day should be $3 for an eight-hour day. This notice was in the form of a demand, and the only answer admissable was yes or no, the cutters claiming that the matter was out of their hands and was therefore not subject to arbitration. Accompanying this demand was the changes desired in the price list for piece work. These, as a rule, called for an increase of thirty-five per cent, so as to equalize the minimum

price for day work. No action has been taken in regard to either matter as yet, and as far as the demand for $3 and eight hours are concerned, the manufacturers are practically in the same position as the cutters; that is, this matter is in the hands of the New England Association, and the local association has no power to act.

Just what the ultimate result will be is not known, but it is hard to see now how it can be otherwise than a suspension of business March 1, or at the latest May 1, which is said to be the date fixed for the new law to go into effect by the National Cutters' Association. At any rate the outlook is anything but bright, and a canvass among the manufacturers find them all refusing work that cannot be completed before March 1.

The general opinion of granite men is that the market is in no condition to stand an increase of thirty-five or forty per cent, and that even if the manufacturers said yes to the demand, there would be little work. A well known Quincy manufacturer, in conversation with your correspondent, said that if he had his way he would give the cutters all they demanded, feeling sure that the result would be so unsatisfactory that the cutters would be glad to return to the present minimum.

His explanation of why he thinks so is, that if the demand is not granted a strike results, and the men all being out will draw strike pay and will make a long fight. On the other hand, if the demand is granted, there will be but little work, as the market will not stand the increased price. The result will be that, instead of a firm giving employment to three gangs, one will be sufficient to do all the work. In other words less than one-third of the present force of cutters would be required to get out the work. There would therefore be a large force of unemployed cutters who not only could not get work, but as there was no strike could not draw strike pay, and in a short time they would become so jealous of those fortunate enough to have work that the whole thing would be bursted and a return made to something like the present bill.

The general impression seems to be that the manufacturers would be perfectly willing to grant the men an eight-hour day with the present minimum.

Joss Bros. Co. report that they have work enough on hand to keep their gang at work until the first of

March, although, as a rule, it is medium sized work. They have recently made improvements to their plant, which enables them to handle stone more readily. A twenty-five foot addition was built to their polishing plant, which permits a team to drive in so that the stone can be loaded or unloaded without handling by a travelling derrick, which runs to all parts of their mill. They are also arranging to operate the travelling derrick in their yard by steam power.

Granite shipments for the month of November fell off a little from all points. This is not surprising, considering the time of the year. As a whole, shipments have; held up remarkably well, which, in a great measure, is due to the unusually favorable weather; and if it only continues to hold good, this year's shipments will surpass any other year in Quincy, as far as known. As it is, as will be seen by the table of shipments for the year published elsewhere, this year has been the banner year for shipments. The total shipments for the month of November was 23,442,823 pounds, or 2,093,096 pounds less than the previous month, which was unusually large. The November shipments were as follows: West Quincy, 9,713,320 pounds; Quarry Railroad, 9,028,060 pounds; Quincy Adams, 4,701,443 pounds.

It is a true saying that quality counts in the end, and one of the busiest firms in Quincy today are Kavanagh Bros. & Company. They make a specialty of the highest grade of monumental work in Westerly granite and Tennessee marble. No better work has ever been shipped from New England than that which is being turned out by this firm. They know just what the best dealers want, and are furnishing it to them. They have shipped several large and very artistic Westerly granite monuments during the season just closed, and have at the present time several very finely carved monuments in process.

W. T. Spargo is as busy as ever, and has about all the work he can get out before the first of March. His work is largely of the medium size kind, although he has a few jobs that are larger than the ordinary run. Among his new work are four ledgers or grave covers, which are to be cut of dark Quincy stock, and all polished. The size of the bases are 7-6 x 3-6 and the ledger 6-6 x 2-6.

McGillvray & Jones are hard at work finishing up several large jobs, of which mention has been made in previous issues of GRANITE. They also have an order for another large tomb job, which will be cut from Deer Island, Me., granite. They report that they are taking no orders that cannot be completed before the first of March, as there is no knowing what the price will be then.

Alexander Marnock & Co. and the Merry Mount Granite Co. report that work remains about the same with them this month as last. They have considerable work on hand, but could do a little more if they had the orders. Their work is largely of the medium size

kind, although they have some that is above the ordinary size, upon which there is considerable polishing.

Herbert W. Beattie, the modeller, is at work upon a number of models to be cast in bronze.

Quincy granite men will, as usual, be well represented in next year's Quincy city council. Past city councils have proved them to be valuable additions to this body.

Fuller, Foley & Co. report that business continues good with them, and that it is too bad that labor trouble should threaten the trade just when business seemed likely to revive and flourish. The outlook they do not consider bright for they do not see how the market will stand the increase in price that must be demanded, if the demand of the cutters is granted.

M. H. Rice, a Kansas City granite dealer, has been in town this month, and has placed a large number of orders for stock monuments, to be delivered on or before March 1. To ship the amount he has contracted for will require at least four or five cars. Mr. Rice says in regard to his large purchase, that the price of finished monuments will be increased at least thirty-three per cent after March 1, and he is buying for speculation.

A call at the works of Deacon Bros., Joseph Walker of the Aberdeen Granite Works, and T. F. Mannex, brought forth the same report: nothing special, but a lot of medium work. All of these firms are taking advantage of the excellent weather, to rush their orders along so as to have everything cleared up by March 1.

A. Malnati has recently secured the contract for a duplicate of the Nichols monument, which is one of the most elaborate memorials erected in Forest Hills cemetery, Boston. It consists of three bases, die, plinth and cap. The die, plinth and cap are elaborately carved. Mr. Malnati states that he can cut in granite any design that can be cut in marble, and it would certainly seem so, as they have finished during the past year many elegantly carved monuments which it would only seem possible to execute in marble.

McIntosh & Sons have improved their plant by the purchase of an air compressor and engine for operating it and the derrick. This is one of the many improvements which this firm have made to their plant during past years.

John Horgan, sculptor, who has been for a number of years in the employ of one Quincy firm, recently completed a model for A. M. Deane & Co. of the "Angel of Peace." The figure is finely modeled, the drapery is flowing and easy, the face is full of expression, and the whole figure shows good taste and judgment. It is to be cut in granite standing in front of a rock-faced cross, the extended arm dropping a flower, and when completed will be erected in the cemetery at Lynn, Mass.

Woodbury Granite Company.

Two of the sights in Vermont worth seeing are the granite quarry owned and operated by the Woodbury Granite Company at Woodbury, Vt., and the recently completed plant of Bickford, More & Company, located at Hardwick, Vt. The two companies are entirely distinct, one firm confining itself to quarrying and the other to cutting granite, both being under the management of George H. Bickford, who is a stockholder in both companies; with Allen Ainsworth, sup-

erintendent of the quarry, and J. D. Sargent of the cutting plant. Our illustrations can only convey to the mind a faint idea of the possibilities of the quarry. It might well be considered the quarryman's dream of what a quarry should be, as it is capable of producing any sized block of granite at any time. This can be illustrated from the following order recently received by the company and carried out on time. On November 1st they received the contract for a vault job to be completed on the 20th of the same month. Two of the roof stones measured 17 ft. 3 in. x 5 ft. x 1 ft., and the ridge stone 17 ft. 3 in. x 3 ft. 6 in. x 1 ft. 8 in. The quarry is located ten miles from Hardwick and connected with the cutting shed of Bickford, More & Company, at Hardwick, and the main line of the Boston & Maine railroad by the Hardwick & Woodbury railroad practically owned and operated by the stockholders of the Woodbury Granite Company, thus giving them ample shipping facilities to all points. They place at the disposal of their patrons two large cars built for their special use. Each car is capable of carrying 100,000 pounds, one of them being a short heavy car, built for transporting large blocks, and the other a long car with a slot in the centre capable of carrying a stone 20-0 x 14-0 x 4-0. A stone this size would rest on its edge within ten inches of the track. The railroad is now planning to continue operations throughout the winter, while last winter

that was shut down from December 31 to April 1, thus showing that the business of the railroad is on the increase as the following figures will also show even more forcibly: The gross earnings for the quarter, including the months of September, October and November of this year, are 55 1-2 per cent greater than for the same quarter of 1898. The quarry equipment is not excelled by any in New England, as the following description will prove: A derrick capable of lifting 50 tons operated by steam power both for lifting and turning; a derrick capable of lifting 25 tons operated in the same way, two other smaller derricks operated by steam power, and one of the largest and most powerful locomotive cranes manufactured by the Industrial Works, Bay City, Mich., capable of switching five cars and lifting twelve tons, and is operated on the tracks in any part of the quarry. The quarry is also equipped with steam drills, both large and small sizes, and in fact with everything in the way of machinery to facilitate the quarrying and handling of blocks of granite of any size required. The sheets have been opened up in an unusual manner in the last few months, and they are now at work on four large sheets which lie one above the other. These sheets vary in thickness from twelve feet to twenty-five feet. Among the long breaks that have been made during the past season is one in a sheet fifteen feet in thickness back thirty feet from the edge and two hundred feet long; another fully three hundred feet long, back from the face twelve to fifteen feet and in a sheet from fifteen to twenty feet thick. These breaks can be made at almost any time, and nearly all of them are capable of being extended when required. Beneath the four sheets on which they are now at work is one that will be opened up

Floor shown in picture is top surface of sheet, 15 feet thick, edge of which is shown in our first illustration. It has been worked off fully 200 feet, can be extended at least 300 feet more. The same of the sheet running through the centre of the picture which is 12 to 14 feet thick.

early in the spring in which there has been made a break fully 150 feet long and 20 feet back from the edge. This sheet is over thirty feet thick. Under the

present management the quarry has improved greatly, as the sloping faces have been squared up, and the
quality of the stock shows marked improvement as
they get deeper into the ledge. It runs absolutely free
from iron and other common imperfections. A large
amount of stock has been shipped during the past
year, and at the present time the company is not able
to keep up with its orders, though an average of 3 to 5
car-loads a day has been shipped for many weeks.
Large quantities have been shipped to New York city
and Buffalo for building purposes, besides the stock
required for the vault work and monuments being cut
by Bickford, More & Company. The company has a
large number of orders on hand for winter delivery, as
well as 20,000 feet of stock to be shipped in the rough
in the spring. Operations on the quarry are to be continued throughout the winter, and they are now building a shed over part of the quarry to prevent the possibility of snow stopping operations during the winter
months. There is an increasing demand for Woodbury granite, as indicated by increased shipments from
Hardwick for use in the better grades of monumental
work. The firm of Bickford, More & Company has
nearly completed its plant, which it aims to make one
of the most modern plants in the business. The cutting shed is 200 feet long, 65 feet wide, with wing
67 x 24 feet, the maximum height of the main shed
being 45 feet. In the shed is a travelling crane, which
is the largest ever built by the Lane Manufacturing

Engine room at quarry showing large hoisting engine and turning
gear of the 50-ton derrick shown in second illustration on previous page.

Company, Montpelier, Vt., and is fully capable of
carrying 60 tons. This crane has a clear space below
it of 25 feet, and is therefore capable of handling the
larger class of work to the best advantage. The plant

is also equipped with air compressor, pneumatic tools,
pneumatic stone dressing machine, polishing wheels,
and two saw gangs equipped with Rapid Stone Saw
Company saws. One of the gangs is capable of taking
a block 12-0 x 6-0 x 7-0, and the other a block

Roof stone 17-1 x 13 x 1-6, cut at quarry. Shipped on special car by
H. & W. R. R. and built for the purpose.

8-0 x 8-0 x 7-0. The main machinery is run by a sixty
horse-power electric motor, the compressor being
operated separately by steam from a boiler of seventy
horse-power. The air compressor is one of the largest
size and capable of 225 feet free air per minute. The
shed is heated throughout by steam with eight coils
1 1-4 inch pipe running entirely around it. A spur of
the Hardwick & Woodbury road runs from the
quarry directly into the shed and the firm is thus able
to handle orders for stone of large dimension with
ease and at low expense. This firm has just closed a
contract with the Harrison Granite Company for the
Scranton soldiers' monument. It will stand, when
completed, 87 feet high, surmounted by a bronze
statue 13 feet high. The monument will be octagonal
in shape at the base and will measure forty feet in
diameter. The main shaft is round and will be five
feet in diameter; there are included in this contract
sixteen turned columns thirteen feet long. It will require eight thousand feet of stock, all to be finely axed.
The cap surmounting the main shaft will be cut in one
piece, 7-2 x 7-2 x 5-0. To show how busy the firm is
at the present it is running three full gangs of men
and has put in electric lights to enable it to run on full
time. The Harrison Granite Company, which has
the general contract for the two pedestal jobs for the
Stanton Avenue entrance to Schanley Park at Pittsburg, Pa., has contracted with Bickford, More & Company for these pedestals, the bottom bases of which
will be 12-0 x 9-0 x 1-2, and the dies just received from
the quarry weighed thirty tons each.

"GRANITE," JANUARY, 1900.

BOTTOM BASE . N — T x E — Y x C — R
SECOND BASE . I — Y x R — T x C — A
THIRD BASE . T — C x A — I x Y — I
DIE . . . . . R — Y x A — 1½ x A — N
PIECE ON TOP OF COLUMNS . C — T x A — N x V P½
COLUMNS . . . Y — N x Y — N x A — R
CAP . . . . . T — I x R — A x C — T

PRICES: { Westerly or Milford, N. H. . . . . . C A E Y
         { Barre . . . . G T Y

"Granite," January, 1900.

Bottom Base . N x E x C — C
Second Base . T x R x C — R
Die . . . . . E x A x C — C Y
Cap . . . . . P — C Y x C — C Y x C — C C

Prices: { Barre . . . . T E Y
Westerly . . . . N E Y
Milford . . . . I A E }

"GRANITE," JANUARY, 1900.

BOTTOM BASE . E — P x R — P x C — P'

SECOND BASE . P — A x A — A x C — Y

DIE . . . . . R — T x C — T x A — C Y

PRICES: { Quincy . . . . A E Y

{ Barre . . . . A R E

"GRANITE," JANUARY, 1900.

BOTTOM BASE	.	T — Y x R — E x C — Y
SECOND BASE	.	P — C C x A — P x Y — C Y
DIE	. . . . .	P — E x C — C Y x C — C Y
CAP	. . . . .	P — C Y x A — R x C — R

	Westerly	I Y Y
PRICES:	Milford	T Y Y
	Barre	E E Y

A. MALNATI,

Westerly * and * Quincy * Granite.

ARTISTIC MONUMENTS.

STATUARY, PORTRAIT BUSTS AND IDEAL FIGURES

Cut from Granite from my own models.

------ SOLE AGENT FOR THE ------

Celebrated Calder & Carnie Pink Westerly Granite.

FROM MY OWN MODEL, AND RECENTLY ERECTED IN CEMETERY AT PORTSMOUTH, N. H.

Power furnished by My Own Steam Plant for operating Pneumatic Tools, Derrick, etc.

===== QUINCY, ❧ ❧ ❧ MASS. ------

BARRE NEWS

Contrary to the general rule at this season of the year, the condition of the granite industry here in this city and vicinity is very prosperous, and indeed better than the most sanguine have dared to expect. Every business man here, and in fact everyone in touch with the business in any of its branches, can see at a glance that we are entering upon an era of prosperity which has never been excelled in the history of the business.

From all over the country there comes pouring in orders for jobs both large and small, although money is a little tighter than it was in the early summer and fall. Barring the ever-imminent possibility of a serious condition of affairs between the Granite Cutters' Union and the Manufacturers' Association in the coming spring, there is nothing to indicate that there will not be a continuance of the present superabundance of business during the year upon which we are just entering. Every one of the large manufacturers have made preparations to do a larger business another year than they have ever done, and taking the entire situation into consideration, it is only reasonable to suppose that their expectations will be fulfilled.

The orders which are coming in now are orders which are first class in variety and design, and many of them call for immediate construction or as soon as possible, showing that there is a present demand for the class of goods which Barre makes a business of producing.

One of the large quarry owners recently said that during the past year he had taken more stock from his quarries than he had done during the two previous years taken together, and that the demand at this time was far in excess of the average months of the year. He also said that it was his opinion that during the coming year there would be more granite manufactured into monuments and sent out of this city than has ever gone out in any single year in the history of the industry.

We do not wish to seem over-optimistic in reference to the condition of the business here, but we are forced to the conclusion that quarry owners and the manufacturers are talking about that which they know and have reason to expect. There would not be such a consensus of opinion in reference to the volume of business which will come to the city during the coming year, unless there was something substantial upon which to base their opinions.

H. J. Bertoli is comfortably situated in his plant at the Pioneer Mills, in Montpelier, and during the past year has done quite a quantity of very fine work. He makes a specialty of statuary. In this work Mr. Bertoli is an expert, and deserves praise for the style of the work which he sends out and the thoroughness

with which he attends, personally, to every detail. He has had in his employ during the summer about one gang of cutters.

The plant of George Straiton is nearly always well filled with both monuments and cutters, and this present time is no exception to the rule. He has now about two gangs of men at work upon the work which he has on hand, and everything is conducted in a business-like manner. During the past year he has done a larger business than during any previous year since his start in business, and has reasons to believe that there will come a larger volume of business, not only to him, but to all manufacturers, when another spring opens.

Milne & Knox are located in a portion of the Vermont Granite Company's plant and have started quite a respectable little business. They are cutting a sarcophagus job at this time which is quite elaborate, and have on their books several other jobs for monuments of various descriptions.

Hopkins, Huntington & Company have been in their present plant now for nearly a year, and since they have become well-settled their business has improved appreciably. They are operating about three gangs of cutters and are making preparations to increase this number if business opens up well another spring.

Milne, Clarihew & Gray report that during the past year they have been in the swim with the other quarry owners in the city and have had about all the work they could do. Their quarries have been operated for some time; their stock is as good as any that can be obtained in this city, or, in fact, in any part of the country. The demand this year has far exceeded that of any previous year since their knowledge of quarrying began, and the way the orders keep coming in leads them to think that the coming year will be one unprecedented in the history of the granite business.

E. L. Smith & Company have been jogging along in the same good old way in which they have been found during the past few years—having plenty of good orders on their books and always in receipt of some new job, which is an improvement over anything they have ever constructed. They have cut and shipped this past year several large memorial jobs for the Central States, and, on the whole, their work has been more satisfactory this year than in any of their previous experience. The number of men in their employ has been a little larger than usual, and

Novelli & Corti,
Statuary and Carving.

PORTRAIT FIGURES, BUSTS AND IDEAL FIGURES
in all kinds of New England Granite.

STATUE OF ROBERT BURNS,
CUT BY SAM NOVELLI.

GARVING

Executed in any style

Floral Work

...A SPECIALTY....

MODELS FURNISHED
ON APPLICATION.

COTTER'S SATURDAY NIGHT,
CUT BY E. CORTI.

We invite all dealers who need high-art work to correspond directly with us. We can give best of references.

NOVELLI & CORTI,

P. O. Box 87. **BARRE, VERMONT.**

they are making preparations to do more work and employ a larger force the coming spring.

Innes & Cruickshank are having very good business now and report that they have done a larger business this year than they have ever done before by almost one-third. The men in their employ have varied from two gangs to three gangs, and they have been in continual receipt of orders during the latter part of the fall, so that they have been obliged to continue the force of cutters about the same as in the busiest part of the summer.

Emslie, McLeod & Company have on their books more work at this time than they have had before at this time of the year and their plant is well filled with work of a high order, both as to design and manner of construction. All through the summer and fall of the year just past they have had work all of the time, and their shipments have been much larger than they have previously averaged since they have been in the business. It is certain, they say, that money is becoming a little tighter, but this is to be looked for to some extent as the winter approaches, and consequently this is no surprise to them. They have some very pretty jobs now nearly completed, and have recently shipped two or three car-loads of monumental work both large and small. Two medium sized shaft jobs have been constructed and shipped during the past few months and a variety of monuments.

Barclay Brothers have been employing more men this season than they have ever done before, and consequently they have shipped a much larger amount of work than usual. They have been having a pay-roll of above a hundred cutters, and besides they have operated a large force on their quarry. It is thought that they will build a large plant in the early spring equipped with all the latest improvements for the construction of granite monuments on the lot which they have recently purchased at the northerly end of the city. This firm has constructed some of the largest jobs, both building and monumental, which have been shipped from this city; the handling has been attended with an expense and delay which would be entirely done away with in one of the more modern arranged plants. Their shipments during the past year have been enormous, some of their single jobs taking some forty or fifty cars for transportation, and in some instances these have been cars constructed especially for the piece which it carried. They are sanguine to the extreme in reference to the condition of things and the business outlook for the coming year.

Wells, Lamson & Company are well supplied with orders at this writing, and report that during the past year they have done a somewhat larger business than they have usually done. The demand for their quarry stock has increased nearly one-third over that of last year and still continues without any appreciable lessening. Quite a quantity of their shipments this past year have been large orders, and the orders which they have on their books now are above the average in point of size.

Novelli & Corti have only been in business since about the time of the unveiling of the Burns statue in this city. Since they have been in business they have been very prosperous in the lines of work in which they are each expert workmen. They are now very busy on some statues which they are constructing for New York parties, and report that they have work enough on their order books to keep them busy during the entire winter. These parties are worthy of the patronage of the trade and will do anything in their line to the customer's entire satisfaction.

The firm of McMillan & Stephens are now operating two quarries in connection with their plant, and report that they are agreeably surprised every month by the continuous demand for stock which they have from all parts of this section. At their plant they have constructed many excellent pieces of work and the volume of their business has been larger, to say the least, than it ever was before. Two or three column die jobs and several shaft monuments have been shipped of late, and, on the whole, they report that they have no fault to find with the existing condition of things or the outlook for the future. They have employed about three gangs of cutters during the greater part of the season and do not vary much from that number at this writing.

Cross Brothers of Northfield have been at their best this year and nearly all of the time they have had over fifty men in their employ. They have made a business of attending to their business, and consequently have made a success. During the season they have constructed several medium mausoleum jobs which would of themselves be worthy of more particular mention than space will permit us to give them. Their work has all been of the first class order, and consequently they have an order book which is well filled with orders, and further, are receiving more orders every day. They will employ more men during the coming year than ever before if the season opens up with anything like what is anticipated.

Doucette Brothers of Montpelier have been well supplied with orders during the past year, and have now on hand quite a quantity of very good orders calling for construction and delivery as soon as possible. They have employed something like a gang of cutters during the summer, and after the holidays are over will put on about that number. They have only been in business about three years, but during that time they have worked up a good trade. Business has been better during the past year than it has been any previous year since they have been in the business.

Sweeney Bros. Granite Company, Montpelier, have never had such a good business since they were established as they have had this year. All of the time they have had all the work they could handle, and they have sent out more work than one would expect from a plant where about two gangs of men are working. They have a good plant and it is equipped with the modern conveniences for the manufacturing of granite monuments. They are planning to do more work another year than they have this year even, and express the opinion that they will do this because there will be more work on the market and at better prices.

The sentiment among the manufacturers in this vicinity is very much in favor of putting up a fight on the issue which has come between the Association and the Stone Cutters' Union. They almost unanimously

MUTCH & CALDER,

Successors to BURLEY & CALDER,

—— MANUFACTURERS OF ——

Barre Granite Monuments and General Cemetery Work.

Pneumatic Tools and all the Latest Improved Machinery.

Correspondence with dealers desiring first-class work invited.

BARRE, VERMONT.

BECK AND BECK

BARRE VT.

MANUFACTURERS OF

Barre Granite Monuments.

WE GUARANTEE THE BEST STOCK AND WORKMANSHIP.

DIES AND CAPS SQUARED AND POLISHED FOR THE TRADE.

We keep a stock on hand of the Monument represented in this advertisement and can ship at short notice. Prices sent on application.

PNEUMATIC TOOLS.

REMOVED

my offices to below address, which are centrally located, and where
I shall be pleased to hear from the trade in the future.

CHAS. H. GALL,

UNITY BUILDING,

79 DEARBORN STREET, - - CHICAGO, ILL.

A LARGE LINE OF DESIGNS, PHOTOS, CASES, Etc.

My Designs are conceded to be the Best and Most Practical in use.

Series 5, New and Practical, 23 on 14 x 21 sheets, Price, $5.00.

—— SEND FOR PARTICULARS. ——

McMILLAN & STEPHENS,

BARRE, - - - VERMONT.

MANUFACTURERS OF

BARRE GRANITE MONUMENTS,

Quarry Owners.   Medium and Dark.

ROUGH STOCK, POLISHING AND SQUARING FOR THE TRADE.

endorse the sentiments of the other members of the New England Association, that it will be to the detriment of the trade in general to materially advance the cost price of monumental work. This conclusion is reached from the fact that the more costly monuments are not a necessity, and that therefore the general public would not indulge so freely in such luxuries if the price is pushed up far beyond its actual value. There is a feeling among the leaders here that if the matter comes to a head, that it is more than likely that there will be a settlement without any prolonged struggle. They are getting ready for the worst, however, and are not planning to be caught napping if anything serious should come. It has been thought that the cutters here would not be over-anxious for the strike, owing to their remembrance of the conditions which existed after the strike of 1893; but contrary to expectations, the very ones who knew most of the time referred to, are the ones who talk the loudest of ultimate success of the union in pressing their demands against the Association. Come what may, it is certain that business has been good enough this year so that both sides have laid up a little money upon which to exist during a long struggle, and if an out-and-out fight comes it will be a long and bitter one.

Let us hope, in the interest of the trade and of both of the differing parties, that they will not resort to the extreme measure of a strike, but that the differences will be amicably settled, even if it is necessary to compromise, for the old saying is true in this day: "It is better to bend than to break."

Z. Macchi is never left out when a good thing strikes the city, and he has had his share of the good things during this past year. He has been running about three gangs of men, some of the time reducing the number to nearly two gangs. He considers this to have been the best season which he has had since he has been in the business.

It is reported that John P. Corskie & Son will build a modern cutting shed in the early spring to accommodate their increasing business.

We instructed our correspondent to interview each one of our advertisers, but he states at the last moment before going to press that it was impossible for him to do so. Such firms as Mackie, Hussey & Company, Marr & Gordon, McDonald & Buchan, Mutch & Calder, Littlejohn & Milne, and McIver & Ruxton do not require any special mention from us in this issue, as their opinions have been well expressed in the past; suffice to say that upon a recent visit by the editor they were doing a good business and working their plants to their full capacity. Among the other advertisers, namely, Rogers & Arkley, Robins Bros., Mortimer & Campbell, James Sector & Company, Dillon & Haley, Montpelier, and E. W. Carle, in a recent interview by the editor, expressed themselves as satisfied with their past year's business, and in fact, as a rule, too busy to talk.

Beck & Beck are still improving their plant to keep pace with their growing business. A. Anderson & Sons are prosperous, as the additions which they build from time to time to their plant prove. Imlah & Company have long ago outgrown their present quarters,

and we have no doubt that in the near future they will be compelled to build. Sangiunetti & Carusi make a specialty of statuary and carving, and it will well repay one to visit their shed to see the variety of this work which they always have under the hammer.

To the Retail Marble and Granite Dealers.

In July, 1898, at an inter-state meeting of marble and granite dealers, held at Council Bluffs, Iowa, the nucleus of the National Retail Marble & Granite Dealers' Association of the United States was formed and temporary officers elected; postponement was had to the 2d Wednesday of February, 1899, at Chicago. In pursuance thereof, a large number of the retail dealers of the United States convened in Chicago on the 8th day of February, the convention lasting over the 8th, 9th, and part of the 10th, at which meeting the organization was completed by the adoption of a constitution and the election of officers for the year, whose names follow: J. M. Graham, Des Moines, Iowa, president; John H. Merkle, Peoria, Ill., vice president; J. N. Kildow, York, Neb., secretary; T. H. Pritchard, Watertown, S. D., treasurer.

An executive committee consisting of the president and secretary ex officio, and one member from each association, represented in the National Association. "The membership of this National Association shall consist of delegates from state or local associations, each state or local association being entitled to one representative and vote for each ten or fraction of ten of its membership."

This National Association is now well on its feet, and will be successful so far as being profitable to the dealers belonging to the several state associations which are organized. If you have no local association in your state, it remains with you to see that such an association is formed for the mutual welfare of yourselves and the general elevation of the business throughout the nation and the betterment of our condition. It will be well to lose no time in getting to work now to organize this association in your state, so that a meeting can be held in January, perfecting an organization and the election of some one or more, to represent you at the National Association. The president or secretary of the National Association will gladly give you such help and advice as you may desire at any time.

A very enthusiastic meeting was held last February, and a more beneficial one yet will be held in February, 1900. The time is the 2d Wednesday in February. The exact place in Chicago will be given notice of in the next issue of the trade journals. We sincerely trust that you will not wait for the other fellow, but that you will go to work at once, organizing a local association in your neighborhood. Do not postpone it until too late. Earnest, concerted action is the only method which will obtain what we are striving for, viz: a fair remuneration on capital invested, and the rooting out of many of the evils now hanging on to the business. If you know that your state has an association, we trust you will lose no time in getting into it. If your state has no association, lose no time in organizing one, and if after due diligence you cannot complete an organization before the 2d Wednesday in February, 1900, come to that meeting yourself and get as many other good dealers in your state as you can to come with you, and we will give you the rights of the floor for this next meeting, with the understanding that if you are in sympathy with the principles of the association, that you will go out from that meeting determined to organize your state long before another National Convention shall be held. But it will be very much better to organize, so as to send delegates to the next meeting, from an organized association, than to attend as individuals. Hoping that you will appreciate the importance of getting to work promptly, we remain,

Yours very sincerely,
J. M. GRAHAM,
President.

J. N. KILDOW, Secretary.

Among the Retail Dealers.

EVANSVILLE, IND.—The local press speak of F. J. Scholz & Son in the following flattering terms: "The growth from a small beginning of the marble works of F. J. Scholz & Son is not only a matter of pride to the firm, but also to citizens generally. In later years the firm has branched out into larger and more important work, and the fact that it is turning out not only massive as well as superb work, is evidence of the great confidence reposed in its members by the public The works have just completed a massive mausoleum for Dr. W. H. Paden of Princeton, Ky. It is the finest piece of such work in Western Kentucky, costing $3,-500, and is built of Georgia marble throughout, and is not only an ornament to the cemetery in which it is placed, but reflects great credit upon the skill displayed at the Scholz Marble Works. Among the most interesting orders now on hand at these works is one for a mausoleum to be placed in Northern Indiana at a cost of $20,000. It will be of granite, and when finished will be one of the most handsome in any cemetery in the state. Besides this individual contract, the firm has also a number of others, not quite so pretentious, but still in the aggregate is sufficient to indicate that it will start into the new year with a very prosperous beginning.

WOLCOTT, N. Y.—The building occupied by J. E. Lawrence, as a granite and marble shop, was destroyed by fire December 11.

NASHVILLE, TENN.—The John G. Carter monument committee met December 2 and examined several designs. After a full consideration of the matter, it was unanimously decided to award the contract to P. Swan of this city. Mr. Swan's design calls for a plain Barre granite shaft, 33 feet in height, and to cost something less than $3,000. The monument will not be completed before next spring.

GRAND RAPIDS, MICH.—The Grand Rapids Monument Co. has erected on the Nanninga and Haan lots in Valley City cemetery a cottage granite monument purchased by Thomas Nanninga. In Spring Grove the company erected a large sarcophagus, also at Casco. At Scotteville and Sparta memorial tablets for the Henry and Shoemaker lots. The company have had a very busy season and many orders are under way at present.

RICHFIELD SPRINGS, N. Y.—The new granite and marble works of Harry Derrick, in this village, is being stocked ready for business.

WESTFIELD, MASS.—November 17, papers were passed conveying for a consideration of $6,000, the property on Elm street, comprising two buildings and a considerable tract of land to O'Brien & Davine, who constitute the Westfield Granite and Marble Company. The purchasers will locate their granite and marble works in the rear of the present store with a front entrance between the latter.

MARIETTA, OHIO.—Meisenhelder and Leonard have under construction a large monument which will be placed at the grave of the late General R. R. Dawes. The stone is a large shaft 22 feet high and is an exact reproduction of the one at the grave of Major E. C. Dawes. It is to be cut from Barre granite.

WORCESTER, MASS.—Arthur M. Evans, a 33d degree Mason, and a member of the firm of the Evans Marble Company, died November 16. He owns large quarries at Fitzwilliam, N. H.

CLYDE, OHIO.—The building occupied by the Hughes Marble and Granite Company was damaged by fire December 8. The loss will not amount to over $200, and is covered by insurance.

Proposed Monuments and Monumental News.

BALTIMORE, MD.—A manufacturing company was recently incorporated for the purpose of manufacturing and selling a tombstone anchor. The anchor permanently secures tombstones in their relative positions firmly and securely, and prevents the desecration of graves.

Some New England Gravestones.

(Continued from December.)

Perhaps the same reasons that caused the Plymouth people to conceal the graves of their dead militated against the marking of the early graves of the settlements, for the slate of which most of the monuments have been formed seemed to last very well, except where it became fractured. The broad surfaces must have offered a tempting mark for the small boys of the different centuries. Times may change, but the instinct for markmanship and fighting seems to have survived throughout all the ages.

But the time came when the fear of the wolves, which were such a menace to the living and the dead, as the old records show, overcame the fear of the Indians, and the flat stones were laid over the common graves whose owners could not possess a family

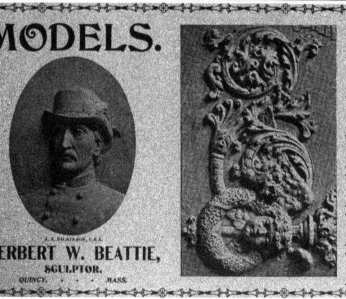

tomb. So, unless somebody was brought from Plymouth in 1620 and buried there in anticipation of the time that Isaac Johnson should buy the land, the stone in the King's Chapel yard bearing that date is quite unaccounted for, for Blackstone had not even arrived. Some have suggested that it might have been some result of Standish's visit to Squantum, but the doughty captain was too busy to come so far to bury anybody, and he would certainly never have carried a tombstone with him for such a contingency. So, if the only evidence Miss Beacon Hill has of her eligibility for the Society of Colonial Dames or Mayflower Descendents rest on one of these tombstone evidences, she is doomed to disappointment.

These discrepancies and wrong marking, which some antiquarians dare aver, is the result of the rival claims of the most ancient cemeteries, and "accidentally done apurpose," can easily be accounted for by some stone cutters supplying the figure 2 in place of the 9 which belongs there. This is borne out, too, by the style of ancient orthography. Neither the 6 nor the 9 fell below the line in any way, and the 2 had a straight line at the base which would more easily be worn off, by the action of the rain, even. At any rate, the cutting of a straight line made a 2 of it, and in cases where this was doubtful, the earliest date would naturally be chosen. This is further supported by the fact that the curl of the letter is almost iden'ical in the case of the 6 and the 9, and is a circle, whi'e in the real 2, as written and printed then, the head is not circular, but open. In many reference books on the old cemeteries of Boston, many of these corrections authoritatively made will be found.

So Dorchester has yet a new claim to distinction in colonial history, and well had she conserved her relics of those far-away days. The historic cemetery is yet "impaled" with its double-railed paling, set now upon a stone wall, and will well repay a curious visitor's interest. For more than the first marked grave in New England tempt the beholder to study the place with attention; and speculation and imagination, and ridiculous mistakes in years and centuries, if you will, recreate historical text-books into romances, and prove your early conscience in regard to them, better than any dreaded "examination" in your school days. And, better than all, in the complications that a study of genealogy involves, you realize that "nobody but a fool is always right."

You will find yourself wondering how Isaac Royal, who died in 1739, was buried here. The last you remembered of him was his departure for Halifax.

There is something ironic in John Foster, the almanac maker's self-written epitaph, "Skill Was His Cash."

You look with a reverent eye upon the grave of the first schoolmaster, and by that gorgeously sculptured tomb of Major Humphrey Atherton you recall the weird story of his death, so much more dramatic than anything which you can ever see as a climax to any play on the modern stage. He died as he came home from the hanging of the witches, falling from his horse not far from the parting of the ways.

A BEAUTIFULLY SCULPTURED STONE AT COPP'S HILL; BUT THE DATE IS CALCULATED TO DECEIVE. SHOULD READ 1695, THE 9 HAVING BEEN CHANGED INTO A 2.

HERE LYETH BURIED y BODY OF GRACE BERRY y WIFE OF THOMAS BERRY AGED ABOUT 58 YEARS WHO DIED MAY y 17 1625

TWENTY-TON TRAVELING CRANE.

ADDRESS

Lane Manufacturing Co.,

MONTPELIER, VT.

WALTER W. FIELD,

117 Main Street, Cambridgeport, Mass.

...TELEPHONE 73 CAMBRIDGE...

NEW ENGLAND AGENT FOR

THE LAMBERT
HOISTING ENGINE CO.

500 Styles and Sizes.
Built to Gauges and Templates.

For Mining, Quarrying, Coal Handling, Pile Driving, Build ers' use, Logging and General Contracting.

Electric Hoists, Single and Double Drums,
with Improved Automatic Brake.
Suspension Cableways.

—— *SEND FOR NEW CATALOGUE B.* ——

Horizontal, Locomotive and Upright
BOILERS.

Engine in Stock for Quick Delivery.

Standard Double Cylinder Double Patent Friction Drum Double Winch
Hoisting Engine, with Boiler and Fixtures Complete.

KAVANAGH BROS. & CO.,

Westerly Granite Tennessee Marble

Artistic Carving a Specialty.
ESTIMATES FURNISHED PROMPTLY.

QUINCY, MASS.

WHY DON'T YOU

have A. ANDERSON & SONS, quote you prices on that work you are about to place? They have all the latest machinery for turning out first-class work, and can guarantee you A1 stock and workmanship. Give them a trial.

PNEUMATIC TOOLS.   DIES, CAPS AND BASES SQUARED AND POLISHED.

A. ANDERSON & SONS, - BARRE, VT.

TO LEASE.

FINE-GRAINED
DARK BLUE GRANITE QUARRY.

—

It will pay
you to investigate this property.

Located near Augusta, Ga. The above property can be leased on very reasonable terms. For further information address A. M. Hunt & Co., Publishers of "GRANITE."

FOR SALE.

QUARRY AT BARRE, VT.,

consisting of about six acres of quarry and dump land. The quarry produces good fine-grained dark and medium stock, mostly medium, and is equipped with a forty-five horse power three drum engine, fifty-five horse power boiler, furnishing power for two derricks, two derricks, also Pulsometer steam pump, one derrick with horse sweep, good engine house, oil tanks, blacksmith shop fully equipped. Will either sell a half interest or the whole. For further information inquire of A. M. Hunt & Co., Publishers of "GRANITE."

FOR SALE.

GRANITE CUTTING, POLISHING MACHIN-
ERY, AND TWENTY-TON TRAVELING
CRANE,

consisting of four Merriam saw gangs, one large and one small granite turning lathe, three large and two small polishing lathes, five Jenny Lind polishing machines, two pendulum polishers, eight verticals, one traveling crane, rope transmission, guaranteed to lift twenty tons. All the above machinery is second hand and will be sold cheap. For further information address "Machinery," care of A. M. Hunt & Co., publishers of "GRANITE."

WANTED.

A salesman, on commission. to handle Quincy Granite in the middle states. Address Mac, care "GRANITE."

Fuller, Foley & Co.,

West Quincy, Mass.

✠

Quincy

Granite.

✠

PRICES RIGHT, - -

= GRANITE· RIGHT.

Fairbanks-Morse
Gas and
Gasolene
Engines
No steam or
coal used.
Send for
Catalogue.
C.J.JagerCo.
174 High St.
Boston.

WANTED, FOR SALE, ETC.

Advertisements inserted in this column, 15 cents a line each insertion; six words to a line. No advertisement to cost less than 50 cents.

FOR SALE.

A second-hand
AIR COMPRESSOR.

Only used a short time.

Address Air Compressor,
Care of "GRANITE."

IMLAH & CO., -:- BARRE, VT.

————DEALERS IN————

BARRE GRANITE MONUMENTS, VAULTS AND ARTISTIC MEMORIALS.

First-Class Work Guaranteed and prices as low as can be quoted for honest work.
Carved Work, Squaring and Polishing for the trade a Specialty.

J. ALBERT SIMPSON,
Treasurer.

L. S. ANDERSON,
Manager.

1826 - 1899.

Seventy-Three Years in the Granite Business.

QUARRIES:

West Quincy, Mass.,   Concord, N. H.

GRANITE RAILWAY
COMPANY.

PRINCIPAL OFFICE: · WEST QUINCY, MASS.

DETAIL OF ILLUSTRATION BELOW:

No 1. Looking West from Quarry No. 1.

No. 2. A corner in Quarry No. 3.   No. 3. A Bird's eye View of Quarry No. 1

No. 4. A Block of Extra Dark Blue Quincy Granite measuring 19 x 16 x 9½ feet,
weighing about 200 tons.

No. 5. Road from Yard to Quarries operated by an endless chain.

February, 1900   Vol. X. No. 2

Granite

A. M. HUNT & CO.

PUBLISHERS

131 Devonshire Street

BOSTON, MASS., U.S.A.

Subscription Price, $1.00 Year

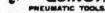

ADVERTISERS' DIRECTORY.

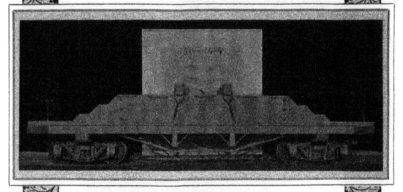

GRANITE

ENTERED AT THE BOSTON POST OFFICE AS SECOND-CLASS MAIL MATTER.

Vol. X.   BOSTON, MASS., FEBRUARY 1, 1900.   No. 2

A. M. HUNT, Editor.

Published Monthly in the interests of the Producer
Manufacturer, and Retailer of Granite as used
for Monumental or Building Purposes.

Terms of Subscription

To Any Part of the United States or Canada:

One copy, one year   -   -   - $1.00, in advance.
One copy, six months   -   -   -   75 cents, in advance.

ADVERTISING RATES FURNISHED UPON APPLICATION.

A. M. HUNT & CO., Publishers,

131 DEVONSHIRE STREET,   -   -   BOSTON, MASS.

Editorials

E could not help being impressed
with the unanimous opinion expressed by the retail dealers, in
letters printed on another page,
regarding the demands of the cutters for eight hours
work and $3.00 per day as minimum wages. They
tell their own story and deal with that end of the business which is of vital interest to the manufacturers, as
this is the source from which they are to secure the
work with which to keep their cutting plants in operation and give the cutters work, which means bread and
butter to them, it seems to us, trying to reason it from
an unprejudiced standpoint, for naturally a trade paper
or any individual has a tendency to favor those who
patronize it and pay him money that there are argu-
ments which should be convincing, aside from the
letters mentioned above, and they should convince
the intelligent granite cutter that such a radical rise
in prices as would be brought about by granting the
present demands are impossible.

There are other features, aside from the demands of
the cutters, which have entered into the cutting and
transportation of monumental work which will serve,
if added to the demands spoken of above, in placing a
prohibitory price upon American monumental work in
granite. We note a few of the articles which enter
into the quarrying of granite and their percentage of
increase. Wire rope, 50 per cent; steel, 25 per cent;
iron, 25 per cent; coal, 65c per ton; hoisting engines
and steam drills have also increased in price, owing to
the increased cost of steel and iron. There has been
an individual increase in wages of the quarry men from
5 to 15 cents per day. To partially cover this increased
cost of material, the quarry owners at Barre have
agreed upon prices, which amount to about 15 per
cent upon certain grades of rough stock. There has
been no change in freight classifications and no increased freight charges upon rough granite.

In the manufacturing department there has been an
increased cost in all material which enters into manufacturing. We note a few: steel, 25 per cent; iron, 25
per cent; carborundum, putty and all material for polishing and sawing granite have increased in price from
30 to 50 per cent; lumber, $2.50 per thousand increase;
nails, 100 per cent; and there has also been a change in
freight classifications on part carload lots which makes
a percentage of increase in freight rates on small shipments of about 25 per cent. On the top of all this,
there has been no material increased price asked for by
the manufacturer for the finished monument, except
within the last two months, and this only to cover
themselves for shipment after March 1st, with the result that there have been but very few contracts taken,
and the average manufacturer will have all work
cleaned up by March 1st. As a consequence, even
if there is no strike, the months of March and April
will find many of the workmen out of a job, owing to
the excessive demands of the National Granite Cutters'
Union, which have made it necessary for the manufacturer to ask from 40 to 50 per cent increase for monumental work to be delivered after March 1st.

HE following letter deals with a matter that
is of vital importance to every retail dealer
and manufacturer in monumental work:

Bryan, Ohio, Jan. 19, 1900.

Can you suggest some remedy for the outrageous
classification of local rates on granite? I would be
willing to share in the expense to fight it. The rate

was high enough as it was. Hoping something can be done to relieve us, I am,

Yours truly,
E. B. WILLETT.

We would suggest that the matter be taken up by every retail dealers' and manufacturers' association, and a protest be sent in to the proper authorities. About one-half of the monumental work that is shipped comes under this change in classification and we believe it to be unnecessary and unjustified.

NFORMATION has reached us that thirty-five members of the Barre Granite Cutters' Union have taken out their cards with the stated intention of cutting monumental work for themselves. We wonder if they will give up business if they cannot earn $3.00 per day, and if they will confine themselves to eight hours for a day's work. We are inclined to think not, if what others who have started in the manufacturing business have done in the past is any criterion to judge from. We should rather expect that their day would commence at six o'clock, and that night would be turned into day to help earn enough to gather from the profits three square meals. We also wonder how this will help them in enforcing the demands. To be sure, this will give them a chance to earn a few dollars, provided they can secure the stock, but it strikes us as one of the best possible ways to defeat their own demands.

We will assume that the demands of the granite cutters are granted. There is no doubt it will give many of the cutters a chance to go to Aberdeen to cut monumental work and it will also have the effect of preventing many a stone cutter from securing a permanent job, owing to their inability to earn the minimum price, and this makes it still harder for the stone cutter to secure a job when he has reached that age where he cannot keep up with the younger man. We will acknowledge that it is hard work—that goes without saying—and that the average stone cutter at the age of fifty has reached that age where he cannot compete with the younger man, from a standpoint of wages, but nevertheless this is no reason why they should insist upon placing a prohibitory price upon American monumental work. It is possible that what they demand may be brought about gradually, but a 35 per cent increase is too radical a change all at one time.

There is no change in the situation at the present time, notwithstanding all rumors which have been published and unpublished. We believe that the manufacturers of monumental work and the granite cutters are nearer together than the average employer and employee, and we look to common sense to be used, and consequently a favorable result from their meetings. We are informed that the committee representing the cutters of Barre, Vt., are the best that possibly can be secured, they are men of intelligence and able to reason for themselves, and the manufacturers' committee is composed of the best talent that Barre can produce.

We understand that the manufacturers have shut down entirely upon taking more work until after the trouble is settled.

Dix Island, Me.—Past and Present.

(Continued.)

Prosperity is all very well, Beals argued, but a man needs a reasonable dose of adversity just to give him a respectful idea of the power of a dollar. When a man has been running behind the game, till he has caught sight of the last dollar of his reserve and then commences to pick up, he is apt to be happy over a margin so small that in flush times he wouldn't have looked at—this was another of Beals's pet sayings.

He was very much of a philosopher in a good many ways and to this day you will find old men who worked for him in their younger days and each of them will have some little anecdote concerning Beals. His philosophy was homespun, but for that reason it was all the better. When Beals talked about hard luck people gave ear, for they knew that he had learned his lesson in bitter experience.

But, as I said before, fortune might throw him down but she couldn't keep him there. He had more grit than any man that ever tackled the Maine granite business. He was first, last and always an optimist, and like all that class was a schemer, and a bold schemer.

He had heard of Maine granite and knew in a general way that it was the best there was, and so one day he dropped into Knox county and began prospecting. He was very quiet about it and apparently had no idea of making a purchase at once. He was a shrewd buyer, was Beals, and when he had looked the field over with a practiced eye, he decided that he could use a part of the Muscle Ridge group in his business. Still very quietly, he proceeded to make a dicker for the one that is now called Dix Island. He drove a good bargain and went back·to Connecticut to see what he could do toward turning his new purchase into a cash-producer.

You will agree that he didn't have a very rosy outlook. He had a claim on a small granite nubble down on the Maine coast, and it was by no means the best piece of ledge in the vicinity of Rockland, either.

And he had his schemes.

That was all. But he started in on a man who was quite prominent in his own state just then. That was Learned of Connecticut, who was making a sensational record in copper mining. He was the principal holder of Calumet and Hecla stock and the market was booming. Perhaps this made him more ready to take chances, but at all events he agreed to go into the Maine granite scheme if Beals could get another man of money to form a third partner.

This Beals did, for he was a good talker, and when he had told his little story to Mr. C. P. Dixon of New York that gentleman surrendered and promised to be No. 3.

That is how the scheme was started and how New York and Connecticut capital was coaxed into coming down to Maine's bleak shore.

Dixon was a typical New Yorker of the prosperous business class. He was a man of middle-age when he came to Maine, but so well-preserved and always so well-groomed that he easily passed for a younger man. He was a man of the world, a good talker, but withal extremely practical and a hard worker. He was hail-fellow-well-met with every one from the new man in the quarry to the special agent of the treasury who was down to make a report on the progress of the work.

In his dealings with the men in his employ he was never extravagant, but on the other hand there was never anything that savored of the niggard.

And these were the men who gave Dix Island its start. Others have had a share since, but they only followed where the big three had blazed the way and it was under these same three that the island reached its flood tide of prosperity.

The first job that came to the new company was the contract for the Treasury building at Washington, and it was of a magnitude which took away the breath of some of the older residents. They said that Mr. Beals might be a very progressive man and all that, but he would find that in this respect he had overreached himself.

"Why," said these people to each other, "there aren't men enough on the whole Maine coast to cut that building out in fifty years. And if there were, they couldn't get 'em all on to the island, for it isn't bigger'n a pint of cider. I don't see why they didn't buy an island that was big enough for something while they were about it. They might as well have had one that they could turn round on without going out in a boat."

Things did look rather dubious to one who was unacquainted with the push of the men in question. But they laughed when people told them that Dix Island wasn't large enough to make a treasury building.

Then they sent to employment agencies in New York and the New York agencies sent to agencies on the other side of the Atlantic. It became noised about in Aberdeen that the Yankees were going to build a big public building in Washington and that though they had granite in plenty they had no workmen who could cut it as it should be cut.

The Scotchmen were told that the pay would be far better than anything they could get at home, and this appealed to the canny Scots. The result was that a few bold spirits started forth and went to Dix Island. Their report was eagerly waited at home and when they wrote that it was all right, there were hundreds of stone-cutters who packed up their kits and took the next vessel for the new country.

At the same time that the Scotchmen were making up their minds to try America there was a similar movement in progress in Italy, for the European agencies had given the tip to the marble-workers of the sunny peninsular. The agents told them that over in America they would cut granite instead of marble and that what they could earn in a day there would be equivalent to all that they could get in a week in Italy.

The Americans, said the agents, do not know how to cut stone with your cunning, but they wish to learn, and they who go to teach them will be able to buy villages when they return.

This and many other things the agents said unto them before they started, for the Italian loves his sun, his wine and his marble, and they were loth to go to a country where the sunshine was snow, the wine raw whiskey, and the snowy marble naught but rough gray granite. But they came just the same, for the offers which the employment agencies held forth were too alluring to be put aside.

Then Rockland began to appreciate the calibre of the men who had bought the little Muscle Ridge island, and Knox county stood looking on in open-mouthed astonishment.

The place began to hum. Men were arriving constantly and there was always employment for them. No matter how fast they came or how thick the population grew, the Dix Island Granite Company had work for them, and what was still better, had the money for them at the end of every month. The place thrived. Wages were high and money coursed freely.

(To be Continued.)

Opinions of Many Retail Dealers Regarding the Demands of the Granite Cutters for Eight Hours and Three Dollars per Day.

In answer to your inquiries of Jan. 12, 1900 in regard to the payment of minimum wages of $3.00 per day to granite cutters for eight hours, we wish to state: Good wages are dependent on the prosperity of the manufacturer. Good wages at the present moment, or additional raise in wages would be a hardship to the manufacturer. The last year, to all we have been able to gather, has been one of exceptional hardship to the retailers. But it is not a matter which a retailer will have any right or privilege to decide. Workmen, and good workmen, are not accessible to any agreements of any kind, as it is human nature to disbelieve the sickness of his fellowmen until actually dead. All retailers, so far as we know, have discounted the raise of wages and are trying to get the additional prices with disastrous results. The majority of people will wait, and may with the additional prosperity, if the same is to come, perhaps order or take to some inferior design. Should the granite industry be tied with another disastrous strike, people will resort to all kinds of substitutes for granite. One idea would be for the manufacturer to grant the demand, and as there will be but very little work the next year, there will be enough men to go around. Should some complication or other prospect give us additional orders, those contracts will have to pay the raise of wages, as all manufacturers have notified their several customers that such raises will take place. If the retailer or manufacturer will make more profits is exceedingly doubtful; on the contrary, the profits will be less. Would a strike increase the profits? We would say, emphatically, No! As the stomach of the human being requires food, so the retailer must have his orders filled. As the majority of people or customers would not shirk from a cancellation of contract if work is not executed on time, we cannot see how a strike can benefit either manufacturer or retailer. If there is plenty of work the retailers and manufacturers will be perhaps able to get better profits next year. But as far as getting better profits this year for the granite trade is out of the question, and a strike would not add to the profits.—Hoffmann & Prochazka, by Ferdinand Prochazka, New York City.

The January number of your journal received this morning, and I have carefully looked over contents of same, and will say that I fully agree with the Quincy manufacturer who had the conversation with your correspondent, namely, "grant the cutters all they demand"; that will avoid a strike and at the same time practically kill the business for 1900, and by the time 1901 rolled around they might learn what was for their best interests, or which side of the bread is buttered. I have been thirty-three years in this business, and think I know enough to "know" that the trade "cannot, and will not" stand any such advance in prices as the present demands would create. For illustration, I will say, in 1899 I put up a monument for the head of quite a large family, costing $275.00, satisfaction given in every way; this year, 1900, I am called upon by some uncle, cousin, aunt or neighbor of this family, saying they have seen this monument, like it, and want one like it in every way (of course they know the cost of same). I give them a price of $400.00. Do you think they ordered it? No! and do you think that I could make them believe that I would make no more on it at $400.00 than I did on the other at $275.00? No! Draw your own conclusions. Many other illustrations could be given. When you cripple or kill the retailer, you kill the whole business. I have old letters now, written me by manufacturers back in 1868 and '69' asking $5.00 and $6.00 per square foot for polishing, and 45 cents each for common sunk letters. If we are coming back to those prices again, I must say I am thankful I am nearing my end. I could write pages pertaining to this business, but you probably would not care to spend the time to read them. I enclose $1.00 for your journal for 1900.—W. G. Potter, of W. G. Potter & Son, Geneva, N. Y.

We think the demand for an eight-hour day may be easily conceded, but $3.00 as minimum wages we think would be equivalent to prohibition at present, and it would require a long time to bring the price up to that point.—McGregory & Casman, Springfield, Mass.

We are sure it will cripple the granite business in the west, and that there will be more marble used than ever.—Hodges & Baldwin, Fremont, Neb.

In reply will say as for the trouble by and between producer and workman, what I may say would not have any bearing upon the question. I think, however, I will say if there is any class of workmen who should be well paid, it should be the monument cutters. At the same time they should not be unreasonable in their demands. $3.00 for eight hours I think unreasonable. — W. H. Crumrine, Akron, Ohio.

We feel and believe the increase demanded by the granite cutters, in connection with the increase in freight rates, will force prices up so high in this section that we will be forced to use more southern granite or marbles. The change in freights to this point is from Barre, Vt., 86 cents to one dollar, other points in proportion. The granite cutters' demands appear unreasonable and unjust, and it is a question whether the manufacturers will stand the increase on labor, stock, etc. Some one is bound to be hurt and we believe it will be the cutters if the manufacturers have the backbone and surplus cash to stand the strain.—Curbow-Clapp Marble and Granite Co., Montgomery, Ala.

I live in a small country town of about 1,500 inhabitants. My trade is mostly from the country. I think to advance the price 25 or 30 per cent, there would be very little granite sold here. Corn at 25 cents per bushel and wheat at 55 cents per bushel, at present prices it would take 400 bushels of corn to buy a $100 monument. It seems to me that monuments are high enough now compared with other things. I don't know how it would be in large places; those that have plenty of money might afford to pay fancy prices.—John F. Greer, Bourbon, Ind.

In my opinion the demands of the granite cutters for an eight-hour day and a minimum price of $3.00 per day is altogether too much, and will in the end result to their disadvantage as well as the manufacturers'. I believe it will raise the price of American granite so high that we will again be importing large quantities of foreign granite, and after so long a continued use of American granite, it will be a change which I think our customers will accept without question, for no matter what we tell them, there is a general feeling among some people that granite imported from a foreign country is certainly better than that quarried at home. This movement will also have a tendency to increase the sale of marble. I have found in my business experience that some of my travelling men who lean towards the use of marble, can sell a much larger proportion than they can of granite, while others who favor granite, can sell it almost exclusively. There is a much larger profit in marble than there is in granite, and if our customers have to pay the increased price which will undoubtedly be brought about, should the granite cutters' demands be acceded to, the dealers will then turn their efforts towards marble and handle granite only when they are obliged to, in which event they will probably push the foreign product.—Philo Truesdale, Port Huron, Mich.

Regarding the demands of the granite cutters, which may appear reasonable in their view of the matter, yet the inevitable result of their demands, if complied with, will greatly decrease the trade of the New England shops and encourage not only importation, but increase the use of southern granite and the manufacture of granite in many of the southwestern states, which is now very much on the increase. We have always employed first-class men and paid satisfactory wages and like to see them do well, but they should consider well the facts and inevitable results of their demands and act slow and reasonable.—J. S. Clark Co., Louisville, Ky.

We believe that demands, if granted, will reduce considerably the amount of granite monumental work. Both the manufacturer and retailer must increase the margin of profit in order to counterbalance certain falling off in sales, or be content with smaller earnings. Will the manufacturer and retailer hold out for a better margin?—Benisch Bros., Brooklyn, N. Y.

Our opinion is that if these demands take effect it will have a tendency to make retailers do more of their own cutting as it could be done cheaper. It would also incline dealers to push other granites where labor demands are not so pronounced.—L. L. Manning, Plainfield, N. J.

In regard to the demand of the granite cutters for the minimum price of $3.00 per day for eight hours' work, we can only express our opinions. We have no organization of granite manufacturers in this state, so each firm will have to decide for themselves. We all have been paying for years $3.00 per day for nine hours' work, so should the granite cutters' demand prove successful in the east, it will place us in this vicinity on a more equal basis with the eastern firms and insure us a large portion of work that was manufactured in the east; but nevertheless it is generally conceded by the manufacturers here that nine hours' work at $3.00 per day the granite cutters are better paid than in any other line of business where the mechanical ability and intelligence of the workman are considered.—Cartwright Bros., Detroit, Mich.

In our judgment the demands of the granite cutters certainly seems unreasonable, and if granted would do the manufacturers, as well as the cutters, great harm. There is no doubt but what a considerable small work, which has lately been made of granite will go into marble. In fact, we have already instructed our salesmen to sell all small work in marble, if possible, as our profit would be more. It will also help to establish a great many plants for the manufacture of granite all over the west, which has heretofore been finished at the quarries. We know at least that we shall go into manufacturing ourselves should the demand be granted. With the change of classification in freight and the advance demanded would certainly raise the price so as to practically make it impossible to close contracts, which very often if not sold in a short time after losing their friends result in their buying no work at all.—A. Black & Son, Hastings, Mich.

We believe that one concession at a time is a fast gain for the granite cutters, $3.00 for nine hours, or $2.65 for eight hours. We are paying $2.75 for nine hours at present.—The Michigan Granite Co., Adrien, Mich.

We believe in the eight-hour rule, but not in the $3.00 minimum pay, as it would advance prices to an unreasonable height too quickly, and have a very bad effect on the business this year. The dealers are just getting in shape again after the hard times and cannot stand the loss of business resultant to the advance.—Edward J. Kishing, Jr., & Co., Newark, N. J.

The granite cutters are demanding too much. If they get $3.00 for nine hours or the present wages for eight hours per day, it is all the men should expect or the business can stand at present.—John J. Kittredge, Worcester, Mass.

Coming upon the heels of six years' adversity and disaster, the advance is so great as to recoil upon the heads of the manufacturers. They (the manufacturers) with too eager selfishness, have already anticipated all demands of workmen three months ahead of the time they are called upon to make any concessions by increasing prices from 25 to 30 per cent. "The goose will not long survive this golden egg."—J. Pajeau, Chicago, Ill.

If the present demand is granted, I believe the pay rolls of Quincy and Barre will aggregate 30 per cent less than in 1899, for the reason that there will be a heavy increase in the imports of foreign granites in small and medium work, and the placing of orders for vaults and large monumental work will be postponed.—M. H. Rice, Kansas City, Mo.

While we have men in our employ who are worthy of the advance, we have others that cannot earn that amount. We think there should be first and second-class wages.—A. J. Harbaugh.

I think eight hours is not enough, it gives men too much time to spend their wages. Nine hours is very reasonable. I always worked ten hours. I do not blame them for trying to get all the wages they can, but they had ought to be willing to work nine hours.—J. J. McCarthy, Anderson, Indiana.

Such an advance in prices as anticipated would greatly reduce sales of American granite and would lead to an improved trade in imported granites. The demand for increase in wages and decrease in time is unreasonable and unjust to the manufacturers, and we trust will not be granted.—M. V. Mitchell & Son, Columbus, Ohio.

If the demands of granite workers are sustained, it is our opinion that our markets will again be flooded with foreign granites, and that marble will be substituted by many on account of prices of granite being too high; that in the end the success of the granite workers will be detrimental to them, is as much as it will to a great extent deprive them of employment. It will injure the manufacturers in the way of lack of orders, and the industry as a whole, which it no doubt has already done; as no doubt others, as well as ourselves, have pushed marble ahead of granite in all of the smaller work for the last six months, which will not be felt by manufacturers until this year.—F. J. Scholz & Son, Evansville, Indiana.

If anything is done to raise the present prices on granite work we believe it will materially affect the granite business in the South. We have over forty agents in this state selling our work, and although our trade has in the past been principally in marble, there has been an increasing demand for granite, and we have been planning to get up a nice design book of granite work to take the place of marble. In fact we have gone so far as to get a great many designs made; but if prices are increased our trade will use dark blue marble as a substitute for granite because it stands this climate very well, and will be considerably cheaper. We have therefore decided to do no more in the granite business until we find out exactly what is to be done in the way of advancing prices. There will, of course, still be a demand for granite for a better class of work, but we are certain that an advance at this time will make it almost impossible to sell granite in this section for medium and low priced work.—The George W. Clark Co., Jacksonville, Fla.

In regard to the demand of the granite cutters for an eight-hour day, and a minimum of three dollars per day, will say that if we are to base our opinion on the kind of figures the manufacturers are sending us, it looks as though the cutters are making a mistake by not making their increase more gradual. We think this big demand, so suddenly, is going to disturb business very much. It makes it very hard on the retailer; he has the hardest end of it; in fact, he is the man in the middle, with both ends hammering at him. We think it will be the cause of a great deal more foreign stock sold, which has been a very small per cent in the last few years.—W. H. Grindol & Son, Decatur, Ill.

*

Quincy Notes.

William Barclay, of Barclay Bros., Barre, Vt., paid his usual New Year's visit to William Spargo. Judging from the reports that we have received he did up the town very thoroughly.

Nichols's Granite Works recently cut letters on a piece of Quincy granite which is quite a curiosity. It formerly formed the keystone for a tomb in Milton, Mass., cemetery, which was torn down and the bodies buried in the ground. The stone, which from appearance is very old, was polished on the back, and the following dates cut: 1786-1799-1788-1795-1793-1829-1830-1843.

As stated in a previous issue of GRANITE, the manufacturers are believed to be willing to grant the men eight hours with the present minimum price, and if anything can be gathered from the men, a good part of them would be only too glad to continue work upon these terms. It would seem that the present trouble is entirely out of the hands of the local manufacturers as well as being out of the hands of the local branch of the Granite Cutters' Union. The manufacturers' side is in the hands of the New England Association, and that of the men in the hands of the National Union. For this reason neither side has, locally, taken any steps to bring about a settlement, and if anything is done, it must be by the New England Association, and the National Cutters' Union.

Up to the present time the New England Association is firm in its resolve not to grant the eight-hour day with the minimum price of $3.00, and the cutters are just as firm in their resolve not to accept anything else. Quincy received a bad set-back years ago during a labor trouble, but has gradually been getting on its feet again until last year, when business was the best that it has been for years, and the prospects for the present year were such as to warrant a belief that this year's volume of business would exceed that of last year, and it is certainly to be regretted that a labor trouble is now threatened. That the demand of the men is unreasonable, any one who has followed or looked into the business will admit, and in the long run it is the men who must suffer the most thereby.

The Quincy Quarry Co. has elected these officers: Thomas H. McDonnell, Barnabus Clark, Clarence ' James Lyons, Michael Meehan, John Swithin, llings, William A. Hodges, James Thomp-

son. At last reports the above directors had not organized. This company is quite busy just at present filling a large order for grout which is being used by the N. Y., N. H. & H. R. R. at Middleboro.

Granite shipments for the month of December were larger than the amounts estimated, in the table published in the January issue of GRANITE. The amount shipped from Quincy Adams was less than estimated, but West Quincy sent out over one million more than estimated, and the Quarry Railroad over two million more than estimated. The total shipped during the month was 21,404,285 pounds, or 3,204,285 pounds more than estimated. This, therefore, makes the grand total for the year 220,247,395 pounds, a remarkable increase over the preceding year. The December figures were: Quincy Adams, 4,596,420 pounds; West Quincy, 5,602,645 pounds; Quarry Railroad, 11,205,-220 pounds.

But little has been heard for a month of the scheme to form a syndicate of the granite quarries in Quincy, and the general belief is that owing to the tightness of the money market and the dubious outlook, the New York gentlemen who were supposed to come forward with the money, have taken another view of the matter. Those who had quarries to sell and were to get a good price for their plants are sorry that the scheme has apparently failed, but the manufacturers who are not fortunate enough to own quarries, are as a rule well pleased that the scheme has failed. The Quincy promoters, however, have not abandoned all hope as yet, of putting it through, and they say that it is only a question of but a short time when the syndicate will become an assured fact.

McIntosh & Sons have just installed a twelve horse power gasolene engine at their plant, which will furnish power for pneumatic tools, and also sufficient power to run their derrick. Later they may put in a polishing wheel. Work continues to hold good with them and they have a large number of orders on hand. These for the larger part are for medium sized monuments, although they have some good sized work on hand. They do not anticipate that the looked-for labor trouble will bother them much, for if the worst comes the members of the firm will do the cutting themselves, and these with the apprentices will give them a gang of twelve.

T. F. Mannex has long felt the need of more yard room at his plant and some time ago purchased a large lot of land just south of their plant. Upon this they have moved their office, which gives them the much desired room. It is their intention at an early date to enlarge their cutting plant. They have a large amount of work on hand, some large and some small, which they are rushing to get completed by the first of March, for after that date no one at present knows whether there will be anything doing in the granite business or not.

Deacon Bros. report that they have a good lot of work on hand, both large and small, most of which is to be cut from Quincy stock. Business with them last

year was much better than ever before, and at present they have more work on hand than they have ever had before at this time of the year, and as the business outlook is so favorable they regret exceedingly that there should be any labor trouble.

Alexander Marnock & Co. report that they have enough work on hand to keep their force of men at work up to the first of March, but that they are taking no orders at the present bill of prices that cannot be completed before that time. They have figured some, according to the price demanded by the cutters, but find it useless. Mr. Marnock, who is president of the local Granite Manufacturers' Association, does not think the prospect of an early settlement is very bright, and at present can see no way out of the matter. His opinion, therefore, is that a strike is almost certain.

McDonnell & Sons report that they have nearly completed all the orders they have that can possibly be completed before the first of March, and they are taking no new orders that can not be completed before that time. Nearly all the large work they had on hand has been completed and shipped, and they are now at work upon some small monuments.

Joss Bros. Co. are fully as busy now as they have been at any time for a year, although they still complain of their inability to get rough stock as fast as they desire. One of the jobs upon which they are at work is an all polished pedestal for western parties. The job is being cut of Middlebrook (Mo.) granite. This is a new stock for Quincy. Its color is a pinkish red of a somewhat deeper shade than the Braintree red granite. It is a fine-grain, hard granite, and takes a beautiful polish.

A number of Quincy manufacturers have received calls for estimates for monuments that it will be impossible to complete before March 1, and in submitting their estimates they figured upon the basis of the terms demanded by the cutters. As yet, however, no manufacturer has been able to secure any contract upon these figures. This only goes to show that the trade will not stand the increased price necessary.

No one regrets more the uncertain outlook in the granite business than does Joseph Walker of the Aberdeen Granite Works. Work has held remarkably good with him, and the open winter has been very favorable to the business, and the result has been that he has been as busy this winter as he was at any time during the year. To be sure much of his work has been of the medium size kind, but he does not mind as long as he has plenty of it. New orders are constantly coming in, but he is taking no work that can not be completed before the first of March.

Several Quincy granite men have received appointments to city offices under Mayor Hall, among whom are James Thompson, for several years president of the Granite Manufacturers' Association, who has been appointed to the position of principal assessor. Joseph

H. Vogel, and John C. Napples, who is treasurer of the Merry Mount Granite Co., have been appointed on the board of managers of public burial places.

The Merry Mount Granite Co. has elected these officers: clerk, Michael B. Seary; treasurer, John C. Kapples; agent, Peter W. Driscoll; directors, John C. Kapples, John Sullivan, Peter W. Driscoll, Enos S. Costa, Michael B. Geary, James H. Sullivan, Lemuel J. Myers.

Messrs. Thomas & Miller intend to utilize the time while the granite cutters are out to remodel their plant and build an up-to-date plant. They will put in all of the latest machinery such as turning lathes, saws and pneumatic tools, and a travelling derrick capable of hoisting thirty tons. They will also put in several polishing wheels.

The firm of Collins & Knight was dissolved Jan. 1. The business will hereafter be conducted under the name of Thomas Collins.

STONINGTON, CT.—Michael Sullivan has brought suit against Orlando W. Norcross, of the firm of Norcross Brothers, for $10,000 for injuries which he alleges were received through the negligence of the defendant in not preparing suitable tools for cleaning out holes made in solid rock for receiving powder during blasting in a quarry.

PENN YAN, N. Y.—The Lewis monument cut by Emslie & McLeod, Barre, Vt., for F. R. Jenkins, was recently erected in the local cemetery. The monument is eight feet square at the base and stands thirty-three feet in height. On the face of the monument to the south is the name, "John L. Lewis," raised in round-headed letters; on the second base, on the face of the die, in bas relief are the square and compass; on the north side of the die, in bas relief, are the 33d degree emblems, the double eagles, the cross and the crown. In bas relief on the east side is the keystone. On the west side are the cross and the crown. The die is concave, with corners finely carved.

CULPEPER, VA.—The Rappahannock Chapter, Daughters of the Confederacy, contemplates the erection of a monument to the soldiers of that county who fell during the war of 1861-1865. Subscriptions to the amount of $330 and a private donation of $100 are already in hand for this purpose.

The National Association of Spanish-American War Veterans has undertaken the work of raising funds for the erection of a suitable monument or memorial to the memory of General Lawton, the same to be placed wherever the family of the deceased may desire. The following officers have been named by the association to take charge of the work and act in conjunction with all who desire to aid in the project: President, General Willis J. Hulings. Oil City; treasurer, Col. E. W. Hine, Orange, N. J.; secretary, Adjutant General W. C. Liller, Lancaster, Pa.; director, Col. Jas. B. Coryell.

"GRANITE," FEBRUARY, 1900.

BASE . . . R — Y x C — T x C — A
DIE . . . . A — A x Y — A Y x R — T

PRICE: Troy Granite, Westerly, and Milford (N. H.) Granite.
  without lettering . . . . $ I A
  Barre Granite . . . . $ T E

Subject to increase of price after March 1

"GRANITE," FEBRUARY, 1900.

BASE . . . P — A x A — N x C — A
PLINTH . . R — E x C — C C x Y — C, Y
DIE . . . A — C Y x A — E x C — Pil

PRICE:
Troy, Westerly, and Milford (N. H.) Granite . $ C T E
Barre Granite . . . . $ C T'Y
Quincy Granite . . . . $ C E N

Prices subject to an increase after March 1

"GRANITE" FEBRUARY, 1900.

Base	. . .	$I - Y \times P - P \times C^L - R$
Plinth	.	$E - C \times Y \times R - A \times C - Y$
Die	. . .	$E - Y \times A - P \times A - Y$
Cap	. . .	$E - N \times R - Y \times C - A$

PRICE:
{ Troy, Westerly, and Milford (N. H.) . $T I E
{ Barre Granite . . . . $T C E
{ Quincy Granite . . . . $T A E

Subject to an increase after March 1

Barre News.

Malcom McIver, a member of the firm of McIver & Ruxton, was married Jan. 26. May his life over the seas of matrimony be as smooth as a calm summer day.

We illustrate in the Hoffer & Corti advertisement, a tablet just completed by this firm. It is without exception the finest piece of flower carving in granite that we have ever seen. The rose branch and stem of the flowers were relieved from the tablet and made as true to nature as it is possible to make in granite. The flower stem is not over a quarter of an inch through and the rose branch about the same. This firm have a large amount of fine carved work on hand which they are thoroughly capable of executing in the best possible manner.

Marr & Gordon are showing an order book full of contracts calling for all grades of monumental work from a 12x10 bottom base to the smallest size tablet. Among them is a mausoleum, several shaft jobs, Celtic crosses, etc. Most of the contracts call for more or less carving.

Barclay Bros.' shed is an object lesson in what it is possible to do in granite, for under the hammer are every grade and size of monuments. It is impossible to pick out anything for special mention as it is all far above the average.

William E. Whitcomb, a member of the firm of Smith, Whitcomb & Cook, machinists and manufacturers of derricks, etc., died Dec. 10. The firm of which he was a member is one of the best known in the trade and Mr. Whitcomb was the active member. We were well acquainted with Mr. Whitcomb, and a more thoroughly honest and whole-souled man it has not been our pleasure to meet. The business will be continued by Will A. Whitcomb, who has long been connected with the business.

There is a better feeling among all classes connected with the granite business here than there was at the time of our last communication, and, indeed, better than it has been before since there was any danger of any trouble the coming March. It seems more probable now than ever that there will not be any prolonged difficulty between the employer and the employees.

The opinion in reference to the advisability of the change is not materially different from what it was months ago, and now, as then, the general opinion is most decidedly against the grand upward turn in prices.

Every plant visited by the GRANITE representative was alive with work, and things look more encouraging than one would naturally suppose with such a radical change staring the trade in the face.

Thus far this winter there has been nothing to hinder work on the quarries progressing at full blast, as there has been only just enough snow for good sledding, and hardly that until January came in. Consequently there has been an unusual amount of stock quarried, not alone for the present need of the jobs upon which work has begun, but for orders which will not be touched for a long time, as well. This will do away somewhat with the not uncommon complaint in the springtime of being behind because stock could not be obtained for the monument.

Money is coming in rather slowly, so say all the manufacturers in the city and it is not improving in that regard either. Every one who has asked for thirty days during the summer and whose usual custom is either thirty, or at most sixty days, now wants ninety, and quite often as long as four months after the bill of lading is received. This is rather distressing to the smaller dealers and necessitates their loosing quite a percentage of their profits in discounting their paper. The banks are flooded with paper, good, bad and medium, and have now got to the pass that they will not handle only the very best notes unless they are backed by parties who have a recognized financial standing.

Work continues to be plenty with the firm of E. L. Smith & Co.; and they are making the business rush. They have recently booked several orders which will take them beyond the first of March to complete unless they make a great extra effort in that direction. They are not willing to express an opinion as to the probability of a settlement of the labor troubles; they only say that they hope that they will not be forced to be idle during one of the most promising seasons which the granite business has ever known. It would be a great loss to the manufacturers as well as to the cutters if a prolonged strike should occur. This concern also owns and operates both a light and dark quarry which it is probable would necessarily lay idle during the trouble.

The Sweeney Bros. Granite Co., Montpelier, is doing a good business. They have a good commodious plant and are running about three gangs of cutters. Work is coming in quite rapidly and the orders which they are receiving, are of a good class.

Doucette Brothers are having good orders come in, and their business has increased during the year which has passed. During the past few months they have made shipments of several good orders to New York parties and have some more work nearly ready for the cars.

Robins Brothers are having their usual amount for this time of the year and consider it very satisfactory. They are employing about one gang of men and are at work upon a large sarcophagus job. The most of their work is of the medium sized class, and every piece of work which goes out of their plant is cut as near the standard as possible.

The Lane Manufacturing Co., Montpelier, Vt., has been the busiest during the past six months that they have been for many years, and during the past month especially they have been so rushed with orders that they have been obliged to put on a night force. They have constructed most of the travelling cranes which have been put into the new plants both in this city and Montpelier during the year, and

NOVELLI & CORTI,
Statuary
—AND—
Carving.

PORTRAIT FIGURES,
BUSTS AND IDEAL FIGURES

In all kinds of New England Granite.

CARVING

Executed in any style.   Floral Work a Specialty.

Models furnished on application.

We invite all dealers who need high-art work to correspond directly with us. ¡We can give best of references.

NOVELLI & CORTI,   P. O. BOX 57.   **BARRE, VT.**

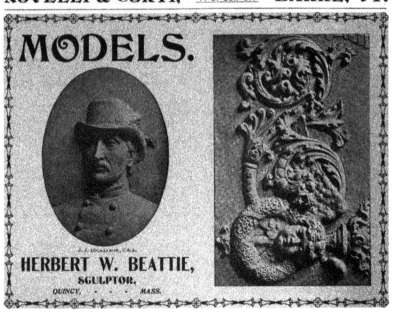

MODELS.

J. J. DICKSON, C.S.A.

HERBERT W. BEATTIE,
SCULPTOR.
QUINCY, - - - MASS.

have also shipped them to almost every one of the New England states and not a few into the Provinces. They built one of the largest and strongest cranes which are constructed in the country, and have the reputation of giving entire satisfaction to their customers.

Mutch & Calder have a shed full of work, both large and small, and are pushing things to their fullest capacity. They are working about three gangs of men just at this time, and consequently their weekly shipments are large. Every facility for handling work well and with dispatch is at their command, and the work which they send out is always first-class in every particular. They have several jobs worth mentioning under the hammer, and orders are continually coming in. Much of the work which they are taking now, they are taking subject to all labor troubles, and on the basis of three dollars for a day of eight hours.

Outside of the probability, or rather the possibility, of a strike in the spring, they report that they are unable to see one cloud above the horizon. Everything looks as though the coming season will be one of the most prosperous which the industry has ever had.

The plant which is operated by George Straiton has a large amount of work on hand of one kind and another, and he reports that work is coming in as fast as one could expect at this season of the year. He has made some extensive shipments during the last few weeks and has several other large jobs which will be ready for the cars very soon. He is of the opinion that the coming year will be the best one which this city has ever known in the granite business. The business has increased about one-half since he entered his new quarters about a year ago, and it is still increasing.

Beck & Beck have a plant well filled with work and are employing about two gangs of cutters at this time. They have on their books also a large amount of orders which call for immediate construction, and several which they have figured upon the basis of an advance in prices resultant upon the increase in wages. Their work on hand includes several sarcophagus jobs, a couple of cottage monuments and one column die job, together with the small work which is always to be found in every plant.

It would be a sad thing, indeed, if there should be any serious and prolonged trouble this spring, for the outlook for a rushing business was never brighter than it is today. The manufacturers in this city and vicinity were never in a better condition to attend to their increasing business than now, and they can produce a class of work which cannot be excelled. Consequently it would produce bad results if the whole business should come to a standstill for a number of months, for besides the loss of profit and interest during the time it would be like starting in new again and working up a business.

We hope for the best, and that best in our humble opinion would be a settlement even with a little "giving in" on both sides.

Monthly Trade Record.

This department is compiled and edited by the United Mercantile Agency. Subscribers, in accordance with the terms of their contracts are entitled to receive further information relative to the parties hereafter mentioned, upon application to the main office. As the names of many business men who are good will appear herein, subscribers can readily see the importance of making inquiries if interested, previous to taking any action.

ARKANSAS.
Fordyce, *M—Clendining, T. D., 76.
Little Rock, *M—Funston Marble & Granite Co., receiver sold assets.

COLORADO.
Denver, *M—Eclat Granite Co., 76.
Denver, *M—Green & Bird, 76.
Denver, *M—Roberts & Jones, 76.
Denver, *M—Staples & Downie, 76.

CONNECTICUT.
Norwich, *M—Frink, L. W., 76.

ILLINOIS.
Chicago, *M—Wright, Harry S., 38.
Fairfield, *M—Dwyer, W. T., succeeds Dwyer & Reinhardt,
Fulton, *M—Doran, M. R., 106.
Kankakee, *M—Faessler Bros., 76.
Lewiston, *M—Lackey, J. W., 76.
Mount Carroll, *M—Ehmer & Ehmer, 86, to T. A. Wachtel.
Olney, *M—Coles, A. H., 76.
Whitehall, *M—Watson & Danforth, 64, Hiram Watson, 58.

INDIANA.
Alexandria, *M—Brenneman, James F., 93 $1,000 and 80.
Columbus, *M—Hutchings & Strickland succeed Hutchings & Phillips.
Lebanon, *M—Dooley, Holmes & Co. succeed S. W. Dooley & Son.
Mooresville, *M—Bryant & Ensminger succeed J. A. Bryant.

IOWA.
Davenport, *M—Iglehart & McKeown, 80.
Fort Dodge, *M—Delano, A. M., 14 $330.
Gladbrook, *M—Delfs & Cobert, 76.
Marshalltown, *M—Woods, W. W. & Son, W. W. Woods, 93 $800.
Perry, *M—Gould Granite Co., 76.
Winterset, *M—Wilson & Clark, J. W. Clark, 93 $600.

KANSAS.
Dodge City, *M—Smith & Kingrey, 76.
Wichita, *M—Penniwell Granite Works, 14 $1,008.

MAINE.
Augusta, *M—Laplante & Lemieux, offering to compromise.

MARYLAND.
Baltimore, *M—Flynn, John J., 32 $5 and 93 $4,500.
Baltimore, *M—Gault, Matthew & Son, Matthew Gault, 20 $112.
Baltimore, *M—Graham, Frank F., 74 $480.
Baltimore, *M—Hellen, George E., 87 $400.
Baltimore, *M—McKnight, John, 74 $480.

MASSACHUSETTS.
Fall River, GZ—Cottrell, William G., 87 $100.
Fitchburg, G—Rollstone Granite & Construction Co., 14 $3,000.

Lawrence, GQ—Lawrence & Raymond Granite Co.
(-Inc.), 76.--
Leominster, *M—Kittredge, M. H., 50.
Middleboro, *M—Surrey & Elliot, 64, D. S. Surrey
58.
New Bedford, *M—Gurd, Frank J., succeeds Wil-
liam Doran.
North Adams, *M—Hosley, A. B., 78.
Quincy, GZ—Berni & Tondini, 14 $300.
MICHIGAN.
 Jackson, *M—Leslie, John G., 14 $321.
Standish, *M—Tribbles, E. R., 76.
MINNESOTA.
Albert Lea, *M—Subby, Nels P., 93 $500.
Renville, *M—Levi, H. J., 106.
Tracy, *M—Harding, E. E., 76.
MISSOURI.
Powersville, *M—Bucher & Ellis, 76.
St. Louis, *M—Douglas, George, & Co., 80.
St. Louis, *M—O'Shea, Jeremiah, 80.
NEW-HAMPSHIRE.
Concord, GZ—Gannon, Michael J., 14 $150.
Concord, GZ—Tressider Bros., J. H. Tressider, 78.
Farmington, *M—Pride, H. W., 76.
NEW JERSEY.
Hoboken, *M—Riley Bros., 14 $2,781.
NEW YORK.
Albany, *M—Milne & Benton, 76.
Kingston, *M—Luther, H.ᵃ B?, 78.'
Little Falls, *M—Johnson, Thomas H., 78.
Lowville, *M—Morrison & Seymour succeed Morri-
son & Williams.
New York, GZ—Edwards, James H., 87 $500.
New York, *M—Presbrey & Coykendall, 76.
Phoenix, *M—Allen, Reuben Y., 106.
Syracuse, *M—Earl, Charles F., 76.
Utica, *M—Salladin, Henry L., 76.
Warsaw, *M—Hanigan, John, & Son, succeed John
Hanigan.
Wolcott, *M—Lawrence, J. E., 70.
OHIO.
Athens, *M—Gleason, John, 93 $925.
Cincinnati *M—Kistner, Henry, 99 $3,000.
Lima, *M—Wells, S. M. (Mrs. E. V.), 99 $550.
New Philadelphia, *M—Wagner, A. J. & Co., 76.
Warren, *M—Trigg, S. J., 78.
OKLAHOMA.
Perry, *M—Amos, P. R., 76.
PENNSYLVANIA.
Butler, *M—Reno, F. M., execution $1,000.
Erie, *M—Weber, S. J., 76.
Pittsburg, *M—Brown, William C., 80.
Sellin's Grove, *M—Miller, M. L., 78.
Wattsburg, *M—Huntley, E. D., 76.
RHODE ISLAND.
Providence, *M—Toye & Holmes, Holmes sues for
dissolution.
VERMONT.
Barre, GZ—McKay & Dowers succeed A. McKay.
WASHINGTON.
Seattle, *M—Puget Sound Marble and Granite Co.,
H. B. Kennedy, 87 $2,000.
Spokane, G—East End Granite Co., 74 $182.
WISCONSIN. --- :
Galesville *M—Hess & Bartholomew 64, Albert A.
Bartholomew 58.

Books, Pamphlets, Etc., Received.

The Ladies' Home Journal for January. This number is fully up to the excellence of this well known
publication. It contains among other articles,
Article No. 4 in the series of the "The Theatre and
Its People." This article deals with the rehearsal of
a play from the first reading to the first performance
and is well illustrated. Another article entitled
"Where the New Century Will Really Begin." This
article should settle many disputes which the uninitiated are liable to fall into. Another article from the
pen of Finley Peter Dunne, the author of "Mr.
Dooley." This article is entitled "Mollie Donahue, who
Lives Across the Way from Mr. Dooley." In fact the
whole issue is full of good things worth reading.

"The Practical Stone Cutter and Masons' Assistant"
is a book of 151 pages and contains a collection of
examples of arches, retaining walls, buttresses, vaults,
tombs, etc., with explanations of the most approved
and economical methods of working them out, together with a description of the tools (illustrated) used
by the stone cutters, by Fred T. Hodgson, architect.
Price 75 cents, Industrial Publication Company, New
York.

Two publications entitled "Air and Gas Compressors" and "Rock Drills and Drill Mountings" issued by the Rand Drill Company, New York. They
are both the best possible production of the press; the
illustrations are the best that money can secure; the
press work and composition are excellent. They stand
at the head of trade catalogues, not only from an
artistic standpoint, but from the plain and thorough
manner in which both air and gas compressors and
rock drills are explained.

A book entitled "The Empire of the South," containing nearly two hundred pages, is without exception the most comprehensive volume that has ever
been issued in the interest of any section, and tells in
an interesting way the rapid strides made in the country east of the Mississippi and south of the Ohio and
Potomac. The Southern Railway is the publisher of
this volume, which is in no sense a railroad advertisement. It contains five hundred half-tone illustrations
from photographs. Copies may be had by enclosing
fifteen cents, the exact postage, to George C. Daniels,
N. E. Passenger Agent, 228 Washington street, Boston.

Among the calenders received is one from E. E.
Hubbell, Elbridge, N. Y. It gives two half-tone views
of his office and cutting shed, and states that he carries
twenty marble and one hundred and twenty-five granite monuments in stock. Surely this is a fair proportion, six to one, and we hope that Mr. Hubbell will
make it sixteen to one. The calender is of the large-
size order, plain and substantial.

A small calendar from George W. Rose, proprietor
of the Sonora Marble and Granite Works, Hamilton,
Ill., with half-tone cut of the proprietor.

From Spon & Chamberlain, 12 Cortland street, New
York city, a "System of Easy Lettering," by J. Howard Cromwell. This book should be of great help to
the granite cutter, as the system is simple and comprehensive. Price 50 cents. For sale by A. M. Hunt &
Co., publishers of GRANITE.

From Alexander McDonald Company, Trenton, N. J., A. R. Baxter, editor, a publication entitled "Trade Notes." It is their intention to publish quarterly, and we wish the new paper all kinds of success.

The Saturday Evening Post, four issues for December and January. It is impossible to separate any individual story or article for especial comment. They are all good. This paper fills in a place not already occupied, and the price brings it within the reach of all.

Notes on Ornament.

By Herbert W. Beattie, Sc., Quincy.

"Style" in ornament is analogous to "hand" in writing, and this is its literal signification. As every individual has some peculiarity in his mode of writing, so every age or nation has been distinguished in its ornamental expression by a certain individuality of taste, either original or borrowed. It is the comprehension of these individual tastes, characterizing various times and people, which must constitute the education of the ornamental designer.

In a review of ornamental styles, we shall find that the elements of form are constant in all cases; they are but variously treated. This, in fact, must be so, if a style be founded upon any principles at all; and those styles which have carried with them the feelings of ages could not be otherwise than based upon some fixed natural laws. The elements of style are of two kinds, natural and fanciful.

The investigation of the principles of ornamental art is an inquiry into the nature and character of these elements; how the effects of certain variations of form and color happen to be so universally appreciated that the varieties of their arrangements have been used by all people from the remotest times. It is highly important that one should endeavor to comprehend the principles of ornament. There are two provinces of ornament, the flat and the relieved. In the flat, we have contrast of light and dark; in the relieved, a contrast of light and shade. Ornament, therefore, is a system of contrasts.

Decoration or ornamentation we may divide into two classes, the flat and the round, or in other words, painting and modelling. That of painting is the far more extensive class, the relieved or modelling is limited to building purposes, monuments, metal work and jewelry, etc.

Ornament is essentially the accessory to, and not the substitute of, the useful; it is a decoration or adornment; it can have no independent existence practically.

In no popular style of ornament have natural details ever yet prevailed. The details of all great styles are largely derived from nature, but for the most part conventionally treated; theory and practice seem to show that this is the true system. A plant is said to be "conventionally" treated, when the national order, or its growth or development, is disregarded. When the exact imitation of the details, and its own order of development are both observed, the treatment is natural.

It is requisite that we should have a clear understanding of the difference between a natural and a conventional treatment of an object. A natural treatment implies natural imitation and arrangement; but an ornamental treatment does not necessarily exclude imitation in the parts; as, for instance, a scroll may be composed of strictly natural parts; but as no plant would grow in an exact spiral direction, the scroll form constitutes the ornamental or conventional arrangements.

We may have, however, conventionalities of detail as well as conventionalities of arrangement. A leaf or a flower, for instance, may be represented as it appears, with all the local accidents of light and shade and color; this would be a strictly natural representation. And it may be represented as a mere diagram, that is, as we "know" it to be, without reference to its appearance; or it may be treated as a mere shadow of itself, as a silhouette; the two latter would be conventional treatments; and it is such representations we find almost exclusively in Egyptian and Greek art.

There can be no question that the motive or ornament is not the presentation of natural images to the mind, but the rendering the object ornamented as agreeable as possible, and therefore the "details" of decoration should have no independent character of their own, but be kept purely subservient to beauty of effect.

(To be continued.)

Correspondence.

We enclose herewith one dollar for subscription to GRANITE for the current year, and wish to say that we consider it of value much in excess of its modest price.

Very truly yours,
C. W. CANFIELD,
New England Monument Co.

Jackson, Mich., Jan. 15, 1900.

Find enclosed post office order for one dollar in payment of our subscription to GRANITE, which we continue to appreciate more and more.

Yours truly,
LESLIE & MITCHELL.

Montpelier, Vt., Jan. 11, 1900.

Allow us to congratulate you on the improvement of your journal, GRANITE, for January, 1900. It certainly commands attention, and as an advertiser we appreciate your efforts. It now looks most prosperous and we trust that it will be a means of prosperity to the publishers of this valuable paper. The reading matter and cuts are worthy of no little perusal and attention and we now hail GRANITE as the coming journal of the trade and can only add the expressive words of the Irishman "More power to you."

Yours truly,
SWEENEY BROS. GRANITE CO.

Woburn, Mass., Dec. 30, 1899.

Enclosed please find $1.00, the price of subscription to your paper. We like it very much and hope this coming year you will give us some granite tablets as well as monuments (in illustration), also some points on lettering. This strike will cripple us terribly, will drive the work back on marble.

Yours truly,
JOHN J. HERN.

Northfield, Vt., Jan. 16, 1900.

We want to say that we were very much pleased with our ad. in your January number; it was arranged very nicely and was very attractive, and we have heard from it very often.

Very truly yours,
CROSS BROS.

Proposed Monuments and Monumental News.

PATERSON, N. J.—It is proposed to erect a monument to the memory of the late Vice President Hobart.

PATERSON, N. J.—In accordance with the bequest of the late William High the Knights of Pythias in this district are making preparations for the erection of a Pythian monument at Cedar Lawn cemetery. Mr. High left $3,000 for the purpose, the sum of $2,500 to be used in the purchase and erection of a Pythian monument and $500 for the purchase of a plot, with the proviso that a sum of not less than $1,000 be raised among the lodges for the burial plot. A committee of five from each of the lodges in the district has been appointed, and they have elected Alfred Crew chairman. It was found that there would be no difficulty in raising even more than the amount required under Mr. High's will.

BOSTON, MASS.—The Victorian club, which hopes to erect a monument to the memory of British dead that lie buried in the Central burying ground, Boston common, has, through its committee, received permission from Mayor Quincy and the cemetery board to erect a suitable monument. "It now remains for the Victorian club to determine upon a design and ascertain the cost of the monument. Respectfully submitted, Thomas T. Stokes, James H. Stark, James Murray Kay, A. A. Haserick, B. R. Ussher, committee on monument." While no design has been accepted, it is intended that Boston men shall be the ones favored. No decision will be reached until those who desire have submitted designs. The offers of contributions to the fund are reported to be liberal and of an encouraging nature.

BOSTON, MASS.—The proposed Parnell monument to be erected in Dublin is attracting considerable interest among the artists of this country, and already one design has been prepared for the memorial by Giovanni Rapetti, a Boston sculptor. The design is now being perfected and will be sent to the Lord Mayor of Dublin in a few weeks. It shows Parnell in life-size standing position making an address. At the base of the monument is Erin with her chains broken, inscribing Parnell's name on the pedestal.

MANCHESTER, N.H.—Senator Jacob H. Gallinger has placed before the senate of the United States a bill calling for the expenditure of the sum of $40,000, or such part of the same as may be necessary, for the erection of an equestrian statue within the limits of this city in honor of Major-General John Stark, the hero of Bennington.

CULPEPER, VA.—The local chapter of Daughters of the Confederacy, of Washington, Rappahannock county, is raising funds to erect a monument to the soldiers of the Confederacy from Rappahannock county. The daughters have already in hand $330 in cash and a $100 donation. They hope to erect the monument next spring.

KNOXVILLE, PA.—The Sons of Veterans have set on foot a plan to erect a monument to General W. P. Sanders, who was killed in the battle of Fort Sanders during the civil war.

ELIZABETH, N. J.—The committee of the Ninth New Jersey Volunteers authorized at a meeting to arrange for the erection of a monument over the grave of the late General Charles A. Heckman met December 10. The bids were opened and the contract awarded to Howell & Sons of Easton, Pa., for $6,000 The monument is to be of Vermont granite and to weigh thirteen tons.

SYRACUSE, N. Y.—$1,400 has been subscribed for the erection of a monument to Fire Chief Philip Eckel. $1,600 will be raised.

MADISON, WIS.—The supreme court have issued a peremptory writ of mandamus, commanding the judge of the Milwaukee circuit court to enter an order dismissing the suit of John S. Conway, the sculptor, against Ex-Senator John L. Mitchell. Mr. Conway has sued Mr. Mitchell for $10,000 for the soldiers' monument which Mr. Mitchell was to give the city. He got a verdict in the lower court, which was reversed on appeal. The costs had not been paid and under the statute the court orders the case dismissed.

BALTIMORE, MD.—Ground has been purchased at Sharpsburg upon which to erect a monument to the Fifteenth Massachusetts Regiment, Second Corps, under command of General Sumner.

BALTIMORE, MD.—The Society of the Sons of the Revolution proposes to honor the memory of Maryland patriots who fought in the revolutionary war by erecting a suitable monument. The organization now has on hand for this purpose funds amounting to about $15,000, and it is proposed to increase this sum by public contributions to $20,000—the cost of the memorial, a design for which is being prepared by J. Appleton Wilson, one of the members.

SCRANTON, PA.—At a meeting held December 4 the county commissioners decided to accept the design of the Harrison Granite Company of Barre, Vt., for the soldiers' monument, and formally awarded the contract to that firm at the sum of $50,000. Six designs were received by the county commissioners. The monument will be of granite throughout, with the exception of the statues on the base and the figure on the top, which will be 13 feet in height, emblematic of Peace. All the figures will be of bronze. The height of the monument will be 100 feet, the base being 30 feet by 40 feet. The diameter of the shaft will be eight feet. The contract for the granite work has been placed by the Harrison Granite Company with the Woodbury Granite Company, Hardwick, Vt.

BINGHAMTON, N. Y.—At a meeting of the Exempt Firemen's association December 7, plans for a monument were presented. It will be 22 1-2 feet in height above the ground, and will have a double base. It will be made of granite, quarried at Concord, N. H. On one side of the shaft will be cut a fireman's hat with two crossed-trumpets, and on the base the words: "Exempt Firemen."

OGDEN, UTAH.—Articles of incorporation of the Utah Volunteer Monument association were filed November 25. The incorporators are William Glasmann and others. The object of the incorporation is "for the purpose of building and erecting a monument and statues in Lester Park in Ogden city, in honor of the Utah volunteers in the Spanish-American and Philippine war, and in memory of those Utah volunteers who died in said war in defence of their country.

BLOOMSBURG, PA.—The Columbia county grand jury unanimously approved of the erection of a soldiers' monument, to cost exactly $5,000. The monument is to be erected on Market square.

PENN YAN, N. Y.—The question of appropriating $3,000 toward the erection of a soldiers' monument in this village will be voted on at the next meeting of the supervisors.

The original burial place of the remains of Sergeant Charles Floyd, the first American soldier to die within the confines of the Louisana purchase, are to be marked with an appropriate monument. The spot on which he was buried is known to have been Sergeant Bluff on the Missouri river, south of Sioux city. For several years past the citizens of Sioux city have been endeavoring to raise the necessary money for the erection of a monument, and it is now understood that the requisite amount has been raised. A bill authorizing the expenditure of $5,000 for the purpose has been passed, and the citizens intended to raise that amount to about $15,000.

OMAHA, NEB.—The fund for a monument to Company H, First Regiment, South Dakota Volunteers, is growing slowly at present, the amount thus far received being $400 short of what is desired.

JANESVILLE, WIS.—Rock county, it is likely, will have a $10,000 soldiers' monument located here. At a recent G. A. R. meeting, held at Beloit, a committee representing the various G. A. R. Posts in Rock county were appointed to push the project. C. E. Lee of Evansville is chairman of this committee, and has caused a resolution to be introduced to appropriate $10,000 by a special tax levy for the monument purpose and to submit the proposition to the voters of the county as provided by law.

WASHINGTON, D. C.—One of the most magnificent and most beautiful memorials in the world will be the bridge, 2,200 feet long and 70 feet wide, which is to be erected across the Potomac river at Washington at a cost estimated at from one to five million dollars. It is to be "A Memorial to American Patriotism" and in its scope will include the valiant men of every period of United States history and of every section of our common country, perpetuating the heroic deeds of all men known as Americans throughout the world.

WASHINGTON, D. C.—Representative Grosvenor of Ohio has introduced the following bill for the erection of a memorial: The secretary of war be authorized and directed to erect at Chattanooga, Tenn., under the provision of the Chickamauga and Chattanooga National Park commission and their engineer, upon such site as the said secretary may deem most suitable, a memorial arch to be known as the Arch of Nationality, to commemorate the heroism of the American soldier, and the complete union which has resulted from the joint military service of all sections in the war with Spain. The several dimensions of the arch shall not be less than those of the Arc de Triomphe in Paris, and its main portions shall be constructed of massive blocks of granite. To enable the secretary of war to carry forward this work, after the adoption of the designs, the sum of $300,000 is appropriated.

WASHINGTON, D. C.—It is proposed to erect a monument to the memory of Eben Brewer, who died in Cuba while he was working for the reorganization of the mail service. The committee is made up from the postmasters of Erie, Pa., Cleveland, O., and Rockford, Ill.

TWENTY-TON TRAVELING CRANE.

ADDRESS

Lane Manufacturing Co.,

MONTPELIER, VT.

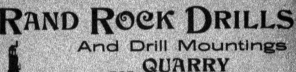

WALTER W. FIELD,

117 Main Street, Cambridgeport, Mass.

...TELEPHONE 73 CAMBRIDGE...

NEW ENGLAND AGENT FOR

THE LAMBERT
HOISTING ENGINE CO.

500 Styles and Sizes.
Built to Gauges and Templates.

For Mining, Quarrying, Coal Handling, Pile Driving, Builders' use, Logging and General Contracting.

**Electric Hoists, Single and Double Drums,
with Improved Automatic Brake.
Suspension Cableways.**

—— SEND FOR NEW CATALOGUE B. ——

Horizontal, Locomotive and Upright

BOILERS.

Engine in Stock for Quick Delivery.

**Standard Double Cylinder Double Patent Friction Drum Double Winch
Hoisting Engine, with Boiler and Fixtures Complete.**

CAN YOU AFFORD TO BE WITHOUT IT?

THE SUBSCRIPTION PRICE TO

Granite is $1.00 Per Year.

Published Monthly. $1.50 with our Imperial Design Book No. I. Look over this issue
carefully, then let us know what you think of it.

McINTOSH
Quincy Granite
Monuments

Let us give you a sample of our work, and then judge for yourself whether or not it is THE BEST.

McINTOSH & SONS, - - QUINCY, MASS.

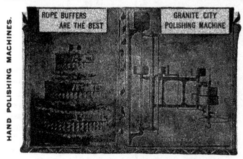

March, 1900

Vol. X. No. 3

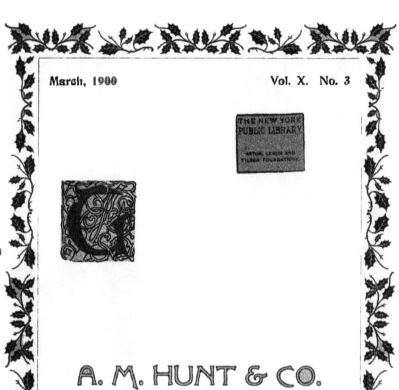

A. M. HUNT & CO.

PUBLISHERS

131 Devonshire Street

BOSTON, MASS., U.S.A.

Subscription Price, $1.00 Year

ADVERTISERS' DIRECTORY.

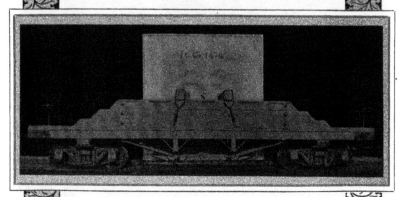

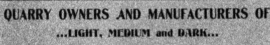

Well, Well! Not Dead Yet,

But you will be, wearing your life away on that hard granite when you can buy of us a light and medium stone that will work in half the time, look just as well

and last just as long. We can get you any size, any shape most any day in the year. Our patterns are excellent and prices reasonable.

VIEWS OF OUR QUARRY.

· Hopkins, Huntington & Co.,

Quarry Owners and Manufacturers. BARRE, VERMONT.

GRANITE

ENTERED AT THE BOSTON POST OFFICE AS SECOND-CLASS MAIL MATTER.

Vol. X.   BOSTON, MASS., MARCH 1, 1900.   No. 3

A. M. HUNT, EDITOR.

Published Monthly in the interests of the Producer Manufacturer, and Retailer of Granite as used for Monumental or Building Purposes.

Terms of Subscription

To ANY PART OF THE UNITED STATES OR CANADA:

One copy, one year - - - - $1.00, in advance.
One copy, six months . - - 75 cents, in advance.

ADVERTISING RATES FURNISHED UPON APPLICATION.

A. M. HUNT & CO., Publishers,
131 DEVONSHIRE STREET, - - BOSTON, MASS.

ditorials

WE have received a number of letters from retail dealers throughout the country asking for suggestions regarding the securing of a reduction of freight rates on monuments and vaults from eastern points to the Missouri River. We suggested in a previous issue that the best way to get at the matter was to enter a protest to the proper authorities against the change in classification of granite work, which went into effect January 1, 1900, and meant an advance on less than carload lots of forty per cent. We can best illustrate as to what it is possible to do in this direction by giving what has been done by the New England Association through work put in by Seward W. Jones, of Jones Bros., a member of the advisory committee, and W. H. Mitchell, president of the Association. The matter was originally taken up with C. E. Gill, chairman of the eastern classification committee, headquarters in New York, on December 22, and relates entirely to less than carload shipments from eastern points to Chicago. The letter called Mr.

Gill's attention to the injustice of the change and protested against it, requesting that he look into the matter. Mr. Gill acknowledged the receipt of the letter, and stated that the matter would be given careful consideration by the classification committee. On December 30th a letter was received from Charles A. Prouty, a member of the Inter-state Commerce Commission, in answer to a protest addressed to the commission, in which he answers in part as follows: "You, together with a great majority of the shippers, have an erroneous idea of the power of the Inter-state Commerce Commission to grant the relief asked for. I express no opinion as to the reasonableness of the proposed advances, but assuming them to be utterly unreasonable as the shippers contend, the commission has no power whatever to grant you any effective remedy. I have been saying this and trying to make shippers understand it ever since my connection with the commission, and now you have a practical illustration of the situation. There is an advance in rates, which, in many cases, amounts to one hundred per cent of the original rate made by concerted agreement of the carriers, without any opportunity for shippers to be heard and without adequate consideration of the effects which such advances will have, and yet the public is entirely at the mercy of the carriers. Railroads ought to be fairly treated, and they ought to be allowed to earn a fair return upon their investment. I do not believe that the shipping community should be entirely in their hands. There is now before congress a bill looking to an amendment of the Inter-state Commerce Act, which I hope shippers will examine and support if it deserves support. We wish to say in this connection that every granite manufacturer, retail dealer or quarry owner can see the advisability of this bill becoming a law. We doubt if much attention would have been paid to it if they had not received recently a practical illustration of the effect of railroads controlling the entire situation. Every retail dealers' association should take it upon themselves and pass the resolutions, which we publish elsewhere, which were recently passed by the Granite Manufacturers' Association of New England and bring it before their representatives to congress. Mr. Prouty further added that the matter had been referred to the Attorney General, who possibly would take some action in the matter, and that if the granite manufacturers desired to make a specific complaint they would notify him, Mr. Prouty, to that effect, but that the decision of the commission would amount to but very little more than a recommendation; and that the railroads had usually treated the commission with great courtesy and usually considered their recommendations. The complaint was drawn up and sent to the Inter-state Commission. The following protest was sent on January 1st to C. E. Gill, chairman of the eastern classification committee. All granite is loaded and unloaded at the expense of the shipper and consignee and is usually shipped in gondola and flat cars; it is securely boxed, and the risk with ordinary handling is normal. Second, the increase amounts to about forty per cent of the rates and will have a tendency to restrict the output of New England granites in favor of western granites. Third, the valuation clause reduces the railroad's responsibility to a minimum, as forty per cent per cubic feet does not represent more than half the value of rough granite before any labor is put on it. To illustrate the cite the following: A piece of granite 4-0 x 2-0 x 2-0 contains 16 cubic feet. The actual market value of this when quarred is $16, while the restricted value under the new classification is forty per cent per cubic feet, or $6.40, being the amount of the railroad company's liability in case of loss or damage. The labor on such a stone varies according to the use to which it is put, but ordinarily it would cost about $75 to manufacture it for ordinary monumental purposes, making the total value of the stone when loaded on the car $91, with the liability of the railroad company, as above stated, $6.40 in case of damage or loss. The present fourth-class rate from Boston to Chicago is thirty-five cents per hundred pounds in less than carload lots. The third-class rate is fifty cents per hundred pounds, making an increase of over forty per cent. Considering the valuation clause, the fact that the goods are loaded and unloaded at the expense of the shipper and consigner, and that it can be loaded into almost any kind of a car, we feel that rather than an increase there should be a decrease in the present rates. It is certainly doing a great injury to the business to increase it as proposed. There was also a protest entered against the classification on statuary. It was proposed to put this in the first class, restricting the valuation to forty cents per cubic ft. The actual increase of granite work in less than carload lots is from thirty-five, the old rate, to fifty cents; differential rate from thirty-one to forty-four cents. As a result of the protest, we are told that the following changes will be made, which means a reduction of about twenty per cent. The rate of fifty cents, which went into effect on January 1, will be dropped to forty cents, or to within five cents of the old rate; differential rate dropped to thirty-five cents, or four cents more than the old rate. We can get no definite idea as to just what date this rate will go into effect, but the Association has been informed that it will be changed in a short time."

We are in receipt of the following letter, which would indicate that any danger from this source has been done away with:

"Referring to the conversation the writer had with you this morning in reference to the classification on granite, we are in receipt of a letter from J. T. Ripley, chairman of the Western Classification Committee, stating that granite and marble have both been restored to the fourth class; so that when the new Eastern Classification goes into effect there will be an increase only of 5 cents per hundred pounds on all western shipments in less than carload lots.

This change in classification, we presume you are aware, only refers to less than carload lots.

Yours truly,
SEWARD W. JONES."

HE absorbing topic in the granite business today is the demands of the workmen and the possibility of a strike on March 1st, owing to the demands of the National Granite Cutters' Union for eight hours' work and a minimum wage of $3 a day. At the present time there does not seem to be anything except a strike ahead. The Granite Cutters' Union at Barre have placed themselves upon record as absolutely insisting upon the demands of the national union. The Association at Quincy has done the same. The New England Granite Manufacturers' Association made a request, through James Duncan, secretary of the National Cutters' Association, that a committee might be appointed to meet a similar committee from the New England Association for the purpose of discussion a compromise, to which Mr. Duncan made the following answer:

Your letter of January 30th was received, and as we were tabulating the vote of our membership as it came in on the proposition contained in your previous letter, we delayed answering until we could report the result. The votes are now recorded. I have been directed by our National Executive Committee to convey the following to your Association: "The subject of your letter of December 7 was voted upon, and by a large majority the motions for a committee under such circumstances was voted down and a resolution not to send a committee unless we had an assurance that your Association would recognize $3 and an eight-hour position our Union has taken, was adopted.

Can Mr. Duncan inform us what would be the duties of the committee appointed under these circumstances? At a meeting of the Granite Manufacturers' Association of New England held on February 13, the following resolution was passed:

Resolved, That the Granite Manufacturers' Association of New England, in annual meeting assembled, indorses the following memorandum:

Whereas, The Granite Cutters' National Union has, through its officers, informed the granite manufacturers of New England, that under its constitution no negotiation for wages and hours of labor will be had with said manufacturers, or any committee by them raised for that purpose, which does not provide in advance a concession and agreement for eight hours labor in a day's work and at least three dollars per day as wages.

Now believing that such a scale of prices will prevent the manufacture of granite, we, the undersigned, hereby agree with each other that we cannot accede to said demands, so required to be complied with.

Resolved, That the Granite Manufacturers' Association of New England indorses and approves the action of its executive committee relative to a conference by committee with the National Granite Cutters' Union, and authorizes and directs its committee to renew such overtures as have hitherto been made to the National Committee of Granite Cutters' Union to the end, that business may not suffer or labor be unemployed.

We quote from Mr. Duncan's letter, published upon another page, "We are informed from many sources throughout New England that employers are satisfied that the conditions we desire are fair." If Mr. Duncan is relying upon individual manufacturers acceding to the demands of the National Union, we will state definitely, from the monumental end of the business at least, that his hopes in this direction will be blasted. We have personally interviewed during the past month every leading monumental manufacturer in New England. There have been rumors of weakness on the part of some of the manufacturers. In other words, it has been stated among the men that certain manufacturers would grant the increase. In every case we have made it our personal business to interview this manufacturer to find his opinion regarding the matter, and in every case we have proved to our own satisfaction, if a man's word is to be relied upon, that there is no weakness among the manufacturers. There are certain manufacturers in Barre, Vt.; they are concerns in good standing in every way and have their own personal reasons for standing outside, but these concerns are as strong in their determination not to grant the men what they ask; simply they cannot do so and live. So much for the monumental end of the business. The building end has placed themselves upon record in the resolution published above, the first part of which is signed by nine out of ten of the large contractors. Personally, we are strongly in favor of associations in the granite business, or any other business; in the granite business particularly, for we realize that the bill of prices paid the workmen have been the only real basis for figuring monumental work. We believe that nine out of ten of the manufacturers have the same feeling as ourselves, but we believe they have ceased to be useful when they make demands which are bound to seriously interfere with the business. We learn from our Quincy correspondent that the workmen are by no means unanimous in their demands for eight hours and a $3 a day, and we can state, personally, from interviews with various granite cutters at Barre, Vt., and other Vermont sections, that the thinking men feel that it is too much to ask all at once. It is more than possible that the future would bring forth what the National Association ask today, but to grant an increase of thirty-three per cent is entirely out of the question. We are afraid that there are hard times ahead for the married men with families, for there is a general determination on the part of local dealers in the necessities of life not to grant the men credit on account of the past record, which has proved very disastrous to the majority of the storekeepers, as many bills contracted during the strike seven years

ago have not been paid as yet. Thus the men who intend to pay will have to suffer for those who don't.

⚜

SOMETIME since we made a statement regarding the condition of the granite business at Groton, Vt., that the business was still in a chrysallis state and would require an investment of considerable money to place it in first class condition. For this statement two of our contemporaries took exceptions. In a recent visit to Groton we found the following condition: Total number of firms employed in the business, four; total number of men employed cutting granite, 36; quarries in operation, one. A member of one of the firms made the statement that they had just received the first piece of granite that they had been able to secure in six weeks. It had then just been blocked up. It is rumored that the Pine Mountain Granite Co., recently formed, two of the members being Alvin Sortwell, president of the Wells River road, and F. M. Ricker, who has large lumber interests in Groton, and practically the owner of the Pine Mountain, which has been prospected over more or less for granite, will build a large cutting shed this spring. We have never been able to prove this statement, but doubt if this is the case, as we think their good business judgment would lead them to rather an investment of money in developing the deposits of granite and the shed would take care of itself in the future. These are the exact conditions, notwithstanding the balloons which have been sent up by our contemporaries. The visit was made during the month of February, and the lack of rough stock from the quarry could be accounted for on account of the bad roads and adverse conditions prevailing in the winter months.

⚜

Important to all Retail Dealers and Manufacturers.

The following resolution was recently passed by the Granite Manufacturers' Association of New England, and should be considered by all associations.

RESOLUTION.

Whereas, The Interstate Commerce Law declares that railway rates shall be just and reasonable and shall not discriminate between persons, localities or commodities, and creates a commission for the purpose of securing to the public the benefit of these provisions; and

Whereas, That commissions, in view of the interpretation which the courts have put upon the original Act, has not at the present time the necessary power to secure the shippers and the public, just, reasonable, and non-discriminating rates, and cannot even exercise the authority which it did in this respect during the early years of its existence;

Resolved, That the Act to Regulate Commerce should be so amended as to give the Interstate Commerce Commission the means to enforce the provisions of that Act, and especially in the following particulars:

1. To give the commission power, after it has upon formal complaint and hearing, determined that a rate or a practice is in violation of law, to prescribe the thing which the carrier shall do to bring itself into conformity with the law. There is no way in our opinion in which the public can be secured in the enjoyment of a just rate, except by compelling the carrier to make that rate.

2. To make the orders of the Interstate Commerce Commission effective of themselves, subject to the right of the carriers to review the lawfulness and reasonableness of these orders in the courts. Under the present system it has required on the average more "than three years to compel" a railroad to obey an order of the commission. After a shipper has tried his case before the commission and obtained an order for relief, he must still spend three years in litigation before that relief is available. No such system can in most cases be of any benefit to the public.

3. To require a uniform classification. The present power of the railways to change classifications at will puts the shipper completely at their mercy. This is illustrated by the action of the railways in putting in effect their new classification January 1, 1900.

4. To compel the railways to keep their accounts in a specified manner and to make those accounts open to government inspection. This is no more than is now required in case of national banks and would be the most effective means of preventing the payment of rebates and similar unlawful practices.

These amendments are embodied in Senate Bill No. 1,439, and we urge upon our Senators and Representatives in Congress to give this bill their careful consideration and support.

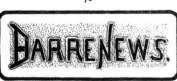

During the past few weeks the feeling in reference to the coming struggle between the cutters and the manufacturers has had quite a change, and today there is hardly one manufacturer or cutter who does not think that the probability of a settlement by March 1 is very remote. The manufacturers are therefore straining every nerve to get the business which must be finished before that time, completed and shipped, and are letting the jobs which they have taken subject to strike conditions wait until the future is outlined a little more definitely. In a conversation with one of the most prominent manufacturers, a suggestion was made by the writer that probably he did not know whether he would be working after March first or not, and the manufacturer, in replying, said: "Oh, yes, I do. I am very certain that we shall have a long rest this time." We have conceded more that two-thirds of the distance and have gone as far, and farther in fact, now that the conditions will warrant us in going, and I am prepared to say that there will not be further

concessions made by the manufacturers. And he went on to say, that if the demands of the National Granite Cutters' Union were granted it would be the ruin of the trade, owing to the fact that the price which they must necessarily get for the manufactured product would be in excess of what it is worth, compared with other goods, and that it can be manufactured in foreign countries, shipped here, and the duty now existing paid, and still be sold considerably less than it can then be produced for here with the wages up where they are demanding them.

They put up the argument, said he, that as long as other classes of workmen are now having their wages increased that they should receive the same treatment notwithstanding and not taking into consideration the fact that while the workmen in other lines have, during the past two years, been having their wages reduced to something like sixty per cent of what they formerly were, the cutters have been getting increased pay all along, the standard having been raised from 28 cents to 29 cents and then to thirty, and now they want to jump it to thirty-six simply because other wages are put back where they were when the cutters were getting about thirty cents or less.

He was very much in earnest in the matter and seemed to believe that the extreme demanded by the cutters would do much more detriment to the general business that is generally supposed.

Further, in relation to the matter of the maintainance of the strike, should one be declared, and in speaking of the caution which the secretary of the Montpelier branch of the Union had inserted in the Stone Cutters' Journal in its last issue in reference to the merchants with whom the cutters ought to trade under strike conditions, the manufacturer said he thought that the secretary was doing the merchants a favor in keeping the cutters away from some of them, considering the fact that only about one-third of the bills which were contracted during the last strike were ever paid. He further said, that as he understood it, that there is and will not be the required amount of money in the treasury of the Union, so that, under their rules, the one dollar per day will not be paid the cutters.

If this is so, there will be only a short time before there will either be suffering or revolt in the Union lines.

Barclay Bros. have had the best year this year that they have ever had since they have been in business, and they think that the business which would come from now out, barring any trouble with the Union, would be in excess of any thing thus far experienced. They are employing at this time all the cutters they can find, which is only about seventy-five.

This is not as large a number as they sometimes have, but it has been impossible to secure enough good cutters here during the past three months. They have work in abundance on hand, and are rushing it along with all the dispatch possible and compatible to good workmanship.

They have as yet not decided just where to build their new plant and have debated between the north and the south end of the town.

But they go on this assumption that there will, sooner or later, be something going on in the granite business, even if there is a strike this spring, and they want a place where they can handle their work with modern machinery and be able to do the work which they have come to them at much less costs than they have been doing during the time they have been in business.

It is generally known here among the manufacturers that there has been a great effort made by the local branch of the Association to make a settlement with the cutters, even by giving them more than the manufacturers can well afford. Consequently, the local committee of the Association have made a proposition to the committee from the Union: That the standard pay should be raised to thirty-four cents and the day eight hours, subject to the ratification by the New England Association. This, the Union, however, would not accept, or, in other words, ask for another proposition, as they have been doing all along, although this was meeting the Union considerably more than half way in the difference between that organization and the Association. It was thought that it was better to go that far than to have a struggle over the matter and to give the cutters to understand that the manufacturers were willing to use them well, and indeed better than they could well afford to the end, that there should be no lull in the business.

At this writing, however, it seems almost inevitable that there will come a strike of long standing, unless perchance there be some disposition manifested by the Union to bring the matter to a peaceful solution by effecting a compromise.

Imlah & Co. are doing good business at this time, having their plant well-filled with cutters, who are working upon jobs of more or less magnitude, and everything looks encouraging. Among the work which is now being constructed in this plant is one column die job, which consists of two bases, die and cap. The cap is an elegant piece of workmanship, it being ornamented with heavy carving. The bottom base is about ten feet square.

William Barclay, of the firm of Barclay Bros., recently gave the fourth annual concert and ball to his employees. The hall was very prettily decorated, among the decorations being a crayon sketch of William Barclay, surrounded by the Union Jack and the Stars and Stripes. Mr. Barclay was introduced as the chairman of the evening and said in part: "It is with pleasure that as your employer I welcome you here and show that I appreciate your labor. Last year I said that the manufacturers and cutters would shake hands over the eight hour day. We both believe that eight hours is long enough to work cutting stone, and I hope that the good sense and strong reasoning powers always shown by the cutters of Barre will be shown now. I think that the men are asking too much when they ask that hours be reduced and the wages increased. Consider, men, the position you are placed in—the prosperity of the city of Barre and the welfare of your families. Beware if you let the sound of the hammer cease in Barre on March 1st, because if you do, you do not know when you will hear it again. (Loud applause.)" The balance of the evening was given to dancing and a general good time.

Emslie, McLeod & Co. are employing fifty cutters and have a number of elaborate carved jobs under construction.

Smith, Whitcomb & Cook have received the contract from the Daniels Granite Co., Milford, N. H., for the entire machinery for their new plant. It consists of a traveling crane, engine (thirty horse-power), boiler (forty horse-power), polishing wheels, steam-heating plant, cutting-off saw, and iron frame for grindling stone. This iron frame is an entirely new feature with Smith, Whitcomb & Cook, and is a very excellent idea.

Dillon & Haley, Montpelier, Vt., have purchased the plant occupied and owned for a number of years by Stafford, McGlynn & Co. This purchase will give them necessary facilities for increasing their work as it comprises not only an excellent cutting, but also a polishing plant.

Wells, Lamson & Co. report a very busy season; their books show a number of more than ordinarily large contracts.

HARDWICK, VT.—Bickford, More & Co. were employing about three gangs of men in February; the greater part of them were at work upon the Scranton soldiers' monument, which was mentioned in a previous issue. This firm has secured a contract from the Culver Construction Co., Springfield, Ill., for the granite for the Lincoln monument, which is to be reconstructed. It will take from ten to fifteen carloads to fill this order.

J. E. Sullivan was employing from 45 to 50 cutters and reports business very good.

G. D. Bailey, as usual, is very busy.

Drew Daniels, Morrisville, is employing thirty men and reports a very satisfactory year's business.

The manufacturers at Barre have been bothered considerably by the lack of soft coal, but we are pleased to say that the coal famine is about over. Then, if there is a strike during March, it will be an excellent opportunity to catch up in this direction.

William Cassie, who for many years has been engaged in the granite business, is very sick with consumption, and has given up his business and sailed to Aberdeen.

Burke Bros. were employing twenty-four cutters during the month of February, and having all the business that they could attend to.

McIver & Ruxton were employing twenty cutters during the month of February. Among their contracts is a soldiers' monument for Connecticut parties.

Among the retail dealers in Barre during the month of February was A. G. Wright, Portland, Oregon. John P. Corskie secured a contract from him for a fountain job, donated by David L. Thompson to the city of Portland. The cost of the fountain will be about $7,000. He also placed with him a shaft job, shaft 24-4 in length. This firm has also received a contract for several tasty carved monuments.

Marr & Gordon have more than the usual number of contracts on hand, calling for all classes of monumental work. One of the contracts calls for bottom base 12-10 x 10-2. Another bottom base 10-2 x 10-2, the last one being a fluted shaft monument with Corinthian cap and surmounted by a figure of Hope.

Rogers & Arkley state that they have done a good business during the last year, and their business has been satisfactory from the standpoint of having pleased their customers and thereby secured duplicate orders. The following is an extract from a letter from Hoffman & Prochazka regarding a monument which they recently shipped: "Very fine and conscientious work."

Ryle & McCormick, Montpelier, Vt., were employing in January thirty-two cutters. This is the average during the year.

John Q. McDonald, of McDonald & Sons, Buffalo, recently paid one of his regular visits to Barre and placed a number of fine orders. They call for all classes of monumental work and are a little above the average which they have previously been placing.

Novelli & Corti have all the work on hand that they can possibly do in the next two or three months. This consists largely of carved work, as this class of work is what they are especially adapted for. Among their contracts are two "Parade rest" soldiers. They have just completed a tablet, which is illustrated in their advertisement in this issue. The carving is notable from the fact that the stems of the flowers are almost entirely relieved from the tablet and will not average over 1-4 in. through. They are shaped as nearly to nature as it is possible to do this class of work in granite. The whole work is artistic and in good taste, and shows what it is possible to do in carved work in granite.

Mortimer & Campbell have on hand more than the usual amount of fine carving, to be completed at the earliest possible moment. Among their contracts is a monument, the bottom base of which is 9-0 x 3-5 x 1-6, panel die, second base heavily carved, cap moulded and carved. This is one of their many contracts.

W. A. Lane has recently purchased for his plant two large electric motors for operating air compressor, derrick, polishing wheels, etc. This is to replace the gasoline engine, which has proven very unsatisfactory.

Cross Bros., Northfield, are employing 75 cutters at the present time. Among the work that they have on hand is a mausoleum 13-6 x 13-6 x 18-0. The order

was taken to be delivered in six weeks, complete. The interior and floor are all constructed of granite. They also have three other orders for mausoleums.

Wells, Lamson & Co. have more than the usual amount of large work on hand; among the work in process is a large job with bottom base 9-6 x 9-6, shaft 2-10 x 28-8. Also sarcophagus monument, bottom base 12-6 x 8-4. Also a vault job, ground measurements 20-0 x 12-2.

Beck & Beck are employing sixteen men; this is the limit of their capacity at the present time. They propose shortly to build an addition to their present plant in order to keep up with their fast-growing business.

McDonald & Buchan have just completed a contract for a mausoleum 18-2 x 18-2; first four courses polished. Each side of the entrance are to be polished columns of Quincy granite surmounted by carved caps.

Mutch & Calder have on hand an unusual number of contracts calling for large work. They have completed during the last year a number of large monuments which call for artistic carving.

Innis & Cruickshank have been employing 60 men, and have just installed a new Ingersoll-Sergeant air compressor.

All attempts on the part of the granite manufacturers to arrange a peaceful settlement of the differences have thus far failed, and therefore the first of March will see a general suspension of the granite business in Quincy for an indefinite period. Until one side or the other gives in there can be no settlement. The cutters are firm in their demand for an eight hour day, and at present writing will accept nothing else. They have also thus far refused to meet any committee from the Manufacturers' Association until this one demand has been conceded. As that is all that has been asked it is rather puzzling to know of what use a conference would be after that one point is settled. That the demand is unjust and that the condition of business is not such as would warrant the increase asked, any unprejudiced layman who takes the trouble to look into the matter for himself will readily admit. The manufacturers as a rule are willing to grant the eight hours with the present minimum, which in reality means an increase of about ten per cent, but the labor leaders have turned up their noses and said no. It is a well known fact that all the cutters in Quincy do not agree with the leaders, but they are in a minority, and it is reported that when they have attempted to council

moderation they have almost been excluded from the hall. It would seem that the Union is not in as good condition to stand a long strike as in other years, for the reason that heretofore when work has been suspended the men have had a month's pay coming to them. This year the weekly payment clause has been in force, and when the men close up their tool boxes on the night of February 28 they will have but one week's pay due. The old cry that strike pay will be received, but as all the strike pay due Quincy cutters on account of last year's strike has not yet been received, and the fact that the American Federation of Labor has several large strikes on its hands now, the amount of strike pay received, if any, will be small. The strike, be it long or short, is bound to create an amount of suffering. To the single man with no family ties to keep him at home it simply means pack the grip and go west, but to the man with a family comes the most wrong and suffering. On the other hand the manufacturers have had full knowledge of what was approaching, and have prepared themselves somewhat. The winter has been unusually favorable for granite cutting, and every manufacturer in the city has made the best of the opportunity, and an amazing amount of work that has been turned out. No orders, however, have been taken for work that could not be completed before the first of March, and therefore it will take some weeks after the strike is settled to get orders and have the plants in working order again.

The Quincy delegates to the annual meeting of the New England Association February 13, were prepared to accept either of the two propositions, viz.: That eight hours shall constitute a day's work with the same price as now in force for nine hours. The second proposition was that eight hours should constitute a day's work and that the average price be 34 cents per hour. If a man was not capable of earning that amount he was to be set at work, and at the expiration of a few days his work was to be figured up and submitted to a joint committee of the manufacturers and cutters, who should fix the amount the man should receive. As will be seen by an account of the annual meeting, neither of these propositions were adopted. Resolutions were, however, adopted relative to the action of the National Cutters' Union in refusing to appoint a committee to meet a like committee from the manufacturers until the latter body had conceded the demand for eight hours and $3. The following evening the Quincy manufacturers held a meeting, when reports from the delegates to the annual meeting were read. The association then passed a resolution endorsing the resolutions as passed by the New England Association February 13, refusing to concede an eight-hour day at a minimum rate of $3 per day previous to the appointing of any committee. The letter of Secretary James Duncan of February 9 to J. W. Frost, secretary of the Granite Manufacturers' Association of New England was read. This letter, with others from Secretary Duncan and James Milne of Quincy was published in the public press the following days. The letter of Mr. Milne calls attention to a few important facts that are perhaps new to the layman, although perfectly familiar to the granite manufacturers. He says:

"It must have furnished all practical granite workers considerable amusement to read the letter of James Duncan, secretary of the Granite Cutters' National Union, which appeared in the 'Boston Globe' of February 15th, in answer to the communication of the Granite Manufacturers' Association of New England, in which he accuses them of forgetting or intentionally omitting some very salient facts in connection with the present situation.

"He then goes on to prove his case and his honesty by 'forgetting' a few things himself.

"It is quite true that the manufacturers have introduced considerable machinery in the past few years, but it is not true that a surfacing machine will cut 60 or 80 feet per day. Forty to 50 feet per day is the largest amount a machine will cut under the most favorable circumstances. Mr. Duncan 'forgot or intentionally omitted to state' that it takes from three to five stone cutters to rough off sufficient stone to keep a machine running, so that instead of one man cutting from 60 to 80 feet, it takes from four to six men including the man who works the machine to surface from 40 to 50 feet.

"Mr. Duncan also 'forgot or intentionally omitted to state' that it cost from $3.00 to $4.00 per day to furnish compressed air to run a surfacing machine. It must have surprised manufacturers to learn that they received two or three times as much work in the way of carving and lettering from a workman running a pneumatic tool, than could be done by hand. Manufacturers have been forced to be satisfied with an increase of 33 per cent over the hand work. It is a well known fact that there is very little profit in running the pneumatic tool; the main advantage being in the better quality of work produced.

"Mr. Duncan then speaks of a few cents increase per hour, a 'slight advance,' he called it, and when he must know that the price asked for will increase the cost of the finished product at least 33 per cent.

"It is quite true that he notified the Granite Manufacturers' Association of New England of the increase asked for one year ago; and it is also true that the New England Association notified Mr. Duncan that the state of trade would not admit of so large an increase in cost, but that they were willing to refer the whole question to arbitration. The gist of Mr. Duncan's reply was 'give us all we ask for, and we will arbitrate the remainder.'

"Mr. Duncan's statement that the manufacturers have made a schedule of prices which is from 13 per cent to 15 per cent higher than the journeymen's advance, is a pure fabrication written with the intention of beguiling an indulgent public.

"If the letter from Mr. Duncan is a specimen of his 'simon pure' honesty, we may well expect some surprising statements from him before the trouble is settled."

The Quincy Quarry Co. have been shipping large quantities of chips to Middleboro, where the New York, New Haven & Hartford railroad are abolishing grade crossings. One hundred and twenty-five car loads were shipped there in January.

(Continued on page 26.)

Quarry Items.

KINGSTON, S. C.—A $100,000 company has been organized to work granite quarries near Salisbury on a large scale.

AUGUSTA, ME.—Both this place and Gardiner are making a strong effort to secure the location of the granite cutting plant where C. E. Tayntor & Company propose to build.

MOUNT WALDO, ME.—The agreement which was signed by Messrs. Duncan and Pierce goes into operation at once; the controversy on the Chicago post-office job is declared to be at an end: at Mount Waldo, eight hours to be a day's work, with wages $3.60 per day. When the job is running on a union basis, the men working by the day will select a committee, who shall prepare a bill, on fair conditions, under which the class above alluded to may work. This bill will be submitted to the union for acceptance, and if satisfactory, it will be incorporated into the general bill of prices; otherwise it must be amended till it is acceptable to the union. Pending the acceptance of this, all men employed on the job are to be paid by the day. There will be no piece-bill at all unless so framed that no unfair advantage can be taken of it. Work is to begin immediately, both at Mount Waldo and in Chicago, and at the same rate—$3.60 per day of eight hours.

LANCASTER, N. H.—Work is progressing finely on opening up the granite quarry in Kilkenny, with every prospect of obtaining plenty of granite.

ELLSWORTH, ME.—At the quarry of the Standard Granite Company, Somesville, a vast amount of business has been transacted this season. A contract for the stone for the mint building in Philadelphia has given employment for from 250 to 500 men during the entire season, and will continue until the contract is finished, which will probably be about the beginning of the new year. The largest pay-day at this quarry was when $16,000 was required to settle with the men for a month's labor.

CONCORD, N. H.—The New England Granite Company has recently received contracts for the granite to be used in the construction of the Continental Trust Company's building in Baltimore, and for a large receiving tomb in Cedar Hill cemetery in Hartford, Ct. It is expected to keep the force of fifty men now at the works employed until the first of May.

TROY, N. H.—The Troy Granite Company will construct a trolley line at their quarry. The road is to be a trolley line of the same gauge as a steam railroad and will be used to haul ordinary railway cars to and from the quarries. The power for operating the railway will be generated near the quarries, and arrangements will be made to use either water power or steam. A brook and pond on the quarry property will, it is thought, provide sufficient power to operate the road a good portion of the time, and a suitable steam plant will also be installed. An electric locomotive capable of hauling several cars will be provided, and suitable switches, side tracks, etc., will be put in at the quarry.

LANCASTER, N. H.—A company has been organized among local business men to develop the Kilkenny granite quarries in East Lancaster. The following officers were chosen: President, John L. Moore; secretary and treasurer, George N. Kent; executive committee, I. W. Quimby, W. H. Hartley, J. I. Williams. Work will be begun at once under the supervision of W. C. Putnam.

NORTH CONWAY, N. H.—Business at Redstone is good. The quarries and cutting sheds will be run all winter. At present work is being done on the Franklin bank building, now being erected in New York city. Some of the work is very expensive. The carving on some of the massive stones going into this construction is a marvel of skill and good taste. The work on some of the carved caps going on top of the great polished pillars that are to be used in the building will cost over $900. There are 300 men now employed at the Redstone quarries.

WESTERLY, R. I.—The controversy between the Smith Granite Company and the Joseph Newall Granite Company was before the appelate court December 2 on the representation of counsel for the Newalls that the receiver had, contrary to the decree of the court, blasted solid rock at the quarries in Westerly. The receiver said he had only complied with the order of the court in regard to furnishing customers with stone. The case went over for a week.

WALDOBORO, ME.—Booth Bros., & Hurricane Isle Granite Company have erected at their works another shed, 140 long and 30 feet wide. They now have 180 men at work there, including granite cutters, quarrymen, engineers, blacksmiths, carpenters and teamsters. The stone for the American Express Company's building in Buffalo, N. Y., is all quarried.

MACHIAS, ME.—E. S. Shattuck & Company are negotiating for land upon which to put up a suitable building in which to set up their polishing works.

LEETE ISLAND, CT.—John Beattie, the veteran quarry owner, died at his home at Leete's, November 23. It is thirty years since Mr. Beattie, then of Newport, R. I., purchased a large tract of rocky pasture on the shore at what was then called Hoadley's Neck. Here he opened a quarry, made a wharf on the water front and transported the product of his quarry in his own vessels. His ability as a contractor is best shown in the work done by him—the pedestal of the Bartholdi statue, the railway stations at Hartford and at Providence, R. I., are good examples of his work. He knew his business from the ground up, having learned the stone-cutter's trade, and more than all, knew men and how to handle them. He was born 81 years ago in the city of Edinburg, Scotland. The remains were lowered upon a huge block of granite weighing about three tons, from his own quarry, and were then covered by a similar slab and left to their rest.

WILMINGTON, DEL.—The Delaware Granite and Mining Company has received a $250,000 contract for the construction of roads and bridges in Porto Rico. The contract was awarded at San Juan, and bridges and causeways are to be erected for the government,

WEST CHAZEY, N. Y.—The West Chazey Granite Company has been incorporated with a capital of $5,-000. Directors, William M. Carnes of West Cazey, Charles H. Booth of New York, and M. F. Parkhurst and John H. Booth of Plattsburg. Mr. Carnes was formerly located at East Barre, Vt.

Proposed Monuments and Monumental News.

ROCKVILLE, MD.—The trustees of the Rockville Academy have decided to erect a monument to the memory of the late Julius West, founder of the institution.

BROWNSVILLE, TENN.—The Hiram S. Bradford Bivouac of Confederate Veterans of Haywood county will erect a monument to the Confederate dead of this county at a cost of about $1,500.

DETROIT, MICH.—The bicentenary of this city is to be commemorated by the building of some form of a monumental work, upon which will be engaged the foremost artists and sculptors of the country.

WASHINGTON, D. C.—The secretary of war has approved the design for the great New York peace monument to be erected on the Lookout Point Park, Chattanooga, Tenn., recently purchased by the government as a part of the national park reservation. The monument will be 100 feet high, 50 feet square at the base, canopy in design, and will contain a roster of all the troops on both sides engaged in the battles about Chattanooga.

LANCASTER, PA.—A movement has been started among the members of the National Association of Spanish-American Veterans in this vicinity to raise a monument in honor of Maj.-Gen. Henry W. Lawton.

DELHI, N. Y.—The proposed soldiers' monument will be of granite, thirty feet high, estimated to cost $10,000.

ROCHESTER, MINN.—Custer Post, G. A. R., is planning to erect a monument in memory of the soldiers of the wars.

JACKSONVILLE, FLA.—Gov. Bloxham has appointed ex-Gov. F. P. Fleming and Mrs. J. N. Whitner as commissioners on the erection of a monument on the field of the battle of Olustee.

GUTHRIE, O. T.—A movement is on foot to erect a monument to Ed Hewins, who was known throughout Oklahoma and Kansas. The monument will be unveiled about July 4, 1900.

READING, PA.—The petition of 250 citizens and soldiers, headed by General D. McM. Gregg, was presented to Judge Ermentrout November 8, asking the court to confirm the report of the Grand Jury in favor of a soldiers' monument. It is proposed to erect the monument on the top of Mt. Penn, 600 feet above the level of the city.

CHICAGO, ILL.—The Lief Ericsson Monument Society have collected $3,000, and will endeavor to raise about $3,000 more.

TORONTO, O.—The ashes of "Mike" Myers, the great government scout and Indian fighter, who died in 1850 at the remarkable age of 107, will be brought to Toronto and reinterred by his grandson, James W. Myers, who will erect a suitable monument.

NEWARK, OHIO.—Congressman J. A. McDowel has made application for the soldier comrades of General W. B. Hazen to erect a monument to his honor at Stone River cemetery.

NEW YORK, N. Y.—Robert B. Roosevelt, a member of the committe of the Holland Society charged with the duty of selecting a design for a monument to the Dutch founders of New York, says that the committee has for four or five years vainly searched for an original idea for this monument. He adds that the model of an equestrian statue of William the Silent, by D. C. French, was accepted in sheer desperation, because it seemed hopeless to expect to get anything more original.

MILFORD, MASS.—The project of erecting a memorial in honor of Adin Ballou, founder of the Hopedale Community and of the central village of the town, is gradually going forward to a successful completion. A statue in bronze somewhat larger than life, surmounting a pedestal seven or eight feet high, will constitute its central feature.

The expense of the statue has been provided for through the generosity of Gen. William F. Draper.

CHICAGO, ILL.—South park commissioners will be petitioned for a site for the colored people's proposed monument of John Brown. Five thousand dollars has already been raised. The sculptor will in all probability be Augustus St. Gaudens.

SPRINGFIELD, ILL.—Governor Tanner, one of the Board of Commissioners of the National Lincoln Monument, November 7, let the contract of the restoration of the monument here to the Culver Construction Company, of Springfield, their bid being $94.500 and the lowest. The work will begin at once on the restoration of the monument, and must be finished by November 1, 1900.

PHILADELPHIA, PA.—A peculiar suit was begun by James B. O'Neill against the Norwood Cemetery Company. Mr. O'Neill alleges that he owns a lot in the cemetery of the defendant, and erected on it a monument costing upwards of $10,000, constructed of granite, ornamented with Italian marble statues. It is alleged that the company contracted to protect the monument from defacement, but that it failed to perform this duty, inasmuch as explosives were stored in the cemetery and not properly guarded. The plaintiff avers that on November 8, 1896, the monument was blown up by dynamite belonging to the company. the statues were broken and injured, and the granite badly cracked. Mr. O'Neill sues to recover $5,000 damages for his losses.

BEAVER, PA.—In accordance with a recent Act of Assembly, the county commissioners have let the contract for a soldiers' and sailors' monument at this place to the Pennsylvania Monument Association, of Philadelphia. It will cost $13,000.

BOTTOM BASE . . . $T - C C \times P - 1 \times C - P$
SECOND BASE . . . $E - I \times R - C \times A - A$
DIE . . . . $P - I \times A - R \times R - R$

PRICE :
Westerly Granite . . . . $E T Y
Quincy Granite . . . . $P E Y
Barre Granite . . . . $P R Y
Troy and Milford (N. H.) Granite . . . . $P A Y

"GRANITE," MARCH, 1900. ORIGINAL DESIGN.

BOTTOM BASE . . . . . E — T x R — P x C — P
DIE . . . . P — A x A — Y x A — A

PRICE:
Barre Granite . . . . $4 A Y
Quincy Granite . . . . $4 P Y
Westerly and Milford (N. H.) Granite . . . $R Y Y
Troy Granite . . . . $3 I E

"GRANITE," MARCH, 1900.

BOTTOM BASE . . E — Y x A — P x C — A
DIE . . . . . P — A x C — T x R — Y

PRICE:
Quincy Granite . . . . $C A E
Barre Granite . . . . $C A Y
Westerly Granite . . . . $C T Y
Troy and Milford (N. H.) Granite . . . . . . $C E E

Association Meetings.

The 12th annual meeting of the Nebraska Marble and Granite Dealers' Association convened at the Lindell Hotel, Lincoln, Neb., January 31, 1899, with the largest attendance that has been had since 1893. Nearly all the leading dealers of the state were present and evidenced a determination not to abandon the organization, but to continue until every reputable dealer in the state had become a member.

In the absence of the president, J. M. Batcheldor was chosen president pro tem. A committee on resolutions, in regard to increase of freight rates, was appointed as follows: I. T. Paine, F. B. Kimball and J. N. Kildow. The meeting then adjourned until February 1st, 1900, at 9.30.

President Alderman having arrived, called the meeting to order. On motion, some of the members were called before the convention and asked to explain what they knew about certain wholesale houses furnishing marble to a certain department store in Chicago. A committee was appointed to draft resolutions, declaring it the sense of the dealers of this state that they would not buy stock of wholesale houses who sell marble or granite to department stores or any person not a legitimate dealer. The committee appointed the following resolutions:

Report of Committee on Department Store Sales of Monumental Work at Nebraska Marble Dealers' Convention, Lincoln, Neb., February 1, 1900:

Whereas, It has come to the knowledge of this association with positive proof, that certain department stores in large cities doing a mail order trade throughout the entire country and have issued price lists on any marble work which they profess to sell at cost, and,

Whereas, We consider this method of doing business derogatory to the best interests of the legitimate trade, both wholesale and retail, therefore be it

Resolved, That this association condemns such practice and believes that no wholesale or retail firm should furnish material for such firms, and feel further that our trade should not be extended to any wholesaler who accepts and fills such orders.

(Signed)
Edw. McLane.
F. B. Kimball.
J. V. Sweeney.

The Committee on Railroad Rates submitted the following:

Whereas, The new classification of freight rates adopted by the railroads of this state arbitrarily, and as we believe unjustly, increase the rates of shipments of marble or granite from points within this state to other points within this state (as per some instances hereto appended), therefore

Resolved, That this association appoint a committee of five to wait upon the State Board of Transportation and protest against this unjust increase in rates and ask them to use all lawful means to prevent same.

By unanimous vote the following letter was approved and a copy ordered sent to the Chairman of the Western Classification Committee of Chicago, Ill.:

Lincoln, Neb., Feb. 1st, 1900.
J. T. Ripley, Chairman, Western Classification Committee, Chicago, Ill.
Dear Sir:—

At a meeting of the Nebraska Marble and Granite Dealers, held in Lincoln, Neb., January 31, 1900, the following letter was considered and ordered placed before your committee:

The Marble and Granite Dealers of this state, 50 in number, desire to enter this protest against the change recently made in the classification of marble and granite from fourth to third, and "D" to fifth classes. We consider this change ranging from 10 per cent to 50 per cent advance on rates from Chicago west, entirely unfair. A moderate advance would receive no opposition, but so large an increase will injure trade, and tend to the use of much native material of poor quality and a loss of business to the roads. We also desire earnestly to protest against the injustice brought upon us when shipping from Omaha, Lincoln and other points to local points in the state, 50 per cent of all material received is reshipped and the classification raises rates from 20 per cent to 30 per cent, and we believe it but necessary to call your attention to this fact to secure a change.

Marble and granite are desirable classes of merchandise for the roads to handle; valuation is restricted to 40 cents per cubic foot, O. R. R., and the roads assume but slight risk.

We most earnestly urge upon your committee to reconsider your action, and if possible put marble and granite back on the old basis.

The association decided by unanimous vote to become members of the National Association, and I. T. Paine of Grand Island was appointed delegate to represent this association. All of the old officers were re-elected. On motion, adjourned to meet at Lincoln, Neb., on the last Wednesday in January, 1901.
Mr. Editor:—

The minutes of the meeting give a very faint idea of what was actually accomplished. The good feeling that prevailed among the different dealers who ordinarily regarded a competitor as something of a "bogy man," gives evidence that in time the dealers of Nebraska will be doing business on business principles, and as men engaged in the same work should do.

The next meeting, in the language of the west, will be a "Cracker-Jack." Every dealer in the state is expected to be present, and every dealer in the United States and Canada are earnestly invited to be present. A banquet will be served, of which the good-looking representative of the Vermont Marble Company—C. J. Field—will have full charge. No other guaranty need be made that for once in our lives at least, the dealers in this state will have a square meal. You are cordially invited to meet with us on that occasion.

Respectfully yours,
J. N. Kildow, Sec.

Yankton, S. D., Feb. 8, 1900.
Editor Granite, Boston, Mass:—
Enclosed find copy of a resolution adopted by the South Dakota Marble and Granite Dealers' Associa-

tion at Sioux Falls February 6, and ordered sent to GRANITE.

The meeting at Sioux Falls was profitable and well attended by local dealers. Dealers reported good business prospects for the coming season.

Yours respectfully,
M. M. BENNETT, Sec'y.

The following resolution was adopted by the South Dakota Marble and Granite Dealers' Association in their annual session at Sioux Falls, February 6, 1900. This resolution was drafted and adopted by the marble dealers of Nebraska in session at Lincoln and reaffirmed by the South Dakota Association later,

Whereas, It has come to the knowledge of this association, with positive proof that certain department stores in large cities, doing a mail order trade throughout the entire country have issued their price lists on marble work which they profess to sell at cost, and

Whereas, We consider this method of doing business derogatory to the best interests of the legitimate trade, both wholesale and retail, therefore be it

Resolved, That this association condemns such practice and believes that no wholesale or retail firm should furnish material for such firms, and feel further that our trade should not be extended to any wholesaler who accepts and fills such orders.

Points of interest from proceedings of convention of Marble and Granite Dealers of Iowa:

The attendance was not large, owing mostly to the very unpleasant weather. But there was a spirit of determination to push the organization to a successful issue that spoke well for the good men back of it. There was a flattering increase in membership. No less than ten dealers making application, they were all elected to membership. They also demonstrated that they were there for the purpose of doing what good they could, and their efforts were intelligently and forcibly carried out.

Charles O' Donnell of 101 Locust street, Des Moines, Ia., was elected to the office of president for the year 1900. Ed. H. Prior, of Postville, Ia., was chosen secretary and treasurer. Either of these men will be pleased to hear from any and all who are seeking to establish associations of this kind, or who may wish to join the Iowa Association.

The state was divided into eight districts. There were four under the original system. The districts are comprised and officered as follows:

No. 1.—Consists of the counties of Lyon, Osceola, Dickinson, Sioux, O'Brien, Clay, Plymouth, Cherokee and Buena Vista. F. M. Schwartz of Storm Lake is vice president for the district.

No. 2.—Emmet, Kossuth, Winnebago, Palo Alto, Hancock, Pocahontas, Humboldt, Wright, Worth, Cerro Gordo and Franklin. C. G. Dayton of Mason City is vice president.

No. 3.—Mitchell, Howard, Winnishiek, Allamakee, Floyd, Chickasaw, Fayett, Clayton, Butler, Bremer. Ed. H. Prior of Postville, Ia., is vice president.

No. 4.—Woodbury, Ida, Sac, Monona, Crawford, Carroll, Harrison, Shelby, Audobon. W. B. Wayt of Sac City is vice president.

No. 5.—Calhoun, Webster, Hamilton, Hardin, Greene, Boone, Story, Marshall, Dallas, Polk, Jasper

Grundy, Tama Poweshiek, Guthrie, Madison, Warren, Marion and Mahaska. W. J. Cadd of Jefferson is vice president.

No. 6.—Blackhawk, Buchanan, Delaware, Dubuque, Benton, Linn, Jones, Jackson, Iowa, Johnson, Cedar, Clinton, Scott, Muscatine. Geo. Lutz of Cedar Rapids is vice president.

No. 7.—Clarke, Decatur, Union, Ringgold, Adair, Cass, Adams, Taylor, Page, Montgomery, Pottawattamie, Mills and Fremont. J. C. Sullivan of Creston is vice president.

No. 8.—Keokuk, Washington, Louisa, Wappello, Jefferson, Henry, Des Moines, Davis, Van Buren, Lee, Lucas, Wayne, Monroe and Appanoose. Henry Melcher of Mt. Pleasant is vice president.

It should be the ambition of each vice president to secure the co-operation and membership of every dealer in his district. Keep after them. Get them. The matter of freight readjustment to which this organization has pledged its efforts should, alone, be sufficient to induce every dealer in the state to join us.

The following resolutions were adopted:

Whereas, The various Trunk Lines have, by combining, raised the rates on marble and granite by changing the classification from fourth to third (in less than car lots) ; and

Whereas, The goods are heavy and imperishable, and are therefore frequently side-tracked, taking from 11 to 22 days for transportation from Vermont to Iowa, and

Whereas, The restricted value is still kept at 40 cents a cubic foot,

Resolved, That the Marble and Granite Dealers' Association of Iowa, now in session, most respectfully, yet emphatically, protest against this high rate, and that the said trunk lines be requested to give a hearing to the committee appointed on this question by this association.

J. M. Graham, president of the National, and Charles O'Donnell of the Iowa Associations, were elected a committee to look after the freight interest of the Iowa dealers.

Whereas, It is a known fact that certain marble companies are furnishing their products to certain department stores, who are retailing inferior marble in such manner as to be detrimental to the legitimate trade,

Resolved, That the Iowa Marble and Granite Dealers' Association condemns the practice of selling to such stores, and will not recommend the said marble dealers or companies to the legitimate dealers in marble anywhere.

Resolved, That a copy of these resolutions be published in the Trade Journals.

Whereas, It has pleased the Grand Architect and Master Builder of the Universe to remove from the trials and tribulations of this sphere to a life of endless duration, our esteemed members, B. F. Wayt of Jefferson, who died February 4, 1899, Jordan McCann of Bloomfield, who died January 18, 1900, and our fellow tradesman, F. M. Havens of Boone, who died December 29, 1899, be it

Resolved, That in the loss of these fellows' craft, we believe the state has lost three of its good, square, legitimate dealers, and that their successors must aim high to become their equals.

Resolved, That we extend our heartfelt sympathy to the families of the deceased brothers, and that a copy of these resolutions be forwarded to the families of each and that a copy be furnished the Trade Journals, and that they be spread upon the minutes of the Association.

Resolved, That we deprecate and condemn the oft repeated statements of a certain concern in this state, to prospective customers, that "We furnish the other dealers in the state the goods they sell and can therefore save you money."

On February 8 we ascertained that no member of our association has purchased a dollar's worth of stock from this small concern. Therefore their statement is false, and said firm is obtaining orders by fraud. (Winterset.)

All of the foregoing resolutions were prepared by committee consisting of J. M. Graham, J. M. Ruge, J. W. Lundy.

The directors for this year are C. D. Oldham, J. S. Agnew, W. B. Wayt, J. C. Root, William McHogan.

J. M. Graham and Ed. H. Prior were elected delegates to the convention of the National Association, to be held at the Revere Hotel in Chicago, February 14 and 15, 1900. Ed. H. Prior was elected to represent Iowa on the Executive Committee of the National Association.

The Constitution was amended, so that the president, secretary or any vice president is empowered to receive into full membership, any firm or dealer at any time upon receipt of application properly presented.

The convention believed that the rate of taxation now prevailing in the National Association is excessive.

Every officer elected and every resolution offered received the unanimous vote of the members, thus demonstrating the thorough harmony which prevailed.

The association was never so strong as it now is and all are determined to make it one of the most powerful and highly respected organizations in Iowa.

I want every man in Iowa, in any way connected with the trade, to send me his name and address. I've got something for him.

ED. H. PRIOR,
Sec'y and Treas., Ia. M. & G. D.'s Assn.
Postville, Iowa.

Correspondence.

You would be doing the granite trade a great service by agitating a reduction of freight rates on monuments and vaults from eastern points to the Missouri river.

The recent advance is equivalent to an advance of 15 cents per 100 pounds less than car load lots. There is also a discrimination in favor of marble as against granite.

The old rates were surely high enough and it would seem possible, if this matter were forcibly brought to the attention of the proper railroad authorities, to have the old rates restored to the mutual benefit of the eastern quarries and the western dealers.

M. H. RICE,
Kansas City.

(This letter is effectually answered under editorials.)

Am in favor of paying mechanics good wages, but I have my doubts about such a great change in wage and hours of work. Hope if the change does come it will be better all around. It is hard work to sell at present prices; do not know how it will be under the proposed change. Twenty to twenty-five per cent will be quite a rise.

GEO. H. CURREEN,
Albany, N. Y.

Omaha, Neb., Jan. 25, 1900.
My opinion is that the demands of the granite cutters are "unreasonable." But as the outlook for trade was "never so promising" as this year, I would suggest that you conform to their demands for the present, and the time may not be far distant when the manufacturers can turn the tables on them.

W. Y. TEITZEL,
Omaha, Neb.

I enclose one dollar for another year's subscription for GRANITE. I can assure you that it gives me pleasure to forward the required amount for another year's subscription.

JOHN CRAUGHWELL,
Sanford, Me.

Please find check in settlement of my subscription for GRANITE. What is the outlook at present in Barre and Quincy? Strike or not?

CHARLES S. CHISOM,
Prattsburgh, N. Y.

The Recent Flood at Montpelier, Vt.

Many retail dealers and others who have visited Barre and Montpelier on business or pleasure will be

Ice jam in the Winooski River, at Montpelier, Vt.

interested in the illustrations below. They can convey to the mind a more definite idea as to the conditions

NOVELLI & CORTI,

Statuary

——AND——

Carving.

PORTRAIT FIGURES,

BUSTS AND IDEAL FIGURES

in all kinds of New England Granite

━━ CARVING ━━

Executed in any style.   Floral Work a Specialty.

Models furnished on application.

We invite all dealers who need high-art work to correspond directly with us.   We can give best of references.

NOVELLI & CORTI,   P. O. BOX 57.   **BARRE, VT.**

MODELS.

J. J. DICKISON, C.S.A.

HERBERT W. BEATTIE,

SCULPTOR,

QUINCY,   .   .   .   MASS.

prevailing in Montpelier on the morning of February 14. The rain had come down in a perfect deluge for a day and a half, and taking that, together with the melting snow, the ice broke away and formed a jam in the Winooski river, which runs through the valley in which Montpelier is situated, and the water backed up into the city. The first general idea that people had of the danger was at about half past one in the morning of February 14, when the fire bells were rung and people flocked out to see the fire and to find that it was the enemy of fire, water, that brought forth the call. The water at that time had filled the basements of every store in the city, and was gradually crawling up to the first floor, and when it reached its height it covered the first floors of two of the principal hotels in the town to the depth of three feet. To illustrate the rapid rise in the water, it is related that one firm of druggists had stored in the cellar five thousand cigars. Upon the first call the cigars were placed upon a shelf three feet from the floor. At that time there was about six inches of water in the cellar and apparently falling. They were then called outside to view the river, which was carrying everything before it and were gone about a half an hour. When they returned they found three feet of water in the cellar and the cigars beyond their reach. Among the amusing incidents of the night was a rescue on the part of three of the leading spirits in the town of a very elaborate music box, or rather an attempt at rescue. The box was taken from the store

Taking the guests from one of the hotels to the depot across the road. The mark on the steps shows the highest point the water reached.

and the rescuing party was wading through the water when one of them stumbled and the box was dropped, and now the owner of the box is not their friend. An attempt was made to rescue a horse, which finally had to be abandoned for the night, but in the morning the ice was chopped from around him, and he came out apparently without any serious harm. A phenomenon was noticed in back of the principal club in the city underneath which is the liquor agency, for be it known every city in Vermont has a liquor agency, and it is the only place in town where liquor can be secured (?) strictly for medicinal purposes. As we started to say, the phenomenon consisted of empty bottles apparently

having contained whiskey, ale, beer and other medicinal drinks, resting on top of the newly formed ice. It is supposed that owing to some unknown pressure

Looking up State Street from the hotel.

from underneath that the bottles were forced to the surface of the ice as the water froze. Possibly what liquor was left in the bottles was strong enough to do this. Anyway, on the morning of the 14th they were there, and we leave it for those who are thoroughly posted to account for the apparently impossible freak of nature.

Stock Monuments.

A splendid lot of monuments, head stones and markers, about fifty in all, of a variety of granites, but mostly Quincy, all finished new and ready to ship. You can easily make up a carload and get the reduced carload rates. Apply early for stock sheets to Swingle & Falconer, Quincy, Mass.

Monthly Trade Record.

This department is compiled and edited by the United Mercantile Agency. Subscribers, in accordance with the terms of their contracts are entitled to receive further information relative to the parties hereafter mentioned, upon application to the main office. As the names of many business men who are good will appear herein, subscribers can readily see the importance of making inquiries if interested, previous to taking any action.

ALABAMA.
Anniston, *M—Gains, D. R., 76.
ARKANSAS.
Clarksville, *M—Collier, J. J. & Co., 80.
Clarksville, *M—Sharer, A. C., 76.
Little Rock, *M—Funston, W. L., 106.
CALIFORNIA.
Ripon, *M—Kewin, T. H., 88 to Salida.
COLORADO.
Denver, *M—Olinger, David V., 14 $1,367.
CONNECTICUT.
Hartford, B—Kelly Bros., 34.
DELAWARE.
Wilmington, *M—Davidson, William, 105.

FLORIDA.
Ocala, *M—Leavengood, A. J., will admit partner.
GEORGIA.
Brunswick, *M—La Mance, Reed E., 20 $75 and $50.
Macon, *M—Artope & Whitt, T. B. Artope, 78.
ILLINOIS.
Evanston, *M—Moore, John, 78.
Kewanee, *M—Craig & Johnson, 64, George Craig, 58.
Pinckneyville, *M—Finnell, A. R., 76.
Sterling, *M—Johnson, F. L., 99 $1,100.
INDIANA.
Anderson, *M—Brenneman, J. F., 93 $500.
Elkhart, *M—Tibbitts, Nathan, warranty deed $2,500.
Lebanon, *M—Dooley, Holmes & Co., succeed S. W. Dooley & Co.
Lebanon, *M—Inks, C. V., 86 to Peter Paulus.
Madison, *M—Crozier, James E., succeed J. H. Crozier & Co:
Sullivan, *M—Sullivan Marble & Granite Co., 43.
Terra Haute, *M—Wagner, William F., 106.
IOWA.
Bonaparte, *M—Fuller, C. E., 20 $282.
Collins, *M—Murray & Gerard, 76.
Davenport, *M—Iglehart & McKeown, 64, C. S. McLeown, 58.
Eddyville, *M—Lafferty, A. M., 93 $400.
Emmetsburg, *M—Godden & Ballard, 99 $2,000, 93 $3,000 and Mr. Ballard, 32 $500.
Marengo, *M—Stoddard & Wood, 64, S. M. Stoddard, 58.
Marshalltown, *M—Woods, W. W. & Son, 87 $450.
Spencer, *M—Shaffer, W. T., 74 $116.
KANSAS.
Cottonwood Falls, *M—Moon, T. E., 86.
Kingman, *M—Cates Bros., 14 $278.
Marysville, *M—Bittel, E. A., succeeds Stuart & Bittel.
Smith Centre, *M—Allen, R. W., 14 $451 .
MAINE.
Auburn, *M—Haskell, R. C., 14 $1.
Berwick, *M—Downs, Herbert N., 93 $550.
Buckfield, *M—Libby, A. W., 76.
Mount Desert, *M—Campbell & Macomber, 14 $2,000.
Newport, *M—Fernald & Norton, F. E. Norton, 93, $400.
Stonington, GZ—Warren, T. & Co., Frank S. Warren quit claimed R. E. $115.
Yarmouth, *M—White, E. M., 93 $300.
MARYLAND.
Baltimore, *M—McKnight, John, 20 $142.
MASSACHUSETTS.
Fall River, *M—Cote, Flavien, 14 $972.
Fitchburg, G—Roolstone Granite & Construction Co., 14 $3,000.
Ipswich, *M—Barton & Williams, William M. Williams, 78.
Quincy, GZ—Burns & Cormack, 64, Mr. Burns 58.
Quincy, GZ—Scandia Granite Works 104.
Salem, *M—Curtis, Charles E. & Son, succeed C. E. Curtis.

Springfield, *M—Casey & Buckley, 76.
Taunton, *M—Cullen, Patrick, 93 $200.
MICHIGAN.
Jackson, *M—Leslie & Mitchell, John G. Leslie, 14 $321.
MINNESOTA.
Crookston, *M—Sundet, Thomas O., 99 $800.
Lake City, *M—Smith, W. C., 76.
MISSOURI.
Palmyra, *M—Ragar, James, 76.
St. Louis, *M—Fitze, Alex C., 106.
Vandalia, *M—Gallagher, J. W., succeeds Gallagher & Weathersford.
NEW HAMPSHIRE.
Concord, GZ—Gannon, M. G. & Son, 14 $250.
Manchester, *M—R. P. Stevens Co., 39 cap. $20m.
West Concord, *M—Clark, Frank R., 93 $1,650.
Portsmouth, *M— Moon & Davis, 64.
NEW JERSEY.
Jersey City, *M—Kelly, John & Sons, 14 $1,596.
NEW YORK.
Bath, *M—Wilson, J. B. & Co., 64, J. B. Wilson 58.
Kingston, *M—Luther, H. B., R. E. deed $1,575.
Middle Village, *M—Eff & Seitz, Anton Eff 78.
New York, *M—Canfield, C. B., 87 $100.
Petersburg, *A—Robertson, A., 76.
Troy, *M—Shea, John F., 78.
OHIO.
Athens, *M—Gleason, John, Jr., 93 $925.
Chillicothe, *M—Harris, John B., 99 $1.500.
Cooperdale, *M—Perkins, T. P., 76.
Fostoria, *M—Robbins, W. D., 84.
Hamilton, *M—Horssnyder, F., 93 $2,711.
Hamilton, *M—Menchen, Henry, 93 $1,000.
Jefferson, *M—Western Reserve Marble & Granite Co., 76.
Montpelier, *M—Weaver, W. O., Frank Weaver, 60.
Newark, *M—Felumlee & Co., 76.
Newark, *M—Griffith, Thomas H., 14 $279.
Springfield, *M—Kelley, I. H., 14 $717.
West Milton, *M—Wallace, L., 76.
OREGON.
Dallas, *M—Comini, Louigi, 76.
PENNSYLVANIA.
Allegheny, *M—Rees Bros., 64, David E. Rees 58.
Bangor, *M—Owens, Thomas, 76.
Duncannon and New Bloomfield, *M—Lupfer & Flickinger 64, Flickinger & Snyder 58.
Erie, *M—New Dunning Marble & Granite Co., 20 $1,300.
Greenville, *M—Halpin & Lewis 64, P. J. Halpin 58.
Grove City, *M—Lewis, C. E., 76.
Kingston, *M—Chapin, W. H., execution $240.
Scranton, B—Carlucci Stone Co., succeed Frank Carlucci.
York, *M—Schrenker, John, 90.
RHODE ISLAND.
Providence, *M—Toye & Holmes, 89.
SOUTH CAROLINA.
Greenville, *M—Clark Bros. & Co. succeed Clark & Cooper.
Pacolet, *M—Stephen & McKie succeed Stephen & Lane.

Spartanburg, *M—Claxton, G. E., 88 to Abbeville. .
Spartanburg, *M—Geddes, George, 14 $162.
Spartanburg, *M—Geddes & Clark, 64.
Spartanburg, *M—Walker & Amos, 76.
SOUTH DAKOTA.
Sioux Falls, *M—Ballard & Son, 76.
TENNESSEE.
Pulaski, *M—Bennett & Ragsdale, 76.
TEXAS.
El Paso, *M—Moretti, John, 84.
VERMONT.
Barre, GZ—King, J. C., 106.
Barre, GZ—Newhall & Tracey, succeed C. D. Newhall.
Bradford, *M—Wilson, A. G., 105.
Bristol, *M—McGee, William N., 80 to C. W. Dunshee.
Morrisville, *M—Pike & Boynton, succeed Walter W. Pike.
St. Albans, *M—Moore, J. G., 80.
WASHINGTON.
Spokane, *M—United States Marble Co., suit dismissed.
WEST VIRGINIA.
Phillippi, *M—Phillippi Marble Works succeed Koon Marble Co.
Weston, *M—Weston Marble Works succeed Koon Marble Co.
WISCONSIN.
Milwaukee, *M—Stampa, William, 14 $200.

Quincy Notes.

(Continued from page 18.)

Nothing new has developed in relation to the proposed granite syndicate to operate the quarries in Quincy. The promoters, however, say that the scheme has not been given up by any means, and that the formation of the syndicate is an assured fact. There have been rumors during the past month that the New York end of the plan has been dropped, as it was costing the Quincy men too much money, and that the plan had been taken up by several Massachusetts men who were now working to carry out the original plans for organization. How well they will succeed remains to be seen.

Herbert W. Beattie, the sculptor, has just completed the model of an elaborate cap for the Scranton, Pa., soldiers' monument. The cap is of massive design, the dimensions being 8-6x7-6. On the front and back, standing forth in bold relief is a large American eagle, while on the two sides are large shields showing thirteen stars and thirteen bars. It is one of the best things that Mr. Beattie has turned out from his studio for some time.

The strike will not affect the Merry Mount Co. to any great extent, from the fact that the firm owns its own quarry, and that all of its cutters are members of the corporation. They have quite a lot of work on hand of the medium size kind, and are taking what orders they can get, feeling confident that they can deliver them all right.

Granite shipments continue to hold up well, and it is probably a fact that never were shipments as large in winter months as this year. January was a good month, February will be better, and March will see the great bulk of the work piled up in the several yards shipped, and the agents at the several terminals expect to have all they can jump to next month. The total amount shipped in January was 18,617,428 pounds. This is 2,786,857 pounds less than in December. Quincy Adams shipped over two million pounds less than in December, and West Quincy also over two million pounds. The Quarry railroad, however, increased its tonnage by over one million pounds. Much of the Quarry railroad shipments, however, were of grout. The January figures were: Quarry railroad, 12,891,380 pounds; West Quincy, 3,316,985 pounds; and Quincy Adams, 2,409,063 pounds.

McDonnell & Sons have a large amount of work on hand, the larger part of which they expect to have completed ready for shipment by the first of March.

Joss Bros. Co. are very busy this month trying to finish up what orders they have on hand before the first of March. The indications in the middle of the month were that they would have about everything cleaned up. In their yards are several large monuments all completed and will be shipped to their destination just as soon as spring opens. These jobs have all been described at length in previous issues of GRANITE.

Joseph Walker of the Aberdeen Granite Works says that he completed more work in January than ever before in that month. This was partly due to the exceptionally fair weather, and partly because he, like the other firms in Quincy, expect to see work stop March 1. Usually on that date manufacturers are getting ready for spring work, but this year the most of them seem to be getting ready for a spring and summer vacation.

The Granite Railway Co. has elected the following officers: president, John A. Lamson; vice president, Harold J. Cooledge; treasurer, J. Albert Simpson; directors, John A. Lamson, Harold J. Cooledge, Otis H. Luke, William S. Patten, T. Francis Meany, George Lewis. William B. Sewall, who has been president of the company for several years, retires from that office and from the directory.

M. H. Rice of Kansas City was in town early this month trying to place $25,000 of orders under the bill of prices of 1899, but could find no taker.

J. C. Sullivan of Crescent City, Iowa, was in town this month and placed a few orders for medium sized work.

Deacon Bros., McIntosh & Sons, and other firms about the Centre street district have been very busy all the month, and will have about all of their orders finished by the first of the month. Nearly all of the yards are filled with finished work, and the firms will be kept busy for some weeks shipping away the finished work.

The Smith-Newall Trouble.

The controversy between the Smith and Newall interests in the granite quarries at Westerly, formerly managed by both parties, was heard again Jan. 8. Three motions were before the court. Two of them were made by the counsel for the Smiths and asked that the powers of the receiver be extended. The motion of counsel for the Newalls was to do away with the receiver altogether on the ground that the amending of their bill of complaint by the Smith interests opened the whole question of whether there should be a receiver or not.

Walter B. Vincent said that the receiver had to refuse a large number of profitable contracts, as his restrictions prevented him from blasting or channelling for new stone.

William S. Martin, a witness called by Mr. Vincent, testified that he knew the receiver had been forced to refuse contracts to the extent of $40,000. The profits on these contracts would be from $6,000 to $10,000. In order to do the channelling or blasting necessary to get new stone no new machine or tools would be necessary.

On cross examination the witness refused to admit that certain losses of the Smiths in 1896, 1897 or 1898 were due to his mistakes in making estimates. He admitted he was not a practical quarry man, but had been in the office of the Smiths for a long time.

James Gourley testified he had been 25 years in charge of a granite quarry. The general understanding in the country was that the Smith Granite Quarry Company was not in the market for work. The declining of orders, as stated by Mr. Martin, was very injurious to the Smith company's business.

Augustus S. Miller, counsel for the Newalls, read a number of affidavits from men who had worked in quarries, which were to the effect that the receiver's work was not of advantage to the plant. Joseph Newall in an affidavit stated that he was informed by parties who were in touch with the trade that the receiver had sold a large quantity of tools and ropes. Furthermore he was informed by the receiver that when a case got into equity it would remain there a couple of years. This led Mr. Miller to remark that if there had not been a receiver the case would have been settled long ago.

Mr. Vincent retorted: "Yes, the lamb would have been inside of the lion." The affidavits all stated the filing of the orders referred to by the receiver could not be done without great and disproportionate expense.

Mr. Miller argued that the amended bill did not authorize the appointment of a receiver pedente lite, but asked that if the court should deem it best to continue the receiver his instructions be made specific.

Mr. Vincent recalled Mr. Gourley to the witness stand, and that gentleman said he did not believe there would be any large expense in filling the orders the receiver had declined.

After Mr. Gourley had made his statement, Mr. Vincent argued that it was plain enough common sense for the receiver to have the power necessary to work the quarry in a profitable manner. The court held the case for advisement.

LATER.—The Appellate division of the Supreme Court has granted the petition of the receiver of the Smith & Newall Granite Company of Westerly, extending his powers.

The court in its decision says that the best interests of the business and the party to whom the quarry shall ultimately come will be preserved by extending the power of the receiver in accordance with the complainant's motion, which is therefore granted.

The decision allows the receiver to secure all contracts possible, and work the quarries practically as he sees fit. Granite workers will be pleased to see work resumed.

Settlement at Barre. No Result at Quincy.

Just before going to press the following comes to us:

At a meeting of the granite manufacturers, on the evening of Feb. 28, at which about seventy firms were represented, it was voted to accept the compromise of thirty-five cents an hour as proposed by the cutters. This action averts a strike of the 1400 or more cutters and sharpeners, and these men will all go to work March 1, under the new schedule.

The manufacturers had previously conceded the demand for eight hours a day for six days a week, but refused to pay more than an average thirty-four cents an hour.

The chief places in which strikes will occur in March and the number of cutters to be ordered out in each place is approximately as follows:

Montpelier, Vt., 250; Hardwick, Vt., 100; South Ryegate, Vt., 120; Redstone, N. H., 30; Concord, N. H., 200; Milford, N. H., 50; Troy, N. H., 20; Hallowell, Me., 100; Vinal Haven, Me., 75; Hurricane Island, Me., 100; North Jay, Me., 100; Blue Hill, Me., 25; Charles Island, Me., 10; Waldoboro, Me., 50; Bangor, Me., 15; Portland, Me., 25; North Sullivan, Me., 35; Calais, Me., 35; Quincy, 1000; Milford, Mass., 250; Worcester, 35; Chester, Mass., 15; Westerly, R. I., 250; Niantic, R. I., 15; Millstone Point, Ct., 75; New London, 30; Groton, Ct., 50; New Haven, 15.

There will be many men beside the cutters idle because of the strike, and it is estimated that fully 5000 people will be thrown out of work.

Meetings are now being held at Quincy, between the cutters and manufacturers, and before this paper is received by our subscribers a settlement will probably be made at this point also.

The settlement made at Barre will have an effect on settlements at all points at which granite is cut for monumental work, especially at Montpelier, Vt., Hardwick, Vt., Northfield, Vt., Morrisville, Vt., and all Vermont points.

SUFFEREN, N. Y.—William Copeland has purchased a lot on Wayne avenue, and will remove his granite and marble yard there early next spring.

Among our visitors in February was Henry Trieble of Trieble & Sons, Peoria, Ill. Mr. Trieble was making his usual visit to the east. It is a great pleasure for us to meet the western retail dealers, and we trust that those who visit the east will not neglect us.

Among our callers this month was I. N. Webster, Des Moines, Ia. Was very sorry to have missed this gentleman, but was glad to see that he was using dis-cretion in travelling through the streets of Boston under the directions of a guide. Call again.—Ed.

ADDRESS

Lane Manufacturing Co.,

MONTPELIER, VT.

48   -GRANITE-

Rough Stock
or
Finished Monumental Work
in
Quincy or Concord
Granites.

Send for
Estimates.

J. ALBERT SIMPSON,
Treasurer.

L. S. ANDERSON,
Manager.

1826-1900.
Seventy-Four Years in the Granite Business.

QUARRIES:
West Quincy, Mass.,   Concord, N. H.

PRINCIPAL OFFICE: - WEST QUINCY, MASS.

DETAIL OF ILLUSTRATION BELOW:

No. 1. Looking West from Quarry No. 1.
No. 2. A corner in Quarry No. 2.   No. 3. A Bird's-eye View of Quarry No. 1
No. 4. A Block of Extra Dark Blue Quincy Granite measuring 19 x 16 x 9½ feet, weighing about 300 tons.
No. 5. Road from Yard to Quarries operated by an endless chain.

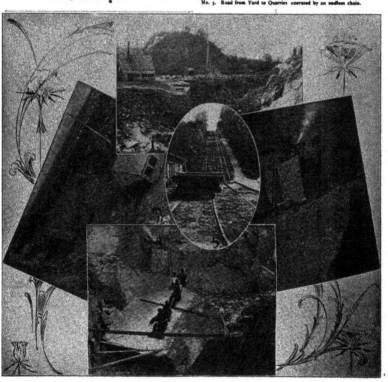

pril 1900   Vol. X. No. 4

ranite

A. M. HUNT & CO.

PUBLISHERS

31 Devonshire Street

BOSTON, MASS., U.S.A.

Subscription Price, $1.00 Year

ADVERTISERS' DIRECTORY.

Reports on Troy Granite.

ORDNANCE DEPARTMENT, U. S. A.

Report of Mechanical Tests Made with U. S. Testing Machine, Capacity 800,000 Pounds, at Watertown Arsenal, Mass., April 15th, 1891.

FOR TROY GRANITE COMPANY, WORCESTER, MASS.

Test by Compression of One Six-Inch Cube of Troy Granite.

Compressed Surfaces faced with Plaster of Paris to secure even bearings.

TEST NUMBER.	DIMENSIONS.		SECTIONAL AREA.	ULTIMATE STRENGTH.	
	LENGTH.	COMPRESSED SURFACE.		TOTAL LBS.	LBS PER SQ. IN.
7419	5.95	5.84 | 5.90	35.01	630.100	17.950

First crack at 525,000 lbs.
Pyramidal fracture.

Correct:
J. E. HOWARD.

D. W. FLAGLER,
Lieut. Col. Ordnance Dept., U. S. A., Commanding.

Chemical Laboratory, Worcester Polytechnic Institute.

CERTIFICATE OF ANALYSIS.

GENTLEMEN :   WORCESTER, MASS., May 4, 1891.

The sample of Troy Granite submitted to me for examination contains :

Silica,	-	-	-	73.15 per cent.	
Alumina and Iron Oxide,		-	-	17.04 " "	
Lime,	-	-	-	0.81 " "	
Magnesia,	-	-	-	0.80 " "	
Potassium Oxide,	-	-	-	5.74 " "	
Sodium Oxide,	-	-	-	2.05 " "	
Loss and Undetermined,	-	-	0.91 " "	

Total, - - 100.00

Respectfully yours,

TO TROY GRANITE CO.   LEONARD P. KINNICUTT, PH. D.

ALL TOGETHER.

Every piece finished and FITTED under personal supervision and shipped from the same place at the same time.

Don't allow your orders to be peddled to parties you would not patronize yourself. — A guarantee of replacing defective work is very good, but — it pleases your customer better to have it right FIRST TIME.

We will make it an object—and no expense—for every dealer unacquainted to carry our samples of the HARDWICK GRANITE,—The Darkest Fine Grained Stock and Absolutely Free From Iron

WRITE FOR SHEETS OF COMPARATIVE PRICES.

25 Years Experience in the Business.   ### GEO. D. BAILEY, Hardwick, Vt.

FRONT PANEL.

BACK PANEL.

BARCLAY BROS.,
OWNERS OF
Dark and Light Granite Quarries.
SPECIALTIES :
Vaults and Large Monuments.

Pneumatic Surfacing Machine.
Pneumatic Tools.

Column Cutting Machinery and
Polishing Mill.

SIDE PANEL.

SIDE PANEL.

ROBERT BURNS MONUMENT,
Unveiled at Barre, Vt., July 21, 1899.
Monument and Statue cut entirely from Barre Granite.
Designed by William Barclay, and executed by
Barclay Bros., in their own Sheds at Barre, Vt.
Bottom base of Monument, 8 feet square.
Total Height, 22 feet 10 inches.

Well, Well!   Not Dead Yet,

But you will be, wearing your life away on that hard granite when you can buy of us a light and medium stone that will work in half the time, look just as well

and last just as long. We can get you any size, any shape most any day in the year. Our patterns are excellent and prices reasonable.

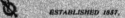

VIEWS OF OUR QUARRY.

Hopkins, Huntington & Co.,
Quarry Owners and Manufacturers.   ⟶ BARRE, VERMONT.

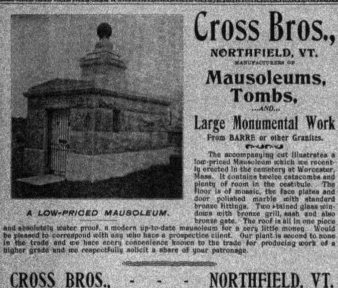

GRANITE

ENTERED AT THE BOSTON POST OFFICE AS SECOND-CLASS MAIL MATTER.

Vol. X. BOSTON, MASS., APRIL 1, 1900. No. 4

A. M. HUNT, EDITOR.

Published Monthly in the interests of the Producer, Manufacturer, and Retailer of Granite as used for Monumental or Building Purposes.

Terms of Subscription

To ANY PART OF THE UNITED STATES OR CANADA:

One copy, one year - - - - $1.00, in advance.
One copy, six months - - - 75 cents, in advance.

ADVERTISING RATES FURNISHED UPON APPLICATION.

A. M. HUNT & CO., Publishers,

131 DEVONSHIRE STREET, - - BOSTON, MASS.

I MUST most emphatically enter my protest against the system in connection with the illustration of designs for monumental work now practiced by certain trade journals, that of giving prices under a so-called key. Another journal practicing a similar baneful system, used a supposed undecipherable key, which required a matter of only some ten minutes' time to put it into plain United States. I lose patience with journals stooping to such methods, while professing to be issued for the purpose of enlightening the trade public.

On the same plane is the publishing of priced designs in the trade journals and should be discountenanced by every respectable publisher. Any dealer can get prices by writing for them, and the cost is so trifling that he certainly will go to the expense for any design he may be pleased with.—I. H. Kelly, Springfield, Ohio, in Monumental News.

We have cut out of the above letter only such matter that we consider refers to us. We

have no apologies to offer for publishing sizes and prices under a key. Our reasons for doing so are for protection. We in common with other journals send out a number of sample copies each issue. We have a regular mailing list which includes our subscribers, those who have paid their dollar for subscription, and the principal idea in publishing sizes and prices under a key is to protect those who paid their money, and not give the same benefit to those who receive sample copies. - Mr. Kelly is not a subscriber, but evidently from the letter above he never will be, for to be consistent he cannot possibly patronize us, but he has certainly taken interest enough in our methods of quoting prices and sizes to puzzle out the key, and we will guarantee that it took more than ten minutes of his valuable time. We can plainly see that it is necessary to change the key, and sometime in the near future we will give Mr. Kelly another chance to figure out prices and sizes. The subscription price to GRANITE is $1 per year, this includes a key to the sizes and prices. We do not think that this is an exorbitant price, and many of our subscribers have assured us that it is not. We are endeavoring to publish a paper which will be of some benefit to the trade, but we are not in business altogether for our health and consequently it is necessary for us to secure paying subscribers, and the way of publishing sizes and prices is one of the methods we use with that idea in view. We do certainly agree with Mr. Kelly that the publishing of prices on designs should not be done, but nine out of ten of our subscribers call for them, and we have complied with their requests. If Mr. Kelly will devise some way of stopping this demand we will be only too much pleased to drop all reference to price. Any other shortcomings that Mr. Kelly may notice in sample copies which come to him, we trust that he will not hesitate to criticise. We should feel sorry indeed if we were not noticed at all.

*

THE advisability of the retail monumental dealers in each state organizing associations and combining with the National Association for mutual benefit has been recently shown in what has been done by this association. The very serious matter of increased freight rates which place upon work at the quarries an almost prohibitory price upon granite work has been overcome, if not directly through the National Association it has had its influence. As a result a protest was entered by the National Association and the Granite Manufacturers' Association of New England in common with others, the high rates which went into effect upon January 1st have been reduced to near their former price. As a result of the combined efforts of the National Association the wholesale houses selling marble to department stores have agreed to a large extent not to do so, and the others are being followed up vigorously. No individual can hope to bring forth a similar result, and we trust that all dealers who are not members of some organization will see the necessity of forming an association with the idea in view of joining the National Association, for in numbers there is strength and there are many matters of importance which will come up in the future which can be handled easily by numbers. In the time of peace prepare for war, for war comes when least expected.

WE published a letter in the March issue among the editorials, from Seward W. Jones, stating that he was in receipt of a letter from J. T. Ripley, chairman of the Western Classification Committee stating that granite and marble had both been restored to the 4th class. It seems that this letter and the change in classification related to sawed marble or granite only, and therefore did not change the rate upon granite in less than carload lots which went into effect January 1st. Upon investigation we find that the rate upon finished granite in carload lots was changed from D to 5th class. Upon strong influence being brought to bear upon the Western Classification Committee to bring back the old rate, they stated that there would be no meeting of the Western Classification Committee until November, but it was agreed among the members of the committee to put the following to a vote of the various roads running west of Chicago: That finished granite in carload lots be subject to C classification and rate, and in less than carload lots back to the 4th class where it was formerly. To cite the difference in carload lots between classification C and the old classification D we quote the following rate: The rate under the old classification D from Chicago to Sioux City was 18 1-2 cents, under the proposed change it will be 22 cents. In less than carload lots it is proposed to bring it back to the old classification 4th class. This relates only to shipments from Chicago west. The rate from east to Chicago, as we explained in our previous issue, has been brought back to near the old rate. We are told by Seward Jones of Jones Bros., that he has every reason to believe that when this matter is put to a vote that it will be voted upon favorably without a question, as he has had numerous letters from the representatives of western roads in the east that they will vote that the change be made, and before this paper is received by our subscribers, in all probability the above change will have gone into effect.

UNDER the head of Quincy Items it will be noticed that the long-looked-for combination of the quarries at Quincy has been effected, at least it has been partially successful, yet there are a number of the best quarries outside of the

combination. Prominent among them is that of the Granite Railway Co., which is one of the best known and has the best quarries in Quincy. The Merry Mount Granite Co. is also outside of the granite combination and a number of others of the best known quarries. The whole situation is practically explained under the head of Quincy Notes and a list of the officers given. It would certainly seem that if it were possible to make a success of the trust that the officers mentioned could make it successful, as among them are the best business men that Quincy produces. It is understood that it is proposed to figure upon some large contracts which New York City has on hand at the present time, and in the future we hope that the new combination will be a help to the Quincy granite industry..

VERY thoroughly explained under the heading of Quincy Notes, is the strike situation at Quincy. We publish below a facsimile of the agreement signed at Barre by the secretary of the Barre Granite Manufacturers' Association and secretary of the Granite Cutters' Union. Each one who reads it can judge for himself as to the

demands made by the cutters in Quincy that average means minimum. Hardwick, Vt., Groton, Vt., Northfield, Vt., and Montpelier, Vt., have all settled upon the basis of the Barre settlement printed above. Milford, N. H., has practically made the same settlement. Reported under date of March 22 that it was generally understood that Concord, N. H., had made a settlement, both parties agreeing upon an eight-hour work day and a minimum wage of thirty-five cents an hour, that the cutters had accepted for the manufacturers a piece bill on monumental work which was said to average an increase of thirteen per cent for the men, and a uniform pay day on the tenth of each month was granted. No settlement has yet been reached at Westerly, R. I. It was reported under date of March 22 that the trouble at Waldoboro between the manufacturers and the stone cutters had been adjusted. The manufacturers conceded an eight-hour day and the cutters accepted thirty-five cents an hour as a minimum price and 16 2-3 cents on piece work. It is understood that this arrangement holds good only while the conference of the Granite Cutters National Union is pending. Booth Bros. & Hurricane Isle Granite Co., Rockland, Me., have offered to put cutters to work under the same conditions as the settlement at Barre, subject to the approval of the Granite Manufacturers' Association. The association, however, refused to ratify the proposition.

The looked for and expected strike in Quincy is on, and from present indications it seems likely to continue for an indefinite period. Efforts have been made by the manufacturers to reach an agreement, and although several conferences have been held they have been fruitless as far as a settlement is concerned. The manufacturers offer a proposition which the cutters refuse and retaliate with a demand.

The strike, however, up to the present time has developed one thing, and that is that the demand of eight hours and $3 was a big game of bluff. It was skilfully played but did not work.

For a year nothing has been heard but that the National Cutters' Union had incorporated in its constitution the clause that after a certain date in 1900 eight hours should be called a day's work with a minimum price of $3. When approached, the cutters said they had no authority to accept other than these terms, and that clause could not be arbitrated. When the New England Granite Manufacturers' Association notified Secretary Duncan of the National Union that they would like a conference, the answer came back that no conference could be held until the demand for eight hours and $3 had been granted. Yet a little later comes the report that Barre had settled on an average of 35 cents an hour. It was also reported that Secretary Duncan had advised them to settle for 34 cents if more could not be obtained, and that he had advised the Quincy cutters to settle on the same basis. No denials of these rumors have come from Secretary Duncan, and others are right in believing the demand to have been a bluff. Early in February the Quincy Manufacturers' Association appointed a committee to meet a like committee from the Cutters' Union to see if a peaceful settlement could not be reached. This committee was composed of John L. Miller, Andrew Milne, Harry S. Nicol, R. S. Seaver, J. McGillvray, W. T. Spargo, Walter R. Fagan, Peter T. Fitzgerald and Alexander Falconer. The first meeting of the two committees was held Wednesday evening, February 28. The two committees discussed the situation for an hour or two, at the end of which the manufacturers offered a proposition to settle on an average rate of 30 cents for eight hours. This proposition the cutters refused. At this point word was received by telephone from Barre that a settlement had been reached there on a basis of an average of 35 cents for eight hours. This report was doubted, and a recess taken, during which the report was confirmed. Upon reassembling, the manufacturers raised their offer to 33 cents per hour. This proposition the cutters said they would present at a mass meeting of the union the following day. At the cutters' meeting on Thursday, its messenger, who had been deputised to communicate with Barre, reported that the settlement there was a minimum price of 35 cents. Thereupon, the cutters voted to settle upon a minimum price of 35 cents for eight hours.

The two committees met again that evening when the manufacturers renewed their offer of an average of 33 cents and the cutters made a demand for a minimum of 35 cents. Another adjournment was taken until the following Monday night. The question of whether the Barre settlement was an average or a minimum was one upon which there was a difference of opinion, and until that was settled no action seemed possible. When the two committees met again on Monday night the manufacturers were fortified with copies of the Barre agreement. This was exhibited, and while the cutters' committee admitted that the agreement certainly read average, they fell back upon the statement that while it may state average it means minimum. Then the manufacturers renewed their proposition of an average of 33 cents, and the cutters their demand for a 35-cent minimum. There they stuck, and as neither would give in, an indefinite adjournment was taken.

The general public of Quincy were blaming first one side and then the other for not bringing about a settlement as had been done in Barre. Some were sure the Barre settlement was an average wage, while others were equally as sure that the settlement was a minimum. The manufacturers determined, in view of the newspaper and sidewalk talk about average and minimum price, to settle that question once for all, and sent to Barre and had a photograph taken of the agreement. A photo-electrotype was then made of the agreement, which was published in a local paper. This apparently settled that question. A fac-simile of the letter is published elsewhere in this issue of GRANITE.

It is worthy of note that during these conferences nothing whatever has been said about the minimum price of $3 a day, about which there was so much talk, and members of the cutters' union who have been asked can advance no excuse nor cannot explain how it is that settlements have been made for less than that demand, although they personally would be glad to settle for a smaller figure.

No provision was made for calling another joint meeting of the committee, but the chairman of the joint committee sent out a call for a meeting the day after the New England conference committee meeting was held. This meeting was held Friday evening, March 16. The situation was discussed, after which the manufacturers' committee made the following propositions:

That eight hours shall constitute a day's work for six days a week.

That the standard wage shall be $2.65 a day.

That the minimum wage shall be $2.40 per day.

That there shall be an increase of ten per cent on the price list of 1899.

That the new terms shall remain in force until March 1, 1905.

The cutters' committee retired, and after consultation reported that they were not prepared to accept the proposition without further consideration; the cutters then renewed their proposition to settle for a minimum wage of 35 cents per hour, which the manufacturers refused.

The following day the several cutters' branches held meetings, at which the new proposition of the manufacturers' committee was submitted. With but little discussion the unions refused to accept the proposition. On Monday evening, March 19, the two committees held another conference; the cutters reported that the unions would not accept the offer made on the 16th. The manufacturers then submitted what they call their ultimatum proposition, which was as follows:

"Eight hours to constitute a day's work; six days in a week, as already agreed to; the pay to be the same as paid for nine hours in the bill of 1899, with an 11 per cent increase in the piece price list of 1899: the agreement to remain in force until March 1, 1905. This practically means $2.52 per day as the minimum price. This proposition the cutters' committee said they would submit to the unions on Wednesday, which they did. The next joint meeting was on Thursday evening, March 22, at which the manufacturers were informed that the branches had voted not to accept the proposition. The manufacturers' committee gave the cutters to understand that they had reached their limit and should make no more offers, and that they should open their yards for business and should endeavor to obtain men at the price they had offered. The meeting then adjourned without date.

The manufacturers are in no hurry to open their yards, and it will probably be the first of April before any attempt is made to resume work. It has been unofficially announced by cutters who attended the last meeting of the branches that the sentiment expressed was, that if the manufacturers did not grant the demand for 35 cents minimum for eight hours before midnight, March 24, that they would not settle for less than $3 for eight hours. This means probably a long fight in Quincy.

Since that time up to the time of writing this letter, nothing has been done toward a settlement. There have been no meetings of the committee, and both sides seem to have settled back, determined to wait for future developments. The men who had unfinished stones on March 1, were permitted to return to work and finish them up, and they have done so.

There has been quite an exodus of cutters from Quincy since the strike commenced, one hundred or more leaving town during the first week. Some of these went to Barre, but a larger part of them went south, where it is reported they were promised $3 a day for eight hours.

The firm of McGrath Bros. was dissolved by mutual consent on January 1. James McGrath retires from the business, which will hereafter be managed by Henry McGrath. This firm is one of the oldest concerns in Quincy. The business was originally established by Patrick McGrath, father of the above, in 1854.

It is hardly to be expected that there would be any increase in the amount of granite shipped during the month of February, yet as a whole shipments the past winter have held up remarkably well. Many of the manufacturers have a large amount of finished work on hand, but it is a little early to ship much of it, although from now until the middle of May there will be quite a rush of shipments. In February the amount shipped from Quincy Adams was over a million more pounds than in January; West Quincy billed off a million pounds, and the Quarry Railroad about six million pounds. The total amount shipped in February was 12,633,344 pounds against 18,617,428 pounds in January. The amount shipped from the several terminals in February were: Quincy Quarry Railroad, 6,885,080 pounds; Quincy Adams, 3,604,534 pounds; West Quincy, 2,173,730 pounds.

Herbert W. Beattie, the sculptor, is modelling a portrait statue of Master Freddie Alley, the boy soprano of Montreal, Canada. As a boy of delightful manners and great promise, his sudden death, which occurred the night following his masterful singing of the piece entitled, "Where is Heaven?" was a sad bereavement to all acquainted with him and his art. In the statue he is represented as resting easily, with his arm against a doric column, with head well posed and holding in his hand his last piece, "Where is Heaven?"

The quarry syndicate of which there has been so much talk for nearly a year past has at last assumed definite shape, and the deal consolidating many of the granite quarries in Quincy can be said to have become an assured fact. On the morning of March 21, the deeds conveying the property to the syndicate were filed with the registrar of deeds at Dedham. At the same time there was filed with the city clerk at Quincy the first mortgage bond of the company given by them to the American Loan and Trust Co. of Boston. The mortgage bond is for $1,750,000, to run thirty years at five per cent from March 1, 1900.

The property or quarries named in the mortgage, which is practically that acquired by the company is as follows: Quincy Quarry Co, Berry Bros., John Cashman, Prout Bros.' Granite Co., Andrew Milne, W. R. Thomas, Fallon & Sons, Frederick S. Field, Adams Temple and School Fund, George S. Paterson 126 shares of the Blue Hill Granite Co., 201 shares of the Lyons Granite Co., and 107 shares of the O. T. Rogers Granite Co. It is also understood that the quarries of L. Dell, Elcock & Sons and George H. Hitchcock & Co. are included in the deal, although their names do not appear in the list of property named in he mortgage. The new company, which was organized under the laws of New Jersey, is known as the Quincy Granite Quarries Co., and the mortgage is signed by John Swithin as president and John K. Hayward as treasurer. According to the prospectus issued by the company some months ago, the capitalization is $1,-750,000. The common stock 25,000 shares at $100 per share. The average annual net earnings are estimated at $128,280; interest on bonds, $80,000; surplus earnings, $91,280. The approximate assets are: 530 acres of quarry land, $1,334.500; granite blocked out, $1,-628.496; quarry railroads, $98,068; engines, machinery, etc., $219,095; salable property not needed in business, $91,000; cash for new power plants, $300,000; total, $3,681,159. It is also understood that the selling agency of the company will be in New York, and will be known as the Quincy Commercial Granite Co. The complete directory of the company had not been given out at this writing, probably for the reason that the complete organization has not been perfected. From reliable sources, however, it is learned that the board of directors will not be far from the following: John Swithin, John K. Hayward, George H. Hitchcock, Andrew Milne, James Thompson, Thomas Swithin, Marshal P. Wright, John W. McArarney, Barnabas Clark, Mr. Ferdinand, a well known Boston clothier, and Mr. Nulty, a Boston banker. There are also two New York men whose names have not been learned. John Cashman of Quincy has been appointed general superintendent of the company and has already assumed his duties as such, the new company having begun to operate the quarries as soon as the deeds were transferred. The plans of the new company are numerous, according to report. Perhaps the most important is to acquire what is known as the Brackets wharf property on Quincy Bay as a shipping terminal. If this is done the intention is to connect the wharf and quarries with the Quincy and Boston street railways systems and to obtain a right from the legislature to transport granite over the line at night from the quarries to the wharf. If this is done it will materially reduce the transportation rates and enable Quincy to better compete with other centres in building material.

It is also understood that the company does not intend to bind itself to sell stock to any but members of the Manufacturers' Association, but will sell stock to anyone who wants to purchase.

It is early as yet to tell what effect the new company will have on the granite cutting business in Quincy. One thing is known certain, and that is they cannot get a corner on Quincy granite at present as there are several large quarries which they have not acquired.

Since the first of March, when it was supposed that there would be the beginning of a long struggle between the Manufacturers and Cutters Union, there has not been very much going on in the plants around this city with the exception of the working of the apprentices in the various sheds.

The difficulty has been settled as far as the local branch of the Association, and the Union can adjust the matter, but during the period of suspense the Manufacturers did nothing about getting in orders or stock and consequently they have not a great quantity of either on hand just at this time. As a result there are more men out of work in this city now than there has been for a long time before. Early in the month just passed there was a fall of about three feet of snow, and the quarry owners thinking that there would not likely be a demand for stock for a little did not clear their quarries as soon as they would have done under ordinary circumstances. More snow has been coming of late and there are quite a number of quarries which will not be opened without a deal of expense. So it is about impossible for the Manufacturers to go on with orders which they may have had before the first of March or may have had come in since the news of the settlement here became known to the public.

The failure of the Union and the Association to reach any settlement in other parts of New England has had some effect on the feeling here.

There is still a possibility of the agreement made between the Cutters here and the Manufacturers not being endorsed by the National Organizations, and it is understood that there is no disposition, as has been reported, to run business "on our own hook" regardless of the National Association.

All work is being conducted on the scale of eight hours at 35 cents per hour for the average cutter, thus increasing the cost of the manufactured product about thirty per cent.

There is a feeling here among the well-informed that the terms which have been arranged to settle the strike will prove a detriment to the trade in the long run, but with business good as it promised to be this year it was thought the wiser plan to compromise rather than to have the hammers idle during the summer with no knowledge as to when they might be heard again.

Sweeney Brothers Granite Co., Montpelier, have received several orders for medium sized jobs since we last visited their plant. They have been doing some work this month but are running pretty short of stock.

They report that they have orders on their books sufficient to keep their men working during the next month if they can only get the stock as they want it.

Some stock is being brought in from some of the quarries, but it is very difficult to get any large pieces without waiting for a long time.

This sort of thing is not expected to continue for a great while, for every effort is being put forth now by the quarry owners to clear out the snow so that operations may be renewed.

Geo. Straiton has been doing a large business during the past year and has now on his books a variety of orders of which no manufacturer in the city would be ashamed. He has nearly completed a large sarcophagus job which is going to Illinois upon which there is quite a large amount of carving, and he has also a very pretty column die monument well under way. Stock has bothered him somewhat, but he has managed to get along thus far without serious inconvenience.

Robins Brothers are having a good run of work just now as they did not plan to stop work if there should be any prolonged difficulty with the Union. They have several medium sized jobs under the hammer and have several orders for spring work upon which they will begin work as soon as those now being cut are finished. They express themselves as expecting a good season for the business and are prepared to make the most of it. During this month they have made shipment of quite a number of the jobs which were constructed in the past month and have but little of the finished product in their plant at this writing.

McMillan & Stephens are getting their quarry into shape again so that they can fill all orders for stock.

They report that orders for stock have been coming in very fast since the settlement with the Union and quite a number of large orders have been received.

Orders for medium and large monuments have been received by them since they began to figure on the new schedule and they report that it is their opinion that the coming season will be all that could be expected.

McIver & Ruxton have just completed two large and very pretty cottage monuments and are now at work on a column die job which they are constructing for western parties. They are receiving orders steadily and say they see no appreciable difference in the ease of getting work now from when they were figuring on the old basis of thirty cents per hour.

One of the jobs upon which they are now at work is a sarcophagus monument, the die of which is embellished by a line of heavy carving surrounding the upper portion, and with a heavy leaf over the upper rounded corners. This is only one of the pretty jobs which they will have under way soon if they are able to secure the stock as they are in need of it.

Mackie, Hussey & Co. are operating about two gangs of cutters just at this time but will put on more as soon as the conditions will warrant an increase. The suspense in which the public participated during the latter part of the month of February resulted in the scarcity of orders and especially for large work. Some of the smaller class of work came in about as usual but not enough to keep a large plant well supplied.

This, together with the fact that they have been unable to get the stock for the larger monuments for which they had orders on their books, has sort of stagnated the business during this month. However, they are looking forward to a prosperous season and are preparing to do a large business.

Z. Macchi has quite a little work on his books and is working his usual number of cutters at this writing. He is constructing a few medium sized monuments which will be finished in a short time and for which he has the stock early in the last month. Some orders are coming in from retailers but there is no such rush as there was before the probability of a strike existed, or as there doubtless would have been now had it not been for the difficulty with the Union.

Mr. Macchi does not think that the business will be as good under the new schedule of prices as it would

have been under the old, but is in favor of making a settlement of the matter in the way it has been settled here rather than to have a long period of wrangling and uncertainty.

Sanguinetti & Carusi are engaged upon the construction of two pretty pieces of statuary, and some monuments upon which the carving is the principal feature, as well. They are employing about one gang of cutters at this time and report that the business from their point of view is very encouraging. They do nothing but statuary and carving and every man in their employ is an expert in the business.

They are now working upon the statue of Patience just at this time and will have it finished and ready to ship in about another month.

Association Meetings.

Editor of GRANITE, Boston:

The following is the report of the National Association meeting held in Chicago, February 14 and 15, 1900.

Meeting called to order by the President. All states having local associations were represented by delegates and a large number of dealers, not delegates, were present. A committee was appointed to wait upon the Western Classification Committee which was then in session, and protest against the increase of freight rates. Mr. Pierce of the Vermont Marble Co. reported that some concessions had already been granted on car-load rates but believed more might be secured with proper effort.

Considerable discussion was had in regard to wholesale houses furnishing marble to department stores. Messages were sent to two marble firms asking if they were furnishing stock to any department store. One firm answered that it had done so but would refuse to do so in the future. The other had not been guilty of the offense. The following motion was unanimously adopted:

"That it is the sense of this Association that no dealer in the United States should buy stock of a wholesale dealer who furnishes marble to any department store, and all persons are hereby urged to refrain from patronizing any such wholesale dealer."

On motion, a vote of thanks was tendered H. D. Pierce of the Vermont Marble Co. for his efforts in getting the increase of freight rates so satisfactorily adjusted.

On motion, a committee was appointed to ascertain where a certain department store was obtaining stock, and when done to notify the Secretary of the Association, he to notify the different state Associations.

The old officers were all re-elected. Meeting adjourned to meet in Des Moines on the second Wednesday of February, 1901.

Mr. Morse, Secretary of the Vermont Marble Co., was a welcome visitor and gave an encouraging talk.

J. N. KILDOW,
Secretary.

Mr. Editor, I wish you would give us a strong editorial upon the necessity of the different states organizing. More states should be members of the National Association. Perfect unity of purpose should exist between the retail Association and the wholesale.

Notes of Ornament No. 2.

BY HERBERT W. BEATTIE, QUINCY, MASS.

Every design is composed of plan and details—as in a vase or urn the shape of the vase is the plan; whatever decorations it may have are the details of the design, or their enrichments, as medallion pictures or pieces of sculpture; so with a candlestick, iron work or a silver casket etc. In all cases where elaborate works of fine art are introduced as enrichments of an ornamental scheme—as the sculpture in the pediment of a building, or a picture in the panel of a wall—it is only the general form and arrangement that they share in the ornamental effect; they are no longer ornaments when examined in detail; but independent works of Fine Art.

The ordinary details or accessory decorations may be of various kinds; they may cover the entire surface of the plan or only portions of it; the covering of only portions of a plan involves, of course, far higher ornamental principles than the uniform covering the entire surface. Decorations which are spread uniformly over a surface are commonly called diapers—an expression supposed to be derived from Ypres, the name of the Flemish town where cloths so decorated were first or largely manufactured. They are composed of a repetition or series of the same ornament, in a vertical, horizontal, or a diagonal order. Diapers are suited for flat or round work in every class of carving. Units of repetition, or repeats of irregular shapes, arranged diagonally, have the finest effects. Geometric diapers are infinite, and by a judicious narration of color may be made extremely beautiful. The majority of ancient mosaics are diapers of this character, and they are good illustrations of the carrying out of the principle of fitness in design.

The diaper, then, is a uniform decoration of a surface and all such decoration is very simple; it is mere filling, but to uniformly cover a surface is, however, but the beginning of a designer's labors; his great business is to produce pleasing variety of surface, not only in the flat but in the round; not only upon regular but upon irregular surfaces. If we suppose a cylinder to represent the block of a column it will not be sufficient to merely cut the surface of this cylinder, and call it a column. We must, in the first place, give the cylinder a shape which shall correspond with its destined use; we must so balance the two ends that it will stand firmly upon one of them, and then, by varying the form of surface, give it a pleasing individuality of character consistent with its destination; and this is the process wherein the designer shows his skill. The principles applicable to one article may be quite the reverse of those applicable to another, and it is the designer's duty to suffer no mere ornamental predilections to interfere with the mechanical or practical excellence of his design. These are conditions of use, and it is these conditions by which a designer must test his designs.

Taking it for granted that the eye requires variety of surface to gratify that faculty of the mind called taste, how is this variety to be effected? By dividing surfaces into sections or compartments, and by making some portions more prominent than others and thus produce that contrast which we assume to be the element of all ornamental effects.

These compartments are known as panels, borders, cornice, frieze, basement or dado; capital, shaft base, pedestal; neck, body, foot, and so on; all designating the ornamental divisions of the general schemes of objects; though these things may not be ornamental, the mere division of an object into such parts is done for the sake of variety of effect, in obedience to one of the necessities of the mind.

These various compartments are separated or made prominent by mouldings; mouldings may be either mere suits of concave and convex members, as in many Gothic examples, or the concave series may be filled in with ornamental details. These may be plain or enriched mouldings; and, as boundaries of compartments it is necessary that they should be particularly distinct, and we accordingly find that they are, in nearly all cases, the part of the design which has been most elaborated.

As no border is introduced into a design for its own sake, but only as a contribution to the general effect, that is sure to be the best which is designed with a view to a principle rather than for any special detail of its own; thus we find a part, which shall contain an elemental principle, is superior to a prominent succession of elaborate and varied imitations, because special attraction to secondary details is not a merit, but a capital defect in a design. The border or moulding is the ornament, and not the details of which it is composed.

The truth of this principle is proved by the practice of all ages; we have not now to create ornamental art, but to learn it; it was established in all essentials long ago. As a proof of this I would instance the most popular decorations of the present day; we find that they are identical with the favorites of nearly all ages.

We still use the forms, and indeed, the very details, adopted by the Greeks upwards of two thousand years ago. Why is this? Certainly not from their specialty of detail, but rather because it would be impossible to select others of a less decided individuality. The ornaments I refer to are—the zigzag, the fret, the echinus, the astragal, the anthemions, the guilloche varieties and the scrolls. In the zigzag we have the simplest variety of lines we can well conceive; in the frets we have a more complicated order of right line series; in the varieties of the guilloche we have a similar simple series of the curved line or interlacings. In the echinus or what is commonly called the egg and dart, we have another character, a bold alternation of light and shade and we have a similar result on a smaller scale in the astragal; both belong essentially to the solid or round.

In the scrolls we have a regular running series of spirals, or any materials treated in that order of curve; use among the Romans has established an extraordinary prestige for the acanthus, but any other materials would answer the purpose. In the anthemions we have a compound element, a succession of alternation of an harmonic group of curves, in a conventional adaptation of floral forms, as the name anthemion itself implies. In Greek examples we have a smaller and larger cluster alternated, generally connected by a hand or some simple scroll. No two Greek anthemions are alike, but there are some few which contain a member a good deal resembling the honeysuckle; this ornament is simple and beautiful, but modern imitations overlooking its principle have assumed it to be an imitation and have called it the honeysuckle ornament. All established styles of ornament are founded upon the same principles; their differences, which I shall in the following issues of GRANITE endeavor to point out, are differences only of the details, more or less developed, some for one reason, some for another. The peculiarity of Egyptian and Byzantine ornament is owing to their symbolism, and the Saracenic is exactly the opposite character.

We do not admire the egg and dart and the astragal because we believe them derived from the horsechestnut or the hucklehone, but because they are admirable details for that prominent contrast of light and shade which is so extremely valuable for edges or mouldings.

To be continued.

*

A Blind Sculptor.

Possibly the most astonishing of all blind men is the French sculptor, Vidal, who is stone blind, but models wonderful statues of animals. How can he do this without seeing? Simply by touch. He lives surrounded by animals of all kinds, and is ever patting and caressing them. When he wants to model a horse, he begins to studying the legs. He stoops down by the animal, talking to it and patting it constantly, and says: "Come, I must examine your legs. Don't you move. Now I must examine your chest. Come, my friend, be quiet, or I shall fail to catch your likeness."

When he wanted to study a wild animal the task was more difficult. Vidal first studied the works of other sculptors, the skeletons of the animal, even stuffed specimens. One day, when he had decided that he wanted to model a lion, he felt that he must study a living model. He did not hesitate to face the danger, but entered a lion's cage, accompanied by the trainer. He felt him, caressed him, studied him attentively and for a long time, and when he came away he modelled his "Lion Roaring," one of his masterpieces. Seen in his studio at work, it could hardly be believed that the sculptor was blind, were it not that at times he goes over his work by feeling it with those 10 sensitive fingers that take the place of his eyes.

*

A Monument that is Bound to Rise.

The city authorities are deeply agitated by the discovery that the base of the Trenton battle monument, which was erected about eight years ago, is being gradually lifted into the air and is carrying the shaft with it. The monument is 110 feet high, built of gray granite and is surmounted by a colossal bronze statue of General Washington. It stands on elevated ground in the northern section of the city on soil of a clayey nature, and to that fact is ascribed the upward tendency of the shaft.

Surveyors who were making observations near the monument the other day discovered that the "bench" works, placed on the base by the engineers at the time of its construction, are nearly a half inch above the level.

The base of the monument is of granite and cement set nineteen feet in the freaky soil, which, it is feared, will eventually overthrow the structure. The estimated weight of the monument is 2,000 tons.

*

We'll Have Em' Yet.

The Plumbers' Trade Journal published the following pathetic appeal to delinquent subscribers:

Lives of poor men oft remind us honest toil don't stand
 a chance;
More we work we leave behind us bigger patches on
 our pants;
On our pants once new and glossy, now patched up of
 different hue,
All because subscribers linger and won't pay us what
 is due.
Then let all be up and doing; send your mite, however
 small,
Or when the snows of winter strike us we shall have
 no pants at all!

They received a number of humorous replies to effusion, but it remained for a Canadian subscriber to dispel delusion of becoming pantless by forwarding the following poetical gem—together with the wherewith:

Editor of The Plumbers' Trade Journal.

Sir, your words have touched me deeply!
 I can't help but feel for you,
As I dive into my pocket
 For the money that is due.

Let me "on the dead" advise him,
 Should that "parson" come, by chance,
Not to try our winter weather,
 Walking round without those pants.

He may think it nice and balmy,
 Things aren't always what they seem;
And forty below in a smile and breast pin,
 Makes a chill pass through your dream.

Should you e'er run short of trousers,
 Try this: get right up and dance,
And you'll find, if I mistake not,
 Breath will come in good "short" pants.

One word: Your Journal is a good one,
 And although 'tis rather late;
Here I send my little "billet,"
 Compliments of Charles E. Gates.
　　　　　　　　　　WINNIPEG, Aug. 2.

If the plumber scribe will take it, he will have a "lead
 pipe cinch:"
Emulate our wise example—then you'll have all kinds
 of pants—
Do as we do, ask subscribers for the shekels in advance.—American Undertaker.

All scribes please take notice of the advice the fledgling gives us.

When years have passed and he is with us still, perchance

If he depends upon asking only, he will go without his pants.

CROSS	E — A x A — R x Y — C — Y
FIRST BASE	A — Y x A — I x C — T
SECOND BASE	Y — N x R — A x A — Y
BOTTOM BASE	C — A x T — T x R — E

"GRANITE," APRIL, 1900.

BASE	Y — C Y x P — Y x A — Y
DIE	P — T x A — N x Y — C C
CARVED CROSS DIAMETER IN CIRCLE .	C — N
BOTTOM OF CROSS	C A inches

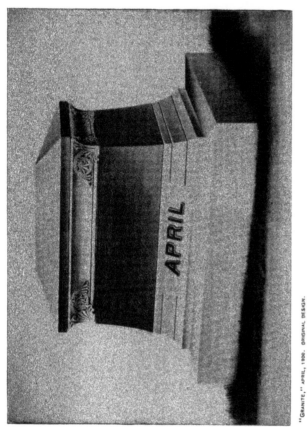

"GRANITE," APRIL, 1900. ORIGINAL DESIGN.

BOTTOM BASE	. . . . .	R — N x C — N x C — R		
SECOND BASE	. . . . .	R — I x C — I x C — P		
DIE	. . . . .	P — Y x A — V x Y — C V		
CAP	. . . . .	E — Y x R — V x C — C		

PRICE:
{ Barre Granite . . . . $A G Y
  Quincy Granite . . . . $R A Y
  Troy Granite . . . . $R E Y
  Milford (N. H.) Granite . . . . . . $R T V

"GRANITE," APRIL, 1900.

BASE . . . . A — N x Y — C V x P — T
DIE . . . . R — T x C — N x C — R

Our Callers.

Among our callers this month was Mr. Fox of Fox & Becker, Middletown, Conn. This firm is about to put in an air compressor and pneumatic tools. He states that business is good and there is a good outlook for the future.

W. F. Fraser representing Bickford, More & Co., Hardwick, Vt., was also one of our callers. Mr. Fraser was starting on a western trip which he proposed to take in the larger cities of the west. We wish him luck.

A. R. Gold, Tompkinsville, N. Y., made a short call. Mr. Gold was visiting Quincy for the purpose of purchasing rough stock. He reports business good.

John E. Staples, York, Me., paid us a short call. Mr. Staples states that he is coming in competition with white bronze monuments. We were of the impression that this class of material for monuments had gone by. He states that four have been recently erected in and around York, and this is the greatest number we have ever had a knowledge of as being erected in any one place. There must have been some particularly big incentive in the way of a money consideration to have brought this matter about for certainly there is nothing artistic in a white bronze monument.

*

It fills The Bill.

Here is a unique sign, said to be posted on a building in an enterprising Georgia settlement :—

· Teeth Pulled Cheap for Cash
—Also—
Music Teached on the Pianner
Coffins on the Installment Plan
Now is the time to Bury your
Friends at a Reasonable Cost
We also Dig Graves.

You can't get ahead of that kind of enterprise. The firm, as Frank Stanton suggests, forgot to add, however, that they served ice cream in season, and did first-class embalming.

—Kansas City Journal

*

Monthly Trade Record.

This department is compiled and edited by the United Mercantile Agency. Subscribers, in accordance with the terms of their contracts, are entitled to receive further information relative to the parties hereafter mentioned, upon application to the main office. As the names of many business men who are good will appear herein, subscribers can readily see the importance of making inquiries if interested, previous to taking any action.

ALABAMA.
Anniston, *M—Box & Claxton, 76.
ARKANSAS.
Camden, *M— Roberts, P. H., 76.
ILLINOIS.
Charleston, *M—Briggs. Alex, warranty deed, $7,000.
Jacksonville, *M—Raedner & Nues succeed D Raednor.
Salem, *M—Slack, W. S., 50.

Savanna, *M—Ivy, George, 76.
INDIANA.
Madison, *M—Crozier, James E., succeeds James H. Crozier.
Richmond, *M—Williams & Tingle, 14 $146.
Shelbyville, *M—Stace & McGeeney, 76.
Sullivan, *M—Sullivan Marble & Granite Works Co., 43.
INDIAN TERRITORY.
Talequah and Wagoner, *M—Hosey, R. A., 106.
IOWA.
Corydon, *M—Niday, C. A., succeeds C. A. Niday & Co.
Jefferson, *M—Arnold, C. F., 76.
Leon, *M—Harris, A. J. & Bro., J. A. Harris 32 $500.
Muscatine, *M—Vanatta, W. J., 32 $2,800.
Perry, *M—Gould Granite Co., 76.
Red Oak, *M—Cole, Z. W., 14 $2,500 and 87 $1,095.
KANSAS.
Fredonia, *M—Prange, S. P., 86.
LOUISIANA.
New Orleans, *M—Kursheedt, Edwin J., 74 $35 and $70.
MAINE.
Newport, *M—Fernald & Norton 64, Fred A. Fernald 58.
South Berwick, *M—Goodwin, A. L., 50.
MARYLAND.
Baltimore, *M—McKnight, John, 20 $54.
Baltimore, *M—Rieger, H. P. & Co., succeed Henry P. Rieger.
Elkton, *M—Sloan, D. L., 78.
MASSACHUSETTS.
Boston, *M—Hall, Charles E. & Co., Francis L. Maguire 62.
Haverhill, *M—Drinkwater, Frederick I., 14 $100.
Milford, *M—Fair, C. L., 50.
Quincy, GZ—Collins & Knight, 58.
Worcester, *M—Evans Marble Co., 84.
MICHIGAN.
Albion, *M—Sebastian, L. P. & Son, succeed Barry & Sebastian.
Byron, *M—Bennett, W. O., 50.
Cass City, *M—Sworm, Charles, 76.
Owosso, *M—Pond, Rollin J., 50.
MINNESOTA.
Renville, *M—Levi, H. J., 106.
Winthrop, *M—Osborn, Eugene, succeeds Theo. Dolger.
MISSOURI.
Augusta, *M—Turner & Brown 64, J. K. Brown 58.
Kansas City, *M—Miller & Johnson 64, W. O. Miller 14 $1,142.
NEBRASKA.
Ansley, *M—Lewis & Cox succeed Lewis & White.
NEW HAMPSHIRE.
Lancaster, *M—Emerson, John H., succeeds Hartley & Emerson.
Manchester, *M—Stevens, R. P. Co., succeed R. P. Stevens & Co.
Nashua, GZ—Cummings, Charles E., 99 $1,500.
Nashua, *M—Fuller & Winslow, 14 $400.
Portsmouth, *M—Leavitt & Lester, 64.

Portsmouth, *M—Moon & Davis 64, Calvin P. Moon 58.

Rochester, *M—Weston, John P. Co., 39.

NEW YORK.

Elmira, *M—Ayers, A. W. & Son, Frederick Ayers 78.

New York *M—New England Monument Co., 37 cap $35m.

Phœnixville, *M—Allen, R. Y., 106.

OHIO.

Chillicothe, *M—Barnhart Granite Co., Harley Λ Barnhart, 93 $1,700.

Cleveland, *M—Uher, James, 50.

Delaware, *M—Griffith, Thomas H., 14 $175.

Granville, *M—De Bow Bros., John De Bow, individual deed $800.

Hamilton, *M—Mencher, Henry, 93 $500.

OKLAHOMA.

Chandler, *M—Sennett, P. F., 76.

PENNSYLVANIA.

Harrisburg, *M—Fraim, H. S., 80.

Mohnsville, *M—Wolf, Howard, 76.

RHODE ISLAND.

Providence, *M—Toye & Holmes 64, Robert G Toye 58.

VERMONT.

Barre, GZ—Cassie, William, 106.

Bristol, *M—McGee, William, 86.

Rutland, *M—Kinsman, W. R., 93 $3,500.

VIRGINIA.

Charlottesville, *M—Kerr, A. M., 76.

Marion, *M—Clark, R. J., 76.

WASHINGTON.

Spokane, *M—East End Granite Co., 20 $3.35.

Obituary.

ADDISON C. RAND.

A. C. Rand, President of the Rand Drill Company, died the evening of March 9th after an illness of a little over a day. His age was fifty-nine years.

Mr. Rand's name will always be linked with the development of rock drilling and air compressing machinery. He was one of the first in this field of work, and guided its growth from the smallest and most uncertain beginnings to its present large proportions. While much work with drills had been done at the Hoosac Tunnel before his connection with the industry, it is well known that their use then was only possible because that enterprise had the State of Massachusetts behind it. The real use of rock drills in civil engineering work, and on an economic basis, began with the West Point Tunnel of the West Shore R. R., though the Haverstraw and Weehawken Tunnels soon followed. Following this came the tunnels of the abandoned South Pennsylvania R. R., and soon after the Washington and New York aqueducts. It seems impossible that an appliance, without which no large work of this character would now be attempted, could have been of so recent origin, but such is the fact. Machine drills became an accepted fact in mining, before they did in civil engineering work, the place of their birth, in an economic sense, being the iron mines which center about Port Henry, New York, though the iron and copper regions of Lake Superior district soon followed.

JOSEPH B. DYER.

Joseph B. Dyer, editor and proprietor of the Stone Trade News, died March 11. In November, 1878, he was elected secretary of the National Granite Cutters' Union and held that position until 1895, when he was succeeded by James Duncan, the present secretary. Immediately after he commenced the publication of the Stone Trade News, which he continued up to the time of his death. In his position as secretary of the National Granite Cutters' Union, he was of course many times antagonistic to the interests of the granite manufacturers. After his resignation he placed himself as publisher of the Stone Trade News in a position to ask favors of those whom he had previously antagonized. The hold that he held upon the esteem of the manufacturers was plainly shown in their desire to assist him in subscriptions and advertising for his publication. All who had known him for years agreed that he was a man of the strictest honor and integrity in all his dealings.

Proposed Monuments and Monumental News.

ELKINS, W. VA.—A monument will be erected at Capon Bridge, Hampshire county, West Virginia, to the memory of Captain David Pugh, the last survivor of the Virginia Legislature that passed the ordinance of secession.

AURORA, IND.—The old soldiers here contemplate the erection of a monument in honor of the men who fell in the battle of Laughery Creek.

ALBANY, N. Y.—If the bills introduced become laws Capitol park will have two monuments. One of its measures provides for the erection of a soldiers' and sailor's monument in Capitol park at a cost to the State of $100,000, to be paid for in two equal parts. A commission is appointed by the terms of the bill consisting of Daniel E. Sickles, John Palmer, Henry H. Lyman, Herman Bendell, William Blasie; the state commander of the Grand Army and the adjutant general to superintend the work. The other is a bill to erect a statue to General Phil Sheridan in Capitol park at a cost of $25,000.

Continued on page 33.

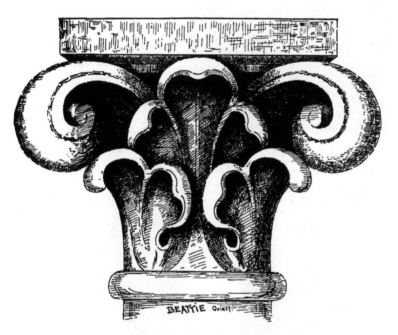

SUGGESTION FOR A CARVED CAP.

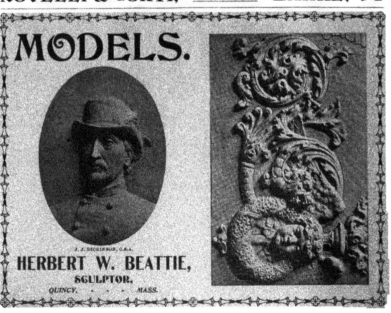

Proposed Monuments and Monumental News.

Continued from page 30.

COLUMBIA, S. C.—The Chickamauga monument commission met recently and decided to call for plans and specifications for a monument to cost $10,000.

COLUMBUS, OHIO.—The house passed Mr. Mitchell's senate bill appropriating $53,000 for the erection of monuments to the memory of the Ohio soldiers engaged in the battle of Shiloh.

MINNNEAPOLIS, MINN.—A movement is on foot for the erection of a monument to the memory of the late Colonel W. S. King.

INDEPENDENCE, KAN.—The cattlemen of this section of Kansas have organized what is known as the Hewins Monument Association, for the purpose of raising a fund for the erection of a monument to the memory of Edwin M. Hewins. The plan is to have the monument unveiled on July 4 next. The statue is to be of bronze.

WRAY, COLO.—The local G. A. R. post has petitioned Congress to appropriate $10,000 for the establishment of a monument in memory of Gen. Forsyth and his band of scouts on Beecher Island.

SPRINGFIELD, MO.—It is the intention to erect a confederate soldiers' monument to cost $10,000: $5,000 has been subscribed.

MANCHESTER, MASS.—An effort is being made by the local members of the G. A. R. to collect money enough for the purpose of erecting a monument.

Through Charles Sumner Post, No. 9, Grand Army of the Republic, department of the Potomac, Washington, D. C., the colored people of the United States are asked to contribute for the erection of a monument to the late Hon. Charles Sumner of Massachusetts. The governor of each state has been requested to appoint a representative colored citizen as a member of the monument committee.

PRINCETON, N. J.—Princeton University is to be enriched by a monument by Thomas Shields Clarke, who has modelled a figure symbolizing Alma Mater, described as a goddess seated on a throne, ornamented with the ram's heads of Pallas. In one hand she holds a branch of bay, and in the other a winged skull. An athletic alumnus advances to lay at her feet his trophies, a sword, a sceptre and a laurel wreath.

ELIZABETH, N. J.—After thirty-four years of effort this city is now likely to have a soldiers' monument. In 1866 the project was started by veterans in Elizabeth, and a subscription of $400 was raised, but the plans fell through and the money was placed in a Savings Institution, where, with the interest since accumulated, it amounts to quite a sum, and an effort will be made to collect enough more to build the monument.

NORTH ADAMS, MASS.—The members of the Notre Dame parish are making plans to erect a large monument over the grave of their former pastor.

NEWBURGH, N. Y.—This city is to erect a $10,000 soldiers' monument.

NEW YORK, N. Y.—At a meeting of the National Sculpture Society, February 10, William Ordway Partridge presented designs for a monument to be erected in Fort Greene Park, to the memory of the prison ship martyrs. The designs are those of the front elevation. The design represents an Ionic colonnade, to which access is given from the rear by means of a broad, semicircular stairway, connecting the two wings or pavilions which flank and terminate the colonnade, one wing to be dedicated to the heroes of the Army and the other to those of the Navy. Each wing forms an open loggia, entrance to which is given through the colonnade by means of the stairway spoken of.

LITTLE ROCK, ARK.—$4,000 has been collected for the purpose of erecting a soldiers' monument. The contract will not be let until $6,000 more has been secured.

HUNTSVILLE, ALA.—Ladies of the Confederacy are inaugurating a concerted effort to secure the erection of an appropriate monument in honor of Dick Dowling.

POTTSVILLE, PA.—The proposition to build a monument to the memory of Philip Guenther, the discoverer of anthracite coal, has again been taken up, with the probability that it will soon be accomplished. It is the desire of those interested that the monument shall be "coal stone," which has contributed much to the material and commercial wealth of the state and especially to this section of it. Guenther, who first brought coal into successful use, lived in a rough cabin in the forest on the Mauch Chunk mountain, Carbon county. While in quest for game for his family, whom he had left at home without food of any kind, his foot stumbled against a black stone. By the roadside not far from the town of Summit Hill he built a little fire of wood and threw pieces of the supposed stone about it, so that the embers might last longer, while roasting fowl.

The President recently signed a bill granting permission for the erection of a monument in Washington, D. C., in honor of Samuel Hahnemann.

ABILENE, KAN.—Contributions are being solicited for a monument to be erected in memory of Tom Smith, the cowboy marshal, killed in 1871.

LAWRENCE, KAN.—It is proposed to erect a soldiers' monument to cost about $1,000.

MEMPHIS, TENN.—It is proposed to erect a monument to the memory of Gen. N. B. Forrest, the confederate cavalry leader.

HOPKINSVILLE, KY.—There is a movement on foot to collect the necessary funds for the purpose of erecting a monument to the memory of the late Gov. William Goebel.

CHICAGO, ILL.—It is Mrs. Geo. M. Pullman's purpose to apply $20,000 to the erection of a monument in Graceland cemetery to the memory of her husband.

HARTFORD, CT.—It is proposed to erect a monument to the memory of General John Sedgwick from a design by George Keller. It will consist of a Greek stela of granite twelve feet in height.

KANSAS CITY, MO.—The Daughters of the Confederacy are securing funds for the erection of a monument to confederate soldiers at Forest Hill cemetery.

It is proposed to erect a monument to the memory of Eben Brewer, the first United States postal agent in Cuba, who lost his life while on duty.

TOTTENVILLE, L. I.—The Joseph Decker monument committee are again pushing the raising of subscriptions. It is proposed to pay $1,000 for a monument.

HUNTSVILLE, ALA.—The members of the Daughters of the Confederacy. have begun a canvass for subscriptions to a fund that is being raised to erect a monument to Confederate soldiers who are buried in the City cemetery. Quite a large sum has already been raised.

PLAINFIELD, N. J.—The attempts made by pulpit and press to arouse enthusiasm to build a soldiers' monument have failed, and the committee which has been working on the matter of subscriptions for a year past, after discussion of their work, have given up the project.

For more than two years a mammoth monument of granite, weighing upwards of 10,000 pounds, has laid unclaimed at the Perryville, N. Y., station on the Lehigh Valley railroad. The freight charges on it must amount to $400. The property was sold by the railroad on board cars at the station, January 25th. The monument was consigned by a Boston concern and the purchaser is supposed to live somewhere in the west. Probably the stone was intended as a memorial of some person or persons at rest in the cemetery at Perryville but just who will doubtless not be learned until the granite is unboxed at the sale.

INDIANAPOLIS, IND.—At a meeting of the Indiana Lawton Monument Commission held recently, the Executive Committee reported that nearly $4,900 had been subscribed.

BROWNSVILLE, TENN.—A movement has been started by the Hiram S. Bradford Bivouac of Confederate Veterans of Haywood county looking to the erection of a handsome monument to the Confederate dead of the county. The indications are that the funds will be forthcoming. The monument will cost between $1,500 and $2,000.

NORFOLK, VA.—The memory of Father Ryan, poet laureate of the Southern Confederacy, is to be honored by a monument to be erected. The project is in the hands of the Daughters of the Confederacy.

WASHINGTON, D. C.—The House committee on library has favorably reported a bill making an appropriation of $5,000 for the preparation of plans or designs for a memorial or statue of Gen. Grant to be erected in Washington. The same committee also reported favorably on a bill appropriating $50,000 for the preparation of a site and the erection of a pedestal for the statue of the late Maj. Gen. Geo. B. McClellan.

SEATTLE, WASH.—It is proposed to erect a monument to the memory of the soldiers of the various Washington companies who have been killed or died while on duty in the Philippines.

INDIANAPOLIS, IND.—Steps to erect a monument over the grave of Nancy Lincoln, the mother of Abraham Lincoln, near Lincoln city, Spencer co., were taken March 1, at a meeting of the Nancy Lincoln memorial association.

A Plutocrat in Graveyards.

"You Eastern people are not the only enterprising inhabitants of the globe," said an enthusiastic man in a New York business house. "I have a neighbor in Pemiscot county, my state, Missouri, who is a sort of plutocrat in graveyards. Some years ago he opened a tombstone factory in his part of the state, and as he marked down the price, he had quite a boom in his business. In a short time there was a monument or headstone at every grave in the cemetery, and as live people do not buy tombstones, this man's business was hit by what your Wall street folks call a flurry. What does he do but go to another town not far away and buy a graveyard of his own, and put down the price of lots. This caused quite a cemetery boom until all the lots were disposed of. As soon as some of the people began to die the enterprising tombstone dealer was again in the whirl, or, as my old friend, Wilbur F. Storey was wont to say of his paper, on the top crest of the advancing wave. In a year or so he had every grave in the cemetery marked with his goods, and another thud hit his business. But he rallied, went to another town, invested in another graveyard site, and manipulated this scheme as he had the others and with like result.

"That makes three cemeteries he has started, filled and marked, and the last time I saw him he told me he was looking for another. He is now known as the graveyard promoter."

Barnard's Statue of Pan.

It has been asserted that Barnard's statue of Pan, recently cast in New York, is the largest bronze statue that has ever been cast in one piece. This statue weighs about 2 1-2 tons. A correspondent of the Revue Scientifique (Paris), Frederic Oom, writes that Portugal did still better than this more than a century ago. He says: "I may be permitted to recall the fact on October 15, 1774, nearly one hundred and twenty-five years ago, there was cast in one piece, at the cannon foundry of the Lisbon arsenal, a piece seven or eight times as large as this—the equestrian statue of King Joseph I., which is still standing in this city. I quote Ferdinand Denis's work on 'Portugal' (Paris, 1846, p. 406): 'There were used 656 1-2 quintals (85,000 pounds) of bronze to cast the colossal statue of Don Joseph; after the conduits of metal had been removed it was calculated that there remained only 500 quintals (65,000 pounds); the interior core of iron, made by Bartholomew da Costa, weighed 100 quintals.' Bartholomew da Costa was a lieutenant colonel of engineers and director of the gun foundry where this memorable feat was accomplished. It took twenty-eight hours to melt the bronze, but only eight minutes to run it into the mold. This distances the New York record, a century and a quarter in advance of it. The statue still stands where it was erected on May 20, 1775, and dedicated on June 6, following. It is seven meters (23 feet) high, and the whole monument, with its pedestal, is artistically very remarkable. Those who do not know the facts generally consider the horse too massive; but it was modelled faithfully from the finest stallion of the royal stables."—Translation made for the Literary Digest.

Interesting Law Decision.

The Law court has rendered a decision in favor of plaintiff in the Knox county case Arthur C. Dutch vs. Bodwell Granite Company, Rockland, Me. The case was tried at the December term, 1898. Plaintiff is a resident of Vinalhaven, and was in the employ of defendant company in their granite quarries at Jonesport, driving a team. He was on a truck loaded with granite, when a bolt broke, and he claims to have been thrown from the truck, and his leg broken so that he is permanently lame. He claimed that the accident was caused by a defect in the bolt that broke, for which defendant company was legally responsible. The jury returned a verdict for plaintiff and assess damages at $1,623. The case went to Law court on motion for new trial and exceptions. The verdict is sustained.

Among The Retail Dealers.

AMERICUS, GA.—Miller & Clark are cutting the pedestal for the monument to be erected by the Daughters of the Confederacy, in the memory of the Confederate Soldiers.

TOLEDO, OHIO.—Loyd Bros.' Co. have received the contract for a soldiers' monument to be erected in the local cemetery.

MOODUS, CT.—This village is to have a soldiers' monument, made possible by a bequest of $2,000 by the late Mrs. Eliza Miller. It will be of granite and will stand about twenty feet in height. It will be over eight feet square at the base. The pedestal will be surmounted by a figure of the Civil War volunteer wrought in granite, eight feet high. The contract for its erection has been awarded to Stephen Maslen of Hartford.

RUTLAND, VT.—W. R. Kinsman has bought the entire stock and machinery of Everson & Co.'s marble and granite works and will continue the business, both wholesale and retail.

UTICA, N. Y.—A building has been erected for the monumental works of Henry L. Salladin. Mr. Salladin was for many years foreman in the works of Hughes, Evans & Co.

TORONTO, ONT.—Duncan McIntosh, president of the McIntosh Marble & Granite Co. died January 19.

ELMIRA, N. Y.—Frederick C. Ayers, the surviving member of the firm of A. W. Ayers & Son, died March 4.

SKOWHEGAN, ME.—Turner & Moore have gone out of the granite and marble business.

Quarry Items.

WESTERLY, R. I.—The property of the Dixon Granite Works was sold at mortgagee's sale, February 20, by order of the Westerly Savings bank. The bidding was spirited, being apparently among local persons. The property was finally sold to Judge John W. Sweeney for $14,500. The new owner states that it is his intention to operate the quarries.

EAST CANDIA, N. H.—A new industry is soon to be established near this village. A company, represented by Otis N. Trussell of Lawrence, has been prospecting for granite on the mountains near the railroad station. It has leased the property for a term of twenty-five years. A derrick has been ordered and an acre of land purchased, located near the railroad station, on which sheds are to be erected.

MILFORD, MASS.—Articles of agreement signed March 1 by representatives of the Drapers of Hopedale and Darlings of Worcester provide for the consolidation of the Shea and Darling quarries, so-called, under the name of the Bay State Pink Granite Co. of Milford, with a capital stock of $500,000. The company will be incorporated in Saco, Maine.

The combination and interests will give it control and ownership of 800 acres of quarry lands. Its main office will be in Worcester, where the company will also have a large stone yard on the line of the New York, New Haven & Hartford railroad.

The company is to erect a big shed for cutting the granite 200 feet long by 60 feet wide, which will be equipped with electricity as a motive power. It will be supplied with all the latest machinery for cutting and handling stone, and a new machine, invented by Daniel W. Darling of Worcester for cutting stone, has been constructed and placed in the quarry.

The present working force of the quarries that have been combined is less than 100 men, but as soon as things are in working order the force will be increased to between 400 and 500 men.

SALISBURY, N. C.—F. N. May, of Rochester, N. Y., who has been in the city for several days, has concluded a deal for the old Phillips granite quarry, consisting of 34 acres, in the heart of the granite belt of this county.

The Southern Railway is now building a spur track about one mile in length from Woodside to the granite property recently purchased by Northern capitalists.

NEW YORK.—Richard Croker has invested in a new scheme. The Tammany chieftain has become the American director of the Granite Industries of Donegal, Limited, and, as a result, the monument to Parnell, to the fund for which Tammany Hall subscribed $15,000, will probably be constructed with stone taken from the company's quarries, in the extensive estate known as the "Rosses of Donegal," near Dunloe, in the northwestern part of Ireland.

Associated with Mr. Croker on the Board of Directors of the company are the Duke of Abercorn, who is Chairman; the Hon. John Herdman, Strabane, County of Tyrone; Colonel Dickenson, of Earlsfort Mansions, Dublin, and the Hon. Frederick J. Abbott, of Liverpool. The company has just been incorporated, with a capital stock of £100,000, which will be increased as soon as occasion warrants it.

The quarries are situated in one of the poorest and most congested districts of Ireland, and the working of the quarries on a large scale will give support to hundreds of families who are now practically existing under conditions of semi-starvation.

*

Dix Island, Me.—Past and Present.

(Continued.)

At that time there were few if any men on the Maine coast who knew the art of cutting granite into fanciful shapes and the Scotchmen and the Italians at once found themselves looked upon as teachers. And they found apt pupils. The boys who had been brought up to a fiisherman's life went into the granite business and under the tutelage of the Italians they became master cutters and in time became teachers themselves. It was surprising to note with what ease these sons of the ocean picked up the mallet and chisel and began to cut Corinthian cap pieces.

In this way Dix Island became known as the best school of stone-cutting in America and its graduates went far and wide. The best of work was turned out at Dix Island, and when a stone-cutter said that he hailed from here he was sure of work if there was any to be had.

Even to this day in divers parts of the country you find a cutter who has grown gray in the business; he will tell you that he worked on Dix Island in his youth; or, more likely, he will tell you that it was on Dix Island that he learned the business. The men who worked there are scattered from Dan to Beersheba, but they enjoy nothing so much as to forgather of an evening, fill their pipes and talk of all the things that happened when Dix was in its hey-day.

———

In the days that were Rockland was a regular mining town. It was the sportiest place in the East and it had the money to back that statement. Wasn't afraid of spending its money, either, was old Rockland. During the rush times when Dix was on the boom a man could get anything he wanted—from a prayer meeting to a cock-fight, but I am sorry to say that so far as Dix Island went the latter were far more popular than the former.

It is true that in the big hall visiting preachers used to hold services, but if it happened that on that particular day the pride of the Shamrock was billed to go against the pet bird of the Aberdeen, the minister would find himself minus an audience unless he journeyed down to the cock-pit where the main was to be decided.

The Shamrock and the Aberdeen were the two big

boarding houses and it won't be necessary to say which belonged to the Scotch and which to the Irish. A Scotchman would have slept on the ledge before he would have staid in the Shamrock all night, and the Irish would no more have demeaned themselves by asking lodging at the Aberdeen. By the same token, it is very much of a doubt whether the proprietor of the Aberdeen would have taken a son of the ould sod into his house, supposing the favor had been asked.

Race feeling ran high at times and the man who wasn't ready to fight for the honor of his house didn't stay on the island for long. It was fight first and explain afterward, and rough as the life was it bred that manliness which is only born of boom and bustle.

The Irish were in the ascendent, but the Scotch were a close second. After them came the "minkholers." Ever hear of minkholers? Probably not, unless you are acquainted with the vernacular of this particular part of the State. Where the name came from no one knew, but all the same, there it was.

In general terms, a minkholer was a man who came from anywhere along the river from Frankfort to Bangor, but it wasn't a name of which the minkholers themselves were overly proud, and it wasn't a good thing to call another man unless you were pretty confident that you could lick him.

The remaining class was Italian, and though not large in comparison with the others, there were enough of them to stand by one another when they thought they were not getting a square deal.

All together there was nothing lacking for the ingredients of a first-class shinry and the men who worked there were not the ones to cross the road to get out of the way of trouble. Consequently there were some exceedingly lively mix-ups during the hours that the crew were off duty.

The Shamrock was the largest building on the island and had accommodations for 625. The Aberdeen—now no more—came next, but though it was a monster structure it was not to be mentioned in the same day with the Shamrock. There were a number of minor boarding houses, but there really wasn't room for the entire crew on the island and a part of the men lived on shore, rowing out every morning and back at night.

Most of these lived on Ash Paint in South Thomaston, and to get back and forth from the island they used whaling boats built for them in New London, Ct. This led to another form of sport and many a hundred dollars changed hands on the result of races between the different whale boats.

Cock-fighting and boat racing were all very well for tame sport, but it was over the cards that men went broke from month to month. Rockland at that time was the Mecca of sharpers, and at any and all times the man who was in the mood for tempting fortune could usually get accommodated.

Every saloon—and there were lots of 'em—had its regular following. Highlow-Jack was a favorite game, but it was the truly American game of poker that had the call for the heavy betters.

Stakes ran high just after pay-day, and when the players settled down to it for business the limit was waived and a man bet everything he had in the world.

(To be continued.)

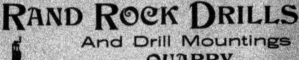

WALTER W. FIELD,

117 Main Street, Cambridgeport, Mass.

...TELEPHONE 73 CAMBRIDGE...

NEW ENGLAND AGENT FOR

THE LAMBERT
HOISTING ENGINE CO.

500 Styles and Sizes.
Built to Gauges and Templates.

For Mining, Quarrying, Coal Handling, Pile Driving, Build
ers' use, Logging and General Contracting.

Electric Hoists, Single and Double Drums,
with Improved Automatic Brake.
Suspension Cableways.

—— *SEND FOR NEW CATALOGUE B.* ——

Horizontal, Locomotive and Upright
BOILERS.

Engine in Stock for Quick Delivery.

**Standard Double Cylinder Double Patent Friction Drum Double Winch
Hoisting Engine, with Boiler and Fixtures Complete.**

FOUNTAIN AIR BRUSH.

SEND FOR CATALOGUE.

THAYER & CHANDLER, 146 WABASH AVENUE, CHICAGO.

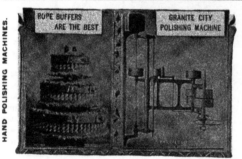

J. ALBERT SIMPSON,
Treasurer.

L. S. ANDERSON,
Manager.

1826 - 1900.
Seventy-Four Years in the Granite Business.

QUARRIES:
West Quincy, Mass., Concord, N. H.

GRANITE RAILWAY
COMPANY.

PRINCIPAL OFFICE: - WEST QUINCY, MASS.

DETAIL OF ILLUSTRATION BELOW:

No. 1. Looking West from Quarry No. 1.
No. 2. A corner in Quarry No. 2.   No. 3. A Bird's-eye View of Quarry No. 1.
No. 4. A Block of Extra Dark Blue Quincy Granite measuring 19 x 16 x 9½ feet,
weighing about 200 tons.
No. 5. Road from Yard to Quarries operated by an endless chain.

May 1900   Vol. X. No. 5

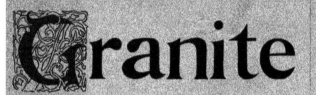

ranite

A. M. HUNT & CO.

PUBLISHERS

131 Devonshire Street

BOSTON, MASS., U.S.A.

Subscription Price, $1.00 Year

Established 1868.

E. L. SMITH & CO.,
QUARRY OWNERS, MANUFACTURERS AND
WHOLESALE DEALERS IN
Barre Granite,
BARRE, VT.

Dark, Medium and Light Rough Stock

of any dimension to the limit of transportation.

Modern Equipped Cutting Plant especially designed for
handling Large Work.

☞ SEND FOR PRICE LISTS AND ESTIMATES. ☜

Wedging out a Spire. Upper Quarry.

ADVERTISERS' DIRECTORY.

Reports on Troy Granite.

ORDNANCE DEPARTMENT, U. S. A.

Report of Mechanical Tests Made with U. S. Testing Machine, Capacity 800,000 Pounds, at Watertown Arsenal, Mass., April 15th, 1891.

FOR TROY GRANITE COMPANY, WORCESTER, MASS.

Test by Compression of One Six-Inch Cube of Troy Granite.

Compressed Surfaces faced with Plaster of Paris to secure even bearings.

TEST NUMBER.	DIMENSIONS.		SECTIONAL AREA.	ULTIMATE STRENGTH.	
	LENGTH.	COMPRESSED SURFACE.		TOTAL LBS.	LBS PER SQ. IN.
7419	5.95	5.84 | 5.90	35.01	630.100	17.950

First crack at 525,000 lbs.
Pyramidal fracture.

Correct :
  J. E. HOWARD.

  D. W. FLAGLER,
  Lieut. Col. Ordnance Dept., U. S. A., Commanding.

Chemical Laboratory, Worcester Polytechnic Institute.

CERTIFICATE OF ANALYSIS.

GENTLEMEN :   WORCESTER, MASS., May 4, 1891.

The sample of Troy Granite submitted to me for examination contains :

Silica,	-	-	73.15 per cent.
Alumina and Iron Oxide,	-	-	17.04 " "
Lime,	-	-	0.81 " "
Magnesia,	-	-	0.30 " "
Potassium Oxide,	-	-	5.74 " "
Sodium Oxide,	-	-	2.05 " "
Loss and Undetermined,	-	-	0.91 " "
Total,	-	-	100.00

Respectfully yours,

To TROY GRANITE CO.   LEONARD P. KINNICUTT, PH. D.

ALL TOGETHER.

Every piece finished and FITTED under personal supervision and shipped from the same place at the same time.

Don't allow your orders to be peddled to parties you would not patronize yourself. — A guarantee of replacing defective work is very good, but — it pleases your customer better to have it right FIRST TIME.

We will make it an object—and no expense—for every dealer unacquainted to carry our samples of the HARDWICK GRANITE,—The Darkest Fine Grained Stock and Absolutely Free From Iron.

WRITE FOR SHEETS OF COMPARATIVE PRICES.

25 Years Experience in the Business.

GEO. D. BAILEY, Hardwick, Vt.

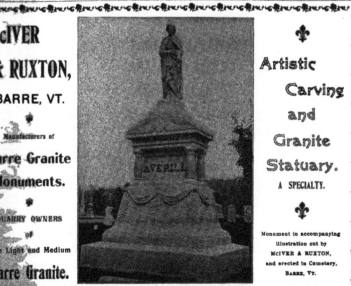

GRANITE

ENTERED AT THE BOSTON POST OFFICE AS SECOND-CLASS MAIL MATTER.

Vol. X. BOSTON, MASS., MAY 1, 1900. No. 5

A. M. HUNT, EDITOR.

Published Monthly in the interests of the Producer,
Manufacturer, and Retailer of Granite as used
for Monumental or Building Purposes.

Terms of Subscription

To ANY PART OF THE UNITED STATES OR CANADA:

One copy, one year - - - - $1.00, in advance.
One copy, six months . - - 75 cents, in advance.

ADVERTISING RATES FURNISHED UPON APPLICATION.

A. M. HUNT & CO., Publishers,

181 DEVONSHIRE STREET, - - BOSTON, MASS.

Editorials

THE labor situation at the present writing, April 21, is as follows: The situation at Quincy and Barre is explained under Barre News and Quincy Notes. The situation at other points in Vermont, including Hardwick, Northfield, Groton and Montpelier, is the same as at Barre. The situation at Milford, N. H., is the same as on April 1st. All plants are working at this point. The cutters at Westerly are still out, no agreement having been reached. At Concord, N. H., a settlement has been made, and all trouble is over, for the present at least. This practically covers the monumental centres in the east. At the principal points where building granite is produced, the situation is as follows: Settlement has been made at Bar Harbor, the men being granted an eight-hour day, minimum rate of thirty-five cents an hour. At West Sullivan, Me., the cutters have produced a schedule for an increase of two cents on all kinds of curbing at the rate of $3 a day for a day's work. No trouble is anticipated. An effort was made on April 14, by the Booth Bros. & Hurricane Isle Granite Co. at New London to compromise on the basis of 32 1-2 cents an hour on eight hours work. The cutters refused to consider anything less than the standard of thirty-five cents, minimum, per hour. As a consequence all employees of the company have been discharged and the plant shut down indefinitely. At Gloucester, Mass., the Cape Ann Granite Co. and the Stone Cutters' Union of Cape Ann have come to an agreement by which the cutters secure thirty-five cents an hour minimum wages and eight hours. This is an increase of 16 2-3 per cent over the wages of 1898, and it is a settlement on the same basis as has been adopted at Barre, Vt. The cutters have been out since March. At Milford, Mass., the striking quarrymen at Darling Bros.' quarry have returned to work on an eight-hour day pending the mutual adjustment of the price per hour. The Milford Pink Granite Co., Milford, Mass., have acceded the stone cutters' demands for an eight-hour day and thirty-five cents as a minimum. No settlement has been made by Norcross Bros. at Milford. It is rumored that a committee from the New England Granite Manufacturers' Association has been in consultation with the Barre Granite Manufacturers' Association. The principal business was to see if Barre concerns would stand by the New England Association if an agreement could be reached, but it is understood that Barre dealers are satisfied with their own position towards the cutters and refused to join the Association in its plan. This plan, it is rumored, was to order a general lockout. The Branford (Conn.) branch of the Granite Workers' Union have come to an agreement with their employers for an eight-hour day, and from 33 to 34 cents per hour for the minimum price, contract to hold for five years. The secretary of the National Union wrote the officials of the Branford Union, informing them that they had no right to agree upon a contract for five years, also contended that the settlement was made upon too small a money basis and ordered the strike renewed. After a conference it was decided that a majority of the men were satisfied with the present agreement, and they declined to renew the strike. A letter was sent to the secretary of the National Union, saying that if the National Union wanted the charter of the local union, they would only have to call for it.

ELOW we publish a letter which will prove interesting, from Mr. H. G. Locke, representing the Chicago & Alton R. R. Company, Boston, from which we quote:
"March 31st. Proposition to rate Marble, Jasper, Onyx, Granite and Slate Blocks, etc., including tombstones, sawed, dressed, chiseled or polished, at 4th class L. C. L. and class C., C. L., not having received a sufficient number of affirmative votes, no change in rating will be made.—Jones Bros."

The above letter refers to shipments from Chicago west. What a pity it is that the prosperity of any industry is practically placed in the hands of the various railroads of this country, for this is practically the meaning of the above decision. What is to prevent the representatives of the various roads throughout the country making the rates still higher. Certainly enough influence has been brought to bear to bring about the change in rates desired, but nevertheless above is the result and we can truly say it was not expected. We understand that there is no appeal from this decision. The Interstate Commission has no power to grant the relief asked for, but still if we recall it there is another chance, as we understand the matter has been referred to the attorney general, who has not as yet given a decision. There is now before congress a bill looking to the amendment of the Interstate Commerce Act provided by Senate Bill 1439, generally known as the Cullom Bill.

This bill provides that the Interstate Commerce Commission shall be authorized and required to prepare and publish within one year from the passage of the act a classification of freight articles and rules, regulations and conditions for freight transportation which shall be known as the National Freight Classification. Provision is also made for the hearing of the complaints of any carrier or shipper against such classification, and for such amendments as may be necessary to remove any injustice to carriers or shippers, and we certainly advise all shippers of granite to examine and support it. Let all the associations take up this matter vigorously, and if the present members of the National Retail Dealers' Association desire the future prosperity of this organization, now is the golden opportunity to show its worth, and now there is something for each and every association to fight for. Let every association whose members desire lower freight rates join with the national association, for more attention can be secured from a combined effort. Individuals who are not members of associations join one and make it strong in numbers so that any request that might be made by this association will not be passed by as not worthy of attention. We feel assured that the New England Granite Manufacturers' Association will be glad to co-operate with the National Retail Dealers' Association in anything that will make an impression upon the powers who control the freight rates. This is the worst possible trust that can exist.

*

E publish below a letter which will explain itself:
"We notice in your paper this month (April), the wail of a neighboring dealer in regard to your plan of publishing designs. We want to do you the justice to say that we have been in the monument business for forty years, and GRANITE is the first journal to come under our notice, that has published good, up-to-date practical designs with the necessary information to make them valuable and available to dealers for 'immediate' use, without waiting to 'write for sizes,' etc. Many good designs have been published by other journals, but without sizes and scale, and are therefore only of value to use as suggestions, and not in a practical way. We congratulate GRANITE upon their good designs, and upon what is better, the desired information in regard to same, to make them valuable. The 'kick' of the dealer is only another example of the many fellows, like the Rev. Mr. Sheldon, who 'know how to run a paper better than the editor.' With best wishes for your continued success, we are,—M. V. Mitchell & Son, Columbus, Ohio."

It is certainly gratifying to us to have this expression from one of the leading monumental firms in the west. It is our earnest endeavor to place before our subscribers thoroughly practical, up-to-date designs, together with prices which will not be misleading. This latter is the hardest feature that we have to contend with. We have experimented in this direction by securing prices from many concerns, and no two would agree, and we are consequently placed in a position of doubt as to the advisability of publishing price given. Possibly our subscribers have noticed that we occasionally omit prices. This is done on account of reasons stated above.

*

NDER Barre News we publish the result of a meeting and vote of the Barre branch of the National Granite Cutters' Union. Those who have closely watched the course of events in the granite business cannot but be convinced that in matters of this kind Barre holds the key to the situation. In other words they can afford to be independent, as Barre and other near by towns in Vermont control about three-fourths of the manumental granite business in the country. Not only do the manufacturers control their end of it, but the granite cutters also are in control, as the membership of the Barre branch is larger than at any other point, and numbers give them the power. We look to see settlements made in the future on the same basis as the Barre settlement.

*

Seventh Annual Banquet of the Barre Granite Manufacturers' Association.

The seventh annual banquet of the Barre Granite Manufacturers was held at the Pavilion in Montpelier on the evening of the 28th of March, and was in every way the most successful one which the Association has ever held. In point of numbers it was the largest, and in the joyful, almost hilarious feeling which prevailed, it was away ahead of any previously held.

The menu, which was as follows, was cleared away about 10.30:

Raw Blue Points.
Consomme Royale.
Lettuce.   Radishes.
Broiled Schrod, Butter Sauce.

ences held. In the course of this report the committee said, that as all propositions looking to a settlement, up to the present time, had come from them, and that the proposition submitted at the last conference was the utmost they could possibly afford to offer, they had reached the conclusion that any further meetings of the two committees would be useless, unless the workmen were prepared to accept the last proposition made.

The association gave the committee its approval and voted not to increase their last offer, which was practically a minimum of $2.52 for eight hours, and to stand by that offer to the end, as it was all they could possibly pay, and a fact was more than they should pay, considering the condition of business. During the discussion that followed the committee's report, several of the manufacturers claimed that they had reason to believe the cutters did not understand that the proposition made at the last conference was a final one. Upon these grounds the association voted to instruct the committee to hold another conference with the cutters' committee, and again submit the proposition as made at the last meeting.

In accordance with this vote another joint meeting was held April 4. At this meeting the situation was discussed informally and the manufacturers' committee again submitted its proposition, assuring the cutters that it was the best they could possibly make. The cutters' committee said that they were not prepared to give their answer then, and suggested an adjournment until the following Friday evening, with the understanding that in the meantime the matter would be placed before the Cutters' Union, and if the result was favorable, another joint meeting should be held, but if unfavorable, no further meetings would be held. With this understanding the conference adjourned.

On Friday morning the cutters held a mass meeting. The action of their committee up to that time was endorsed. It was then proposed that a secret ballot be taken to see whether its committee should be given full power to settle. The proposition to take a secret ballot was voted down, and the meeting adjourned without further discussion. Since then there has been nothing done by either side looking to a settlement, and there is no prospect of a peaceful settlement in the near future.

Many of the cutters seen do not hesitate to express their disapproval of the union, but say that they are powerless to do anything, for if any attempt is made to urge a settlement upon the terms offered, the member so doing is almost hustled from the meeting. The best cutters, men who are able to earn and can command good wages, are the ones who advocate a settlement upon the basis of the last proposition made. Then again the strike pay is not coming as regularly as the men could wish and there is considerable dissatisfaction notwithstanding the statement given out by the cutters' press committee that everything is satisfactory and the men remain firm. Many believe that had the cutters' committee been given full power to settle, that the strike would have been ended early this month. Several attempts have been made to have a vote of this kind passed, and as the votes in favor are increasing at every meeting, it is believed that before many days the committee will be given the power to settle. The opposition to this seems to come from the Italians and young men, and as they hold

the balance of power they can do as they like. It might be well to state, however, that the Italians who are holding out for 35 cents are those who either do not speak English or so little that they do not really understand how the are voting. The more intelligent Italians have been doing considerable missionary work in enlightening them of the true situation, and the result is that the sentiment to give the cutters' committee full power is growing. When this comes, as it doubtless will before the end of the month, it is said that the cutters' commmittee will offer a proposition to settle for a minimum price of 33 cents per hour, and the feeling among the manufacturers is that while it is more than they should pay, that they will grant that amount rather than prolong the strike, which is slowly but surely killing Quincy as a granite centre. Meetings of the several branches of the cutters were held in the middle of the month, but nothing could be learned in relation to any action taken.

The returns of granite shipments for the month of March show a large increase over the month of February, the exact figures being 11,640,471 pounds. This increase is due to two reasons. From Quincy Adams and West Quincy from the fact that the manufacturers are shipping the large amount of work which had been accumulating in their yards during the winter months. The other reason is the large orders that have been received by the Quarry railroad for grout, large quantities of which are being used by the N. Y., N. H. & H. R. R. in abolishing grade crossings on its Plymouth divisions. The increase at this terminal over the previous month was over 6,000,000 pounds, and this was largely grout. The shipments for April are expected to fall off some as many of the yards have been cleaned up, and as no new work is being done. It will be some time before the shipments run up to any large figures again. The total for March was 24,303.815 pounds, divided as follows: Quincy Quarry railroad, 13,073,790 pounds; Quincy Adams, 6,619,-725 pounds; West Quincy, 4,610.300 pounds.

Herbert W. Beattie is busy making models for a lot of special work. Mr. Beattie finds that it is necessary at this time to be connected with the outside world by telephone. and a long distance instrument has been installed at his studio.

The well known firm of McDonnell & Sons was dissolved by mutual agreement April 4, Thomas H. McDonnell retiring from the firm. Mrs. Emily A. McDonnell, wife of the late John G. McDonnell, the remaining partner, has purchased the assets of the firm, including the name and good will, and will continue the business at Quincy, Buffalo, N. Y., and at the various branch offices heretofore conducted by the firm. In connection with the above dissolution there is a rumor that James S. McDonnell, who has been connected with the Quincy office of the firm for many years, contemplates the forming of a stock company to purchase the plant.

The Quincy Quarry Granite Company has been doing business in Quincy now for a month, but the general public seems to be as much in the dark as to what the company proposes to do as they have been from the start. All inquiries are met with a request to wait a day or so. It is, however, known that the company are getting things into shape, and probably in their own good time they will give the public the information desired. The stockholders met in Quincy early this month and elected a board of fifteen directors; nine of them are Quincy men. All attempts, however, to obtain an official list of these directors has been a failure. No reason is assigned for withholding the list only that they are not ready to give it out at present. It is rumored among the granite men that the nine Quincy men as the board of directors are John Swithin, Thomas Swithin, Andrew Milne, James Thompson, Herbert F. Doble, John W. McAnamey, George H. Hitchcock, Marshal P. Wright and R. F. Claflin. Mr. Nulty, Mr. Ferdinand and Barnabus Clarke are the three Boston directors, and there are three from New York. Executive Committee: John Swithin, Thomas Swithin, James Thompson, Andrew Milne, Mr. Nulty. President, John Swithin. Mr. Nulty, Treasurer. The new company has opened an office in Durgin & Merrill's block in Quincy Centre, which is in charge of a clerk, who is as mum when any question is asked concerning the company as are other persons who know and could tell if they would.

A trip through the several yards this month found a little something doing at each, the work, however, being confined largely to apprentices. Nearly all of the finished work has been boxed ready for shipment and the first of May will see about everything sent away. The manufacturers as a rule were found at their offices at work upon their books and getting their accounts into shape. All regretted the present situation, but saw no way out of it unless the cutters came to their senses. All say that they have offered really more than they can afford, but they desire to get a settlement. The summer business is done for, no matter what happens, but they are in hope that an agreement of some kind will be reached, so that the fall trade may not be interfered with.

We are in receipt of the following letter from Mackie, Hussey & Co.: "This firm have sold out their business to Barclay Bros., who will take possession May 15th."

We wish to congratulate Barclay Bros. in securing the finest granite cutting plant in the country, in fact we might say in the world. It will give this firm the facilities which they have been sadly in need of to carry out their large contracts, which have been delayed in the past on account of lack of shed room and modern appliances, which it was impossible to install in the old-fashioned circular sheds which they formerly occupied. This plant has been described in the past and the majority of the leading granite manufacturers are familiar with it. We dislike even to entertain the idea that George C. Mackie and W. E. Hussey are to dissolve their connection with the granite business permanently. Mr. Mackie has been prominent in the granite business for a number of years, and is known as a careful and conservative manager and a man of

sterling worth. It is not necessary for us to recall the good qualities of Mr. Hussey, who is well and favorably known to the retail dealers as one of the leading salesmen in his line, and one whose word can be relied upon. We assume that Mr. Hussey will still continue on the road.—Ed.

The following comes to us just before going to press:

The widespread granite cutters' strike, which is now practically ended, because the compromise of Barre cutters was generally followed, is likely to be definitely settled for some time to come this week.

The Barre compromise was termed at other granite centres "the Barre scale," and in brief was 35 cents per hour scale for an eight-hour day. The acceptance of this scale by the Barre cutters prevented a strike here, and at many other places a tentative agreement was reached between the cutters and employers, by which the 35-cent rate for an eight-hour day would remain in force while the Barre men were at work under it.

At other places, notably Quincy, Mass., the employers failed to agree to the 35-cent scale, although agreeing to the eight-hour day, an increase in hour wage and a new bill of prices for piece work.

The Barre scale is satisfactory here, and the Barre branch of the Cutters' National Union has been called to meet tomorrow to act upon the question of suspending from the constitution that article which declared for a $3 eight-hour day. The polls will be open three hours on April 28, and a majority for or against what is practically an elimination of the article, will count. More important still, the National Union has agreed that the Barre scale is satisfactory. No change in the schedule could be made at this time in any event, owing to the great rush of work in all the yards.

The harmony between the cutters and the employers has done great good to Barre. The population has increased 500 in 30 days and is still increasing. Italians and Scotchmen are sending for their friends, and manufacturers from Concord and Quincy have asked for shed room. Many new sheds will be built, one large Quincy firm being ready to contract buildings at once. Several other out-of-town manufacturers are trying to obtain options on the plants here.

April 27. The result of a meeting of the Barre branch of the National Granite Cutters' Union mentioned above, was that it was voted to discredit clause 198, which in effect regulates that the wages of the cutters shall be $3 per day of eight hours. The men by this action express their favor of a wage of 35 cents as an average.

It is Barclay Bros.' intention to add one hundred feet to the length of the building, which will enable them to employ one hundred and seventy-five cutters. The business and good will of Mackie, Hussey & Co. have been purchased by Barclay Bros.

Anyone at all interested in the success of the granite business here or the general interests of the city and the surrounding country can but feel a thrill of pleasure at the thought that while, in nearly every other granite centre in New England the sound of the hammer is not heard, and the dinner pail hangs empty near the stove, while on the streets the one time busy granite cutters are grumbling because things do not go along smoothly, yet here in the city of Barre and the contingent territory business was never so good as it is today.

Over one thousand men march to and fro, morning, noon and night, and at the end of every month are able to walk up to the man they owe and ask for a receipted bill, knowing that they will have then something to themselves with which to buy the comforts of life. All eyes in the other granite centres in this section of the country are turned to Barre and their thoughts and imaginations are reaching out to ascertain, if possible, how it happens that the cutters and the manufacturers of this branch of the Union and Association, respectively, were able to come to an understanding without any struggle.

As we have before stated in reference to the Manufacturers here, they have all been cutters in their day and in a measure sympathize with them in their struggle to get what is right. Some of them would give them even more than could be afforded for the purpose of making a settlement of the matter so that their plants would not become idle and a drug on their shoulders. Any way the matter is settled as far as this section of the country is concerned, and what is better than all, it is settled to the satisfaction of both of the contending parties.

It is surely to be hoped that the other branches of the Union and the Association will follow suit and arrive at some sort of a compromise in the near future, for as we have said in these columns, "it is better to bend than to break."

A deal has been made recently which will do away with the intended building on the part of the firm of Barclay Bros.

When things really get to going in the new plant they expect to work over one hundred cutters, and will work their plant to its fullest capacity if things keep on, as conditions indicate that they will at this writing.

James M. Boutwell, who is now operating both the well known Langdon Quarry and the quarry formerly owned by the Wetmore & Morse Granite Co., says that business was never better than it is today if the demand for rough stock is any criterion. He is able to meet the demand promptly with both the quarries in full operation, and it seems to be in the increase. The price has been raised slightly during the past year, thus making the working of the quarries a little more profitable.

The firm of Melcher & Hadley have on their books a good assortment of orders, and are receiving more every day. They are working about one gang of cutters just at this time and are cutting some first class work of the various designs. Their shipments have been quite large during the past two months, and in .he near future they will send out several very nice jobs. They are making arrangements to do a larger business this season than they have ever done before, and express the expectation that this will be one of the best years which the granite business has ever known.

Doucette Bros. of Montpelier are doing a good business at this time and have more orders on their books than they have had before for some time. They are working about two gangs of cutters and will put on more in the near future. They are cutting several monuments of sarcophagus designs, and are well satisfied with the outlook for the season. Orders are coming in with unusual frequency, and the prices at which they are able to take them are such that a good margin can be made.

The new, large plant which the firm of Ryle & Crimmins are building in Montpelier is being pushed right along and will be ready for occupancy in about a month.

Obituary.

D. L. Sloan, proprietor of the Elkton Marble and Granite Works, Elkton, Md., died February 13, 1900. He had been in the monumental business at this location for thirty-three years. His son, J. H. Sloan, will continue the business, having learned the business with his father, with whom he has been connected for the past twenty years.

Correspondence.

Find enclosed $1.00 money order for one year's payment to the GRANITE.

As long as the GRANITE will keep up its standard you may count me as a subscriber for same.—M. F. Durlauf, Jasper, Ind.

You may send on GRANITE. We would not be without it.—Thomson Granite Co., Mansfield, Ohio.

I think the cover of your paper is the best in the trade and between the covers better than the cover.—Herbert W. Beattie, Sc., Quincy, Mass.

I did not tell you to stop GRANITE at expiration, and still I have not received it. I have missed the magazine for the past two months very much. You will find a check for $1.50 enclosed for the Imperial Design Book and the GRANITE, commencing January 1, 1900. Please' send January and February numbers.—C. M. Holbrook, Brattleboro, Vt.

You may send GRANITE to me for this year with the January, February and March numbers, please.

I was very much interested in the paper and missed it very much when it was stopped.—Martin Canfield, Honesdale, Pa.

Enclosed please find one dollar ($1.00) for another year's subscription to GRANITE. We should regret to discontinue subscription as much as you would, as we are greatly pleased with your paper.—The McIntosh Granite & Marble Co., Limited, Toronto, Canada.

Enclosed please find $1.00 for which please continue my subscription for your paper, GRANITE, which it would be hard to keep shop without. Hoping you are having success.—G. A. Snere, Glencoe, Minn.

Enclosed please find my check for one dollar to pay for GRANITE to March 1, 1901. Please send me the sizes and price of your designs, which are very fine and practical. and oblige.—Thomas Staniland, Dayton, Ohio.

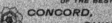

I enclose one dollar for renewal of subscription to GRANITE. It is well worth it.

PAUL E. CABARET,
New York City.

Yours of the 12th received, and see that ———— are a reliable firm. Much obliged. If you would send us the names of two or three more quarry owners and manufacturers, we would be obliged. Also send us your paper; find enclosed draft for one year's subscrip-

FRIEDERICHS & BRAUN,
Peotone, Ill.

(All advertisers in GRANITE can be relied upon. Try some of them and prove it for yourself.)

Proposed Monuments and Monumental News.

DENVER, COL.—The state board of capitol managers has granted permission to the Sons of the Revolution to erect a monument on the capitol grounds. The board reserves the right to pass upon the plans for the monument. The monument will be in granite and bronze.

WASHINGTON, D. C.—Plans have been formulated for the erection of a monument to the memory of General Albert Ordway.

WASHINGTON, D. C.—A bill appropriating $10,000 to secure plans for a suitable memorial to Ulysses S. Grant, to be erected in Washington, was called up March 24. The bill was unanimously passed.

SIOUX CITY, IA.—Ten thousand dollars have been appropriated for the purpose of erecting a 100-foot stone shaft which will mark the spot where 100 years ago Sergeant Charles Floyd, a member of the Lewis and Clark expedition, met his death. Colonel Chittendon, U. S. Engineer, will have charge of erecting the shaft for the Floyd Memorial Association.

TOPEKA, KAN.—Mayor Drew appointed Councilman J. W. F. Hughes, J. S. Warner and M. Snattinger as a special committee to consider the feasibility of the city of Topeka erecting a monument to the memory of the late Colonel Cyrus K. Holliday.

KANSAS CITY, MO.—An effort is being made by Ninth District Republicans to raise the funds necessary for the erection of a monument to the memory of the late Judge Arnold Krekel.

BAY CITY, MICH.—Efforts are being made for the erection of a soldiers' monument.

ATLANTA, GA.—A movement has just been started by the friends of the late Governor Atkinson to erect a monument to the memory of the distinguished dead. The plan is to raise a fund of $2,000, which will be devoted to the building of a monument at Newman, the former home of Governor Atkinson.

MONROE, GA.—The R. E. Lee Camp of Confederate Veterans, in their regular meeting Tuesday, decid-

ed to erect a monument. The monument is to cost $2,000, and will be ready for unveiling exercises on Memorial Day, April 26, 1901.

BELLEFONTE, PA.—At a public meeting April 7, the Centre County Soldiers' Monument and Curtin Memorial Association was formed. President, General James A. Beaver. It was decided that the proposed soldiers' monument should not be started until $25,000 had been raised. Of this amount $15,000 will be devoted to the soldiers' monument and $10,000 to the Curtin memorial. General Beaver stated that he had already in sight over $2,500 for the Curtin fund.

PUTNAM, CT.—The ladies of the Woman's Relief Corps have been discussing and planning how to honor the soldier dead with a commemorative monument, and have decided to go about the work at once to raise funds to carry their purpose into effect.

BOSTON, MASS.—The following bill is before the common council: That the finance committee be requested to appropriate the sum of $50,000 for a monument to be erected in memory of the citizens of Boston who died in the military and naval service of the Spanish-American war.

MONTREAL, QUEBEC.—The citizens are raising a fund of $100,000 for the purpose of erecting a monument to the soldiers from the city who have given their lives in South Africa for the empire. They intend that it shall be the most magnificent monument in Canada.

BALTIMORE, MD.—The Maryland Daughters of the Confederacy are energetically at work in raising the fund for the monument to the Confederate soldiers and sailors of Maryland.

HAMILTON, OHIO.—The Soldiers', Sailors' and Pioneers' Monument Association met April 5. A concentrated effort will be made by the members of the association to have congress pass the bill appropriating $25,000 for the erection of a monument to commemorate old Fort Hamilton.

ALBANY, N. Y.—This bill was advanced by the assembly: Appropriating $2,500 for the erection of a monument to the memory of the soldiers of the Ninth Regiment, New York State Volunteers.

YEADON, PA.—At the suggestion of Archbishop Ryan, a committee has undertaken to raise $3,000 with which to erect a monument in Holy Cross cemetery to mark the last resting place of departed priests.

RALEIGH, N. C.—The monument to be erected to Zebulon Vance will cost $7,000, $2,000 of which was subscribed and $5,000 appropriated by the State.

DES MOINES, IA.—A bill, appropriating $50,000 for the erection of monuments to Iowa regiments on the battlefield of Shiloh, and offered amendments providing that the commission may use the unexpended balance of the appropriation, if any, on the state monument, and may cause the regimental monuments to be constructed of granite and bronze. The amendments were adopted. The bill provides for one state monument to cost $15,000, and eleven regimental monuments to cost $3,000 each.

(Continued on page 27.)

"GRANITE," MAY, 1900.

BOTTOM BASE	E — T x E — T x C — A
SECOND BASE . .	P — A x P — A x C — A
DIE	R — Y x R — Y x P — Y
FIGURE	A — T x A — T x E — C Y

PRICE: . . . . $C E Y Y

"GRANITE," MAY, 1900.

BASE . . . . C — R x A — C Y x C — T
DIE . . . . A — T x A — E x ⟨V — N Top / C — Y Bottom⟩
FINISHED FRONT . . . C — T x A — Y
BEVEL ON BASE . . . Y — T

"GRANITE," MAY, 1900. ORIGINAL DESIGN.

BOTTOM BASE . . . . E — T x R — T x C — V
SECOND BASE . . . . P — Y x A — Y x Y — N
DIE . . . . . . R — N x C — N x C — C V

PRICE : { Barre Granite . . . . $A E V
Quincy Granite . . . . $A I V
Milford or Troy (N. H.) Granite . . . $R V V

Among The Retail Dealers.

CALAIS, ME.—E. E. Shattuck & Co., the granite workers, finding their quarters too small for their extensive business, have removed to larger quarters. An addition 20x30 to the building will be used as a polishing room. The front room in the store will be used as a display room, and the rear will be used as a workshop.

E. E. Shattuck & Co., the granite workers, finding their quarters too small for their extensive business have removed to larger quarters. An addition 20x30 to the building will be used as a polishing room. The front room in the store will be used as a display room, and the rear will be used as a workshop.

CHAMBERSBURG, PA.—Forbes & Berger, marble and granite manufacturers, have leased the ground from the Cumberland Valley Railroad Company upon which they are erecting a marble and granite works.

HARTFORD, CT.—Stephen Maslin has obtained the contract for erecting State headstones to the memory of Connecticut soldiers who died in the Spanish war.

SPRINGFIELD, ILL.—At a meeting of the Nancy Hank Lincoln Memorial Association held in the governor's office March 10, it was decided to accept the proposition of J. S. Culver, to erect, free of charge, a monument over the grave of Lincoln's mother near Lincoln City.

HASTINGS, NEB.—The committee having in charge the matter of erecting a monument over the grave of the late William A. McKeighan, have let the contract to Miller & Bigelow. It is to cost $600.

BEALSVILLE, PA.—J. M. Miller has sold his stock of marble, granite and sandstone to the California Marble and Granite Co.

QUAKERTOWN, PA.—George Hintzel, marble dealer of this place, will shortly move to Tamauqua, where he will engage in the same business.

INDIANAPOLIS, IND.—A deal that has been pending for some time, was completed April 2, by which Willis Miller of Danville, Ill., and H. A. Rockwood of this city will start a new manufacturing plant. The enterprise will be called the Willis Miller Milling Company, and is organized for the purpose of dealing extensively in marble and granite, the rough material to be brought to this city from the quarries and worked into proper shape for the monument-makers and dealers. The site on which the new plant is to be located immediately has been leased for a period of five years. Messrs. Miller and Rockwood will at once begin making improvements to the building and will add several other small structures. The necessary machinery has been contracted for and will soon arrive.—Exchange.

HYDE PARK, MASS.—George O. King of the Hyde Park Monumental Works, has just finished and placed in position a handsome monumental tablet over the

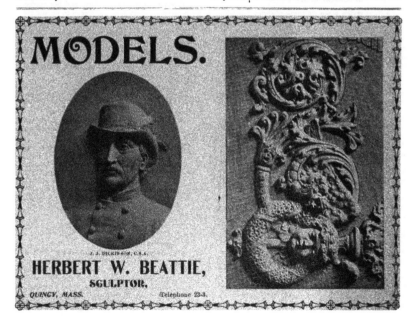

remains of the late Gridley J. F. Bryant, the famous Boston architect. Mr. Bryant built, as supervising architect, many of the notable buildings in Boston belonging to the city and national government.

NYACK, N. Y.—C. M. Travis has a contract to build a monument for the grave of Bill Anthony, the hero of the Maine, in Evergreen cemetery. The monument is to be built at the expense of Richard Croker of New York. The monument will be four feet high and three feet wide. It will be of granite, with rough rock face work. On a raised panel will be this inscription: "Sir, I have to report that the ship has been blown up and is sinking." It will be finished in February.

EASTON, PA.—The committee of the Ninth New Jersey Veteran Volunteers appointed to award the contract for the monument to be erected over the grave of General Charles A. Heckman at Easton, Pa., awarded the contract to Howell & Sons.

WESTERLY, R. I.—Edmund Keleher, formerly senior partner in the granite firm of Keleher & Flynn, died Dec. 29 at the age of 39 years and 10 months. For a long time Mr. Keleher had suffered from a cancer on his jaw, and though he suffered severely he bore his affliction patiently to the end.

*

Notes of Ornament No. 3.

BY HERBERT W. BEATTIE, SC.

In a short review when we speak of styles it is with broad distinction only; there are, of course, many varieties of nearly every great style, but as long as the chief characteristics remain unchanged, the style is the same. From this point of view the styles become comparatively few. We find that nine will comprise the whole number, viz.: three ancient—the Egyptian, the Greek and the Roman;three medieval—the Byzantine, the Saracenic and the Gothic; and the three modern—the Renaissance, the Cinquecento and the Louis Quatorze.

Several of these styles have their recognised varieties. Of the Greek there are the Doric and the Alexandrian; that is, the severe and the florid. Of the Byzantine, there are the Romanesque, Lombard and Norman varieties, etc.; and of the Renaissance, also, there are several varieties.

These various styles extend over a period of upwards of three thousand five hundred years, of which two thousand may be considered the ancient period.

About one thousand years may be considered the medieval period; and the last five centuries may be considered the period of the Renaissance or modern period.

Style is only another name for character. Every style, as such, depends, of course, upon what is peculiar to it, never in what it has in common with other styles. These peculiarities are what we term characteristics.

Sometimes a style is merely a modification of, or peculiar elaboration of, the features of another style. It is, then, only a variety or a derived style; and such varieties are common, especially in later times, the natural result of the accumulation of materials. These

varieties may be invented at pleasure, when one is once master of the essential characteristics of the great historic styles.

As a matter of course, the earliest styles are the most simple, and also the most original, as each successive style has been gradually developed out of its predecessor, viz.: the Roman from the Greek, the Romanesque from the Roman, and so on.

It does not follow that an ornament is in a certain style because it belongs to the period of that style, for a style is defined not only by its time or period, but by the prevailing peculiarities or characteristics of that period; and it is not at all the case that every work of a period possesses these peculiarities. Let us examine the pecularities of the nine historic styles which illustrate the history of ornament. The Egyptian, Greek and the Roman—the ancient; the Byzantine, Saracenic and the Gothic—the middle ages; and the Renaissance, Cinquecento and Louis Quartorze—the modern.

EGYPTIAN.

The earliest style of ornament of which we know anything is the Egyptian, dating 1800, B. C., when it was already established. As a rule the elements of Egyptian ornament have a peculiar meaning; they are not chosen for the sake of beauty or effect. The style is therefore very simple and limited in its arrangements. The details are not mere crude imitations of nature, but natural objects selected by symbolism and fashioned by symmetry into ornamental decorations. So that we have here one great class, and the earliest systematic efforts in design in the world's history.

The Egyptian artist, was by birth and not choice, in his profession; every man was forced to pursue the occupation of his father.

Many Egyptian ornaments are still popular ornaments, as the fret, wave scroll, spiral, zig-zag, water lily, star and palm. The frieze is the commonest form of decoration, and the details are generally some of the more important symbols, as the lotus, or water lily of the Nile, and the zig-zag, the type of water. The fret is of less frequent occurrence. There is, however, one particular ornament which is more common than all others in Egyptian decoration. This is what is sometimes called the Scarabæus or beetle, or rather the winged globe; it occurs in all sizes and almost in all materials, and is a species of talisman or invocation of good luck. The globe is supposed to represent the sun, the wings providence, and the two asps, one on each side of the globe, dominion or monarchy. This ornament is placed over doors, windows and in passages, and sometimes of an enormous size. There are several other winged figures found in Egyptian friezes, natural and conventional, the vulture, the winged asp and the human winged figure, corresponding apparently to those described in the works of the Jews.

The sphinx, a remarkable object in the Egyptian art, does not come under the category of the winged creatures. In this it is distinguished from the Greek creation of that name, which is always winged, and always female. The Egyptian sphinx, on the other hand, is always male. It is supposed to represent the combination of physical and intellectual power, and its principal position was on either side of the path leading to the temple. The most essential symbolic characteristics of an Egyptian design are the winged globe, the lotus, the papyrus, the zig-zag, the asp and the cartouche containing hieroglyphics. The lotus is, perhaps, the most common. These are mixed up with many arbitrary or geometrical forms, as the fret, spiral or wave scroll, star, etc., and with many of the natural productions of Egypt, conventionally treated, and in simple symmetrical progression, every detail having a symbolic meaning beyond its mere ornamental service in the design.

General gaiety of color is likewise characteristic of the Egyptian taste, but the colors are generally limited to red, blue, yellow and green, though the Egyptians were acquainted with nearly all other colors.

A simple progression or repetition is characteristic of the Egyptian style, and it is certainly very rarely we find anything else, yet in the cluster of the lotus, in the form of its leaf, we have a very beautiful compound example. And this ornament is important, as anticipating the anthemion or most popular floral ornament of the Greeks, so common in architecture and the terra cotta vases.

Every Egyptian capital is a variety of the lotus-bud, lotus-bell, or Isis-head, but the lotus-bell is the most common. The abacus is, on all occasions, the width only of the pillar, and invariably narrower than the capital, which is a valuable feature, and very essential to the effect of stability. The Egyptian pillars vary in their height from four to nearly seven diameters, the longer being the most common.

The Egyptian style of decoration was not without its influence upon all people connected with Egypt: the Jews, the Greeks, the Persians and we still see the remains of their influence in the whole basin of the Euphrates and borders of the Persian Gulf. In Egypt we find grandeur of proportion, simplicity of parts, and splendor and costliness of material, gold, silver and ivory, precious stones and color as the great art characteristics. And we find throughout that the prevailing characteristics of Asiatic art also is sumptuousness. It is equally displayed in the works of the Tabernacle, Temple of Solomon and in all palaces of Persian kings.

Jewish ornament, like the Egyptian, appears to have been purely representative. The only elements mentioned in Scripture are the almond, the pomegranate, the palm tree, the lily, or lotus, oxen, lions and the cherubim. The only example we possess of Jewish ornamental work is the bas-relief of the candle-stick of seven branches, still partly preserved among the sculptures of the Arch of Titus of Rome.

Extending our view still farther east we find the most characteristic feature of Hindu art seems to be the fantastic, and though possessing the same jewelled richness as the Egyptian, it wants its simplicity and grandeur. Its most striking peculiarities are its fantastic animal devices, and its profusion of minute foliage.

It is not till we come to Greece that we find the habitual introduction of forms for their own sake, or for their æsthetic value or effect, purely as ornamental; this is the greatest step in art.

(To be continued.)

Monthly Trade Record.

This department is compiled and edited by the United Mercantile Agency. Subscribers, in accordance with the terms of their contracts, are entitled to receive further information relative to the parties hereafter mentioned, upon application to the main office As the names of many business men who are good will appear herein, subscribers can readily see the importance of making inquiries if interested, previous to taking any action.

ILLINOIS.
Jacksonville, *M—Rowe, Harvey, 43.
Lacon, *M—Kirk & Smith, 64, Thomas D. Kirk 58.
INDIANA.
Logansport, *M—Billman, C. D., 50-43.
IOWA.
Boone, *M—Cadd, W. J., 76.
Fairfield, *M—Messett & Lynn succeed Harry Messett.
Jefferson, *M—Arnold, C. F., 76.
Marion, *M—Kaley & Lyttle succeed W. H. Kaley.
Marshalltown, *M—Woods & Sherlock succeed W. M. Sherlock.
Red Oaks, *M—Cole, Z. W., 86 to Greeley & Davis.
KANSAS.
Abilene, *M—Stewart & Son, 76.
MAINE.
Augusta, *M—Turner & Brown, 64.
Bangor, *M—Fletcher & Butterfield, George M. Fletcher, et al., 14 $850.
Lewiston, *M—Johnson & Taylor, 76.
MASSACHUSETTS.
Mansfield, *M—Freeman, John, 76.
Oxford, *M—Bergren, Claus, 76.
Quincy, G—Swithin Bros. Granite Co., 39 cap $10m.
MICHIGAN.
Adrian, *M—Woodard, J. J., 76.
Albion, *M—Sebastian, L. P. & Son, succeed Barry & Sebastian.
Ann Arbor, *M—Harvey & Lane succeed R. C. Barney.
Downington, *M— Brown, A. S., succeed Southworth & Paige.
MINNESOTA.
Fergus Falls, *M—Partridge, Richard, succeed Partridge & Chantron.
MISSOURI.
Jefferson, *M—Schmidt, G. J., 76.
Jefferson, *M—Vetter, F. J., 76.
Kansas City, *M—Miller & Johnson, 64, W. O. Miller 58.
NEBRASKA.
Nebraska City, *M—Neidhart & Forbes, 64, W. A. Forbes 58.
Oxford, *M—Boyd, J. A., 76.

NEW HAMPSHIRE.
Milford, GZ—Lovejoy Granite Co., 99 $300.
NEW JERSEY.
Bridgton, *M—Ogden & Platt succeed John Ogden & Son.
NEW YORK.
Amsterdam, *M—Bostwick, John M., dced $1,900
Flushing, *M—Sugden & Keeler, 64, Alfred R. Keeler 58.
Goshen, *M—Corbett, James J., 76.
New York, WG—Leland & Hall Co., 39 cap $50m.
Oswego, *M—Salladin, Charles F., 20 $180.
Redwood, *M—Force, H. M., 76.
Sandy Creek, *M—Sherman & Co., 88 to Watertown.
Schnectady, *M—Gardner Bros. succeed Charles Schreiber.
NORTH DAKOTA.
Hillsboro, *M—Knutsson, K., succeeds Morgan & Gordon.
OHIO.
Cincinnati, *M—Schwartz, Fridolin, 104.
Circleville, *M—Marshall & Renick, 76.
Fostoria, *M—Robbins, F. E., succeeds W. D. Robbins.
Granville, *M—De Bow Bros., 99 $200.
Hamilton, *M—Horssnyder, F., 93 $2,200.
PENNSYLVANIA.
Birdsboro, *M—Rea, John, 76.
Reading, *M—Eisenbrown, P. F., Sons & Co., H. W. Eisenbrown 78.
Scranton *M—Carlucci Stone Co. succeed Frank Carlucci.
RHODE ISLAND.
Providence, *M—Burns, John Granite Co., 39 cap $25m.
SOUTH DAKOTA.
Sioux Falls, *M—Ballard & Son, 76.
TEXAS.
San Antonio, *M—Mierow Marble Co., 39 cap $5m.
VERMONT.
Barre, GZ—Beach & Jones, 76.
Hardwick, GZ—Brush, Emerson, 86 to Clark Trow.
Montpelier, GZ—Bertoli & Peduzzi, 76.
Williamstown, GZ—Rowell, Ira H. & Son, 76.
NEW BRUNSWICK.
St. George, GZ—Messenett & McDougall, 87 $1,700.
ONTARIO.
Collingwood, *M—Walker, Pease, succeeds I. A. Johnson.
Leamington, *M—Pengelly, J. H., 80.
Ottawa, *M—Shields & O'Connell, 76.

What's the matter with this for an epitaph and a little laudable advertisement: "Here lies Jane Smith, wife of Thomas Smith, marble cutter. This monument was erected by her husand as a tribute to her memory and a specimen of his work. Monuments of this same style are two hundred and fifty dollars."

The following is gracefully put: "Here lies Bernard Lightfoot, who was accidentally killed in the forty-fifth year of his age. Erected by his grateful family."

Dix Island—Present and Past.

(Conclu'd.)

There is on record the memorable game of poker which was played by Horace Beals and John Greenwood, one of his head men.

Beals didn't quite approve of Greenwood's going up against the game, but he had his own way of making his wishes known. He didn't call Greenwood into the office and tell him that he must either quit the game or his job. That wasn't his way.

Instead of that he dropped in one night where the boys were congregated. There were several games in progress, and in one of them sat Greenwood playing with luck which was better than a license to steal, as the old man Beals put it. Beals watched the game through and when Greenwood had his man trimmed he sauntered up to the table.

"Playing in pretty good luck, then't you, John?" he asked.

"Pretty fair," was the response.

"Rather better'n fair, I should say," said Beals, "but all the same I think I should like to try a game with you. I saw the new moon over my right shoulder to-night and that usually means that I'm going to have good luck. What do you say to a quiet little game?"

"Be more'n glad to accommodate you," said John, for he had the card-player's belief in his lucky nights and he was fully convinced that he was having one of them. Beside that, he didn't reckon that Beals knew the game as well as he did, and he was counting on adding to the comfortable little roll that he already possessed.

The cards were dealt for the opening hand and the game was started. For a time things ran about even and then Greenwood began to pull ahead. Beals said nothing, and his face was as void of emotion as a plaster cast.

The cards only ran that way for a short time. Then Beals began to win, slowly at first, but as the stakes went up in Greenwood's desperate efforts to get back what he had lost, the money changed hands more rapidly. Beals was a steady winner. He won all the cash that Greenwood had with him, and when the workman staked the month's pay that was coming to him, the proprietor won that also. That wound up the game. Greenwood was worse than busted, but he was taking it with a steady nerve.

Beals gathered up his earnings slowly, making them into an imposing a pile as possible.

"That's quite a bit of money to be losing in an evening, John," he said.

"Yes, sir," answered John.

"In fact, it is rather too much. Now I tell you what I'll do. If you'll promise never to play poker again so long as you work for us on the island, I'll give this pile of boodle back to you. What do you say, is it a bargain?"

Greenwood did not answer for a minute or two. His eye rested first on Beals and then on the pile of money.

"Yes," he answered at length, "I guess you're right about it, Mr. Beals, but I'll be blamed if I ever looked at it in quite that way before. Yes, I'll take your offer, an' I'll keep my word."

"John," said Beals, as he handed back the money and the order for Greenwood's next month's pay, "it wasn't necessary for you to make that last statement. When John Greenwood tells me that he's going to do a thing he hasn't got to say that he'll keep his word. That goes without saying."

That is the story of the most famous poker game that was ever played on Dix Island, and it is a story that any of the old settlers of this locality will tell you for the asking.

During the palmiest days of the island, from '72 to '75, wages were way up. The monthly pay-roll of the company was in the neighborhood of $100,000. It never ran below $80,000 in those days and sometimes up to $115,000 and $120,000. That money used to come to the Rockland banks, and the paymaster would take it from there in a big grip-sack. Very often he would row over to the island by himself, and if he didn't happen to finish his work in one day he'd tote what there was left back to Rockland and lock it up over night.

People along the shore took a great interest in the paymaster's visit. Down round Ash Point today there are men who recall being led up, when they were small boys, to the paymaster and being allowed the privilege of peeping into and "hefting" the big valise that held such a fortune.

At that time stone-cutters were paid from $4.00 to $4.50 per day. Quarrymen got from $2.00 to $2.50. Foremen were paid their five plunks per day, and a chief foreman did not get less than $6.50 or $7.00. Clerks and time-keepers got $5.00. Rodney L. Fogg, who was the government superintendent, was paid $8.00 per day, rain or shine, Sundays and all. David Smith, who had general charge of the island for the company, received $7.00, and of all the old-timers he is the only one living.

The men worked ten hours per day, and as the law says that men shall work only eight hours when in government employ, the employes of the Dix Island Granite Company have always felt that they had something coming to them. But it has never come. They claim that for that extra two hours every day the government should settle, and they have tried in every way to effect a settlement, but no Congress has ever seen fit to take the responsibility of paying the bill. Commission after commission has been sent down to Congress, and that has always been the end of it. If the question of back pay is ever settled in favor of the workmen there will be thousands of dollars paid over to old workmen and their heirs, and assigns not only in this country, but all over the country where Dix Islanders have settled.

Men who have traversed the length and breadth of the continent in the interests of the granite business say that you cannot go into a single quarry of any size from Maine to California, but what you will find men who either worked on the island themselves or are sons of men who did. It was the greatest stone-cutters' school that this country ever had.

Many of the men who now work on Hurricane of Vinalhaven got their training on Dix. Mr. L. M. Crockett, who is a chief foreman at Vinalhaven, drove a string of oxen in the old days at Dix. He is one of the veterans of the business. He was made chief foreman in '69, and today he is chief foreman in the same quarry. That's a thirty-year record and is one not often equalled. During that time men have come and gone, but he has staid at his post and lost hardly a day from sickness.

And in that time no man has ever worked for him who could do him up at wrestling. It is a custom of his to approach a new man with an off-hand remark like this:—

"H'm, your name is Clark, isn't it?"

The newcomer admits that such is the case.

"Well," Crockett will answer, "as long as I have been here I never have allowed a man whose name ends in k to work for me till I've found out whether he's a better man than me."

That means a wrestling match, and there have been some withy tussles on the rocks of Vinalhaven, but the man who can throw Foreman Crockett has yet to put in his appearance.

The present keeper of Dix Island remembers this trait of Crockett's. His name is also Crockett, and the first day that he went to work the foreman told him that he never allowed a man of his own name to work for him without finding out who was the best man.

"Well," answered the other Crockett, "that's always been my plan, too."

"Good!" exclaimed the foreman, heartily; "we'll find out about this on the first snow."

"That was years ago," said Keeper Crockett, as he told me the story the other day, "but I've never forgotten the fall I got that day. I thought that I was something of a rooster myself, but the old man took that notion out of my head so quick that I didn't know I ever could wrestle. He tossed me into the air as though I had been a feather, and when I struck the ground I only wished that the snow was about twice as deep as it was."

The work that goes on today on Dix Island is not even an echo of the old days. The present owner, Mr. Thomas Dwyer of New York, uses the island only for getting out such stone as he needs in his contracting business in New York. He came into possession of it five or six years ago by the purchase of a mortgage for something over $7,000. After the boom dropped out of the island it went down as rapidly as it had once grown.

When Horace Beals died he left it to his widow. She subsequently took unto herself another husband, a Mr. E. L. Dwyer. Things did not result pleasantly from the match and Mrs. Dwyer gave her husband the deed of Dix, Andrews and several minor islands in the Muscle Ridge group, and later married a foreigner of rank and settled down in New York as the Countess de Castelusia.

Many a fortune was made in the little island only to be lost in unlucky investments elsewhere, and the personal history of some of the men who were concerned in its up-building would be most interesting reading, even at this late day.

But what Dix Island was, it will probably never be again, and the yarn I have spun today is but the fragmentary story of what was once the busiest spot on the Maine coast.

Washington Monumental Case.

Peter Reinhalter, late trading as P. Reinhalter & Co., to the use of the P. Reinhalter Company vs. John Spence and others, now or late doing business under the style of the Washington Memorial Association. The defendants are, or were in 1894, members of the Junior Order of American Mechanics, residing in Coatesville. A movement was started for the erection of a monument to General Washington, to be erected on the Battlefield of Brandywine, but the monument never was erected. The plaintiff claims that a contract was given him, and that he prepared to do the work, getting the granite out of the quarry, and partly dressing it but was obliged to cut it up and use it for other work, by which its value was depreciated one-half. He claimed he should be paid for his loss and sued to recover $5,000.

Three of the defendants were not served with the writ by the Sheriff, because they could not be found. These were John Spence, W. D. Doan and M. D. Lichliter. It was alleged by the plaintiff that at a meeting of the defendants with himself and others, the design presented by him for a monument was accepted, and subsequently a contract was signed between himself and John Spence, President of the Fund, and William Doan, Secretary of the Fund. If this agreement was authorized by the defendants it follows, of course, that they are responsible, otherwise not.

On the trial of the case, in February last, the plaintiff came very near being non-suited, because of his failure to show that the defendants were responsible for the contract made by Spence and Doan, who have since disappeared. After inspecting the affidavit of defense Judge Butler, who tried the case, held that it so far supplemented the plaintiff's testimony as to admit that they were all present but two. The defendants having been required to answer, testified. They claimed that while they selected the design presented by Reinhalter & Co., they did not authorize a contract, and declared their conviction at the time that no contract should be entered into until two-thirds of the money was raised. The jury rendered a verdict for defendants and the plaintiff asked for a new trial. As two of these defendants were not present at the time that the plans of the monument were discussed it is plain that they could not be held responsible, this Washington Memorial Association not being a chartered organization. The fact that they were included as defendants complicated matters somewhat. The court held that they should have been eliminated from the case. Question as to whether or not a new trial should be granted is held under advisement.

Put on Their Aprons Again.

Ten wealthy stone contractors, whose firms have an aggregate capital of $4,000,000, are working in the yards of the John Tait Cut Stone Company, Chicago, Ill. They are engaged in hard manual labor as an evidence of their loyalty to a common cause.

Two months ago the journeymen stone cutters were locked out of the yards of the Tait company on account of the difference between the associations of contractors and workmen. Mr. Tait abided by the decision of his associates, hoping the trouble would be settled at an early date or soon enough for him to finish a contract he had on hand.

When it became apparent that the differences might not be adjusted for several months, Mr. Tait became alarmed. He saw he was in danger of losing a large amount of money if he did not fill his contract on time, and he applied to his fellow-contractors for assistance. They responded in the only way open to them, putting on aprons and going to work in the yards.

The contract will be finished in time and Mr. Tait's money will be saved.

Art ?

"Art?" said our friend, the sculptor, with a gentle smile. "Art? It's sad and amusing. Let me relate an experience. A committee from an historical town waited upon me once and talked about a statue to be put up in the town square. I asked them how much money they had to spend. The sum they mentioned was about enough to pay for the casting of a bronze of heroic size ; just about enough and no more. That's what I told them, and they talked among themselves and came to the conclusion that perhaps a granite statue would do. I gave them my opinion of granites in two words ; and then, seeing that they had reached the end of their rope, I said that if they would give me my own way I would agree to offer them a regular bargain—a bronze at cost. Mind you, I asked nothing. They hesitated for a moment, as if they were suspicious. Finally they agreed that it seemed to be a fair offer. I asked them how much time they could spare me. They said a month. I said that I would have the statue ready in a few years. I visited the town and determined upon an heroic figure of a village artisan—the typical colonial soldier. The committee again nearly took the job away from me. A village artisan seemed too common a figure to them. They must have thought that a minute-man was a dignified warrior in gold lace or khaki. But they yielded, and I gave the best that's in me to the work. Fickle fame was my only reward. Yet, I'm satisfied. A few mortuary busts keep the pot boiling nowadays"—Exchange.

No Rest for Lincoln.

Fate seems to have denied rest to the great emancipator even in death. When the body of Abraham Lincoln was taken to a temporary vault in Oak Ridge cemetery, at Springfield, Ill., a few days ago, it marked the eleventh removal of the remains of the martyred President. For thirty-five years the metallic casket has been shifted hither and thither to meet the exigencies of time and change. The following table gives the history of the unquiet remains of Lincoln, from the time of his death, thirty-five years ago:

Died in house near Ford's theatre, Washington, in which he was assassinated, April 14, 1865.

Removed to White House.
Removed to Capitol building.
Removed to funeral car.
Removed to Capitol building, Springfield, Ill.
Removed to receiving vault, Oak Ridge cemetery.
Removed to temporary vault.
Removed to sarcophagus, Lincoln monument.

Removed to space between walls.
Removed to bed of cement.
Removed to temporary vault.

For several years the Lincoln monument at Springfield has steadily fallen into decay. It was completed seventeen years ago, after fifteen years of labor. Soon after it was finished the base of the knoll on which it rested began to shift. Gaping seams appeared in the masonry, and the monument, which was one of the finest in the country, has long been in danger of total collapse. Recently enough money was appropriated by the State Legislature to raze the old structure and rebuild it on a foundation which goes down thirty-five feet to bed rock. This last removal of Lincoln's remains was made necessary on account of the rebuilding of the monument. The metallic casket now rests in a crude wooden box in a temporary vault in Oak Ridge cemetery.

Soon after the body was first placed in the monument in 1876 an attempt was made to steal it. After this the coffin, which had been exposed to view behind iron gratings, was walled up in the tomb with a solid cement barrier. In making the removal some days ago it was found that great disintegration and decay had taken place in the casket and contents during the past few years. For a week workmen dug in a bed of solid concrete, in an endeavor to locate the remains of the great emancipator and his wife. The moisture had soaked through the cement and had formed a frost, possibly an inch thick, around the casket in which Lincoln was buried. This moisture is undoubtedly responsible for the advanced state of decay in which the cedar casket was found. Fortunately, Lincoln's body was buried in a metallic coffin made of lead and copper, and were it not for this fact, the probabilities are that the remains could not have been transferred to a temporary resting place intact.

When the casket was taken from the cement the outer wooden box was, as might have been expected, badly decayed. No other box had been prepared, and the wooden box in which the body of the great emancipator is now resting was made with a hatchet, a saw, a few nails, and some unplaned boards. It was constructed upon the ground within a few feet of the tomb, as were five similar boxes in which were placed the decayed caskets containing the remains of Mrs. Lincoln, the three sons, and the grandson. Plans are now being considered with a view of placing the casket so that it can be seen, and at the same time be safe from further efforts to steal it. It is believed that by placing the casket above ground it will not disintegrate and corrode so rapidly.

When the other coffins were removed that of the infant son was so badly decayed that the bottom came out and the small skeleton was exposed to view. It was placed back in the casket, in which a metal bottom was placed.

The temporary vault is constructed in such a manner that half a dozen persons could not reach Lincoln's remains in many hours. The vault is surrounded by a stone wall two feet thick and strongly cemented with mortar. The cap stone covering weighs five tons, and was placed with a steam derrick. The vault contains two decks. In the bottom Lincoln's remains and those of his wife lie side by side. In the upper deck are the remains of the three sons and the grandson.

(To be Continued.)

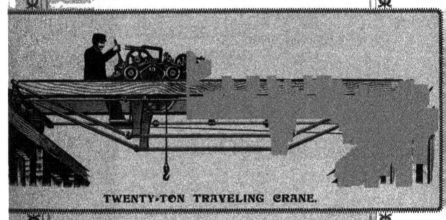

WALTER W. FIELD,

117 Main Street, Cambridgeport, Mass.

...TELEPHONE 73 CAMBRIDGE...

NEW ENGLAND AGENT FOR

THE LAMBERT
HOISTING ENGINE CO.

500 Styles and Sizes.
Built to Gauges and Templates.

For Mining, Quarrying, Coal Handling, Pile Driving, Builders' use, Logging and General Contracting.

Electric Hoists, Single and Double Drums,
with Improved Automatic Brake.
Suspension Cableways.

—— *SEND FOR NEW CATALOGUE B.* ——

Horizontal, Locomotive and Upright

BOILERS.

Engine in Stock for Quick Delivery.

**Standard Double Cylinder Double Patent Friction Drum Double Winch
Hoisting Engine, with Boiler and Fixtures Complete.**

FOUNTAIN AIR BRUSH.

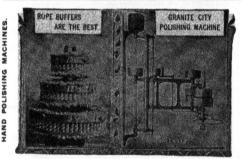

Vol. X. No. 6

ranite

M. HUNT & CO.

PUBLISHERS

Devonshire Street

STON, MASS., U.S.A.

cription Price, $1.00 Year

ADVERTISERS' DIRECTORY.

Reports on Troy Granite.

ORDNANCE DEPARTMENT, U. S. A.

Report of Mechanical Tests Made with U. S. Testing Machine, Capacity 800,000 Pounds, at Watertown Arsenal, Mass., April 15th, 1891.

FOR TROY GRANITE COMPANY, WORCESTER, MASS.

Test by Compression of One Six-Inch Cube of Troy Granite.

Compressed Surfaces faced with Plaster of Paris to secure even bearings.

TEST NUMBER.	DIMENSIONS.		SECTIONAL AREA.	ULTIMATE STRENGTH.	
	LENGTH.	COMPRESSED SURFACE.		TOTAL LBS.	LBS PER SQ. IN.
7419	5.95	5.84 | 5.90	35.01	630.100	17.950

First crack at 525,000 lbs.
Pyramidal fracture.

Correct :
J. E. HOWARD.

D. W. FLAGLER,
Lieut. Col. Ordnance Dept., U. S. A., Commanding.

Chemical Laboratory, Worcester Polytechnic Institute.

CERTIFICATE OF ANALYSIS.

GENTLEMEN :   WORCESTER, MASS., May 4, 1891.

The sample of Troy Granite submitted to me for examination contains :

Silica,	73.15 per cent.
Alumina and Iron Oxide,	17.04 " "
Lime,	0.81 " "
Magnesia,	0.30 " "
Potassium Oxide,	5.74 " "
Sodium Oxide,	2.05 " "
Loss and Undetermined,	0.91 " "
Total,	100.00

Respectfully yours,

TO TROY GRANITE CO.   LEONARD P. KINNICUTT, PH. D.

ALL TOGETHER.

Every piece finished and FITTED under personal supervision and shipped from the same place at the same time.

Don't allow your orders to be peddled to parties you would not patronize yourself.—A guarantee of replacing defective work is very good, but—it pleases your customer better to have it right FIRST TIME.

We will make it an object—and no expense—for every dealer unacquainted to carry our samples of the HARDWICK GRANITE,—The Darkest Fine Grained Stock and Absolutely Free From Iron

WRITE FOR SHEETS OF COMPARATIVE PRICES.

25 Years Experience in the Business.

GEO. D. BAILEY, Hardwick, Vt.

ARE YOU

▬▬WEDDED TO ANY PARTICULAR CONCERN?

If not give **US** a share of your patronage.

We can name you prices on

🌸 *Polished Work*

that will fairly daze you. All our work guaranteed.

Hopkins, Huntington & Co.,
Quarry Owners and Manufacturers. BARRE, VERMONT.

ESTABLISHED 1857. QUARRIES, QUINCY, MASS., BARRE, VT.

McDonnell & Sons,
Lock Box 85, - Quincy, Mass.

**Quarry Owners, Polishers
and Manufacturers of the Finest**

DARK BLUE QUINCY AND DARK BARRE

GRANITES.

Rough Stock FURNISHED TO THE TRADE.

GRANITE

ENTERED AT THE BOSTON POST OFFICE AS SECOND-CLASS MAIL MATTER.

Vol. X.   **BOSTON, MASS., JUNE 1, 1900.**   **No. 6**

A. M. HUNT, EDITOR.

Published Monthly in the interests of the Producer,
Manufacturer, and Retailer of Granite as used
for Monumental or Building Purposes.

Terms of Subscription

To ANY PART OF THE UNITED STATES OR CANADA:
One copy, one year - - - - $1.00, in advance.
One copy, six months - - -   75 cents, in advance.
ADVERTISING RATES FURNISHED UPON APPLICATION.

A. M. HUNT & CO., Publishers,
131 DEVONSHIRE STREET, - - BOSTON, MASS.

ELOW we publish a letter which
will no doubt prove interesting to
many :

Springfield, O., April 16, 1900.
The Monumental News.

Dear Sir:—A friend has handed me a copy of
"Granite" for April and called my attention to a reply
to a letter published in the February number of The
Monumental News. I do not seek a controversy with
the editor of "Granite," for I could not hope to cope
with him at so great a disadvantage, he, having the
control of his own columns, and no censorship would
prevail against his utterances, whilst I would have to
depend on the kindness of others for the publishing of
whatever comment I felt disposed to make.

I think, however, his editorial invites a reply, and
relying on your kindness to put it into print, I will
make an effort to show the reasons for the views set
forth in my former communication.

I have always considered "Trade Journals" the most
efficient helpers, and instructors that could have been
devised, whose influence when rightly directed molds
public opinion in Art Memorials, elevating the standard of excellence of the work produced and making
the producers better workmen and more liberal minded
men. But Trade Journals whose influence is thus felt
are not governed solely by the "love of gain," to such
an extent that they are willing to permit their visions
to be eclipsed when the right is assailed. They take no
part in that selfish prayer of the old deacon :

> "Lord bless me and my wife
> My son John and his wife
> Us four and no more."

But looking upon their vocation in a higher light
seek to do the greatest good to the greatest number,
although for the present a few paltry dollars may be
diverted from their coffers. Such journals need no
"protection," desire none, content in the belief that
what they have sent forth to the world will be as bread
cast upon the waters which in due time will be returned.

On the other hand the system of "Key" publications
bears upon its face a most pernicious influence, particularly when coupled in many cases with that other
enemy to true business interests, the frequent wholesale scattering of cheap priced designs, putting them
into the hands of unprincipled agents who are filling
our beautiful cemeteries with monumental monstrosities to the sore hurt and detriment of legitimate and
experienced manufacturers and dealers, and to the injury of all that is good, beautiful and elevating in fine
artistic memorials. They thus pander to a class who
care not what they sell nor how much they stand in
the way of progress towards a higher and better grade
of work.

The department store catalogue with its price-list of
monuments is far less injurious to the business of the
retail dealer than is the trade journal that makes a
practice of publishing designs with sizes and prices attached. It is the principle involved against which I
protest.   I. H. KELLEY.

If Mr. Kelley did not desire criticism he should refrain from writing letters for publication upon subjects on which he is not thoroughly posted. If Mr. Kelley has seen fit to forward his letter, or letters, direct to us, we should have published them in full, as we are not afraid of his criticisms; therefore he is not placed at a disadvantage and he simply assumes that they would have been censored, and no doubt he feels that they should have been. We do not believe that anyone is in a position to criticise our publication who is an acknowledged non-subscriber and simply depends upon his friends for securing a copy of the paper which he is pleased to criticise. We defy Mr. Kelley to prove that we have published in our journal monuments which are not artistic. The original designs which we publish are drawn for us by what we consider one of the best and most practical designers in the business, and those which are illustrated from photographs we know and are told that they are the best than can be secured. If Mr. Kelley can, upon a thorough perusal of our year's edition, which no doubt he will not peruse on account of his not desiring to become a subscriber, state that if there has been anything better published in any of the trade journals since trade journals were published in the business, we will then try not to believe what others tell us who are better posted than ourselves. We fail to see exactly wherein Mr. Kelley draws a line between publishing sizes under a key, for which we have plainly stated our reasons, and printing them out in full. Cheap priced designs we never have published, as we stated above, and if Mr. Kelley will point out in any of our papers which we have published in the last two or three years "monumental monstrosities" or anything in the way of illustrations which have been in any sense an injury to the trade, we will feel that we have labored in vain, for we have put into this department the best that is in us. We think that Mr. Kelley is perfectly honest in what he says, but in this case he is talking without knowledge and simply is bearing in mind some design sheets which he receives from some wholesale dealers.

🌣

WITH a sigh of relief we are glad to say that the labor troubles are about over as far as the monumental part of the granite business is concerned, with the exception of Westerly, R. I., and before this paper goes to press we are in hopes that a settlement will have been made there also. The members of the Granite Cutters' Union and the manufacturers are having meetings together, and no doubt as other places have settled it will not be long before Westerly will settle also. The settlement at Quincy is thoroughly explained under Quincy Notes. It is very satisfactory from the standpoint of the length of time for which the settlement is made, namely, five years. Every year since our connection with the business there has been trouble ahead which has served more to retard the development of the granite business than anything in the way of hard times or other complications. Those who contemplate building new cutting plants, developing quarries, or adding to their quarry or cutting plant anything in the

way of improved machinery were always held back by the cry of strike if certain demands were not granted; but now the way is clear for five years at least. We are informed that although everything seemed to be smooth and pleasant as far as the Quincy settlement was concerned, the last meeting was an all night session and came within a very narrow margin of precipitating trouble, the result of which could not have been foreseen. Not only would it have included Quincy, but all other points in the granite business. Barre is having trouble with the granite polishers, and there seems to be an inclination on the part of the polishers to settle. There is another matter to be settled, that is the usual half holiday on Saturdays. This, no doubt, will be settled by the individual firms. Those who are pushed with work will no doubt keep their plants open on Saturdays and those who can will close them. The half holiday on Saturday is almost as much a necessity for the manufacturer as for the workmen. It gives the workmen a period of rest and it gives the manufacturer a chance to clean up his shed, attend to office work which may have been neglected and do other things which are necessary. No doubt during the warm months of summer there will be a general closing up. At the centres where building granite is produced there have been settlements made, notably at North Jay, Me., where two hundred workmen are employed, among which were seventy stone-cutters that were affected with the trouble. The cutters at West Sullivan, Me., are out, the manufacturers having refused to sign the schedule presented by the union. Work at Norcross Bros. Granite Co. at Stone Creek has been resumed, settlement having been made satisfactory to the stone-workers which gives them an eight hour day and a minimum price of 33 to 35 cents an hour. The situation at Frankfort, Me., where the Mount Waldo Granite Co.'s quarries are located, are still complicated, as non-union men are employed in the quarries; less than two hundred men are now at work and of course the work on hand is progressing very slowly. Non-union men are constantly at war with the union men and rows are frequent. The company had recently made two contracts, involving $3,000,000 in all, and of course the two hundred men will be insufficient to carry out the contracts. Everything has been settled as far as labor troubles at Milford, N. H., is concerned and the business is running smoothly. In other words, all labor troubles as far as the granite business is concerned, both in the monumental and building departments, are about over. (Later) We are just notified that settlement has been made at Westerly, R. I., on the following basis:

1. Eight hours to constitute a day's work.

2. Thirty-five cents per hour minimum wage for competent men; aged, incapacitated and incompetent men, not less than 33 cents an hour, and employers at no time shall employ more than 25 per cent of their men for less than 35 cents per hour, the percentage to apply strictly to day work.

3. Competent men, and men of extra abilities, 35 to 40 cents and over, as may be agreed upon.

4. Piece work at the option of the employers.

5. Fifteen per cent general rise on the piece bill of 1899.

6. Pay day every two weeks, with one week "lie time."

7. At any contention which may arise during the period this agreement is in force as to the performance in good faith of section 2 by the employers or employes, there shall be a joint committee appointed by the branch and employers, the employers to give all necessary information.

8. The bill of prices to remain in force until March 1, 1903.

Should any change be desired three months' notice is to be given previous to that date.

A meeting of the employers' and tool sharpeners' committee was held May 21, when a bill for 33 1-2 cents an hour, for an eight-hour day, was signed.

*

Detroit's Great Plan for a Monument.

The plan for a monument to commemorate the two-hundredth anniversary of the foundation of the city of Detroit, Mich., is stupendous and magnificent. The American artists who coöperated in the making of the design are of the most eminent members of their respective professions—Stanford White, architect; Augustus St. Gaudens and Frederick Macmonnies, sculptors; Dwight W. Tryon and Thomas W. Dewing, painters. The location, on an island in the Detroit River, is excellent. The design calls for a Doric column twenty-four feet in diameter at its base, and two hundred and twenty feet high, surrounded by groups of sculptors in the water, within the court of a marble colonnade 900 feet long, with a wing at each end 300 feet long. The colonnade will furnish places for statues of Cadillac and others noted in the eventful history of Detroit. Above the colonnade on the land side opportunity will be afforded to construct an artificial lake fed by decorative fountains, with an ornamental aquarium and horticultural building at either side. The top of the column will be accessible to visitors, commanding an interesting view; and it will be marked by a flash light at night. The cost of the work will be one million dollars. The funds are to be raised by popular subscription. We have no doubt they will be raised, for the majestic character of the scheme, its splendid site, and the appeal that the project must make to every patriotic citizen of Michigan, cannot fail to assure a general and generous response.—Boston Transcript.

*

Mutilation of Public Memorials.

The Washington correspondent of the New York Sun makes some extraordinary statements concerning the mischief done in the Washington monument by barbarians who regard themselves as civilized men and women. A few days ago a bridegroom, visiting the place with his bride, broke off with his heavy cane the head of a miniature Diana, one of the ornaments of a memorial tablet. He picked up the fragment and gave it to his bride to carry home as a souvenir of Washing-

ton. A park policeman saw the act, took away the head and took bridegroom and bride to the police station. The local magistrate fined the man $1 for destroying public property. The head cannot be replaced.

An examination has since been made of the actual condition of the memorial stones, many of them noble gifts of great artistic beauty from foreign nations, in honor of the great Washington. The investigation shows that of 177 memorial tablets there are only seven that remain unmutilated, and these are the plainest, with little lettering and no ornamentation. The wantouly injured stones can never be replaced or restored. Some beautiful stones, elaborately ornamented, have been so mutilated that they are eye-sores. The superintendent of public buildings and grounds says that the records show that eight out of ten of these vulgar vandals who are caught prove to be ministers visiting Washington on excursions. We should say that a minister who would do such an act deserved to be dismissed from his church and have his license to preach revoked. It is a more unmanly crime than some for which church members are excommunicated.

Colonel Bingham, the superintendent, will make a report to Congress recommending the passage of a new statute against it with severe penalties. This comes late. What has the superintendent been about all these years while irreparable mischief was doing? We suggest a month in jail as a part of the penalty, not to be remitted. This might have some deterrent influence upon ministers and bridegrooms.

The strike in Quincy is ended and business has been again resumed; the settlement reached is a most satisfactory one, and the manufacturers and cutters believe it to be the best of any made in New England, from the fact that it runs for five years, and everybody knows just what to expect during that term at least. Manufacturers can figure upon work in one year, to be delivered the next year, knowing as they will just what they will have to pay for labor. Work was resumed in all yards on Monday, May 7; and while the manufacturers were not over-burdened with orders, they all had some work on hand. They were not able, however, to give employment to all the cutters who desired it, and only the best workmen have been employed. It will take several months to get business in good running order again, and as business picks up men will be put on. Many of the cutters who left town during the nine weeks of the strike and obtained work elsewhere in New England are returning to Quincy, which is, in itself, evidence enough that the men are satisfied with the settlement made. The first step toward the final settlement was made on April 26. when meetings of the two cutters' branches were held.

Just what was done at these meetings was not given out, other than their committee was instructed to hold another conference with the manufacturers' committee. This conference was held on the afternoon of May 1. In the absence of the chairman, Andrew Milne of Milne & Chalmers occupied the chair. The situation was discussed at length and both sides renewed their former propositions, and the meeting adjourned. That evening the regular meeting of the Granite Manufacturers' Association was held and the strike situation was the one matter discussed. The result was that the manufacturers instructed its committee to hold another conference and draw up a proposition for them to submit to the cutters. The conference was held May 2, and the proposition submitted by the manufacturers' committee. It was immediately accepted by the cutters' committee, who, however, said their action must be ratified by the unions. This, the unions did, at a meeting held the following day.

The news that the cutters had voted to accept the manufacturers' proposition was received with many a sigh of relief in Quincy. On the following Friday evening the two committees met again to sign the bill. There were many minor details to adjust in the price-list and two committees kept at it all night, their labors not being completed until after 5 o'clock the following morning. While the committees were in session a group of reporters held forth in an adjoining room ready to send the news broadcast throughout the world. As the hours slowly wore away these reporters became uneasy and tired, and doubtless thought many unkind things about the committee that they did not hurry faster. At 3 o'clock, seeing no prospect of getting the news in the morning papers, they left for home, leaving the committee still in session.

The agreement, as finally signed by Andrew Milne, representing the manufacturers, and Alexander C. Smith, representing the cutters, was as follows:

ARTICLE I.—It is hereby agreed by and between the Granite Manufacturers' Association of Quincy, Mass., and the Quincy Branches of the Granite Cutters' National Union that the bill of prices agreed upon shall remain in force until March 1st, 1903, without change, and two additional years under the following conditions:

If either party desires a change, to take effect March 1st, 1903, they shall submit their demands to the other body not later than December 1st, 1902. Committees shall immediately be appointed to consider and act upon the changes desired, and all matters not fully adjusted by January 20th, 1903, shall be referred to a board of arbitration, and no suspension of work shall ensue.

The composition and duties of said board to be as follows: To be composed of three members from each side, whose first duty will be to appoint two disinterested persons, one to be appointed by each side, and these two to choose a third disinterested party to act as arbiter. The board thus constituted shall consider and decide all matters referred to it and in all cases where the arbiter is called upon to render a decision it shall be the right of the members of the board to present all evidence bearing on the question.

The board to render a decision on all matters not later than February 25th, which shall be final and binding.

The expense attending said board to be apportioned equally to the two bodies.

Should no notice of desired change be submitted by December 1st, 1902, the present bill of prices to continue in force until March 1st, 1905, and from year to year thereafter, unless a notice of desired change be submitted by December 1st of any year.

ARTICLE II.—It is also agreed that all disputes arising in regard to this scale of prices shall be referred to the joint figuring committee, consisting of three workmen and three manufacturers, who shall meet each alternate week. They shall hear the case, and failing to agree by a two-thirds vote, shall proceed to choose a disinterested party to act as arbitrator, who shall be chosen by at least a two-thirds vote of each committee. Said arbitrator to hear the case and make a decision within two weeks, which shall be final. Said committee shall keep a record of all decisions. The association losing the case to pay the expense of the arbitrator.

All other disputes shall be referred to the joint executive committee, who shall render a decision within twenty-one days, or upon failure to agree by a two-thirds vote, shall proceed to choose an arbitrator, as provided for in Section 1 of this article.

Pending arbitration it is mutually agreed that there shall be no strike lockout or suspension of work during the term of this bill of prices, except as provided in Article 7 of miscellaneous.

ARTICLE III.—To more effectually enforce the provisions of this agreement and bill of prices, it is hereby mutually agreed by and between the Granite Manufacturers' Association and the branches of the Granite Cutters' National Union of Quincy, Mass., that any member of said association or branches of said union found intentionally violating said agreements or bill of prices, or offering or paying less, or offering to, or found working for less than the sums and prices named therein, shall cease to be a member of said association or branches of said union, until they comply with the conditions as made by the joint executive committee. If the workman and employer disagree, and each believe their construction of the bill or their figures correct, they shall refer the matter to the joint figuring committees and upon their decision correct the price.

ARTICLE IV.—The foregoing articles, numbered I. to III. inclusive, with the accompanying bill of prices for granite cutters and tool sharpeners, including cuts and former decision of joint boards (changed to conform thereto), are hereby agreed to and ratified by the authorized committees of the Granite Manufacturers' Association of Quincy, and the Quincy branches of the Granite Cutters' National Union, who are empowered by their associations to make these settlements.

The settlement of the bill of prices was that of 1899, as a basis upon which an increase of fourteen per cent was made. In computing the same on each item where a fraction of a cent appears a whole cent is to be allowed. The other changes and additions in the price-list were as follows:

BOTTOM BASES.

ARTICLE 11 (New).—If the top bed of a bottom base has to be lowered so that the stone will be a required thickness both beds will be paid for.

MOULDINGS.

ARTICLE 28 (New).—Corners taken off wash of rock-faced bases 1 inch each way, per lin. ft., 10c.

MARGIN LINES ON ROCK-FACE WORK.

ARTICLE 23 (New).—A hammered wash dropping 3 inches or over on a rock-faced base, pay for pitched lines on bottom of wash and corners, per lin. ft., 6c.

MISCELLANEOUS.

ARTICLE 1.—The pay of a competent workman shall be 35 cents per hour, but in cases where a workman cannot earn that amount on the basis of this price-list he may be employed at his average rate per hour, to be in no case less than 33 cents.

ARTICLE 2.—All work not specified in this bill shall be cut by the hour, with the exception of carving, draped urns, draped shafts, and draped crosses; but in no case shall this be construed to mean that a stone which can be figured by the bill of prices, with the exception of carving, may be cut as a special bargain. All work not covered by the bill of prices to be subject to the inspection of a joint committee.

ARTICLE 3.—Eight hours shall constitute a day's work.

ARTICLE 6.—Diagram and price on same to be given with stone when practicable, in all cases within two days, but in case of a man starting in a yard diagram with price marked thereon to be given when stone is taken up unless arrangements have been made to work by the day.

BLACKSMITHS.

ARTICLE 1.—Eight hours to constitute a day's work.

ARTICLE 2.—Thirteen men shall constitute a gang at 36 1-2 cents per hour (if extra men are employed, the right to substitute is allow) or $2.90 per eight hours' work.

ARTICLE 3.—All extra men to be 22 1-3 cents per day per man.

ARTICLE 4.—All piece men to be 25 cents per day per man, no deduction to be made for less than one day's absence.

ARTICLE 5, 6, 7, 8.—No change.

Terms of settlement same as stone-cutters.

Hours to be worked, 8 to 12 A.M., 1 to 5 P.M.

Hardly had the men returned to work when National Secretary Duncan of the Cutters' Union, who has all along been opposed to the settlement made in Quincy, and who, it is alleged, has uttered dire threats against the Quincy branches should they settle for less than a 35 cent minimum, made himself manifest by notifying the two Quincy unions that they were requested to surrender their charters. This action did not please the members of the unions at all, and it is reported that they held a mass meeting on Sunday, May 13, at which his request was considered, and it was decided to invite Secretary Duncan to come to Quincy and state his reason for refusing to sanction the Quincy agreement and demanding their charter. The regular meeting of the unions was held on the following Wednesday when it was expected that Mr. Duncan would be present, but for reasons best known to himself, he failed to appear. At this meeting, among other matters, it was voted to stand by the agreement made of a 33 cent minimum and a 35 cent average for eight hours.

The Quincy cutters can not understand how Secretary Duncan can sanction the Barre, Vermont, agreement, which is a 35 cent average, and refuse Quincy, which is also a 35 cent average, and a minimum of 33 cents. It is said that in spite of the fact, which everybody admits, that Barre, Vermont, settled for a 35 cent average, Mr. Duncan declares it was a 35 cent minimum and he was opposed to Quincy settling for less than a 35 cent minimum. The Quincy cutters further claim that Secretary Duncan has no authority to demand the surrender of their charter, which can only be done by a majority vote of the unions throughout the country. Quincy Union has always been loyal to the National Unions and is furthermore one of the strongest unions in the country and it is not believed that they will be forced to surrender their charter, and if they are, it is believed that they will do so before they will bend to what is termed the return of the National secretary. Nothing new has developed since the regular meeting of the cutters May 9.

Although Quincy was suffering from the effects of a strike last month, the shipment of granite did not give any indication of it, for the total amount shipped was 12,547,243 pounds more than in March. The largest increase was over the Quarry Railroad, which showed a gain of 9,846,210 pounds. West Quincy showed a gain of 3,888,360 pounds and Quincy Adams a loss of 1,187,327 pounds. The figures for April were: Quarry Railroad, 22,920,000 pounds; West Quincy, 8,498,660 pounds; Quincy Adams, 5,432,398 pounds; total, 36,-851,058 pounds.

A trip through the cutting district found all the manufacturers feeling happy that the strike had been ended and that business had settled down once more. Nearly all the manufacturers have a few orders on hand, but it is all small work. Practically, there is no large work in Quincy at present other than that mentioned previous to the strike. The manufacturers do not feel at all down-hearted, however, as they feel that it will not be long before some of the big jobs in the market are landed for Quincy to cut.

The granite polishers of Quincy, who have no organization, are taking steps to form a polishers' branch of the union.

Kavanagh Bros. & Co. are employing twenty cutters and have a number of fine jobs under way in Westerly and Quincy granite.

John Horrigan, who for some time has been connected with F. Barnicoat as modeler and carver, has started in business. We cheerfully recommend Mr.

Horrigan to the trade as a man thoroughly acquainted with the business. He will make a specialty of granite figures and modeling in clay.

We reported, in the May issue, that the firm of Mc-Donnell & Sons had been dissolved, Thomas H. Mc-Donnell retiring from the firm, and that Mrs. Emily A. McDonnell, wife of the late John Q. McDonnell, Buffalo, the remaining partner had purchased the assets of the firm and would continue the business at Quincy and Buffalo. It was also reported that James S. McDonnell, who has been connected with the Quincy office for some years, contemplated forming a stock company. An option was given to him and said option has expired without anything having been done in that direction. We are in a position to state that the business of McDonnell & Sons, at Quincy, will be continued on a much larger scale than heretofore under the new management. Mrs. Emily A. McDonnell is well-known to all connected with the granite business as having assumed the management of the Buffalo business upon the death of her husband and has, by her ability and push, not only retained the business, but largely increased it. There are not many instances of this kind on record, and Mrs. McDonnell deserves great credit for what she has done. Of course it has required close application and long hours of work to have brought about the present prosperous conditionof business. The services of George H. Ruxton, of the firm of McIver & Ruxton, Barre, Vt., have been engaged as superintendent for the Quincy plant. We have known Mr. Ruxton ever since his first start in the granite business as a member of the firm of McLeod & Ruxton, and later McIver & Ruxton, and to those who know him he needs no introduction from us, but to those who do not we recommend him as a man with a thorough knowledge of the granite business and who built up the Barre business by push, hard work and ability, and we have no doubt he will meet with success in his new undertaking.

Monumental Gate of Exhibition a Monument of Ugliness.

The Eiffel Tower, ugly as sin in the daytime, is gloriously redeemed at night. Illuminated it is fair as an angel of light. It is to be hoped the same will prove true of the Exposition's Monumental Gate, for by day it would be the ugliest thing in Paris if there were no Eiffel Tower. It is unworthy of the simple majesty of the Place de la Concorde, in which it is situated, and unworthy of the matchless architectural spectacle which it precedes. Paris, quick to sense and label the absurd, has named it "The Salamander" ("La Salamandre") from its pronounced resemblance to a species of up-to-date, economical parlor heater. The recent crowning of this unlovely gate with an enormous painted image of a Parisienne in street attire, as much out of keeping with the gate, which is Oriental in style, as the gate is with the Place de la Concorde, evoked from the public and the press howls of anger and derision which do infinite credit to their taste. Several

direct demands for the removal of the statue have been made. The ministry, forced by the hue and cry to take cognizance of the matter, has solemnly declared that it will not take action since it is for "the people" to decide the fate of the Parisienne. How the people are to register and enforce their decision the ministry cunningly fails to specify, and, as it is not to be supposed "the people" will go to the (almost justifiable) length of toppling the offending object over, the incident may be considered closed. The retention of this monumental horror is the more unpardonable in that it is located in a corner of the Exposition grounds where nothing is demanded architecturally, and where a simple, inconspicuous, vine-covered turnstile would answer all æsthetic as well as practical ends.

Every exposition that has ever been has had one or more egregrious blunders to answer for. The Salamander is the blunder of the Exposition of 1900. I have gone out of my way to denounce it as I daily go out of my way to avoid passing beneath it, in order to clear it off the ground, so to speak, before beginning the descriptions of the exposition's wonders which will be necessarily in order soon. There! A disagreeable duty is done!—Boston Transcript.

The contract for the erection of the Ehret Mausoleum which amounts to $50,000 has been awarded to Wells & Lamson.

George Ruxton, of the firm of McIver & Ruxton, has accepted a position as superintendent and manager for the firm of McDonnell & Sons, Quincy, Mass., of which business Mrs. Emily A. McDonnell is the sole partner in both the Quincy and Buffalo business.

During the last two weeks business has shown signs of greater prosperity than have appeared before during the present year and indeed, more business is being done here than at any other time for a long while. Large orders for work are on the books of almost every concern which pretends to do any amount of business and all of the little firms are having all they can do to keep up with the orders which they receive. All around there has been a grand hustle on the orders calling for shipment before Memorial Day and as a general rule they have been shipped before this writing. There has been quite a considerable work done here for Memorial Day this year, and some of it has been work of a costly order. The general class of work this season has seemed to be somewhat above the average on both size and the amount of carving to be done. The bill of prices which was agreed to between the Union and the Association has been signed for the period of three years, and consequently we are safe from any trouble from anything of that sort for that

length of time. The strike of the polishers, however, has remained unsettled up to this time. Quite a few of the manufacturers of Montpelier and several of this city have signed the bill, but it is generally opposed on account of the clause which does not allow an apprentice in any plant unless there are four machines. Under this rule there would not be a half dozen apprentices in both cities and it seems that in a short time the polishers would have things all their own way as there would be only a few places where a man could learn the business. Consequently the manufacturers, as a rule, are refusing to sign the bill, and it is quite probable that the men will be back at work in the near future. Not that we pretend to say that there is no virtue in the demands of the polishers, for we think they are entitled to an eight hour day as much as the cutters, but this clause in their demands makes a very unfavorable impression, not only upon the manufacturer, but also upon the general public, in that it gives the impression that they are attempting to "corner the market," so to speak.

We hope, however, that some settlement will be made soon, so that there may be nothing to retard the progress in the business which has started along so promisingly this season.

Arrangements have been made by the firm of Barclay Brothers to install themselves in the plant which they have recently purchased of the late firm of Mackie, Hussey & Co., about the first of June. They have some large work yet to be finished at their old plant, but will have all the jobs which it will not be practicable to move, finished and shipped before the time for moving will have arrived. They have a large amount of large work on their books, and quite a quantity which will have to be sent to be finished when they go to their new quarters. There they will have ample room for the large amount of business which they will carry on, and they will do a larger work than they have ever done before. Already they have made arrangements to increase the force of cutters by about one-third of their present number.

They report that work is "booming." Anyone at all acquainted with Mr. Barclay knows what he means by that. Orders are coming in rapidly and steadily and the best of it is the money seems to be ready when the work is done. There is a good deal of difference in the ways of a manufacturer when he is getting his returns promptly.

Then business seems to be good and he has no fault to find, and this is the condition of most of the firms of this city and especially at this time of the firm in question.

The hustling firm of McIver & Ruxton have their plant well filled with monuments of almost every description, and ranging from jobs having a bottom base 12x8 to a small marker. At this time they have six or eight large jobs, one having the bottom base as indicated above and a die of corresponding dimensions, upon which there is extensive carving, and another having a cluster of four finely hammered columns on each corner of the die. This is an elegant job, and one of good size too, it having a bottom base 11x8 and the die being 6 ft. 9 in. x 3 ft. 10 in.

Nearly all of the work which they have on hand and now under the hammer is all hammered work, thus making it easy for them to get along during the strike of the polishers. They report that they have been in receipt of orders during the past few weeks quite a deal in excess of the amount usually received at this season, it being just before the work for Memorial Day is all finished and shipped. Everything seems to look favorable for one of the best seasons which the industry has ever known, and this concern is in a position to take advantage of the conditions by working more men and making every day and hour count for all it is worth.

Emslie & McLeod have on their books a large amount of orders for first-class jobs, some of which they are now finishing for shipment. Some of their jobs are of sarcophagus design and are large and elegantly carved. Orders are coming in quite rapidly at this time, and there seems to be every reason to believe that the coming season will be one of the best which they have ever had since they have been in business. Shipments for the Memorial Day trade have been large this year, and some of the jobs which they have sent out have been large and very pretty. About the usual number of men are being employed by the concern and they have work enough on their books to keep them busy for quite a time.

We are informed that Mr. W. E. Hussey, of the late firm of Mackie, Hussey & Co., who have just sold out their plant to Barclay Brothers, will enter the employ of the purchasing firm and that Mr. Mackie will retire from business.

The partnership which has heretofore existed between J. E. Sanguinetti and E. Carusi has been dissolved by mutual agreement, and the business will be continued by Mr. Sanguinetti. The same class of work will be carried on as in the past, and a specialty will be made of carving and statuary. They have on their books quite a quantity of orders, and six or seven statues are under the hammer. Among these are statues of Hope, Soldier at parade rest, and Contentment. The work done by this concern is of the highest order and is admired by all lovers of fine statuary. The carving done is of the best style known to the art and in every way gives the trade entire satisfaction. Mr. Sanguinetti is now employing about one gang of cutters and will put on more in the near future, if business keeps up to the point it now is.

Robins Brothers have their plant well filled with stock which they are working in to all sorts and styles of monuments and they have also a good assortment of orders on their books. Business is good and the prospect seems to be very bright for the future. They shipped quite a quantity of finished work for Memorial Day and have several pretty jobs nearly ready for shipment at this writing.

The Ingersoll-Sergeant Drill Co., New York and Boston, had all its air compressors at the Paris Expo-

Continued on page 27.

"GRANITE," JUNE, 1900.

TABLET . . . . . R — Y x $\begin{cases} C -.N x Y - T - \text{TOP} \\ A - A x Y - C Y \text{ BOTTOM} \end{cases}$

BASE . . . . . . C — Y x R — P x C — C Y

Cap . . . . Y — G x R — T x C — T
Die . . . . A — N x R — T x C — T
Bottom of Die . . . . . . A — N x R — C Y x C — C C
Base . . . . V — C V x P — N x A — I
Bottom Base . . . . C — A x E — T x R — T
Carving R Inches Wide All Around

"Granite," June, 1900.

Die	R — R x R — T½ x C — G½
Base	V — C V½ x P — T x A — T
Bottom Base	C — C x E — T x R — P

WILLIAM H. LEARNARD, JR.
JAN. 8. 1828
JUNE 21. 1895.

"GRANITE," JUNE, 1900.

TABLET . . . . R — C Y x A — A
TOP . . . . Y — C C
BOTTOM . . . . C — P

Continued from page 18.

sition erected and ready to run on the opening day, being the first American exhibitor to operate and the first exhibitor from any country to run its exhibit by steam. Mr. John J. Swann, late Associate Editor of Engineering News, is in charge of this exhibit.

Notes of Ornament No. 4.

BY HERBERT W. BEATTIE, SC.

The next historic style is the Greek. We see that Egyptian ornament was derived from natural inspiration, that it was founded on a few types, and that it remained unchanged during the whole course of Egyptian civilization, except in the more or less perfection of the execution. Greek art, borrowed partly from the Egyptian, was a development of an old idea in a new direction, and, unrestrained by religious laws, it rose rapidly to a high state of perfection and Art becomes now for the first time purely æsthetic. It is, in fact, the substitution of the æsthetic principle in place of the symbolic that constitutes the originality of Greek art, and the perfection of pure form is carried to a point which has never since been reached. It is meaningless, purely decorative, never representative, and can hardly be said to be constructive; for the various members of a Greek monument rather present surfaces exquisitely designed to receive ornament, which they, at first, painted, and in later times both carved and painted. The ornament was no part of the construction, as with the Egyptians; it could be removed and the structure remain unchanged.

On the Corinthian capital the ornament is applied, not constructed; it is not so on the Egyptian capital. There we feel the whole capital is the ornament:—to remove any portion of it would destroy it.

In the well-known honeysuckle ornament it is difficult to recognize any attempt at imitation. What is evident is, the Greeks, in their ornament, were close observers of nature, and although they did not copy or attempt to imitate, they worked on the same principles.

The three great laws which we find everywhere in nature—radiation from the parent stem, equal distribution of areas, and the tangential curvature of lines—are always obeyed, and the perfection with which they are obeyed is only realized by an attempt to reproduce Greek ornament, rarely done with success.

A very characteristic feature of this style, continued by the Romans, is, the various parts of a scroll grow out of each other in a continuous line.

The three historic periods of Greek art are the Doric, Alexandrian or Ionic, and Corinthian, and the distinctive ornament of these three periods is the capital.

The Doric capital consists of a round flat cushion, called the echinus, and a large square abacus, the lower diameter of the echinus being that of the pillar, its upper that of the abacus. The cushion is called the echinus from its being invariably painted with that ornament. As this ornament is so constant, the Doric order may be descriptively termed the echinus order;

and the echinus is the principal ornament of the period, with the wave scroll, the fret, the zig-zag, the anthemion, and occasionally the astragal; foliage performs a very secondary part in Greek ornament.

The second Greek period enriches all these forms, and some are made more familiar, as the astragal, the spiral, the guilloche, the acanthus; and in a very simple way the scroll as a succession of reversed spirals. It further carved the ornaments instead of painting them as was the custom in the Doric period.

The Ionic capital now supplants the Doric; and the volutes are added to the echinus, the characteristic ornament of the Doric capital.

After the establishment of the Ionic order, in which the volute is so prominent, we find the curved lines being more in harmony with the volute.

The ordinary scroll and acanthus are kept subdued in Greek work in comparison with the echinus, anthemion, etc., as the former are more characteristic of Roman than Greek art.

In the Corinthian period the acanthus capital was used with slightly more acanthus foliage. The capital was called "Corinthian" from its reported discovery by Callimachus of Corinth.

The Acanthus order, so little used by the Greeks, was a favorite with the Romans. The only Greek scroll worthy of the name is a very simple one on the roof of the choragic monument of Lysicrates.

The most simple form of the scroll is of rare occurrence and there is always a great simplicity—both in the details and in the arrangement of the materials of Greek ornament; it is generally the various elements arranged in simple horizontal series, one row above the other, and when we consider that each stroke was done with a single touch of the brush, and that from the differences which appear we may be sure no mechanical aids were employed, we must be astonished at the high state of art which must have existed for artists to be found in such numbers able to execute with unerring truth what is almost beyond the skill of modern times even to copy, with the same happy result.

It is now almost universally recognized, that the white marble temples of the Greeks were entirely covered with painted ornament. Whatever doubts may exist as to the more or less coloring of the sculpture, there can be none as to the ornaments of the mouldings. The traces of color exist everywhere so strongly, that in taking plaster casts of the mouldings the traces of the pattern are strongly marked on the cast. What the particular colors were, however, is not so certain. Different authorities give them differently; where one sees green, another finds blue, or imagines gold where another sees brown. We may be quite certain, however, of one point—all these ornaments on the mouldings were so high from the ground, and so small in proportion to the distance from which they were seen, that they must have been colored in a manner to show them distinct and to bring out the design.

The next will be the third and last ancient style, the Roman, an enlargement and enrichment of the florid Greek.

(To be continued.)

A Question of Liability.

The case of Patrick Hoctor against Samuel Lavery, which, owing to the peculiar questions involved, has excited more than ordinary interest in its progress through the courts, has just been decided by the appellate division. The action grew out of the following circumstances:

Hugh Lavery, for many years a citizen of Glens Falls, N. Y., died in 1884. He left a will in which he made certain specific devices, and also set aside for his executor, in trust, the sum of $700 for the purpose of erecting a suitable monument over the remains of himself and mother. The surrogate appointed John Lavery, a brother of the testator, as administrator. The latter, pursuant to the provisions of the will, contracted for a monument with Mr. Hoctor, who at the time conducted a marble shop in Glens Falls.

John Lavery died on May 20, 1885, before the monument was erected or paid for, and on June 24, 1885, letters of administration, with will annexed, were issued. It was found that after the specific bequests and legacies had been paid, with the costs of administration and debts, there was no money belonging to the estate of Hugh Lavery to make up the trust fund provided by his will to build a monument.

John Lavery left a will in which he bequeathed to each of his four children, including the defendant, Samuel Lavery, the sum of $350, and making each of the legacies a charge upon a farm owned by him. He also gave Samuel Lavery a farm upon which he lives. The rest of the estate, real and personal, was left to the widow, who was named as executrix. She took possession of all of the property except the farm, and raised the money to pay the legacies by mortgaging the real estate.

Mr. Hoctor, finding that there was no money belonging to the Hugh Lavery estate, began proceedings to collect from the estate of John Lavery, to whom the monument had been sold, but the bequests made by John Lavery had been paid, and suit was brought against Samuel Lavery, one of the heirs, as a test case, for his proportionate share of the claim. The trial was had before a referee, who decided in favor of the plaintiff. An appeal was then taken to the appellate division, which sustains the findings of the referee.

At the trial the defendant contended that John Lavery was not personally responsible for the purchase price. Judge Herrick, who wrote the opinion, in which the other members of the appellate division concur, holds that the indebtedness incurred constituted a valid claim against John Lavery personally, and that Samuel Lavery, as one of the legatees, is liable for his proportionate share.

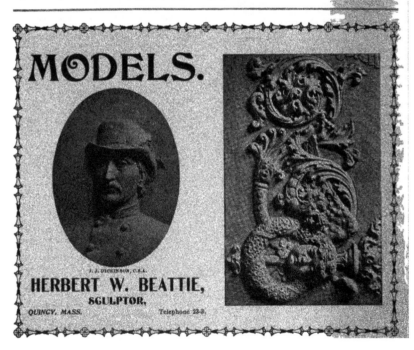

No Rest for Lincoln.

Concluded.

The question of opening the casket before the transfer to the temporary vault was raised, but it was decided not to do so. It may be opened before being placed in the new tomb.

The body and that of the other members of the family will remain in the temporary vault about a year, by which time it is expected the monument will be rebuilt.

The vault in Oak Ridge cemetery is in fact the eleventh resting place of Lincoln's body, and the seventh spot on which it has been deposited since it was brought to Springfield from Washington, thirty-five years ago. Upon the arrival of the remains at Springfield, they were taken from the Chicago and Alton depot to the hall of Representatives, in the state house, and there remained in state for several days. From Representative hall they were taken to Oak Ridge cemetery, and placed in the temporary receiving vault of the cemetery, where they were under a guard of soldiers for a long time. The body was next removed to a temporary vault on the side of a hill.

Next all that was mortal of Lincoln was taken to the sarcophagus inside the north part of the Lincoln monument, this constituting the third removal.

While here an attempt was made to steal the casket. After this the remains were secretly conveyed to the south side of the monument, carried through Memorial hall, and three well-known gentlemen were selected from the Lincoln guard of honor to secrete the casket. These three persons took the body into the superstructure of the monument and hid it in a narrow passage between two brick walls, which formed a part of the foundation of the monument, this constituted the fourth removal. The remains were removed a fifth time thirteen years ago, when they were taken from between the walls and placed in Memorial hall.

Here the casket was opened for the purpose of identification. The sixth removal occurred when the casket was placed in the bed of cement, from which it was removed March 10 and placed in a temporary vault beside the body of Mrs. Lincoln and the five other members of the Lincoln family, who had been entombed in the old monument.

On election night, 1876, an attempt was made by two men to steal the body. J. C. Powers was the custodian at the time. He had received intimation that such an attempt would be made, and watche l with the utmost diligence for several nights. On election night he was aroused by hearing noise of hammers, and hastily rushed to the door of the sepulcher. But the vandals heard him coming, and escaped. They had already forced the door into the tomb, and were at work on the casket. They were captured later, and inasmuch as the laws of Illinois did not provide any punishment for those who stole the dust of her dead, a case was made out for breaking the lock of the sepulcher, and they were sent to the penitentiary for one year. Some months after this the members of the Lincoln Guard of Honor took the casket and buried it in six feet of cement, beneath the crypt.

The new Lincoln monument will be a duplicate of the old one, except that it will be fifteen feet higher. Work on the monument was begun in 1869, and the last group of statuary was put up in 1883. Larkin G. Mead designed the monument, and it was built at a total cost of $215,000.

The tomb proper was in the north end of the monument. Six crypts were arranged side by side where the five members of the Lincoln family, who have already died, were originally placed. In the centre crypt were the remains of Lincoln. On the end of this casket, now that it has been exposed to view, may be seen in a semi-circle his immortal words, "With malice toward none; with charity for all." On the left of this crypt were the remains of his wife, and on the right, side by side, his three sons—Edward, who died before the war; William Wallace, who died at the White House at the age of 12, and Thomas, or Tad, who died in Chicago several years later at the age of 18. The unoccupied crypt was for Colonel Robert T. Lincoln.

At the south end of the base of the monument was memorial hall. Here was a bust of Lincoln, a cast of his right hand, with which he wrote the emancipation proclamation, one of the old chairs from his law office, surveying instruments which he used in early life in the regions round about Springfield, the powder horn worn by his grandfather, Abraham Lincoln, during the revolutionary war as a soldier from Virginia, and a variety of other valuable relics.

From four groups of statuary forming a square rose a plain granite shaft 100 feet high. The statue of Lincoln stood on a shaft thirty-five feet from the ground.
—Chicago Inter-Ocean.

Proposed Monuments and Monumental News.

RED WING, MINN.—The monument board of the fire department has decided to erect a monument over the graves of deceased firemen. It will consist of a pedestal inscribed with the names, surmounted by a statue of granite representing a fireman in full uniform. It will cost $750.

BAY CITY, MICH.—The movement started recently for the erection of a soldier's monument at Oak Ridge cemetery is making fairly good progress. The monument is to cost about $1,000.

PADUCAH, KY.—The Daughters of the American Revolution have a scheme on foot to erect a monument at some public place in the city, in memory of Gen. George Rogers Clark, a revolutionary hero.

BOSTON, MASS.—It is proposed to erect a gate at the entrance of the Charlestown Navy Yard. The gate will take the form of an arch to commemorate the deeds of the most famous naval heroes. $30,000 has been appropriated for the purpose by Congress. The plans call for a building the face of which will be of limestone or granite.

JERSEY CITY, N. J.—W. B. Cushing Command, No. 1, Union Veterans union are agitating the question of erecting a soldiers monument.

NEWPORT NEWS, VA.—The Daughters of the Confederacy are collecting money for a monument.

EPHRATA, PA.—Residents of Ephrata will complete the erection of a monument at that place to the memory of the revolutionary war soldiers who died at the Ephrata hospitals after the battle of Brandywine.

TOPEKA, KAN.—Articles of incorporation have been filed by the Halliday Monument Association which has been formed for the purpose of erecting a monument to the memory of Colonel Halliday.

MACON, GA.—A monument is to be erected to the memory of the late S. B. Price, mayor of this city for ; number of years. The city will probably contribute a large amount toward that end.

FREDERICKSBURG, MD.—A committee of lawyers, ministers and business men of Winchester, representing the Morgan Monument Association, of that city, visited Washington, D. C., recently, to secure the endorsement and co-operation of President McKinley in the plan to erect a monument over the grave of Gen. Daniel Morgan, the Revolutionary soldier buried in Mount Hebron Cemetery, that city.

PHILADELPHIA, PA.—An effort is being made to secure the necessary funds for the purpose of erecting a monument in memory of the army nurses of the civil war.

PASSAIC, N. J.—An association has been organized by the telegraph officers and operators of the Erie Railroad company and the Western Union Telegraph company to raise funds for the erection in Laurel Grove cemetery, Port Jervis, of a monument in memory of the late superintendent of telegraph, W. J. Holmes. The officers of the association are Chief Operator of the Erie C. D. Reed, president; Operator R. H. Carson, secretary; Chief Clerk S. S. Thompson, of New York, treasurer, and Manager J. H. Arnott, of Binghampton, vice-president. Each person will canvass his territory for popular subscriptions and it is hoped that $2,000 will be subscribed for the fund.

SIOUX CITY, IA.—The commission to provide for the erection of a monument to the memory of Sergeant Charles Floyd, the first Iowa soldier to fall on the Louisiana purchase territory, was appointed May 2. It consists of Hon. G. D. Perkins, Asa H. Burton, Hon. C. R. Marks, all of Sioux City, and Mitchell Vincest of Onawa and C. J. Holman of Sargent Bluffs. An appropriation of $5,000 was made by the legislature for the erection of the monument.

BALTIMORE, MD.—The Sons of the American Revolution have decided to go ahead at once with the erection of the proposed Maryland Revolutionary monument and not wait for an appropriation for the purpose by Congress. William Ridgely Griffith is chairman of the committee. The monument will cost about $20,000, of which the society has $15,000 in hand.

FORT WAYNE, IND.—The Lawton home monument association of Ft. Wayne. Directors—John B. Harper, Andrew J. Monihan, Thomas W. Blair, Alexander Johnson, William Geake, Charles Haag, David N. Foster, H. C. McMaken, Isaac N. Metzger, Frank Alderman and Henry C. Zollinger. The object of the association, as set out in the articles of incorporation, is to erect a monument in Ft. Wayne to perpetuate the memory of Gen. Lawton. .

JEFFERSON CITY, Mo.—The commission which has in charge the erection of a monument to the memory of John S. Marmaduke, late Governor of the State of Missouri, met at the capitol recently to consider designs and bids and let the contract. Quite a number of very handsome and tasteful designs were submitted by the Pickel Marble Company, St. Louis; Hodges & McCarthy, St. Louis; B. H. Rucker. Rolla; Vetter & Schmidt, Jeerson City, and J. H. McNamara. St. Louis. The contract for building the monument was awarded to Hodges & McCarthy, of St. Louis. The monument will be of Missouri syenite granite. The base will be 6 feet square; the second base 4 feet 6 inches square; the die will be 3 feet 6 inches square by 4 feet 5 inches in height, and the shaft 2 feet 2 inches square, the whole monument above the foundation being 20 feet 5 inches in height. The design is plain, but massive.

BROOKLYN, N. Y.—Architect Albert E. Davis and other citizens have started a movement in Bronx Borough to secure the erection of a memorial to the soldiers and sailors from that borough who fell in the war with Spain. At a meeting recently held plans were formed for raising the necessary funds, about $10,000. The model, which is being prepared by Piccirilli Bros., sculptors, will shortly be placed on public exhibition.

PITTSFIELD, MASS.—The project to erect a soldiers' memorial in this city is meeting with great success and the promoters are much encouraged.

ALEXANDRIA, VA.—The Washington Monument Association of this city has been chartered. The association has a capital stock of $500 and is authorized to acquire land to the value of $25,000. The officers are William B. Smoot of this city, president, and Alexander J. Wedderburn of Fairfax, treasurer. The purpose of the association is to erect a monument in this city to the memory of George Washington.

WASHINGTON, D. C.—Mr. Fitzgerald of Massachusetts has introduced a resolution in the House to appropriate $100,000 for the purpose of erecting a monument in Arlington cemetery close by the graves of the known and unknown dead of the Spanish-American and Filipino war as a memorial to the heroism and bravery of these men in the recent struggle.

Granite and Bronze.

WASHINGTON, D. C.—Mr. Payne has introduced a joint resolution in the House, providing that permission be granted the Woman's Relief Corps of the United States of America to erect a statue in memory and honor of the late Annie Wittenmeyer, past national president of the Woman's Relief Corps of the United States of America, on one of the public reservations of the city of Washington, to be designated by the Secretary of War, the joint committee on the library, the superintendent of public buildings and grounds and the committee of the Woman's Relief Corps appointed by it for that purpose: Provided, That the statue with pedestal shall cost not less than $15,000, and that it shall be presented to the people of the United States by the Woman's Relief Corps.

PATERSON, N. J.—$3,575 has been collected towards the erection of a monument in memory of Alex Hamilton.

MILWAUKEE, WIS.—The National Society of Colonial Dames will erect a bronze tablet to the memory of the soldiers who died in the Spanish-American war.

SOUTH FRAMINGHAM, MASS.—The descendants of Thomas Eames, who was one of the earliest settlers in Framingham, will set a memorial to their ancestor, in the form of a five ton boulder. Upon the boulder will be placed a 16x20 bronze tablet, with this inscription, in raised characters: "Here stood the house of Thomas Eames, burned by Indians in King Philip's war. Feb. 1. 1676. His wife and five children were slain, and four carried into captivity. This memorial is placed here by his descendants, A.D. 1900."

WASHINGTON, D. C.—A bill has been introduced in the House providing that the sum of $50,000 be appropriated "to be expended under the direction of the Secretary of War, in erecting at the city of Albany, N. Y., a monument to commemorate the birthplace of Gen. Phil Sheridan. This sum shall be expended under the direction of the Secretary of War or such officer as he may designate."

TOPEKA, KAN.—The monument which is to be erected to the memory of Colonel Halliday will probably be modeled after the style of the General Grant monument erected at St. Louis, Mo. It consists of a statue of bronze, nine feet in height, and stands on a granite pedestal ten feet high.

WASHINGTON. D. C.—Mr. Wetmore, from the committee on the library, May 1 made a report to the Senate on Senate joint resolution 48, directing the selection of a site for the erection of a bronze statue in this city in honor of the late Henry Wadsworth Longfellow. A substitute was submitted by the committee for the bill as introduced by Mr. Hoar, which excepts the Capitol and library grounds from the places that may be selected as a site for the statue. The original bill appropriated $6,000 for a pedestal for the statue, but the substitute appropriates only $4,000 for this purpose, together with such superintendence, etc., that may be involved in the work.

Among The Retail Dealers.

KENTON, OHIO.—White & Price have secured the contract for a soldiers monument to be erected at this place.

ROME, N. Y.—John H. Cross has secured the contract for the soldiers' monument. It is to be cut from Barre granite.

OTTAWA, ONT.—Acting under instructions from the master-in-chancery, the stock and plant of the Canadian Granite Company was sold at auction, April 12. The most of the stuff was sold and about $2,000 realized, which was considered fairly good, considering the character of the articles and stock. The granite was sold to Messrs. Jones & Steele, former employees of the company, who intend going into business as a firm.

HAMMONDSPORT, N. Y.—The contract for the erection of the soldiers' monument has been awarded to Charles S. Chisom of Prattsburgh.

READING, PA.—Ernest Epp, proprietor of the Central Steam Granite and Marble works, 428 North Eighth street, will have to double his present force of sixteen workmen in order to meet the demands of his trade.

NORTH JAY, ME.—The granite for the exterior walls of the palatial residence to be constructed on Fifth avenue, New York, for William A. Clark, the Montana millionaire and candidate for United States Senator, will be furnished by two New England granite manufacturers. The granite for the basement and first story will be taken from Redstone, N. H., and the white granite will be cut from North Jay, Me., for the superstructure. It is said that about $1,000,000 worth of stone will be taken from the quarries. The ornamental work on the granite will be the most elaborate ever cut for a private residence in this country, and will cost in the neighborhood of $225,000. The 600 cutters employed in both places have been out on a strike for the past few months, and returned to work since last Friday, their employers having granted them an eight-hour work day and a minimum wage of 35 cents per hour.

BELFAST, ME.—Work has begun at the granite plant at Mosquito mountain. There are about forty men in the crew. Lumber is on the ground for a large stone shed.

MARINETTE, WIS.—Inducements are being offered to the Amberg Granite Company to remove its granite cutting works from Amberg to this city. The works employ from 300 to 500 men.

RED BEACH, ME.—The Beaver Lake granite quarries, owned by the Maine Red Granite Company, are to be reopened and a crew of men are already at work preparing for active operations. The stone found in this quarry is of an unusually fine quality. The handsome soldiers' monument in Memorial Park, Calais, is made of Beaver Lake granite, as was also the pedestal of the Grant monument in Chicago.

ROCKLAND, ME.—The machinery, blacksmith shop, boarding house, etc., connected with the Hewett's Island granite plant were sold at auction April 30th, and about thirty-five gentlemen went from here on the steamer W. G. Butman, to participate in the event. The bidding at times was pretty lively and more than ordinary interest attached to the sale. The proceeds were a little short of $3000. The Hewett Island plant was formerly operated by the Maine Granite Co., but the concern failed and the property was sold on an execution by the sheriff.

Monthly Trade Record.

This department is compiled and edited by the United Mercantile Agency. Subscribers, in accordance with the terms of their contracts, are entitled to receive further information relative to the parties here. after mentioned, upon application to the main office As the names of many business men who are good will appear herein, subscribers can readily see the importance of making inquiries if interested, previous to taking any action.

ARKANSAS.

Russellville, *M—Hill, William H., Jr., succeeds T. H. Elgin.

COLORADO.

Colorado Springs, *M—Camp, Biehl & Co., succeeds Banning & Camp.

CONNECTICUT.

Hartford, BZ—Collins, Samuel & Co., 86 to Watson & Jackson.

New London, *M—Kopp, J., succeeds W. E. Ohaver.

GEORGIA.

Brunswick, *M—La Mance, Reed E., 20 $51.

ILLINOIS.

Chicago, *M—McGowan, Dorrell, 76.
Chicago, *M—Scholz, Grotefeld & Co., 76.
Gilman, *M—Lutton, Charles H., 76.
Rockford, *M—Best Bros. succeed W. G. Best.

INDIANA.

Indianapolis, BZ—Schmid, J. C. Sons, 86.
Muncie, *M—Smith, James M., 78.
Richmond, *M—Tingle & Tingle succeed Williams & Tingle.

Shelbyville, *M—Ham Bros. succeed Ham & Son.

Terre Haute, *M—Sullivan Marble & Granite Works Co., 43.

Williamsport, *M—Rariden & Rariden, Samuel J. Rariden, 93 $150.

IOWA.

Bloomfield, *M—McCann, A. T., succeeds Jordan McCann.

Carroll, *M—McNeil & Schroeder 64, Schroeder & Wilmers 58.

Corydon, *M—Niday, C. A., 32 $1,600.

Fort Dodge, *M—Delano, A. M., 99 $500.

Guthrie Centre, *M—Frink, W. C., 93 $108.

Oskaloosa, *M—Thompson & Roux succeed E. C. Thompson.

Red Oak, *M—Cole, Z. W., 87 $1,165 and 14 $2,500.

Washington, *M—Neiswanger, D. & Son, D. Neiswanger, 32 $2,000.

Woodbine, *M—Greenizer, R. W., 76.

KANSAS.

Salina, *M—Kingrey & Smith, 76.

MAINE.

Bangor, *M—Fletcher & Butterfield, 87 $850 and 90 at 25 cents.

Alfred, *M—Hodsdon & Linscott. Willis Linscott, 78.

Bath, *M—Rogers & Curtis, C. F. Curtis quit claimed R. E. $1.

Foxcroft, *M—Sampson & Bragg. O. H. Bragg 99 $1,000 and 32 $2,000.

Lewiston, *M—Johnson & Taylor, 76.

MARYLAND.

Baltimore, *M—McKnight, John, 20 $829.

MASSACHUSETTS.

Quincy, GZ—McDonnell, E. A., succeeds McDonnell & Sons.

Quincy, GZ—McQueen, John, 14 $2,000 and $1,700.

MICHIGAN.

Jackson, *M—Union Granite & Marble Co., 14 $24.

Woodmere, *M—Peel, Frank W., 89.

MINNESOTA,

Fergus Falls, *M—Partridge, R., succeeds Partridge & Chantron.

Lake City, *M—Snyder, Wesley, 76.

Minneapolis, *M—Higgins, A. M., 106.

MISSOURI.

Gallatin, *M—Tillery, Lynn & Harris succeed Tillery & Brown.

NEBRASKA.

Red Cloud, *M—Boyd, J. A., 88 to Oxford.

NEW HAMPSHIRE.

Nashua, *M—Fuller & Winslow. 14 $400.

NEW JERSEY.

Hoboken, *M—Riley Bros., 87 $1,000.

NEW YORK.

Auburn, *M—Ten Eyck, Fred G., 20 $278.

Baldwinsville, *M—Blanchard, J. R., 20 $432.

Binghampton, *M—Barnes, E. J. & Son. 86 to G. A. Chaplin.

New York, *M—Caterson, W. H., 20 $337.

Plattsburg, *M—Heath, E. H., 93 $1,000.

Poughkeepsie, *M—Miller, M. J. (Mrs. P.), 87 $700.

Saranac, *M—Lobdell, Lared W., 106.

Saratoga Springs, *M—Thomas & Miller succeed W. H. Thomas.

OHIO.

Cincinnati, *M—Schwarz, Fridolin, 104.

Cincinnati, *M—White, Alfred & Sons, Albert White, 78.

Hamilton, *M—Horssnyder, Fred, 93 $2,200.

Leipsic, *M—Shoemaker & Co., mortgage deed, $500.

St. Bernard, *M—Schwarz, Fridolin.

Toledo, *M—Crosby & Devlin, 74 $240.

Troy, *M—Kester, George J., succeeds Ritter & Kester.

OKLAHOMA.

Enid, *M—Pearce & Jones, Willis Pearce deed $1,800.

OREGON.

Tillamook, *M—Arthur F., 76.

PENNSYLVANIA.

Reading, *M—Eisenbrown, P. F. Sons & Co., Harry W. Eisenbrown, 78.

RHODE ISLAND.

Providence, *M—Burns John Granite Co. succeed John Burns & Son.

Westerly, G—Dixon Granite Works, 86 to Sweeney Granite Works.

VERMONT.

Northfield. *M—Sawyer, C. D., 70.

VIRGINIA.

Luray, *M—Bradley & Williams, J. S. Bradley 20 $123.

Marion, *M—Clark, R. J., 76.

NEW YORK.

Wirt Leland, formerly a member of the firm of S. A. MacFarland & Co., dealers in statuary at No. 39 West Forty-second street. has filed a petition in bankruptcy. In his petition Mr. Leland says the firm owes $18,245 and its assets are $8,615. MacFarland, he says, is in Italy and refuses to join in the petition to have the partnership declared bankrupt.

Consolidation of the Granite Industry of St. George, N. B.

The latest regarding a granite trust that comes to us is the consolidation of all the granite industries of New Brunswick, which is being brought about by Charles Campbell, late of Eastport, Me., formerly a hotel clerk in that city. Mr. Campbell has been at work obtaining options upon all the granite properties in the Province of New Brunswick. and especially those at St. George, N. B. He has succeeded in obtaining options for purchase upon all the granite properties, together with mills, waterpowers, etc., situated at St. George upon the Magaguadavic river. The mills get their power from the falls of this river, where there can be obtained 20,000 horsepower or more, when all the plans and improvements are carried out that the company has in view.

At present there is only a very small part of this great power used for the granite mills. The total amount of acreage that these options cover is upwards of 10,000 acres, extending from Lake Utopia to within two miles of the salt water at Bocabec.

Under the contemplated consolidation the plants, mills and quarries will be equipped with all the latest and most modern machinery, and railroads will be built between the quarries and the mills and also to the salt water for the shipment of stone. The railroads will be equipped with electric power. Mr. Campbell has secured options upon other valuable granite quarries in the Province, and rumor has it that he has also secured the "Spoon Island" quarries; if so, he or his company have the monopoly of the granite business of the Dominion of Canada.

The granite industries at St. George at present employ about 300 men.—Exchange.

Quaint Epitaphs.

Susan Darling Safford, has some choice specimens. Here is one sample:—

"He got a fishbone in his throat,
And then he sang an angel's note."

This fine specimen is from Block Island:—

"He's done a-catching cod,
And gone to meet his God."

A Tennessee matron has this touching tribute:—

"Some have children, others none;
Here lies the mother of twenty-one."

Hetty Green's Great Riches.

"Hetty Green's wealth consists largely of government bonds, railroad stocks and mortgages," writes Leigh Mitchell Hodges of "The Richest Woman in America," in the June Ladies' Home Journal. "She says she is not so fond of government bonds since the finances of the nation have become polluted with politics. Good mortgages of any kind are now her favorite form of investment. If all the mortgages she holds were foreclosed to-morrow twenty-eight churches of various denominations, in almost as many States, would become hers, and four cemeteries would be added to her real estate. Besides these there would be blocks of great business buildings and splendid city houses, theatres, livery stables, hotels, etc.

The Newspaper Man.

You fancy you'd like a newspaper career? Why
    certainly, certainly, son;
You think it's a picnic, year in and year out, and
    that 'twould be nothing but fun
To sit at a desk and write verses and such, just
    grind 'em out any old way,
It's as easy as lying and pays most as well; in
    fact it's nothing but play.

You fancy you'd like a newspaper career, for news-
    paper men, as you know,
Go to every attraction that comes into town and
    have seats in the bald headed row;
And if they are on to their jobs, it is said, that
    some of them even can get
Permission to go to the rear of the stage, where
    they flirt with the antique soubrette.

A newspaper man doesn't need an hotel, one room
    is a plenty for him.
For he's always invited to banquets and such, and
    he's aye in the social swim;
His wardrobe most always has one suit of clothes,
    and at times there's as many as two.
And he spends his spare moments in dressing him-
    self, and in telling himself that he'll do.

The newspaper man, when he wishes to go to
    some city other than his,
Or whether for pleasure his journey is made, or
    whether it's strictly on biz,
Can ride on a pass, without paying a cent, get his
    sleeper D. H. clear through,
And the porter reserves him a seat that affords of
    the scenery the very best view.

All these you imagine, O son, pertain to the news-
    paper man of the day,
But don't give your fancy too much of a rein, and
    don't let it sweep you away;
For the truth of the matter, my boy, is this, the
    average newspaper man
Looks back with a shudder upon his career, and
    regrets the day when he began.

It's true all the labor he has to perform is to sit at
    the desk and write,
And dig up subscriptions and hustle for ads, and
    keep the shop running all right;
His bills must be met on the day they come due, or
    the very first thing people say
Is that he is a goner, and that they can see his fin-
    ish not far away.

For every free pass that he gets to the show, he
    gives up its value twice o'er
In free advertising, and often he's cursed when he
    says he won't give any more.
He pays for his ticket whenever he goes, or wheth-
    er on pleasure or biz,
And whenever the porter espies him on board, a
    dark frown steals over his phiz.

At times he gets busy and gives some galoot who
    deserves it a merited rub,
And then when he's going home late some fine
    night, he's hit on the head with a club;
He's damned if he does, and he's damned if he
    don't and his plight is a sorrowful one,
O, the editor's lot is a picnic, my boy, and it's al-
    ways just like having fun.
            —*Minneapolis Journal.*

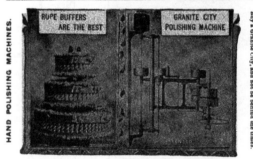

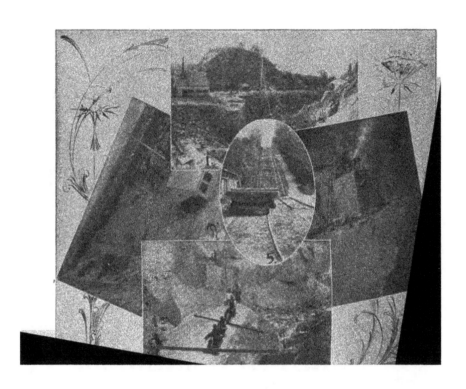

· GRANITE ·

FRONT PANEL.

BACK PANEL.

BARCLAY BROS.,
OWNERS OF

Dark and Light Granite Quarries.

SPECIALTIES

Vaults and Large Monuments.

Pneumatic Surfacing Machine.

Pneumatic Tools.

Polishing Mill.

SIDE PANEL.

SIDE PANEL.

ROBERT BURNS MONUMENT,
Unveiled at Barre, Vt., July 21, 1899.

Monument and Statue cut entirely from Barre Granite.

Designed by William Barclay, and executed by
Barclay Bros., in their own Sheds at Barre, Vt.

Bottom base of Monument, 8 feet square.

Total Height, 22 feet 10 inches.

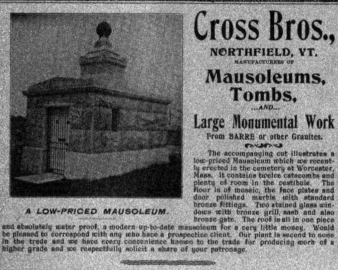

GRANITE

ENTERED AT THE BOSTON POST OFFICE AS SECOND-CLASS MAIL MATTER.

Vol. X.   BOSTON, MASS., JULY 1, 1900.   No. 7

A. M. HUNT, EDITOR.

Published Monthly in the interests of the Producer
Manufacturer, and Retailer of Granite as used
for Monumental or Building Purposes.

Terms of Subscription

To ANY PART OF THE UNITED STATES OR CANADA:

One copy, one year - - - - $1.00, in advance.
One copy, six months - - - 75 cents, in advance.

ADVERTISING RATES FURNISHED UPON APPLICATION.

A. M. HUNT & CO., Publishers,

101 DEVONSHIRE STREET, - - BOSTON, MASS.

Editorials

ARDWICK, VERMONT, has had
a small-pox scare. The following
telegram was received on May
30th:

"Small-pox scare absolutely without foundation.
See letter.

"(Signed) E. R. FLETCHER."

The following letter was received June 7:

"Briefly stated, one of our leading citizens, interested
in copper mining property in Arizona, returned from
there Friday, May 25th, not feeling very well, and our
health officer Monday morning pronounced the disease
small-pox. The patient was quarantined, small-pox
signs were posted on the street corner, schools were
closed, people began leaving on every train, and before
Tuesday night, hundreds had gone. The State Board
of Health came here May 29th, and after a thorough
examination, gave out the information which caused
us to send the telegram.

"Hardwick is having a splendid trade, granite business is better than ever, and we are confident you will
gladly give us such space in your paper as is necessary
to contradict wrong reports and avoid any injury to
one of the most progressive towns in New England.
State official report not yet received. Will send it
later.

"Yours respectfully,
E. R. FLETCHER,
G. H. BICKFORD,
R. E. WALLACE."

It would be a pity indeed to have anything of this
kind happen, as it would seriously interfere with the
season's business.

It is evident that it takes but a very little to scare
people in a small place. In all probability, according
to the stories about the scare, two cases would depopu-
late the town. A health officer who would make such
a report without the advice of others should be made to
suffer.

IN conversation with a prominent granite
manufacturer recently, he bitterly complained about the trouble which he had in
connection with shipments of granite work
with especial reference to claims for breakage. He
stated that, notwithstanding the fact that every piece
of granite was thoroughly boxed and bound with hoop
iron, yet complaints had been received from his customers of parts of a monument chipped and otherwise
broken; also that the parts were received in bad order,
the boxing being entirely destroyed.

There are several ways to account for this. First,
they may not have been properly boxed at the start,
but our informant tells us that in two instances at least
he personally superintended the boxing of stones,
and they were boxed as strong as wood, hoop iron and
nails could make them, and yet there was the same
complaint, broken boxing and damaged stone and

claim for discount. Either of three things must have happened,—the car in which the shipment was made must have been through an accident, in which case it is strange that no other part of the shipment was damaged, or it must have been broken in setting, or the dealer called for discount on general principles. We should advise the manufacturers to carefully inspect the stone and see that it is thoroughly boxed. The shipping receipt should be a guarantee that the goods were in good condition at time of shipment and no part of a shipment should be accepted by the dealers from the railroad unless in good condition.

The manufacturer has troubles of his own at home. He should not be held responsible for the fault of the railroad company or careless handling. On the other hand, if it is the manufacturer's fault, as it occasionally is, it may be due to bad boxing, and as a consequence, damaged stone; or it may have been injured in cutting, and the workman, to cover up his mistake, has so arranged that it should be boxed without inspection, or possibly it may have been a case where a part of the moulding or other parts may have been broken in cutting, and glued on, and in shipping this imperfection became loosened. If the monument is received by the retail dealer in bad condition, it should be shipped back immediately so as to save himself the reputation of claiming unjust discounts, as the manufacturer has that feeling when a shipment is made that the monument was perfect before boxing and after shipment.

*

HE condition of the granite industry at the present writing is, to say the least, encouraging. To be sure, there are certain sections where it is dull, but as a rule, the retail dealers are having more than their usual amount of work. This information is gathered from the various manufacturing centers with especial reference to Quincy, Milford, N. H., Concord, N. H., Montpelier and Barre, Vt.

Of course, it is impossible for us to cover the entire country in order to gather from various sources the volume of business transacted, but the manufacturing centers are the sources which best show the condition of the business throughout the country.

The manufacturers at Milford report, much to our surprise, that they are not having the demand usual at this season of the year, and it is rumored from outside sources that there is a lack of rough stock. We can say understandingly that this is not so. A call at the quarry shows that they are, as a rule, in good condition. We noted a peculiar condition of things at one of the leading quarries, or rather one of the quarries which produce a better quality of stock. During a visit of something over two years ago, this particular quarry was in, to say the least, a discouraging condition. So called "salt seams" which for the uninitiated we described as wavy lines of white quartz varying in width from 1-4 inch to 1 inch, showed almost on every stone, but as the quarry has grown deeper, these seams have gradually come together and ended, leaving the stone on both sides and the sheet underneath entirely free. Of course it took some time for the quarry owners to discover this,—something over two years in the

case mentioned, and certainly it must be very gratifying. Just how to account for the lack of orders for the Milford monuments, it is impossible to state. On the contrary, the Concord, N. H., manufacturers are having all that they can do, and the trouble existing here is something that has not happened in a long time, viz.— the lack of good granite cutters. There are plenty of so called "tramp workmen" who are only taken on under stress of circumstances. One manufacturer reports figuring on three mausoleum jobs with good chances of at least securing two of them. Other manufacturers report enough work on hand to keep them busy for some time.

Quincy manufacturers, although not driven by their work, yet there is something coming in constantly which makes them fairly busy. At Barre, Montpelier and Hardwick, and other Vermont points, including Northfield, plenty of work is reported; of this we will report on more definitely in our next issue. The leading Vermont marble firms report an abundance of orders. As one of the firms stated, "We are snowed under with orders." This is one of the common expressions in Vermont, where, as some people believe, there is good sleighing every month except July, but we can say understandingly that it is not so.

*

E have suggested in previous issues the advisability of establishing schools for the purpose of educating the coming granite cutter in the art of modeling and drawing.

Under the auspices of the Aberdeen, Scotland, Master Masons' Association, the operative masons and Granite Cutters' Union have established at the Robert Gordon College a successful class for training the young workmen in the arts of modeling and sculpture. It is stated that, judging from the results already achieved, this especial and systematic training of the younger craftsmen promises to produce in Scotland a band of skilful sculptors whose work will yet reflect great credit on the whole granite industry of Scotland.

What has been done in Aberdeen can be done in the United States, and to this one thing alone the future of the granite industry will owe its life. There are many granite cutters today who will be only too glad to avail themselves of some such way of educating themselves in case they are given the opportunity.

The best results cannot be expected from the machine trained workman given a piece of work and he follows his sketch or model, but in order to make him a skilled workman he must be capable of thinking for himself. This is the reason why our soldiers make their great success in battle, as they did in Cuba. They thought for themselves. What is true of them is true of the granite cutter. Train his eye and brain and the result will be surprising. The older granite cutters will not find it easy to take up the pencil and produce the same results as from the training of the younger men, but they can try. Here is a good chance for missionary work for the Granite Manufacturers' Association, combined together as they have done in Scotland with the Granite Cutters' Union, to bring forth schools and classes where sculpture, free hand sketching and modeling can be taught, and the future of the monumental industry will be firmly established.

Burke Bros. have just placed a contract with the Lane Manufacturing Co., Montpelier, for a new plant, 60x170, and office, 16x18. This is to be equipped with all modern stone-working machinery, including a ten-ton traveling derrick, Ingersoll-Sergeant air compressor, and is to be complete in every particular.

Since the last issue of the GRANITE there has been no material change in the condition of business in this vicinity with the one exception that there has been a collapse of the strike instituted by the polishers. Up to the beginning of the year there has been no Polishers' Union, at least not well organized, and consequently there was no great force in their demands that they be placed on the same footing as the cutters.

Those of the strikers who did not lose their positions by the action have gone back at the same rate of wages and the same nine hours' work as obtained before the demands were made. Most of the manufacturers made out to get along during the strike by either working the wheel themselves, or trusting the same to their apprentices, of whom there were quite a number in the city. It is said that the polishers will unite and work together so that at another time there will be more chance of winning, and also that it is expected that there will be an understanding with the Stone Cutters' Union that the latter will assist them in their demands to a certain extent.

On the whole the strike was a failure for the polishers only from the fact that they made the manufacturers feel that it meant something to their business to have one branch of their employees go out in a body.

It is certain that there will be no more strikes for wages or shorter hours during the remainder of this year, and it is not probable that there will be anything of the kind occur the coming spring.

Bertoli & Peduzzi, Montpelier, have been enlarging their plant so that they will have more than double the room which they have been having in the past, and consequently they will reach out for a larger amount of business of the same variety as that which they have been turning out since they have been in business. They have now on their books quite an assortment of orders for statues and are cutting several, some of which will be ready to ship in a short time. Other work is also done by them, such as the general run of monumental work, upon which there is considerable carving. Of this class they have a large amount under way, and some already completed.

The firm of Wells, Lamson & Co. of this city have been working for some time on the enormous mausoleum job which they have been fortunate enough to have awarded to them for construction.

This job is known as the Ehret Mausoleum, and when completed will be erected in Woodlawn Cemetery in New York City. The job is a large one and will be more particularly described in some future issue of GRANITE. It is 36 feet square on the ground and is 44 feet high. It is going to be one of the most elegant mausoleums which are to be found among the many elegant ones in Woodlawn Cemetery.

Z. Macchi has now in his employ about two gangs of cutters, and is making things hum. He has a large variety of work, both upon his books and under the hammer, and has also recently shipped quite a quantity of medium-sized jobs to western parties. He is now engaged upon the construction of a very pretty sarcophagus job for B. Thomasi of this city, recently deceased, which will be set in the local Catholic Cemetery. It is an all polished monument and has considerable tracing upon the die.

Mr. Macchi has, among other jobs which he is now cutting, a large column die job which he is cutting for New York parties, and which will be ready for shipment in the near future, and several plain jobs of the varying designs and dimensions. He reports that the future of the business looks brighter than it has for some time, and that he is of the opinion that there will be yet, notwithstanding, one of the best seasons which has ever been known in this city.

The firm of Innes & Cruickshank have something on their books and in their plant which is interesting, and they are always glad to see the representative of GRANITE. At this writing they have on their books a large quantity of orders for all classes of jobs ranging from the ordinary marker to the large column die monument. Among the best of the latter class which are to be seen in the city at this time is a plaster die job which this concern is now cutting. It has a bottom base of about 8x5, and the die and cap to correspond. The job is well cut and is embellished with carving of a heavy order. They have also under the hammer a large sarcophagus job having quite an amount of carving upon the die. At this writing they are employing about three gangs of cutters and will put on more in the near future.

They are very sanguine as to the future condition of the granite business, and say that although the polishers' strike here has set the manufacturer back a little during the past month or two, that business is coming back to the normal condition now and will doubtless be on the incline throughout the summer.

The firm of Mutch & Calder are planning to make a change in their plant during the next month, and consequently they are getting their heavy work out of the way and are now, with one or two exceptions, cutting small work, which can be completed in short order.

During the high water of last winter their plant was three times submerged with about six and one-half feet of water, and when it went out it of course left things in a rather bad condition—the machinery rusty, and everything covered with about six inches of mud. This they intend to remedy by raising their plant about seven feet and filling in the same to that depth. This will put their plant in a condition where it will not likely be submerged again and still will not injure it as to its accessibility. This may take them in the vicinity of about two weeks, and will be done either this month or in August. Among the large jobs which they have yet uncompleted are two large plain jobs having base, cap and die, the base being 7 ft. 4 in. by 7 ft. 4 in. They are finishing a large column die monument which will be ready for shipment within a few days.

Around the plant of Emslie & McLeod there is an air of prosperity which it is pleasing to find, and which gives one the feeling that there is something worth living and working for. This concern is now employing about forty-five cutters and have been turning out a large amount of work during the past few weeks. They have a large number of monuments of various designs and sizes under the hammer, and many more which they will begin as soon as these now being constructed are finished and shipped.

Sarcophagus, spire, column and pilaster die and cottage monuments are to be seen in their plant in a more or less advanced state of construction, and they report that work is coming in as fast as they can care for it. They have on their books one large job which will be shipped to Syracuse, N. Y., when it is completed, and of which a more particular description will be given in some future issue, when the same is nearing completion. It is a monument which is being erected in that city to the memory of the Chief of the Fire Department, and it will be surmounted by a statue of that personage.

The firm of Beck & Beck have recently put in an air compressor, and during the spring they have remodeled their plant so that it is more commodious and better adapted to the needs of a granite manufacturing concern. They are employing about one gang of cutters at this time, but will put on more as soon as they can be secured. The majority of the work which they are now cutting is of a small order, although they have some two or three good-sized sarcophagus jobs which are well under way. Work is coming in in good style at this writing, although it has been a bit slow during the past few weeks, or in fact since their Decoration Day work was finished.

Barclay Brothers have now become settled in their new and spacious modern plant which they purchased of the late firm of Mackie, Hussey & Co., and are doing business in the same old style as in their former quarters, only on a larger scale. They have been doing as large business during the past few years as any concern in the city, but now they intend to employ quite a number more men if the condition of the trade demands or warrants it. They have a large amount of orders on their books for both large and small work, and are rushing the work along in a style which pleases. There is nothing too large for them now to handle with ease, and nothing too small for them to give the same careful attention which all their work has been wont to receive.

E. L. Smith & Co. are working about two gangs of cutters at this writing and are cutting some good work which they will have finished in a short time. They

have two large sarcophagus monuments under the hammer and a column die job which is nearly finished. The books show a goodly number of orders received during the past month and they report that they are estimating upon a large amount of large work which they have reasonable expectations of securing. There is, and has been throughout the summer, a good demand for their dark stock and quite a good demand for the stock from their light quarry, and on each quarry they have a large force working to supply the orders of their customers.

Sweeney Bros. Granite Co., Montpelier, are at work at the present time, among other contracts, on a sarcophagus monument 9 ft. 5 in. by 9 ft. 4 in. The die is very handsomely carved. This firm is employing thirty men at the present time.

Dillon & Haley, Montpelier, are now located in the plant which was formerly occupied and owned by Stafford & McGlynn, both members of this firm having died some time since. They are employing at the present time about 16 cutters, and report an abundance of work.

Ryle & McCormick, Montpelier, are employing 32 cutters. Among their contracts at the present time is a draped shaft monument, of which the bottom base is 8 ft. 6 in. square and the shaft 20 ft. x 2 ft. 2 in. square. They have recently installed Ingersoll-Sergeant air compressors capable of operating fifteen pneumatic tools.

The business of the firm of McIver & Ruxton will be continued by the senior member of the firm. Mr. Ruxton goes to Quincy as superintendent for McDonnell & Sons.

The condition of business in the granite industry in Quincy at present is not all that could be desired. The long strike, coming as it did when everybody should have been rushed, has rather unsettled business, and it will be some months before it gets back to where it was when the strike came on the first of March. During the strike the cutters were frequently heard to declare that the manufacturers had work enough on hand, although they claimed they had no orders. Further, the cutters claimed that as soon as the strike was settled, the people would see that there was a lot of work in Quincy. Well, the strike is settled, and the past few weeks has shown beyond a doubt that the claim of the manufacturers was true. Every firm has succeeded in getting some few orders, but there is nothing large, everything being of the medium size kind. All of the yards are open and working, but with decreased force, kind, although they have a few jobs on hand that are larger than the ordinary run. Mr. Marnock expects that the fall business will be considerable better than at present.

*

Injunction Against Setting a Monument.

The injunction recently asked for by the Rt. Rev. J. S. Michaud, bishop of Burlington, Vt., forbidding the erection of a monument over the grave of the Rev. Thomas Lynch in St. Mary's cemetery at Fairhaven, having been granted by Judge Taft of the supreme court, it is not probable that the monument will be placed in position, although completed by Houlihan Bros. of Rutland, Vt.

At the time of his death it was supposed that Fr. Lynch left considerable property, his wealth being estimated at from $50,000 to $75,000. His unexpected death left many things in an unsettled condition, and it was expected that a will would be found, which would explain some things.

No such document was found, but instead a few penciled notes, which were made by the priest himself years ago, providing for the erection of a monument over his grave, and disposing of a few things among relatives in this country.

Thus far only about $7,500 has been found that belonged to his estate.

Soon after Fr. Lynch's burial, the Rev. Gerald Fagan of Boston and the Rev. Thomas Gaffney of Rutland, acting with other relatives, contracted with Houlihan Bros. for a monument that was to cost $1,200. The design was to be a casket, on which was a recumbent figure of Fr. Lynch.

The bishop was not consulted about the design, and soon after its completion, when the contractors called upon him for permission to place it in the cemetery, he forbid, and asked for the injunction forbidding its being placed upon the church grounds. It was not the erection of the monument that he opposed, but the design. Had it been a statue of the deceased priest no objections would have been made.

In the memoranda that Fr. Lynch left the sum of $1,200 was appropriated for a monument. That was the contract price of the one made, but the administrator of the estate, John O'Neil of Burlington, refuses to pay for it, as it is not satisfactory to the bishop. As Frs. Fagan and Gaffney became personally responsible for the cost of the stone, they are not worrying about that, but there are many who wonder what the outcome will be.

*

Greatness Soon forgotten.

There is nothing that interests a person more than a puzzle except a question of identification. The doubt and absence of proof have a certain fascination that ᴏᴏᴇ on until all roads are found to lead in the ι and absolute certainty prevails.

At the Boston Athenæum there is to be found material enough for any number of ambitious persons whose knowledge of things in general and of the past in particular prepares them for the solving of a series of riddles that many have abandoned.

Four dusty, distinguished and dismal plaster busts await identification there, and while no prize is offered, the glory of discovery seems reward enough for any mortal to ask. There is no question that these plasters are of famous men. That they should repose in their present positions is a wonder, for they would create all kinds of talk were the public to look upon them. It may be great men are forgotten, after all, in spite of the work of the artist and the sculptor. These busts have seemingly been in the Athenæum since the building was erected.

———

The case of the bust in Doric Hall is not yet forgotten. A searching inquiry proved that the person who named it had done so hastily. It was on March 27, 1891, that Gov. W. E. Russell sent a letter to the House of Representatives, in which he called atttention to the report of the commission appointed (under chap. 24, Resolves, 90) to inquire into the authenticity of this bust, which bore the name of Samuel Adams. He declared it to be intended for George Washington and submitted photographs in proof. On the board of inquiry were Edward G. Porter, Samuel A. Green and John C. Ropes. They had received their appointment in October, and after their work had been accomplished they said that the bust had been removed and examined on all sides, no inscription being found of any kind.

No record could be discovered to show when it was placed in the hall. It formerly stood in a niche on the old stairway leading to the green room. This was remodelled in 1868. The bust was of Carrara marble, and was made near the beginning of the century. As Samuel Adams had never sat for a bust, and his faithful biographer never referred to it, that idea was abandoned. It was soon discovered that an exact facsimile was in Christ Church, Salem street, a gift of Shubal Bell. In establishing the fact that the bust in Doric Hall was of Washington, the commission had the statement of Lafayette, who upon seeing it remarked: "That is the Washington that I knew."

———

It is presumed that the men at the Athenæum whom the busts represent had importance, otherwise there would not have been any excuse for the likenesses. For over a year these casts have adorned the reading room. Many visitors have been curious, but could give no light upon the subject, save a casual reference to Dewey, McKinley and Schley, which was an attempt at humor that failed. There was, for a short time, an earnest attempt to solve the mystery, but when the room was remodelled and the readers had to depart to a smaller room to enjoy the books or papers, these casts were taken from their positions and hidden from the public gaze.

That was on March 20 or thereabouts, and today they are almost forgotten. In the smaller room, behind

a huge case in which is packed a large piece of statuary, are two of the busts, black with dust. The third reposes upon a case to the right of the entryway up one flight. In the moving one shoulder of the bust was broken, but that can be mended should enough interest centre in it. The fourth of the group is packed away, and what it looks like the reporter does not know.

The attendant at the Athenæum says that in the days of long ago, when the Athenæum was used in part as an art gallery, there were any number of busts given to it, and among the number many that in the course of moving to the present Art Museum remained unidentified. There are also in the rooms of the Athenæum pieces of statuary, the gifts of families who preferred to have them there rather than in their homes.—Boston Herald.

The granite cutters' strike in Hancock county, Me., seems to have cropped out in some queer places. This is one of the stories told : A stone contractor at Franklin has a flock of sheep. His brother is a sheep-shearer and stone-cutter. The brother was asked if he would shear the sheep, whereupon he made the following answer: "No, sir; not a clip until you sign the bill of prices." At last account the sheep were wearing their winter clothing, with prospects of doing so all summer, unless the strike is settled. Wonder what the sheep think of the conflict.

An American Shaft on Scottish Soil.

The only spot on the globe where Memorial day services are held regularly outside of the borders of the United States is in Edinburgh at the statue of Lincoln, erected in the old Calton burying ground, in memory of the Scottish-American soldiers who fell in the American civil war.

The ceremonies are in charge of the United States Consul in Edinburgh, and were this year attended by hundreds of Americans now traveling in the British Isles, as well as many English. Hundreds of floral tributes were placed around the statue, which has been thus decked every year since it was unveiled on August 21, 1893.

The monument is a work of art. It is fifteen feet in height. It is massive without being heavy. The pedestal, supporting a statue of Lincoln, stands upon two steps of polished red Aberdeen granite. Inscribed on the first of these are the words, "In Memory of the Scottish-American Soldiers." On the second step are the words, "To Preserve the Jewel of Liberty in the Framework of Freedom.—Abraham Lincoln."

The Great Monument to the Confederacy.

The Confederate Veterans' Association appointed to raise funds for the erection of the Battle Abbey of the Confederacy at Richmond have about completed their work. Charles Broadway Rouss, the New York mil-

lionaire, who was himself a confederate soldier, offered three years ago to give $100,000 for that purpose, provided another $100,000 was raised by general subscription. Mr. Rouse also offered to give an additional $10,000 for the same purpose for every additional $10,-000 that was raised by general subscription.

Col. White as chairman of the committee having in charge the raising of the fund, will have the pleasure of reporting that the $100,000 has been raised by general subscription and that the committee now has Mr. Rouss' drafts for $100,000 additional. It only remains for the association to agree on plans and go ahead with the work of the building. While no plans have been agreed on, it is definitely understood that the Battle Abbey will be built in Richmond and it will serve the double purpose of an enduring monument to the soldiers of the lost cause and a permanent home for such valuable relics of the confederacy, and mementoes of its heroes, as may come into the possession of the Confederate Veterans' Association, or be donated by friends.

Bolt of Lightning Strikes Monument.

Memorial day exercises in Byron, Ill., were marred by a highly sensational episode which resulted in the partial destruction by lightning of a beautiful and costly soldiers' monument—the first one erected in Illinois after the close of the civil war—under circumstances which are a source of awe and wonderment to the hundreds who participated and of the people for miles around.

A violent electrical storm following a sultry morning, accompanied by a torrent of rain, forced the participants hurriedly to repair to a hall to conclude the ceremonies. While the speaker of the day was calling the roll of the dead the heavens were rent by an awful crash, accompanied by a vivid sheet of flame, shaking the ground like an earthquake. When the storm subsided it was found that the monument, of marble, in the business centre of the town, had been partially demolished by the bolt. A piece of the shaft proper, nearly five feet long and eighteen inches thick, was ground into fragments and hurled many rods in every direction. The lower portion of the monument, eight feet long and two feet thick, fell beside the foundation stone, while the heavy cornice supercapstone landed in a dooryard ten rods away.

Surmounting this monolith was an American eagle rampant of heroic proportions. The "grand old bird" landed half a block eastward, right side up, on his pedestal, without a scratch. Several bushels of marble ground to powder, resembling fine salt, are strewed about the streets, disintegrated by the force of the explosion.

The medallions bearing the names of the sixty-five dead soldiers from Byron escaped injury.

Another curiosity of the fiery stroke appears in the two "long tom" 6-inch Parrot rifled cannon which guard the monument on either side. Normally their muzzles stand at eighteen degrees elevation. The shock depressed them to an exact horizontal.

R — Y x A — C x Y — E

⸤⸥ Scotland's Granite City.

ery visitor to Aberdeen, the centre of Scotland's
ite industry, is naturally struck with the remark-
cleanliness and beauty of the great silver gray
ings that line the principal streets of the city. No
to impress on him that this is one of the staple
itries of this particular part of Scotland. On every
he sees the amplest evidence of this. At all the
ipal railway stations stand wagon after wagon
with rough unhewn blocks of the familiar red
gray rock. Cart after cart and lorry after lorry
s him on the street, bearing to its destination the
uct of the neighboring quarries. By his side he
the busy clank of hammer and chisel, and anon
teady whir of machinery as the stubborn rock is
y fashioned into the separate parts of the architect
gineer's design.

e granite industry of Scotland practically dates
the beginning of the present century. True, of
e, for simpler building purposes the stone has
tless been used from the time when the prehis-
men raised in the northwestern wilds of Caledonia
mysterious circles of gigantic granite boulders
a still bear testimony to their presence in our
t. But the history of this industry begins with the
eenth century. Prior to this the great public
ings of the Granite City itself were almost wholly
td with stones from the sandstone quarries of the
and south. Decorative work in granite was
y unknown in those days. But enterprising
men were already at work devising newer meth-
f conquering the hard, unyielding granite. That
, which ages before had been polished and carved
cient Egypt in a fashion which our workmen of
have never been able to surpass, and which even
ars testimony to the marvellous dexterity of those
ht craftsmen—that stone was not to lie dormant
iseless in the great granite hill of the north.

e pioneer craftsman, seeing some specimens of
ht polished granite, determined to experiment on
cal Scottish stones. His implements were crude
he hand polishing process infinitely laborious; but
success as he met with encouraged him to go on
rosper, and in due time brought fresh rivals into
irgin industry. The old hewing tools were dis-
d; lighter and more pliant implements took their
; the powerful giant, steam was harnessed to the
ling machinery, and in itself soon revolutionized
ade. From being a purely local industry, supply-
cal needs, it gradually extended its connection to
orth, south, east and west. New quarters were
d throughout the whole of Scotland, wherever
te boulders reared their heads, until today struc-
of Scottish granite may be found in almost every
if the civilized world.

Scotland alone this industry finds employment for
rd of 15,000 men. A glance at the export trade
single year will, however, afford the best con-
n of the various uses to which Scottish granite
w pnt. First, let us begin with the foundations
ies; and from this firm standpoint work up to
ative architecture. For the year ending 1897
were shipped from Aberdeen alone 31,403 tons

of granite setts and 4,500 tons of granite paving. This
represents an increase of 50 per cent in less than five
years, evidently tending to show that in that line granite is more than holding its own against the rival wood
and concrete materials. Vast quantities, too, have been
shipped from the same port for bridges and docks, em-
bankments and sea walls, its great weight and durabil-
ity rendering it an efficient protector from the stormy
waves of winter.

During the year 1898 polished granite to the value
of 26,700 pounds was shipped to the United States. In
this department, however, a steady decline has manifested itself since the enforcement of the McKinley
tariff. In 1892 the export trade to the States amounted
to 123,565 pounds, compared with which the year 1898
shows the startling decrease of 96,865 pounds. This
loss, however, has been more than counterbalanced by
a vastly increased English and colonial trade. South
African and Australian markets have developed rapidly; whilst with London and the larger cities of the
South a successful trade in polished fronts for shops
and public buildings has now been established. As the
cost of an American granite monument averages from
15 pounds to 20 pounds, whilst the cost of a polished
shopfront varies from 500 pounds to 2,000 pounds, it
will readily be seen that the loss of the American trade
has not been so disastrous as it might otherwise have
been. But the trade in polished fronts is not confined
to Britain. Decorative work in Scottish granite now
adorns the streets of the principal cities of Holland and
Belgium, of France and Switzerland. Last year a costly and handsome monument was sent to Buenos Ayres,
there to be erected over the grave of a famous mer-
chant prince; another scarcely less valuable went to
France to mark the resting place of one of her most
famous public men; while yet another specimen of finely polished Peterhead granite went to occupy a prominent place in one of the many temples of the Flowery
Land. An Aberdeen firm is perhaps still executing an
order from President Kruger's government for a lasting monument to commemorate the repulse of Dr.
Jameson and the triumph of law and order in the
Transvaal Republic.

During the last few years special attention has been
paid to cultivation of artistic work in granite. Under
the auspices of the granite association, the Master
Masons' Association and the Operative Masons and
Granite Cutters' Union, there has been established a
class for training the younger workmen in the arts of modeling and sculpture. Judging from the results already
achieved, this special and systematic training of the
elite of the younger craftsmen promises to create in
Scotland a band of skilful sculptors whose work will
yet reflect great credit on the whole granite industry
of the north.

The principal granite quarries in Scotland are Rubislaw, Kemnay, Persley, Dancing Cairns and Dunecht—
all near Aberdeen; and Peterhead, Oban, the Isle of
Mull, the Island of Arran and Craignair and Creetown
in Kirkcudbrightshire. Other districts of course there
are; but they are mainly of lesser repute. The Kirkcudbrightshire granite is largely employed in dock
work and bridges, having been satisfactorily used in

such works as the Swansea docks and the Liverpool, Birkenhead and Newport docks. The famous rich red granite quarried at Stirling Hill, Peterhead, is highly prized for its beautiful color and fine texture, and is largely used for polished columns, pilasters and cornices. Fine specimens of this granite may be seen in the pillars of the Carlton Clubhouse, London, and the handsome columns of St. George's Hall, Liverpool. From Dunecht quarries were extracted the stones used in building Dunecht House, lately the property of the Earl of Crawford and Balcarres. This magnificent building, erected by F. Christie & Son, is undoubtedly the finest specimen of granite architecture in the United Kingdom.

For amount of output, however, Rubislaw quarry remains, perhaps, unrivalled. Standing on the eastern side of the little hill our gaze is soon riveted by the magnitude of the operations. "The half o' Aiberdeen has come oot o' that hole," the workmen there will tell you. Far, far down at the bottom of the jagged cliffs one sees men seemingly scarce bigger than a large doll drilling and splitting great blocks of rock; others are scattered round the rough granite walls preparing for blasting operations. Suddenly the shrill summons of a steam horn breaks through the air, and the pigmy quarrymen with one accord strike for the summit. As they emerge one notes with some amazement that, so

far from being the dwarfs which the depths of the quarry had depicted them, they are as sturdy and stalwart a band of workmen as one could meet in "Aberdeen an' twal' mile roon" (for, sub rosa be it said, to the true Aberdonian the world beyond that limit is of "vera sma' accoont"). No sooner is a place of safety reached than a tremendous report burst forth, accompanied by a shaking of the earth, as if by a tiny earthquake. After the smoke has wholly cleared away we return to the edge of the great granite pit. At the bottom now lie vast boulders of granite, weighing in all perhaps over a hundred tons. Soon the quarrymen are at work again, cutting those boulders into blocks of convenient size.

Nothing—absolutely nothing—is wasted. First, the larger stones are raised by a powerful Blendin crane to the level of the ground, drawn along an enormous overhanging wire rope to the loading-bank, deposited on lorries, and promptly driven off to be hewn and carved into monuments, pillars and pedestals. Follow next the smaller building-stones, then the still smaller blocks for granite setts, and yet, again, still smaller chips for rubble walling. In one of the neighboring quarries in particular this economy of materials is carried yet one step further. Even the stones which the builders reject are cast into a powerful crushing-machine, ground to the required size, and utilized in the

manufacture of adamant paving, and is a partial substitute for granite or sandstone.

A large and most valuable piece of rock at Kemnay quarries, Aberdeenshire, was recently loosened from its bed and shifted to where it could be conveniently cut into the sizes desired. The work preparatory to blasting was in progress for some weeks. Along the back of the huge mass a series of 12 holes, each over 20 feet deep, were bored by means of the steam boring machine. These were charged with powder and fired simultaneously by means of electricity. A succession of eight charges were fired in order to loosen or shake the mass from its "bed" (or, more properly, as applied to granite, "fault"). This having been done, the final or larger charge was given, and so well had the quantity of powder required been calculated that the immense block was simply shifted forward into the desired place. The rock was of first class quality and the block displaced weighs over 9,000 tons. Some idea of the size of this block may be gathered from the fact that 1,125 railway wagons were required for its transport, or a single train over four miles long.

By stepping-stones, such as those we have described, by dint of enterprise, economy and foresight, the Scottish granite industry has reached at last its present proud position in the north. Yet, successful though it has been in the past, there is no reason to believe that the heyday of its prosperity is gone. At home and abroad a growing demand for artistic granite produce still continues. In lands far distant its fame and worth have been discovered, and while the hands of Scotland's craftsmen lose not their cunning nor their eyes grow dim to appreciate the beautiful and artistic in their work, the granite industry of the north will be a source of pride and profit to all who have at heart the prosperity of our national industries—Exchange.

Portable Polishing Machine.

The device we illustrate below is to dispense with the labor usually employed in dragging heavy weights over tile and mosaic floors to produce an even surface. One or two men using this machine, furnished with

suitable electric power, can perform surfacing in a much more satisfactory manner and at an expense hardly to be compared with the old hand method. It is also serviceable for polishing large granite and marble surfaces.

The motor is two-horse power and will be furnished

any voltage required. The surfacing wheel is 20 inches in diameter and of an improved form, which tends to retain the abrasive material. The sand box and water tank are conveniently located, and supply sand and water as desired. The truck wheels have a heavy rubber tire to prevent marring the surface.

The machine is shipped ready for immediate use. Weight, about 800 lbs. Made by the F. R. Patch Manufacturing Co., Rutland, Vermont.

*

MILFORD, N. H.—The condition of the granite industry at this point, as stated under Editorials, is not in the best possible condition. Just how to account for this it is impossible to say. Certainly, the trade was never in a better position to handle monumental work than at the present time. A new plant has just been completed for the Daniels Granite Co. This plant is up to date in every way and is one of the strongest concerns at this location. The machinery at this plant was made and installed by Smith, Whitcomb & Cook of Barre, Vt., and consists of polishing wheel, traveling derrick, air compressor plant, engine, and in fact everything which goes to make a modern plant.

The Milford Granite Co. are not employing their usual number of men at this season, but state that there is plenty of work to figure on, and no doubt the summer's business will average up fully as much as in previous years.

Henry W. Hayden, who has been in the granite business at this location formerly under the name of Hayden Bros., and who at this time is engaged in business for himself, has opened up a new quarry which gives promise of an abundant supply of dark blue, fine granite as good as produced in Milford. Mr. Hayden has abundant experience in the quarry business and we have no doubt but that his present undertaking will give him a good supply of Milford granite.

Burnett Bros., although not one of the largest firms in the place, yet they are absolutely reliable and can be depended upon to turn out as good a class of work as any firm at this location.

Ingram Bros. are also one of the small, reliable firms capable of turning out good quality of work.

The New Westerly Granite Co., which formerly consisted of five partners, has dissolved. Two members of the original firm retain the old business.

The Souhegan Granite Co., which is a corporation made up from granite manufacturers for the purpose of developing the quarries, report an abundant supply of stock and the quarries in excellent condition. The granite produced by this quarry is dark blue in color.

*

CONCORD, N H.—The granite industry at this point is in far better condition than ever before within our remembrance. Previous years have ben a continual complaint, but the year 1900 seems to have brought prosperity to the granite business in this city.

John Swenson is employing two gangs of cutters—at the shed and about 80 men in all. There are two other firms, each employing three gangs of cutters, and another firm employing between 90 and 100 men, making altogether about 250 granite cuttters, saying nothing about the number employed upon the quarry, which would probably add to this an additional 50.

W. N. Howard, who has been in this business for some time, and whose advertisement will be found elsewhere, is one of the small reliable concerns. He can be depended upon to give satisfaction.

Monthly Trade Record.

This department is compiled and edited by the United Mercantile Agency. Subscribers, in accordance with the terms of their contracts, are entitled to receive further information relative to the parties hereafter mentioned, upon application to the main office. As the names of many business men who are good will appear herein, subscribers can readily see the importance of making inquiries if interested, previous to taking any action.

GEORGIA.
Savannah, *M—Ryan, John, Jr. & Co., 80.
ILLINOIS.
East St. Louis, *M—Roux, Louis, 88.
Enfield, *M—McCurdy, O. W., 76.

Lacon, *M—Kirk, Thomas D., succeeds Kirk & Smith.
Lawrenceville, *M—Milligan, A. M., 93 $800.
Mount Vernon, *M—Johnson & Browder, 76.
Peotone, *M—Friederichs, H., succeeds Friederichs & Braun.
INDIANA.
Terra Haute, *M—Clancy, James, succeeds Frank Pratt.
IOWA.
Bloomfield, *M—McCann, A. T., succeeds Jordan McCann.
Bloomfield, *M—McCann, C. C., 76.
Oelwein, *M—Spezia, Charles V., 76.
MASSSACHUSETTS.
Worcester, *M—Murphy, M. H., 76.
MICHIGAN.
Hartford, *M—Clifford, John, 76.
MINNESOTA.
Preston, *M—Spezia, Charles V., 80.
MISSOURI.
Clinton, *M—McNichols, E. S., 80.
Maryville, *M—Richmond, F. G., 80.
Maryville, *M—Simmons, R. M., 80.

Wellsville, *M—Harris, E. A., 88.
NEBRASKA.
　Wahoo, *M—Sickle, J. L., 80.
NEW HAMPSHIRE.
　Exeter, *M—Moon, C. P., 80.
NEW JERSEY.
　Morristown, *M—Dickson, I. B., 76.
　Pleasantville, *M—Froud & Clark, 80.
NEW YORK.
　McGraw, *M—Thompson, D. A., 76.
　Oneida, *M—Madk, E. W., 76.
　Rochester, *M—Sayre & McGee, 76.
OHIO.
　Cardington, *M—Lowery & Curtis, 76.
　Clyde, *M—Wells, Edward B., 93, $3,500.
　Leipsic, *M—Shoemaker & Co., Frank Shoemaker, 99 $500.
　Troy, *M—Prince, John, 80.
PENNSYLVANIA.
　East Downington, *M—McClintock, William, 78.
　Williamsport, *M—Shenton, H. E., 76.
WISCONSIN.
　Burlington, *M—Campbell & Stein, 64.
QUEBEC.
　Beebe Plains, *M—Haseltón Bros., Herbert H. Haselton, 78.

❦

Roman Ornament.

The Roman is simply an enlargement or enrichment of the florid Greek. It did not add a single important element to the Greek, but elaborated the established elements with every possible variety of effect, and with all the richness of which they are capable, developing some into colossal proportions. It was, therefore, original only in its treatment of the Greek materials.

Roman art is accordingly still Greek art, and it is more than probable that nearly all the great artists employed by the Romans were Greeks. The Romans ceased to value the general proportions of the structure and the contours of moulded surfaces, which were entirely destroyed by the elaborate surface moulding of the ornaments carved on them; and those ornaments do not grow naturally from the surface, but are applied on it. The Acanthus leaves under the modillions, and those round the bell of the Corinthian capitals, are placed one before the other most unartistically. They are not even bound together by the necking at the top of the shaft, but rest upon it; and unlike the Egyptian capital, where the stems of the flowers around the bell are continued through the necking, and at the same time represent a beauty and express a truth.

The fatal facilities which the Roman system of decoration gives for manufacturing ornament by applying Acanthus leaves to any form in any direction, is the chief cause of the invasion of this ornament into many works. It requires little thought, and is so completely a manufacture, that it has discouraged many in an indolent neglect of their especial work and decorations have fallen into hands most unfitted for their place.

In the use of the Acanthus leaf the Romans showed but little art. They received it from the Greeks, beautifully conventionalized; they went much nearer to the general outline, but exaggerated the surface decoration. The Greeks confined themselves to expressing the principle of the foliation of the leaf, and bestowed all their care in the delicate undulations of its surface.

Though not original, Roman ornament has its peculiar characteristics as well as every other style. The chief of these is its uniform magnificence. The most simple Greek ornament becomes under Roman treatment a most elaborate decoration. In fact, the most florid Greek example becomes a very simple design in comparison with only an ordinary Roman specimen. The architectural orders, though preserved in nearly their pure Greek form also, have not escaped this enrichment; and the composite, the only distinct Roman order, comprises, as its name literally implies, all three Greek orders at once, the echinus, the voluted, and the acanthus orders.

It may be incorrect to say there is no new element in Roman ornament. The shell, which in after times became so very prominent, is first found in the modillion of the Arch of Titus at Rome. The Roman acanthus likewise had a character of its own. The Greeks used the prickly acanthus; the Romans the soft acanthus. But the Roman acanthus for capitals is commonly composed of conventional clusters of olive-leaves, a modification arising out of the necessity of strong effect in the massive lofty temples of the Romans; but this peculiar conventional leaf does not occur otherwise than on the capitals. There is, further, this distinction between the two styles, that the most rarely used elements among the Greeks are moch characteristic of the Roman; viz., the scroll and the acanthus. The acanthus, in every form except the capitals, is so peculiarly Roman, that its appearance in an ornamental work is good evidence of its belonging to the Roman period. The difference of the two leaves used will prevent any mistakes, and the same may be said of the scroll in anything like an elaborate development and is seldom without the acanthus foliage. Some Roman examples of the echinus from the fullness of curve are especially bold and fine in effect, and are remarkable for deep undercutting. As a rule, Roman ornament consists of a scroll growing out of another scroll, encircling a flower or group of leaves.

We have so far been looking upon the best contained in this style, but we must not overlook those features which show it as a period of decline. In the first place, quantity supplanted quality; and in the second, this quantity was applied without taste.

Greek taste steadily progressed until about the time of Alexander; from this period richness and abundance of ornament gradually supplanted the chaster principles of design. The conquest of Asia introduced a taste for ornamental display, which, ending in pure ostentation, resulted in the utter destruction of taste, and of art itself, under the luxurious example of the Roman Emperors. The Greeks themselves, however, were always lovers of splendor. Their painted sculpture could hardly be surpassed in magnificence; their personal costume was of the richest character; and the splendor of their temples was only characteristic of their mural decoration generally. This splendor was carried out by the Romans on a still greater scale, until a boundless luxury established an indiscriminate extravagance of ornamental detail. Expense was substituted for skill.

This concludes the third and last ancient style, and we will now take up those of the Middle Ages.

JONESBORO, ME.—The Chandlers River Granite Co. have just sold their quarry at that place to Franklin parties. The new owners will begin at once to operate the quarries and thus open up a new business that has for several years lain idle. The stock quarried at this place will be mostly curb stone and paving.

GLOUCESTER, MASS.—The "motion" paving cutters have sold their accumulated stock to an agent of a Philadelphia contractor. They have sold also their output for the next six months to the same man at an advance of $3 per thousand over local buyers.

"Motion" men are those quarrymen who select a boulder in a field, and cut it into paving blocks, and dispose of their product to middlemen, who in turn sell it to the contractors in the large centres. For quite a period there has been a lull in the demand for paving blocks among the middlemen, who offered prices which were too low. The men declined to sell, but kept at work and accumulated a large stock.

SALISBURY, N. C.—The Rowan Granite Co. was chartered May 24. The company is organized for quarrying granite and other rock. It is chartered for sixty years, and the capital stock is $100,000.

PETERSBURG, PA.—The stone cutters employed by the Petersburg Granite Co. went out on a strike June 9. The real cause of the strike cannot be ascertained. The company made a proposition which the men rejected, and they decided to stop work. The company employs about two hundred men.

Proposed Monuments and Monumental News.

HAMILTON, OHIO.—The county commissioners, in compliance with the special law of 1898 and the election of 1899, have levied a tax of 11-12 of one mill for three years for the erection of the Soldiers', Sailors' and Pioneers' monument. It will raise $80,000 in three

years, of which about $7,000 goes to Middletown for the soldiers' monument in Woodside cemetery.

It is expected that plans for the monument will now be prepared and the project pushed.

MARQUETTE, MICH.—Twenty-five thousand dollars is the sum which the Marquette Monument Association expects to raise in a single day when it holds its meeting in July.

As the name of the association implies, the purpose of the fund is to erect a monument to Father Jacques Marquette, the missionary and explorer. This idea first crystallized in 1888. Neither the design of the monument nor the sculptor have yet been selected.

Governor McSweeney and the South Carolina Monument Commission has located eight important points on the battle field held by South Carolina troops at Chickamauga, where markers are to be placed, and also selected the site for the handsome monument to be erected by the state on the reservation.

LYNCHBURG, TENN.—The movement inaugurated by Camp John A. Norman, Sons of Confederate Veterans, to erect at this place a monument to the Moore County Confederate dead, is now well under way, and the monument committee report that several hundred dollars have been subscribed to the monument fund. The monument committee consists of Harry Dance, chairman, and others.

Concerning the equestrian statue of Washington by Daniel C. French and E. C. Potter, which is to be unveiled in Paris on the Fourth of July, the Art Interchange says it is a work of which Americans may well be proud; and it will show to Europeans that we have native sculptors equal to the best of any land, for among the many statues which adorn the streets and squares of Paris, there is none more imposing in dignity nor more sure in artistic knowledge than his.

BROOKLYN, N. Y.—The citizens of Bronx have undertaken to raise $10,000 for the purpose of erecting a soldiers' monument.

CHICAGO, ILL.—Polish-Americans have taken up the idea of a monument to Count Pulaski, the Polish officer who was killed while fighting for the freedom of the republic November 29, 1779. A few weeks after Pulaski was slain at the battle of Savannah, the continental congress passed a resolution providing for such a monument to the hero, but the resolution has ever since lain buried. Poles now wish to revive it and to have an appropriation of $20,000 for the memorial.

SULLIVAN, IND.—Citizens are discussing plans for the erection of a soldiers' and sailors' monument to cost between $5,000 and $10,000.

PITTSFIELD, MASS.—Citizens are discussing the proposition of erecting some suitable memorial to the soldiers of that city who have served in the various wars. The patriotic orders are interested in the matter.

RICHMOND, VA.—An effort will be made to raise the necessary funds for the purpose of erecting a monument to the memory of Gen. A. P. Hill.

BELLEFONTE, PA.—The Center county soldiers' monument and Curtin memorial committee held a meeting June 10. The chairman reported that since the last meeting $12,000 had been raised, with promises and pledges for an additional large amount.

RED BANK, N. J.—Arrowsmith Post, No. 61, G. A. R., is endeavoring to secure a plot of ground upon which to erect a soldiers' monument. The proposed monument will probably cost $7.000.

Quarrying at frankfort, Me.

Frankfort has for years been an important center of the granite industry. Mount Waldo, towering to a height of 1000 feet, is a solid mass of granite, while Mosquito Mountain, near by, is also composed of granite.

The scene of these extensive granite operations is one of the most picturesque in all New England and the view from the quarries of the Mt. Waldo Granite Company, high up on the rugged slopes of Mt. Waldo, is one of great interest. The quarries are at a height of exceeding five hundred feet above the Penobscot river, and it can therefore be readily imagined that the view therefrom is a very expensive one. If time affords a further climb to the summit will disclose to the view a panorama of very wide extent and exceeding attractiveness, and here has been built a commodious camp.

At the base of Mt. Waldo and near the water's edge, is the great building erected last year by the Mt. Waldo Granite Company and in which are a large crew busily engaged in finishing pieces of granite to be shipped to Chicago for the immense government building in process of erection there. This is undoubtedly one of the largest buildings of its kind to be found in any Maine granite quarry and is 209 x 81 feet in size and 33 feet posted. It is well lighted and is admirably adapted for the purposes required. A traveling crane aids materially in moving the massive granite blocks, the crane having a capacity of 25 tons. In addition to this building there are five other cutting sheds, two of these 16 x 130 and three, 30 x 130 feet. There are also two blacksmith shops and an office and draughtsman's building.

Excellent shipping facilities by water are afforded by the south branch of the Penobscot river, there being a wharf frontage of 300 feet, and sufficient depth of water for vessels of good size to load there. At the wharf are two modern derricks of 20 tons capacity each and a hoisting engine with six drums, three of them to each derrick. The shipping of granite is also facilitated by a traveling crane on a car, having a capacity of ten tons.

The granite is brought down from the quarries, which are high up on the rocky side of Mt. Waldo, by a railway. There are in all between 1100 and 1200 feet of railroad track, part standard and the balance three feet guage. The distance from the wharf to the quarries is 5600 feet. The railroad is operated by a cable put in two years ago. There is at the quarry a hoisting engine with a four-foot drum and the round trip from the quarries to the wharf and return is made in twenty minutes, carrying a load of twenty tons. In addition to the above there is also a double drum worked by a lever with windlass. There is also a cable blondin, the cable being 800 feet in length and anchored at both ends; and there is also in connection therewith a double drum hoisting engine. There is also at the quarry a hoisting engine, with three drums to each derrick, for general hoisting purposes. To supply water for the hoisting engines and for other purposes there are tanks of large capacity and water is brought to them through pipes. Steam drills are employed at the quarries, and the equipment is in all particulars the most modern and up-to-date. Within the past two years the Mt. Waldo Granite Company have expended about $75,000 in permanent improvements. In addition to other contracts considerable is done in the line of paving and three-quarters of a million blocks were shipped last year.

Mt. Waldo has long been famous for its granite, and quarrying has been carried on there for an extended period of years. It was in the vicinity of half a century ago that the late Geo. A. Peirce, father of the present proprietors, commenced to operate there and associated with him for many years was John T. Rowe. Originally the firm was Peirce & Rowe, and later Peirce, Rowe & Co. In 1880 the business was incorporated and is now known as the Mt. Waldo Granite Co. Geo. A. Peirce died in 1873 and John T. Rowe in 1898. The directors of the company are John, Hayward and Albert Peirce, all of them sons of the late Geo. A. Peirce, and Albert is secretary and treasurer. John Peirce makes his home in New York city and has become widely known as a granite contractor. Hayward Peirce is a graduate of the University of Maine and makes his home in Frankfort.

There are employed at present at the Mt. Waldo Granite Co. about 110 cutters, 40 apprentices and 75 quarrymen. About two years ago a strike was inaugurated at this quarry and since then non-union men have been employed. The cutters are largely Swedes and Italians but are proving very skillful and industrious workmen. In years gone by many large contracts have been filled here, notable among them being the East River bridge at New York. The Mt. Waldo Granite Company are at present at work on a contract for the big government building in process of erection in Chicago. The granite is shipped from Frankfort by vessel to Perth Amboy, N. J., and thence by rail to Chicago.—Exchange.

The selection of granite as the stone to be used in the work of constructing the rapid transit tunnel for New York, is stated to be in the interests of Tammany politicians who are financially interested in granite quarries in Maine, whence it is proposed to bring the granite.—Exchange.

For Quick Working

TRAVELING CRANES

Up to Forty Tons Capacity, suitable

FOR GRANITE SHEDS,

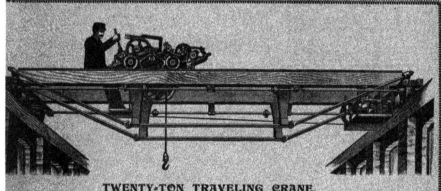

TWENTY-TON TRAVELING CRANE.

ADDRESS

Lane Manufacturing Co.,

MONTPELIER, VT.

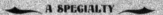

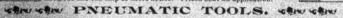

August 1900 Vol. X. No. 8

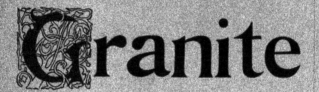

Granite

A. M. HUNT & CO.
PUBLISHERS
131 Devonshire Street
BOSTON, MASS., U.S.A.

Subscription Price, $1.00 Year

Wedging out a Spire, Upper Quarry.

ADVERTISERS' DIRECTORY.

For Quick Working

TRAVELING CRANES

Up to Forty Tons Capacity, suitable

FOR GRANITE SHEDS,

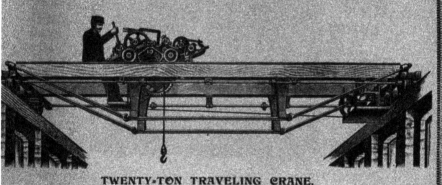

TWENTY-TON TRAVELING CRANE.

ADDRESS

Lane Manufacturing Co.,

MONTPELIER, VT.

ENTERED AT THE BOSTON POST OFFICE AS SECOND-CLASS MAIL MATTER.

l. X.   BOSTON, MASS., AUGUST 1, 1900.   No. 8

A. M. HUNT, Editor.

dished Monthly in the Interests of the Producer,
Manufacturer, and Retailer of Granite as used
for Monumental or Building Purposes.

Terms of Subscription

To any part of the United States or Canada:

copy, one year   -   -   - $1.00, in advance.
copy, six months   -   -   75 cents, in advance.

ADVERTISING RATES FURNISHED UPON APPLICATION.

A. M. HUNT & CO., Publishers,

DEVONSHIRE STREET, - - BOSTON, MASS.

HE condition of the granite industry in Vermont at the present
writing is good, notwithstanding
the prediction of a dull time after
rch 1st on account of the rush of orders from January 1st to March 1st in anticipation of the strike.
re seems to have been a surplus of orders, enough
that since March 1st, taking into consideration the
ers which could not be completed at that date and
new orders placed, it has kept the manufacturers
king to their full capacity ever since the first of
uary. Of course there are firms who are not doing
ch, and no matter what the conditions of business
this is always the case. It can be accounted for in

several different ways : principally because they are not
financially well fixed so they can advertise, or do not
believe in it. The live, up-to-date concern who is continually looking for new business is having all that it
can attend to. A very satisfactory condition of things
we noticed on a recent trip to the granite centres,
namely, a constant tendency on the part of manufacturers to get away from the wholesale dealer and sell
the retail direct. It has taken time for many of the
trade to work up this class of business, but when they
have secured their share of the retail business, invariably it has been satisfactory not only to the retail dealer but to the manufacturer, judging from experiences
reported by both.

E clip the following from an article by Richard Whiteing in the July issue of the Century entitled "Artistic Paris."

Paris lives even more obtrusively for art
than it lives for commerce. There is art everywhere
—in the streets and gardens as well as in the picture-
galleries, in the churches and town halls, decorated by
liberal commissions from government. The very bill-
boards are galleries of black and white. The government does its part just as if the industry were a question of coal or iron. It is fostering and protecting, if
not protective. The elementary school system, as we
have already seen, is a net thrown over all France to
catch children of promise. If they do well in their rudiments of drawing, they are passed on to schools
where they may do better. If they do supremely well
in these schools, they will assuredly be urged to go to
the Beaux Arts.

Of course most of the students enter that institution
without any call but the inner one. However, there
the school is, for all. It is a masterpiece of contrivance
to a given end, with its grade upon grade of teaching
right up to the highest. Nothing is left to chance.
You are supposed to know your rudiments, and more
when you go there ; it is no school for the a-b-c. You
must bring drawings or paintings to the professor as

evidence of vocation. If he thinks there is promise, he gives you leave to "aspire." This means that you may enter the section of the antique, where he will quietly keep an eye on your work. If you fail there you go no further. If you succeed, you one day get your promotion to the life-class, and rank as a member of the atelier of your chosen master. From this time forth he takes something of a personal interest in you. In the atelier you have the stimulus of all sorts of competitions. There is the monthly contest for the right to choose your place. The professor looks at your work, marks it first, second, third, and so on, in the order of merit, and as it is marked, so you have the right to plant your easel where you will for all the month to come. It registers a step in honor, and it precludes bad blood. Then comes the annual competition for the medal, or a tremendous struggle for a place in some special class. Yvon's used to be a favorite for the rigor of the game in drawing. The professor held that, whatever else a man carried away with him from the Beaux Arts, he should not fail to have an impeccable perception of the niceties of form. The other things were for other teaching, for other stages. Yvon's best man was able to draw anything in any position, and to be beyond the reach of surprise by the eccentricities of contour. With this we have examinations in history, ornament, perspective, anatomy. Students are supposed to know something about these collaterals of their great subject. Many take the history and the perspective in a perfunctory way, feeling that the strain is not there, and that drawing and painting are still at the heart of the mystery. In the final heat for Yvon's the few that were left did their best in drawing from the figure, which had to be completed in so many days of two hours each.

The Prix de Rome—restricted to Frenchmen, is something like a prize—the winner has free quarters in the art capital of the world on a liberal allowance from the state. The first heat is a sketch in oils, and the result, of course, leaves many out of the race. The second is a figure in oils. For the third, the few left standing are sent to paint against one another for their lives on a subject given by the school. Now, there are all sorts of possibilities of unfair play in a competition of this sort, and against them authority has taken due precaution. A man may get outside help, and bring in a work that is only half his own; and even if he does every bit of it, he may still have fed his invention on the contraband of borrowed ideas. So, to prevent all that, they put him in a kind of monastic cell in the school itself, and there for three mortal months, until his task is done, he has to live and work, with no communication from the outer world. He is what is called en loge. He brings in his own traps, and he is as effectually under lock and key as any Chinese scholar competing for the prize of Peking. The moving-in day for the Prix de Rome is one of the sights of the Latin Quarter, with its baggage-trains of personal gear, ranging from the easel of study to the fiddle of recreation. When it is all over, and the best man has won, he settles for four years in the capital of Italy to rummage at his ease in its treasure-houses of the art of all time. Of course he has to rummage on a plan. Paris requires of him a work of every year, to show that he

has been making good use of his time. If this is of unusual merit, it is bought by the government.

We publish the above to draw attention again to a matter upon which we have written Editorials in the past, upon a subject which we sincerely believe to be a necessity in order to preserve the granite industry in the future, not that we believe there is any present danger of it collapsing, but we do believe that of necessity there must be some improvement each year, that it may be prevented from a down-hill course, which eventually means ruin at the end.

Then what could be better than to take up the matter of schools where the future granite cutter can be taught art upon the same lines spoken of in the above article.

This should be a matter for the Granite Cutters' Union, the Granite Manufacturers' Association and the town or city in which the granite industry is located, to undertake. Prizes should be offered and it should be made so interesting for the boy that he will be proud to call himself, not a stone cutter, but a sculptor. Of course all boys cannot become sculptors, but they can at least try, and if they fail to gain a prize, yet even then their studies will place them far above the average workman of today. And the object for which the prizes were offered will be gained, viz., an improvement of the present condition of the art of designing and cutting monumental work in granite which all familiar with the subject will agree with the editor, needs it badly.

IN another page we publish a description of Professor Despradelle's design for a colossal monument to be called the "Beacon of Progress." It is stated in the article that the erection of the monument is assured. We trust that this may be so, for the following figures will give a slight idea as to what it will mean to the granite industry, for we assume that granite will be the only possible material that will be considered in connection with the construction of the monument. The main shaft above the bases will contain about 23,437,500 cubic feet. Basing our figures upon the height, 1,500 feet, 200 feet square at the base and about 50 feet square at the apex; 8 shafts setting on the base of the main shaft, each from 250 to 275 feet high, 30 feet square at the base, all would contain about 960,000 cubic feet. One shaft 500 feet high, 60 feet square at the base would contain about 800,000 cubic feet. In front of this shaft set on the same pedestal is a column 50 feet high, surmounted by an eagle; main bases and stairways cover a space of 900 feet square, flanked by lions rampant on bases, all containing 18,000,000 cubic feet. Aside from these are the bases and pedestals proper, which would contain about 5,000,000 cubic feet. We have made no allowance for the foundation, and the above figures we consider very conservative, and amount in round numbers to 49,000,000 cubic feet. To give a slight idea as to what this would mean to the granite trade we quote the following figures estimated as to the output of the Barre, Vt., quarries. We quote

Barre quarries for the reason that they probably produce more granite than any other section at the present time. The dark quarries produce and ship about 7,325,000 cubic feet. The light quarries produce about 700,000 cubic feet per year. We estimate that it would take two thousand men thirty-one years to cut the granite, if only roughly hammered. These figures are given upon the basis of the number of men it takes to cut the granite output of Barre, and is roundly estimated, as the whole output of Barre is not finished at the quarries, large quantities being shipped away in the rough. The Boston Transcript has the following to say regarding the monument:

It is easy to say that mere size in a monument constitutes no artistic merit; yet for the expression of certain ideas and for the commemoration of certain historical events, it is obvious that colossal monuments are entirely appropriate, and, further, that their very dimensions count as an essential part of the conception. Mass without meaning, indeed, may be conceded to be the acme of materialism and stupidity, but there is a legitimate part to be played in monumental art by vast masses, treated in accordance with the special laws of colossal architecture. The imagination is powerfully affected by immensity, massiveness, height and majesty of forms, in art as in nature; by the Egyptian pyramids as well as by the Alps. The stupendous conception of Professor Despradelle for a monument "to the glory of the American people" is one of those projects which, even upon paper, impresses the mind with an irresistible sense of awe by its magnitude and audacity. It is an architectural dream, a bold flight of the imagination, and when we are told that its erection is assured we are inclined to smile. Yet, nothing is impossible, not even a monument fifteen hundred feet high. The chief obstacle to the realization of such a marvellous project would be the enormous cost.

The photographs of Professor Despradelle's prize design show that he has drawn his inspiration in great measure from the ancient Egyptians. This was to be have been expected in a plan of this gigantic character. The Egyptian obelisk, pyramid and temple furnish the type of architectural structure from which all races and periods have derived their ideas of colossal monumental art. The obelisk, from which the artist has taken his central motive, is probably the most ancient form of memorial known. It is the simplest, most logical physical embodiment of the idea of aspiration, ambition, exaltation. The perpendicular movement of its outlines, the upward sweep of its contour, the whole tendency and purport of the form combine to signify a spiritual impulse common to all races of mankind. In setting forth the reasons why the Egyptian obelisk was a work of art, T. H. Bartlett has said: "The Egyptian had an idea to express. He thought of thought, of perspective, of the absorbing value of space, of the imposing effect and power of distance, and of the searching sun as they affected form. All these were influences to be considered in a worthy expression of his life, as centred in his only uprising sentiment of devotion to his divinity. These considerations were solemnities to him. To give shape to them he was obliged to use the meanest, the hardest, the most unresponsive

of materials—granite. But he conquered it. He did not raise it to respectability, but he condemned it forever as a beast of burden to carry to eternity the imperial signet of his genius. He took it as hard and repulsive: he left it a living stone. Like everything that he touched with the enchanted wand of a great purpose, his obelisks are stones dominated by his soul. They have lasted for these thousands of years because they are the best existing expressions of all the art that can be put into such a form. They are the result of a spiritual necessity."

It was left to modern art to utilize the obelisk form for the purposes of national and hero-worshipping memorials, but nothing, in all probability, could have supplanted it to advantage. "To the glory of the American people" is a very large phrase, and calls for a very grand monument. Its art should be commensurate with its bulk, else it will celebrate material and brutal things, not the real glory of a civilized people. It is not possible, and would not be just, to criticise Professor Despradelle's design in detail, without a complete acquaintance with all its parts; but the approval given it by the French architects, and the purchase of the drawings by the ministry of the fine arts, go far to establish the presumption of its distinct artistic merits as a project, to say the least. The feasibility of such a project is a matter of sentiment and finance, and, as a rule the popular enthusiasm requires something less general, broad, and vague than the glory of the nation, if it is to be a continuing and persistent enthusiasm, to be depended on in season and out.

#

Granite and Bronze.

ALBANY, N. Y.—It is proposed to erect a bronze tablet of fine workmanship to the memory of George Rogers Rowell, M. A. The tablet will be erected by the residents of Southampton, L. I., where he was born.

WASHINGTON, D. C.—The report on the bill appropriating $17,500 for the purchase of a bronze portrait statue of George Washington has been presented to the House.

WEST POINT, N. Y.—Bronze life size statues of Grant, Sherman and Sheridan will be placed in Cullum Memorial Hall if the fund which the professors of the military academy are trying to raise reaches the proportions they expect.

#

Among the Retail Dealers.

CUBA N. Y.—The Cuba Granite Works, E. O'Malley, proprietor, recently contracted with G. H. Gentzer of Roulette, Pa., for a large monument in extra dark Barre granite. The design is modern and original, making a fine piece of workmanship.

SYRACUSE, N. Y.—In the case of William H. Harrison of Onondaga Valley against P. L. Dwight of De Ruyter, which went on trial before a special term of Supreme Court, it is asked that Dwight be perpetually enjoined from removing a granite monument which marks the graves of deceased members of Harrison's family. Harrison says that in September, 1898, he and Dwight, who is a dealer in monuments, entered into an agreement whereby the latter erected the monument in Hawk's cemetery, Georgetown Station, Madison county. Dwight, it appears, claims that the monument has not been fully paid for, and has threatened to remove it from the cemetery. The purchaser, on the other hand, alleges that he has paid the full purchase price, which was $325. In his complaint Harrison sets forth that the monument dealer has notified the superintendent of the cemetery by letter that the monument would be removed. Harrison further claims that Dwight threatens to sell the monument at auction, and adds that such an auction would be a desecration of the graves of the people in whose memory it now stands.

WILMINGTON, DEL.—The union granite cutters at the marble and granite yards of B. H. Jones, Fourth and Monroe streets are on a strike, and at a meeting at Union Labor League, decided to remain out until their demands are acceded to. They want a scale of 35 cents an hour and eight hours per day, demand that two men now in Jones' employ be discharged.

LYNN, MASS.—The firm of Blethen & Curry, granite workers, is doing a lively business. It has the contract for the granite for the new Item building, also for the granite engine beds for the new General Electric building on Centre street, for the work on two cemetery lots in St. Mary's cemetery, one in St. Joseph's and two in Marblehead ; also for a large monument and two tablets of red Swedish stone to be furnished as soon as possible, a granite curb job, and a quantity of circle top curbing.

LINCOLN, NEB.—Kimball Bros. have just completed the work of erecting a handsome and massive monument for the Cobb family in Wyuka cemetery. It is an obelisk of Barre granite, distinctive in style, of quite large proportions. A tablet of the same material is placed at the head of each grave, each containing the appropriate inscription. The faultless execution of the work reflects great credit upon Kimball Bros., who are recognized as one of the leading monument firms of the West.

WASHINGTON, D. C.—Work has begun on the new building being erected by J. F. Manning & Co. on the corner of 14th and H streets. It will be a one-story pebble-dash-front building and will be used as an art studio for the display of Italian and other imported marble statuary, bric-a-brac, etc.

The hot weather during the middle of the month of July was so severe that for several days it became necessary to suspend work, and for several days practically no work was done in the cutting sheds or quarries.

Proposed Monuments and Monumental News.

OXFORD, MISS.—The Ladies' Confederate Memorial Association of Oxford have started a movement to raise funds for the erection of a monument in memory of the Confederate dead which lie buried in the vicinity of that town.

READING, PA.—A movement has been started in Reading for the erection of a monument in honor of the Ringgold Light Artillery (First Defenders), which was one of the first companies to march to the defense of Washington when President Lincoln issued his call for 75,000 volunteers on April 15, 1861.

Notice is hereby given that the Ohio Shiloh Battlefield Commission will receive proposals for granite monuments, to be erected in the "Shiloh National Military Park," Pittsburg Landing, Tennessee, at their office in the State House, Columbus, Ohio, up to 12 M., August 15, 1900, for twenty-four regiments of infantry, engaged, costing not to exceed $1,500 each ; six batteries of artillery, engaged, costing not to exceed $1,000 each ; two battalions of cavalry, engaged, costing not to exceed $1,000 ; four regiments of infantry, engaged, costing not to exceed $1,000 each ; and one battalion of cavalry, on detached duty, $500.

Each proposal must be accompanied by specification, statements of the proposed dimensions, design, plan and elevations showing exact measurements, a close estimate of the weight and the kind of granite to be used ; each proposal and accompanying statements to be in duplicate, one marked "Original" and the other "Duplicate."

Each monument is to be erected by the contractor, complete with inscriptions, and in the position designated by the commission, on a foundation furnished by the Shiloh National Park Commission.

Address Ohio Shiloh Battlefield Commission, Columbus, Ohio, or either of the undersigned.

R. B. BROWN, President, Zanesville, O.

T. J. LINDSAY, Secretary, Washington, D. C.

SPOKANE, WASH.—The contract for the Monaghan mausoleum has been let to the Washington Monumental and Cut Stone Yorks for about $4,000. It will be the first of its kind in the Spokane cemeteries, and is to be completed in about three months. The designs for the mausoleum, which have been prepared by an architect, show a granite vault 18 feet square and about 14 feet in height, without the capping and cross, which rise nearly 10 feet higher. It is to be built of Little Spokane granite and trimmed with the dark granite from Medical Lake. Over the heavy iron gate at the entrance will be the family name in polished black granite.

McKEESPORT, PA.—Subscription books have been passed round in various quarters and money is being raised to erect a monument to cost about $3,000 in Richland cemetery for the Grand Army of the Republic Post of Dravosburg.

CINCINNATI, OHIO.—An organization of the citizens of the Fifteenth ward was effected June 14 to further the project of erecting a monument to the memory of Thomas Bland, the fireman who lost his life in attempting to save the life of a child.

LOUISVILLE, KY.—The recent convention of confederate veterans held here voted to accept the offer of $100,000 made by Charles Broadway Rouse of New York, formerly a soldier of the confederacy from Virginia, for the purpose of erecting a memorial to the confederate dead at Richmond, Va. The memorial committee reported that it had secured pledges of $124,437.35 in addition, and that the prospect of raising an amount sufficient to make the total, including Mr. Rouse's donation, $300,000, was excellent. Upon these representations Mr. Rouse has authorized the Confederate Veterans' Association to draw on him for the amount pledged by him at any time it may be thought advisable to begin the work. The Confederate Memorial Association, which has the enterprise in hand, has elected Judge George L. Christian of Richmond, Va., as its treasurer, and the memorial is to be built in Richmond.

TOLEDO, OHIO.—A movement has been started in this county and Bulgaria to erect a monument over the grave of J. A. MacGahan, the noted war correspondent.

WEST CHESTER, PA.—In order to preclude the possibility of a contest over his will after he is dead, J. G. Taylor of this place is now engaged in expending a fortune of $100,000 in monuments. Mr. Taylor's avowed purpose is to use all his money in improving Lafayette cemetery, on the heights of Brandywine battlefield, a short distance from the spot where General Lafayette fell, wounded in battle. The bodies of his father, mother, sister, wife and child are buried there. Quietly and without ceremony, Mr. Taylor yesterday unveiled his fourth monument. The shaft is of white enameled brick, containing a niche in which is a life-size figure of Christ in marble. The statue was made in Carrara, Italy. Near this pile Mr. Taylor has completed the base of a $25,000 monument commemorative of General Lafayette.

YORK, PA.—At a regular meeting of the Rescue Fire Company held July 3, the company ordered the trustees of the company to purchase the $800 statue for the company's monument on Penn park.

COLUMBIA, S. C.—Captain S. E. White, an old confederate soldier, will erect a monument to the dead Indians who helped the confederate cause.

COLUMBUS, OHIO.—The Andersonville Monument Commission met July 8 and organized by electing Daniel S. Wilder of this city president, and N. B. Mason of Cincinnati, secretary.

SOUTH NORWALK, CT.—It is proposed to erect a soldiers' monument at this location.

BATTLE CREEK, MICH.—The citizens' committee on soldiers' monument report that $6,000 of the $6,500 necessary to secure the building of the monument has been raised, and that as soon as the additional $500 is raised, the monument will be ordered.

SOUTH NORWALK, CT.—Nearly $2,000 has been subscribed for a soldiers' monument which the citizens are contemplating erecting as soon as the necessary amount can be raised.

ROCKPORT, IND.—The Spencer county council has voted an appropriation of $800 to buy the tract of land surrounding the grave of Nancy Hanks Lincoln, at Lincoln City, in Spencer county. The property to be bought is a beautiful natural park of sixteen acres. The grave is near the summit of a large hill, almost in the centre of a wood, and at present is marked only by a neat stone of granite and railing of iron. The park will be under the direct care and management of the Nancy Hanks Lincoln Memorial Association. A monument of fitting proportions is to be erected.

LACONIA, N. H.—The matter of erecting a soldiers' monument is being agitated.

SOUTH BEND, IND.—The county council June 4 authorized the erection of the $25,000 soldiers' monument petitioned for by citizens.

PHILADELPHIA, PA.—An ordinance introduced in the common council appropriating $100,000 for the construction of a soldiers' monument, was considered and referred to a sub-committee. The subject of a soldiers' monument has long been agitated in the various Grand Army Posts in the city, and it is proposed by these organizations to raise $100,000 in addition to that asked of the councils, making $200,000 in all, for the purpose of erecting a monument to the soldiers of Philadelphia in one of the public squares.

PETERSBURG, VA.—A. P. Hill Camp has appointed a committee of seven to formulate plans for the raising of the necessary funds to erect a monument to the memory of General A. P. Hill. Robert Gilliam, chairman.

MACON, GA.—Mayor Smith is figuring on a plan to get the school children of Macon to build a granite or marble arch in one of the streets to celebrate the big fair that will be given here in the latter part of September.

MEMPHIS, TENN.—A called meeting of the Forrest Monumental Association, or the women's organization, was held June 9 for the purpose of devising ways and means for co-operation in raising the money to build a monument to General Nathan Bedford Forrest.

LYNCHBURG, TENN.—The joint committee on monument to the confederate dead of Moore county appointed from Woody B. Taylor Camp of Confederate Veterans and John A. Norman Camp, Sons of Confederate Veterans, met June 10 and perfected permanent organization by the election of Hon. James J. Bean of John A. Norman Camp of Sons as chairman.

SAN FRANCISCO, CAL.—Every county in the state was represented at the convention of the Lincoln Monument League of California, held on June 16. The object of the gathering was to formulate a plan for the erection of the proposed monument to the martyr President.

WASHINGTON, D. C.—The monument to be erected to the memory of General Albert Pike, explorer, teacher, soldier, poet and lawyer, will be most imposing, and is the work of Trentanove, the sculptor who has already arrived from Italy. The unveiling, which will be conducted with great ceremony, will most likely occur next May. The pedestal is of red granite from Loke Como, Italy. On the steps is seated a graceful female figure representing Masonry, with the star on her forehead, symbolic of the spread of the light of Masonry throughout the world. She holds aloft the banner of the Scottish Rite. The figure of General Pike is of bronze, cast in one piece at Florence, Italy.

TOLEDO, OHIO.—To Monument Builders: The monument committee for Lucas county, O., have placed at their disposal four thousand dollars ($4,000) for the purpose of erecting a soldiers' monument in Woodlawn cemetery, near this city.

You are solicited to furnish one or more designs for a monument costing the above amount, exclusive of foundations, to be set in place on a foundation prepared by the committee.

The general plan is to be a shaft, comparatively plain, with such ornamentation, as the good taste of the designer may suggest. The material is to be of the best granite or some other stone or material equally durable.

The monument is to be finished by the first of May, 1901, and the contract to be let this summer.

Designers will state the kind of stone or material used, with full description. dimensions and specifications, for the monument all complete and set in place. These designs must be in the hands of the committee on or before August 23, 1900, and will be opened at a meeting of the committee to be held in the parlors of Memorial Building, Thursday evening, August 23, 1900. No design will be opened previous to this date, and the contract will be awarded to the party who will furnish the most satisfactory monument for the money. The committee reserves the right to reject any or all bids. Address the chairman.

By order of the committee.

L . F. LYTTLE,
209 Superior Street, Chairman.
MISS KATE G. RAYNOR,
3339 Cherry Street, Secretary.

LANCASTER, PA.—The Lancaster Monumental Association has elected the following officers for the ensuing year: president, Samuel Evans, Columbia; vice-president, S. Clay Miller; secretary, H. R. Brene treasurer, James H. Marshall; solicitor, A. C. Reir esq.; finance and executive committee in charge monument for the coming year, D. D. Rosenmille L. D. Stauffer and Edward Edgerley.

Byzantine Ornament.

BY HERBERT W. BEATTIE, QUINCY, MASS

We will now run over the Middle-Age styles zantine, Saracenic and Gothic, which to distin from the ancient or "heathen" may be termec "Christian" art.

The terms Byzantine and Romanesque will ably be used in the following as synonymous. are so as regards their architectural features; th zantine being only a variety of the Romanesque the later centuries they may be considered the in all respects, but in the earlier centuries there ornamental distinction, the more strictly Roman being a simple debasement of Roman art; the B tine being this art combined with the symboli ments introduced by the new Christian religion, prising a peculiar symbolic version, also, of the R acanthus foliage. The wide or general significat: Romanesque is to distinguish the early Chr round arch from the Gothic or pointed arch.

Pure Byzantine ornament is distinguished by b toothed and acute-pointed leaves which in carvin bevelled at the edge, are deeply channelled throug and are drilled at the several springings of the with deep holes, and the running foliage generall; and continuous. The introduction of animal or figures is very limited and always in a stiff conven style.

Romanesque ornament, on the other hand, de mainly upon sculpture for effect; it is rich in ligh shade, deep cuttings, massive projections, and a intermixture of figure subjects of every kind wit age and conventional ornament. During the fir second centuries, Christian works of art were li to symbols, and were then never applied as d tions, but as exhortations to faith and piety. A Christian decoration rests on this foundation.

The early symbols were the monogram of C the lily, the cross, the serpent, the fish, the au The fish, from the common Greek word for fish taining the initials of the sentence: Jesus Christ, o the Son, the Saviour; and the circle or nimbus, th ry of the head. These are very important eleme Christian decoration—especially the nimbus, wh the element of the trefore and the quatre-foil, so mon in Byzantine and Gothic art,—the first havin erence to the Trinity, the second to the four Ev lists, or the testimony of Christ, and the cross: . extremities of which we often find four circles, b the circle in the centre which signifies the Lord.

Thus, figures or combinations of three, four an circles are common in mediæval art, and have all s significations. Many crosses are composed near

sively of the five circles as principles, or are promi-
ntly decorated with them. A cross of this character
not uncommon, either with the circle or nimbus in
e centre, and four other circles or nimbi at the ex-
remities, or composed simply of five circles arranged
n the form of the cross—and the centre circle or nimbus having reference to the Lord and the other four to
the Evangelists. Occasionally the symbolic images of
the evangelists, the angel, the lion, the ox and the
eagle are represented in these circles. The hand, in the
attitude of benediction, is another characteristic element in early Christian and mediæval works of art.

There is a distinction between the Greek and the
Latin form—the Greek symbolizing Jesus Christ, expressing his Greek monograms, IC. XC. (Jesou C
Xristo C), by placing the thumb on the third finger,
and slightly curving the second and fourth; the Latin
displaying the thumb and the first and second fingers
only extended, thus symbolizing the Trinity. The Roman prelate blesses in the name of the Trinity; the
Greek in the name of Jesus Christ.

Without some knowledge of these essential points,
the Byzantine decorations are quite unintelligible; for

thus leaf, somewhat resembling the ordinary thistle or
holly leaf.

Why the beautiful styles of the ancients were dis-
carded for such crude elements or ornament, needs no
other explanation than the statement that they were
Pagan.

Paganism, however, consisted solely in forms, not in
colors; and therefore, in respect of color, there never
were restrictions in Byzantine art. The forms of the
ancient, too, as Paganism itself gradually disappeared,
were slowly admitted among the elements of Christian
decoration; and the scroll, under certain symbolic
modifications,—the foliations terminating in lilies or
leaves of three, four and five blades, the number of the
blades being significant,—became eventually a very
prominent feature in Byzantine decoration; and under
the same modifications the Anthemion, and every other ancient ornament, was gradually adopted, and after
a systematic exclusion of about four or five centuries.
But the most characteristic of all ordinary Byzantine
ornamental details is that conventional scroll work and
foliage just described. An important feature always to
be observed in the works of the Byzantines is, that all

Fifth Maryland Regiment closing in upon Roulette's Barns and House, modelled by Herbert W. Beattie, Quincy, Mass.

their early designers would appear to have avoided,
rather than sought beauty in all these peculiar forms;
the principle is exactly the same as that by which
Egyptian art was regulated. The Lily, the emblem of
the Virgin and of purity, is as common in Christian
decoration as the lotus in that of Egypt. It is the
symbol which was eventually elaborated into the most
characteristic foliage of Byzantine and Romanesque
art, still well illustrated in work of the twelfth and thirteenth centuries, and especially in the old iron work of
that time. Conspicuous in their foliage, also, is a peculiar version of the Greek acan-

their imitations of natural forms were invariably conventional; so far they have preserved the ancient custom throughout. It is the same even with animals and
with the human figure; every saint had his prescribed
colors, proportions and symbols.

We find that the most beautiful Byzantine decorations are those in which the symbolism is unobtrusive,
or even wholly disguised; not absent, for that is very
rarely, if ever, the case. A design which contained no
trace of symbolism could hardly be a genuine Byzantine example. Generally speaking, the symbols in
some form or other are paramount, being mixed up

"GRANITE," AUGUST, 1900.

BOTTOM BASE	. . . .	R — C Y x A — A x C — A
SECOND BASE	. . . .	R — A x C — T x C — Y
DIE	. . . .	A — N x C — Y x A — T

PRICE:
Barre Granite	. . . .	$ C Y P
Medium Quincy Granite	. . . . .	$ C C I
Westerly Granite	. . . .	$ C P Y
Milford and Troy, N. H., Granite	. .	$ C R Y

"Granite," August, 1900.

Bottom Base . . . . P — A x A — P x C — A
Second Base . . . . R — T x C — N x C — Y
Die . . . . R — Y x C — A x R — Y

PRICE: { Barre Granite . . . . $ C P I
Westerly Granite . . . . $ C G R
Milford and Troy, N. H., Granite . . . $ C I Y

"Granite," August, 1900.

Bottom Base . . . . C A x T — Y x C — P
Second Base . . . . C Y — T x P — T x C — A
Die . . . . G — T x R — T x R — T
Top of Die . . . . G — R x R — R
Cap . . . . C Y — R x P — R x C — T

Price: In Dark Quincy all polished above the lower base . $C A R Y

with geometrical forms. Many Byzantine capitals may appear to contradict this; but on examination it will be found that the apparently floral forms are combinations only of the conventional types derived from the symbols. The very tracery is sometimes composed of serpents; and serpents are not an uncommon ornament for a capital.

The serpent figures largely in Byzantine art, as the instrument of the fall. The cross planted on the serpent is found sculptured on Mount Athos. The ordinary northern crosses, so conspicuous for their interlaced ornaments, are only modifications of this idea.

The leading forms of Byzantine architecture are likewise due to the same influence—the cross, the circle and the dome pervade everywhere. The dome has its own reference to the vault of heaven.

Some of the principal Byzantine or Romanesque churches are developments of the symbol of the five circles or glories; they are placed in the form of a cross and are surmounted by domes corresponding in size and situation to the circles represented in the pavement below. St. Mark's, at Venice, is a conspicuous example of this symbolic architecture. This species of architecture, with the dome and round arch, is termed Romanesque, as derived immediately from that which prevailed throughout the Roman Empire at that time when from heathen it became Christian. Though not Roman absolutely, it is derived from the Roman; it is debased Roman—Romanesque; it is a general term which distinguishes the round-arch species from the Saracenic and Gothic, which are pointed arch species. The preservation of the dome and arch, however, was probably due rather to the symbolic value of those figures among the Byzantine Greeks than to the more historic example of the Romans.

The chief varieties of the Romanesque are—the Byzantine, the Lombard and the Norman. Both the Lombard and the Norman may, in a technical point of view, be considered mere modifications or varieties of the Byzantine.

There is this difference between the Byzantine and the Lombard and Norman varieties, that the symbolism is mere matter of habit in the two latter, and generally, perhaps, though rudely preserved in many forms, is disregarded in spirit: that is, in mere ornamental detail. such as the zigzag, dog's-tooth, nail head, star chain, and a host of others: but the symbolic figures and other religious decorations mean exactly what they express.

St. Cloud, Neb.—The Arnold Granite Co.'s polishing plant and granite mill was totally destroyed by fire July 5. The loss is estimated at $5.000 on the building and machinery, and $3.000 on material ruined by heat.

Stony Creek, Conn.—The granite cutting business is not booming very loudly at this usually busy centre. But indications point to a revival in that line very soon. Norcross Bros. have about 60 cutters at work and several men are waiting to be called to the sheds this week. The Stony Creek Red Granite Co. are still idle; but as the superintendent has been called away to New York it is to be hoped that he will return with a contract. At Hanna's quarry near Guilford, Conn., they have a contract for a building to be erected at New Britain. A small crew are at work, with Billy Murray, formerly of Vinalhaven, as boss. Beattie Bros. are doing some quarrying for a breakwater culvert. No cutting is being done.

Manchester, N. H.—A. L. Adamson has recently sold two valuable quarries at Chesterfield. The old granite quarry at Granite Station was sold to Lewis J. Dollie of Cincinnati for $3,000. This quarry was opened in 1868 by Messrs. Rothwell, Hartwell, Dick & Co., who operated it for a number of years, working during that time several hundred convicts. The business paid handsomely, and from that quarry the stone used in the erection of the City Hall in Philadelphia was gotten. Mr. Dollie, the recent purchaser of the property, will operate the quarry, and is now arranging to commence work. The famous old Ordway quarry, on James river, was sold by Mr Adamson to Albin Netherwood for $7,000. This quarry, like the granite, has not been worked for several years, but will soon be put in operation. From this quarry came the stone used in building the Army and Navy building in Washington.

Bath, Me.—The Bath Granite Co. has been organized in this city. The capital stock is $10,000, of which $5,000 is paid in. This company will at once commence operating the Pownal quarry and will also work the Freeman quarry, a part of which lies in Pownal and part in Yarmouth, Me., and contains about 39 acres. The Pownal quarry covers about five acres. The Bath Granite Co. will have their headquarters at Bath. W. F. Carleton of Bath is president of the company, and John Hyde is vice president. A portion of the help employed heretofore in the Freeport, Me., quarries will enter the employ of the Bath Co. T. W. Hawes will be superintendent.

Baltimore Md.—The proposed new custom house will cost $1,500,000. The material will be pink granite, with dark stone facings.

Minneapolis, Minn.—W. C. Baxter secured the contract to furnish the cut and polished granite for the family vault to be erected at Lakewood cemetery for Marcus P. Hayne. It will be of Ortonville granite. The interior will be of polished marble and there will be some ornamental bronze work.

Vinalhaven, Me.—Business is on the increase, and it is rumored that the Bodwell Granite Co. is to start six new fires, which means an increase of about ninety men.

Continued on page 30.

The Manufacturing Centers.

The Vermont manufacturing centres outside of Barre, which will be found under Barre News, report a good business. Hardwick particularly is progressing. At the present time it is estimated that two hundred and fifty cutters are employed and the question of housing those who want to and have moved to Hardwick is getting to be quite a serious matter. We noted a number of new dwellings in the course of construction, and there are more in prospect. J. E. Sullivan was employing at the time of our visit three gangs of workmen and report business in good shape and increasing. Bickford, More & Co. were employing thirty-five cutters and had just contracted for a new shed to be built in the half-circle shape, 187 feet long and used as a summer shed to accommodate about four gangs of cutters. Among the contracts were eleven vault jobs ranging in price from $2,000 upwards. We noted a rough stone cutting in their shed 15x13x2, weighing 47 tons in the rough, also the cap of the Scranton soldiers' monument, which when completed will measure 7x9x5. This stone had just come from the quarry in the rough and workmen had just commenced upon it. During the past summer they have erected four derricks at the quarry and are now erecting a seventy-five ton derrick. They contemplate adding 2,200 feet to the quarry railroad and are employing thirty-five men on the quarries. They have also erected a twenty-ton derrick at their wharf at Burlington on Lake Champlain and have built two flat boats for the transportation of stone. We noted a number of new small concerns just started at Hardwick. The chances are that all of them will not last the summer. In the course of events there will be a shaking up and those who mean business will come to the top, the others will go to the bottom and out of sight.

Business at Northfield, Vt., is in good condition. Cross Bros. are employing fifty cutters and their books show a number of good contracts. Among them are two mausoleum jobs. They are contemplating erecting a new straight shed with all modern improvements. Cannon & Slack are doing a good business and improving their plant by the addition of an air compressor and pneumatic tools. E. B. Ellis is doing an increasing business and reports the outlook as excellent.

The granite business at Groton does not show any great increase. The firms there have settled to four, who have evidently come to stay. One of the older plants is being improved by an Ingersoll-Sergeant air

compressor, polisher, hoister and derrick, erected by Smith, Whitcomb & Cook. In all we should say they were employing about forty cutters at the present time and one quarry in operation, that is, only one that produces any great amount of stock. There has been a great deal of prospecting, and it has finally settled the point that there is a lot of good granite in Groton, but as yet is has not been developed. There are many rumors that the Pine Hill Granite Co. are putting in money for this purpose but as yet there are no indication, except rumors, that this will or has been done.

Beacon of Progress.

The Boston Herald published recently the perspective and detail of the grandest, most stupendous and most artistic structure ever conceived by man, the design for which won for Desire Despradelle, the author, the first medal in the Salon for 1900 at Paris and aroused an unparalleled enthusiasm among the noted architects who composed the jury on awards.

The subject of the design is of especial interest to the people of America, being a monument dedicated "to the glory of the American people," and entitled "The Beacon of Progress."

The extraordinary size for which the monument is designed will excite the wonder of nations, and upon its completion will mark a new era of monumental architecture. It will be by far the most colossal of artificial structures.

At a height of 1500 feet from the base, which will measure nearly 900 feet on a side, the capstone of the main shaft will nestle among the clouds.

The magnitude of these dimensions is made more pronounced by a comparison with some of the high structures now in existence. To begin with, Bunker Hill monument, to which Bostonians proudly lead their visitors, is 231 feet high, practically one-seventh the height of this proposed gigantic shaft. The Statue of Liberty in New York harbor, with its height of 306 feet, would barely rise to one-fifth the height of this new wonder. The Washington monument, the object of awe and admiration throughout the country, would have to nearly treble its height of 550 feet in order that its capstone should rest on a level with that of Professor Despradelle's creation.

Among the marvels in colossal structure in the old world, the Pyramid of Cheops measures 486 feet from tip to base, while the Pyramid of Cephrenes is 456 feet high, these two pyramids marking the greatest efforts of an age given to the colossal and grand in sculptural achievements.

The Eiffel tower, a creation of our own age, raised to the tremendous height of 300 metres, or 984 feet, simply as a money-making investment, pales into insignificance beside the magnitude of grandeur of this artistic symbolism of the progressiveness of the American people.

In design, Professor Despradelle has made an adaptation of the Egyptian obelisk, and in creating a structure of such mammoth proportions has shown a loftiness of conception and daring of execution that are worthy of the high position to which his triumph has raised him.

The perspective shows an immense sloping base nearly 900 feet square filled with mosaics of uniform design, the outer border of which is a line of five-pointed stars.

Numerous sets of broad steps lead up to the top of the base on three sides. On the front side is situated a large amphitheatre, with seats, which is designed for witnessing military manœuvres, civic ceremonies, pageants, etc. On either side are broad stairs, each flanked by a row of 12 crouching lions, of gigantic size, on pedestals.

On the pedestals are inscriptions such as the following: "Nothing great was ever achieved without success," "A century from the birth of Washington has changed the world."

On each of three sides of the central shaft rise monoliths of 250 or 275 feet in height.

In front the place for the central of these monoliths is occupied by a shaft which rises about 500 feet.

On a ledge at the bottom of this shaft is a circular column 40 or 50 feet high, surmounted by a globe, upon which rests the American eagle.

The national bird is very much in evidence, and surmounts the peaks of all the lesser monoliths and shafts.

Under the circular column in front is a large space which bears the inscription: "To the glory of the American people."

All of these decorations are filled with mosaics and bear hundreds of names of persons and things distinctly American—the names of the states, the great inventors, the newly acquired possessions, the industries, arts, great statesmen; in fact, nearly everybody and everything that have helped place the United States on the footing it now stands.

The main shaft has a base about 200 feet square, and gracefully tapers away to its almost inconceivable height of 1,500 feet. The sides of this are mosaiced up to a height of 300 feet, and on the front side a tapering panel of decoration runs up about 1,000 feet. The whole structure is one of the most beautiful and graceful imaginable, and is in itself a true beacon of the progress of art at the end of the 20th century.

As creator of a new era in architecture, Professor Despradelle is well fitted to bear the title. He is a man of great breadth of mind, of boundless ideas. He is wrapt heart and soul in his profession, and displays an enthusiasm of purpose, a grandeur of conception and a daring of execution that have made his name famous on two continents.

He was educated at L'Ecole des Beaux-Arts in 1882; received many of the prizes at L'Ecole des Beaux-Arts and Societe Centrale des Architects Francaises; took part in the Concours de Rome four times, and received first and second grand prix in 1889. He was at that time designated laureate du Salon, officier d'Academie, assistant inspector of state buildings and national palaces, and, under this title, helped in the building of the new ministry of agriculture, the National Library, the mansions of M. Wilson and M. Grevy, the ex-President, and various other public and private edifices in Paris.

(To be continued.)

Continued from page 27.

MILFORD, N. H.—The Granite State Granite Co., with a capital of $100,000, has filed articles of incorporation.

;

CLARK ISLAND, ME.—The Clark Island Granite Co. started up their works on July 2, and there will be plenty of work all the summer and fall. The job is a building for the Atlantic Insurance Co., at the corner of William and Wall streets, New York City. There is a large amount of carving and ornamental work, and first-class union help will be employed. From 75 to 100 cutters will be engaged, and it is estimated that it will take seven or eight months to complete the job.

FRANKFORT, ME.—The strike at the yards of the Mt. Waldo Granite Co. still remains unsettled. The company is running what is called an "open yard." The company is willing to settle with the union, but refuses to pay $3 per day for blacksmiths and refuses also to have the men now at work for them fined by the union. The company has said to the committee sent to them by the union that it would pay the same wages as all other places of a similar character pay, and allow an eight-hour day. The Frankfort branch of the union refuses to settle on any terms except 35 cents per hour and a fine for every man now at work in the stone sheds. The company refuses to submit to this proposition.

NEW LONDON, CT.—The striking granite cutters at the Booth quarries in Waterford and the quarries at Millstone Point returned to work June 7, an agreement being reached between the men and their employers on a basis somewhat similar to the schedule now prevailing at Barre and Quincy.

PHILADELPHIA, PA.—A large demand is reported for stock of the Consolidated Granite Company, interested in which are, it is understood, not only prominent stone merchants of New York and the East, but some capitalists of New York and Philadelphia, all of whom express belief in the company developing a large earning capacity. Property controlled by the company consists of three tracts, aggregating 308 1-2 acres, containing extensive deposits of granite at Port Deposit, Md., on the Susquehanna River, and the Central Division of the Philadelphia, Wilmington & Baltimore Railroad, and three miles from Perryville, on the main line of the same railroad. Quality of granite is recognized as standard, the formation being a grade biotite gneiss, with color varying from light to very dark, and having a tensile strength of 25,000 pounds per square inch, and weight of from 165 to 170 pounds per cubic foot. In uniform beds, blocks of almost any dimensions can be obtained, according to the report of an expert. Capital stock of the Consolidated Granite Co. (which is declared to have no bonded indebtedness nor preferred stock) consists of 200,000 shares of par of $25 per share, full-paid and non-assessable.—Exchange.

MONG the many pleasant memories of a recent business trip to the good old state of Vermont was a day's outing to Bluff Point on Lake Champlain in company with the agents of the National Life Insurance Co., of Montpelier, Vt., with their wives and sweethearts. This trip was only one incident in a week's outing which this company gave their agents. The company gathered together represented fifteen different states and the only rank outsider was the editor of GRANITE. When we consider the matter, there is a connection between the granite monumental industry and the life insurance business, and considering it from that standpoint we were not so rank as it would seem upon first thought. We realize that we took many chances in entering, as it were, the lion's den, but having been through the fire consider ourselves fireproof. A better and a jollier party could not have been gathered together, and our illustrations given herewith show samples of what a camera can do when it gets up against a party of insurance agents. Four of the plates exposed by the author were spoiled, evidently the lens could not stand the strain. The gentleman with the extemporized flag, or rather the two flags, is General Peck, who is well known all over the state of Vermont, and to a large extent outside. He is signalling to a newly married couple from Burlington who are spending their honeymoon on Stave Island. The gentleman just beyond is Mr. Houghton, president of the National Life Insurance Co. Others in the picture will be recognized by Vermonters. Among them, the gentleman in the upper left hand

hang back for a while. Then, as it was seen that the price had been fixed permanently, the orders began to come in and they have been coming in a steady stream ever since. Several manufacturers seen report that notwithstanding the seven weeks' suspension of business caused by the labor trouble, this year, to date, shows fully as many orders as last year at the same time. In fact, all the dealers report that they have a good number of orders on hand and that the outlook for fall trade is bright. The Quincy Quarries Granite Co. have increased the price of rough stock a little, but as there are so many quarries not included in the syndicate they cannot advance the price a great deal. Whether they will eventually get control of the remaining quarries is of course something that cannot be told.

Snap Shots Taken on a Day's Outing on Lake Champlain.

corner of our cut being S. S. Ballard, who is general agent for the state of Vermont. Possibly the picture may be slightly exaggerated but he will stand exaggeration.

We trust that all the good boys we met on that trip will sell twice $100,000 during the next year.

The condition of the granite business in Quincy as a whole can be said to be much better than it was last month. All of the manufacturers seen report that business has apparently begun to move upward. For the first few weeks after the strike was settled, it looked as though it would take some time with the increase in price, made necessary by the increased price that would have to be paid the cutters, and in fact customers did

as the officers of the company are just as close as to their affairs as they ever were.

The Granite Manufacturers' Association are talking up their annual summer outing, which will probably be held some time before the first of August. Just when or where is at this writing not determined. A special meeting of the association has been called, at which these matters will be attended to.

At McIntosh & Sons the same story is told—plenty of orders and rushing to complete their orders that must be set before fall. They have several good sized jobs on hand, although the larger part of their work is of the medium size. They find the new power plant installed a great labor-saver, and wonder how they ever got along without it as long as they did.

Fuller, Foley & Co. report that while they are not rushed they are quite busy and have a good number of orders on hand, which they are rushing toward completion to make room for fall orders, which should begin to come in soon.

Joss Bros. Co. report that work continues to remain good with them and that they are having hard work to keep up with their orders. Many new orders have been booked during the past month, some of which call for considerable fine work and carving. These jobs are not confined to Quincy stock, for this firm deal in all known granites, samples of nearly all of which can be found at their works.

Deacon Bros., on Centre street, tell the same story now as a month ago—that is, business is rushing, never was better with us than at present. This, of course, speaks volumes for the character of the work they do. They contemplate enlarging their plant at an early date. Many of the orders they have on hand are for medium size work of Quincy and other well known granites, although they have a few good sized sarcophagi jobs.

Herbert W. Beattie, the sculptor, is one of the busiest men in Quincy. He has just completed the model of a seven-foot figure of "Catharine of Sienna." The saint is represented as being robed in a man's costume with a crown of thorns. The hands are clasped in front of the body, while resting easily over the left arm is a cross. The figures when cut will be placed in Mt. Calvary cemetery, Brooklyn, N. Y. Mr. Beattie has also just completed twelve pieces of Romanesque ornaments and memorial tablets which are to be cast in bronze. Aside from this he has made a number of models for special ornamental work. He also has a number of orders on hand, all of which goes to show that he stands at the head of his profession as a sculptor.

W. T. Spargo has booked several good jobs during the past month, as well as a quantity of smaller work. One sarcophagus has a 6x2-10 base all polished die with a raised carved wreath at each end. Another has a 7-4x4 base all polished die and an elaborately carved cap.

Milne & Chalmers have just completed a handsome fountain cut from a solid block of Quincy stock. The job is finely finished. It was a gift to the city by one of its philanthropists, which name appears in the inscription on the front.

The Merry Mount Granite Co. say that they have nothing special to report other than that they are quite busy; they have a good lot of orders on hand, but nothing very large. At their quarry, however, they are more than rushing and cannot keep up with their orders for rough stock.

Joseph Walker, of the Aberdeen Granite Works, reports that he has been unusually busy this month. A look through his yards showed some fine specimens of work; in fact nowhere can a better class of work be found. He has several handsome dies all completed that would do your heart good to look at. The stock used is dark Quincy and is exceptionally fine stock. The sides and ends are polished and look very handsome. Such work as this certainly speaks for itself.

McGillvray & Jones report that they are busy. They have booked a number of orders during the past month but they are largely of the medium size jobs. These, with the several large tomb jobs they have on hand are enough to keep them busy. A more detailed description of these tombs has already been published in these columns. They have also found it necessary as well as convenient to have their office connected by telephone.

Word has been received from Messrs. McIntosh, Spargo, Barnicoat and Falconer, who are travelling in Europe. They had a good trip and report that they are having a great time. They did not stop long in gay Paris, however, the pressure being too great.

West Quincy outdid itself again in June in the matter of granite shipments as it again had one of the largest months on record in this line. 10,989,090 pounds was the amount shipped from this point during the month of June. Quincy Adams comes next with 3,-933,717 pounds, while the Quarry railroad comes up in the rear with 2,454,310 pounds. The total from the three terminals for June was 17,377,117 pounds. This was 13,088,126 pounds less than the month of May. The greatest falling off during the month was on the Quarry railroad, June figures being nearly twelve million pounds less than in May. Quincy Adams dropped a million pounds, as did also West Quincy. It is thought that July and August figures will show an increase and that they will compare favorably with last year.

Monthly Trade Record.

This department is compiled and edited by the United Mercantile Agency. Subscribers, in accordance with the terms of their contracts, are entitled to receive further information relative to the parties hereafter mentioned, upon application to the main office. As the names of many business men who are good will appear herein, subscribers can readily see the importance of making inquiries if interested, previous to taking any action.

CONNECTICUT.

Bridgeport, *M—Smith, Daniel, 93 $300.
New London, *M—Ohaver, W. E., 86.
New London, *M—Stoll, Charles F., 86 to Frank M. Ladd.

GEORGIA.

Brunswick, *M—La Mance, Reed E., 14 $50.
Carrollton, *M—McNamara, G. G., 80.
Carrollton, *M—Ward Marble Co., 80.
Long Pond, *M—Adams, A. L., 99 $264 and 93 $385.

ILLINOIS.

Cairo, *M—Zeran Marble & Granite Works (Inc.), succeed J. S. L. Zeran.
Casey, *M—Hollis & Sedgwick 64, W. D. Sedgwick 58.
Chicago, *M—De Camp & Bowen, 86 to John Gall.
Rockford, *M—Best Bros. succeed William Best.

INDIANA.

Anderson, *M—Carpenter, C. A., 93 $2,500.
Cambridge City, *M—Peel, O. M., 76.
Columbus, *M—Columbus Monument Co., Benj.

M. Hutchins, 93 $350.
Fort Wayne, *M—Hughes, W. S., 86.
Huntingburg, *M—Funk & Garmon, 76.
Lafayette, *M—Darby, W. W., 76 and 14 $300.
Lafayette, *M—Vitts, Jacob J., 93 $250.
Shelbyville, *M—Ham Bros. succeed Ham & Son.
Terra Haute, *M—Wagner, W. F., 86 to Wey Bros.
Wabash, *A—Forest, Edwin, 80.

IOWA.
Bussey, *M—Bussey, J. A., 70.
Carroll, *M—McNeill & Schroeder 64, Schroeder &
Wilmers 58.
Emmetsburg, *M—Godden & Ballard, Mr. Godden
32 $200.
Fonda, *M—Raymond, L. A., 76.
Keota, *M—Northrup, B. A., succeeds J. T. Fulton.
Le Mars, *M—Smith, J. H., 87 $1,500.
Leon, *M—Harris, J. A. & Bros., J. A. Harris 32
$100 and 99 $800.
Waverly, *M—Hattendorf, A. W., 32 $2,600.

KANSAS.
Downs, *M—Scott, T. H., 76.
Eldorado, *M—Sinclair, Hector, 93 $500.
Englewood, *M—Butler & Bishop, 76.
Great Bend, *M—Brooker, Charles R., 86 to A. C.
Baxter.
Lawrence, *M—Strahm, Frederick, 32 $220.
Pleasanton, *M—Tindell, J. M., 32 $1,000.

MAINE.
North Sullivan, *M—Blaisdell, Havey & Co., 80.
Sullivan, *M—Taylor, Alex & Son, 64.

MARYLAND.
Baltimore, *M—Shamleffer & Bro., 20 $15.

MASSACHUSETTS.
Fall River, *M—Picard, Israel, 93 $500.
Lee, *M—Gross, William H., 93 $1,550.

MICHIGAN.
Buchanan, *M—Beistle & French succeed J. P.
Beistle.
Coldwater, *M—Beard & Son, 84.
Grand Rapids, *M—Schmidt, Matthew, succeeds
Charles Schmidt & Bro.
Marshall, *M—Mumaw & Nye succeed Henry W.
Mumaw.

MINNESOTA.
New Ulm, *M—Ambrosch, I., 32 $1,400.
Owatonna, *M—De Long, C. H., 86 to Owatonna
Marble & Granite Works.
St. Cloud, *M—Arnold, Walter, 70.

MISSISSIPPI.
Brookhaven, *M—Ingram, L. G., 76.

MISSOURI.
Gallatin, *M—Tillery, Lynn & Harris succeed Til-
lery & Brown.
Jefferson City, *M—Vetter & Schmitt, 76.

NEBRASKA.
Ansley, *M—Lewis & Cox succeed A. H. Lewis.
Norfolk, *M—Foster, Walton, 84.
Omaha, *M—Feenan, Martin J., 93 $500.

NEW HAMPSHIRE.
Berlin, *M—Walters & Whitney, 76.

Lebanon, *M—Billings, Henry G., 93 $24,000.
Nashua, *M—Cummings, C. E. & Son, C. S. Cummings 99 $1,200.

NEW JERSEY.
Phillipsburg, *M—Klein & Martin, 76.

NEW YORK.
Binghampton, *M—Barnes, E. J. & Son, 86 to G. A.
Chaplin.
Buffalo, *M—Wegenaar Granite Works, 80.
Fort Plain, *M—Selwood, M. A., R. E. deeds $2,-
700, 20 $6,976.
Oswego, *M—Salladin, Charles F., 14 $180.
Saranac, *M—Lobdell, J. W., 106.
Saranac, *M—Thomas & Miller succeed W. H.
Thomas.
Whitneys Point, *M—Eggleston, M. B., 76.

OHIO.
Bryan, *M—Denel, G. W., 14 $320.
Cincinnati, *M—Great Western Marble Works,
Philip McDonough 36 $336.
Leipsic, *M—Shoemaker & Co., 93 $400.

OKLAHOMA.
Ponca City, *M—Collingsworth & McMurphy, 76.

OREGON.
Portland, *M—Schanen & Neu, P. Neu 99 $1,000.

PENNSYLVANIA.
Allentown, *M—Kramm, R. H., 80.

RHODE ISLAND.
Newport, *M—Stevens, P. Son, Edwin Stevens,
prop., 78.

TENNESSEE.
Chattanooga, *M—Mountain City Marble Works,
36 $290.

TEXAS.
Denton, *M—Simmons, W. T. & Co., succeed Benj.
Bland.
Llano, G.—Llano Granite Co., 39.
San Antonio, *M—Zirkel, Otto, 32 $950.

VERMONT.
Hardwick, GZ—Brush, Emerson, 86.
Newport, GZ—Hazel, John M., succeeds Carrick
Bros.

VIRGINIA.
Alexandria, *M—McKenna, John, conveyed per-
sonality $500.

WASHINGTON.
Walla Walla, *M—Roberts Bros., L. W. Roberts,
99 $60.

QUEBEC.
Beebe Plain, *M—Haselton Bros. & Co., 64.

All of the conditions necessary for a busy season
have been present in the situation here during the past
few months and there seems to be no lessening of the

amount of work which is being turned out from the large plants in the vicinity. Everyone here has quite a quantity of orders of various styles and dimensions on their books and in the plant under way, and nearly all of the manufacturers are very sanguine as to the future of the business, and especially as to the immediate future.

At this time there are about as many cutters employed in the city as there has ever been before, and a reason to expect that the number will be materially increased before the winter days are reached.

The class of work during the last few weeks, with the exception of at a few of the larger plants, is not as large as it sometimes is, quite a little of it being cottage monuments and markers, although there are some large jobs at almost every plant, and several in some of them.

The general feeling is to the effect that there will be a continuation of the amount of work up until the holidays, and all are trying to make the most of the good times at hand. Money comes in rather hard, especially from the western portion of the country, and some of the small concerns feel the strain quite severely.

The old firm of McIver & Ruxton will soon be superseded by the firm of McIver & Matheson. Mr. George Ruxton, who has long been the junior partner of the firm of McIver & Ruxton, is to leave the city for a job with McDonnell & Sons, Quincy, and Mr. James Matheson, who has long been in the granite business in this city, takes his place in the firm. The concern

has now on its books a large quantity of orders and is working about the usual two gangs of cutters with the probability of putting on more in the near future. They have recently shipped several cars of finished work to parties in the central states and have other jobs well under way. Orders come as freely as ever and they have no hesitancy in expressing themselves as fully satisfied with the present condition of the business.

The Vermont Granite Co. have recently successfully quarried and sent to this city a block of their dark stock which is 40x30x20, containing about 24,000 cubic feet of stock and weighing about 4,000,000 pounds. This is one of the largest blocks of granite which has ever been quarried here. It was in perfect condition and created a good deal of interest among not only the men of the granite business, but among all who had the opportunity to see it.

Robins Brothers are doing a good business at this writing and they report that they have no reason to enter any complaint. The work which they have on hand, although not large, is of excellent character and they have a large number of orders on their books. They are working only one gang of cutters this season.

Emslie & McLeod have always had a good business ever since their business was first established, and the class of work which they turn out is such that they find no difficulty in getting in all the good orders which they can well handle. They are able to construct both

September, 1900

Vol. X. No. 9

Granite

A. M. HUNT & CO.

PUBLISHERS

131 Devonshire Street

BOSTON, MASS., U.S.A.

Subscription Price, $1.00 Year

ADVERTISERS' DIRECTORY.

For Quick Working

TRAVELING CRANES

Up to Forty Tons Capacity, suitable

FOR GRANITE SHEDS,

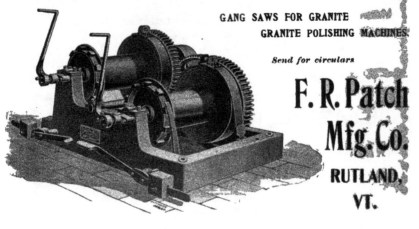

GRANITE

ENTERED AT THE BOSTON POST OFFICE AS SECOND-CLASS MAIL MATTER.

Vol. X.   BOSTON, MASS., SEPTEMBER 1, 1900.   No. 9

A. M. HUNT, EDITOR.

Published Monthly in the interests of the Producer,
Manufacturer, and Retailer of Granite as used
for Monumental or Building Purposes.

Terms of Subscription

TO ANY PART OF THE UNITED STATES OR CANADA:

One copy, one year - - - - $1.00, in advance.
One copy, six months - - - 75 cents, in advance.

ADVERTISING RATES FURNISHED UPON APPLICATION.

A. M. HUNT & CO., Publishers,

131 DEVONSHIRE STREET, - - BOSTON, MASS.

WHO is responsible for this cheap
and shoddy work going into cemeteries, on which nobody makes
anything?—Reporter.

We should say that the Reporter is largely responsible for the majority of this class of work placed in the
cemeteries of Chicago and vicinity. Since our connection with the monumental business dating back
over a period of ten years, the constant cry of the manufacturer has been, when solicited for an advertisement and asked to pay cash, "We can pay the Reporter in monumental work when we have some random job which we cannot sell elsewhere." Or if a
job is refused by a retail dealer within two hundred
miles of Chicago, the manufacturer says, "Ship it to
Chicago; the Reporter will take it." These are facts
which can be proven by any one who will take the
pains to ask the necessary question of the manufacturer or the responsible dealer in Chicago or vicinity.

Is it possible that this method of conducting business does not have its effect upon the prices of monumental work and the quality of the monument? The
retail dealer who is obliged to compete with the Reporter's price finds it necessary to drop the bottom out
of the profits, and the manufacturer who competes
with the Reporter's price to the retail dealer simply
finds himself snowed under. We also say, "What Is
The Use Of It All?" What is the use of all of this
advice, given in the Reporter's July issue, from one
who is apparently doing all that is within his power,
to bring about the conditions which he states as entirely wrong?

Be consistent, brother Nichols; when you have
pulled the mote from your own eye then it will be time
to look into your neighbor's defective orb.

We do not question about the existence of the evils
as expressed in the "Reporter," but it does not sound
pretty for the Reporter to criticise them.

THE matter published below is taken from a
recent issue of the Monumental News,
page 457.
Granite Works at South Quincy, Mass.
Granite Works at Barre, Vt.
Branches at Palmerston Road, Aberdeen, Scotland,
and Carrara, Italy.

"Never before in the history of the granite trade
has there been such poor work manufactured as at
the present time. Truth compels us to make the
statement, much against our inclination. This ap-
plies as well to imported granite as to domestic.

"We anticipate that the time will come, and in the
near future, when we shall be compelled to manufacture everything we have orders for, in order to furnish even good work, and such that will prove satisfactory."

We certainly take exception to the statement that "there is more poor monumental work cut from granite at the present time than ever before." From a general knowledge of the business we find, on the contrary, that there is an improvement all along the line. If the statement had been made that never before in the history of the granite trade has there been such a hustle on the part of some wholesale dealers to squeeze the manufacturer down in price, and, as a consequence, in the quality of his work, it would be correct. Mr. Wholesale Dealer who published the above can secure any quantity of good work by paying the price that such work calls for, and if they do find trouble in placing their orders with manufacturers who are responsible, and cut good work, it is entirely their own fault, as from necessity many of the best manufacturers absolutely refuse to figure for the wholesale dealer.

The latter part of the clipping above—"We anticipate that the time will come, etc ," does not agree with the first part of this clipping—"Granite works at Quincy, Mass., Barre, Vt., branches at Aberdeen and Corrara."

If this firm has manufacturing plants at all these locations, why is it necessary for them to "anticipate the time when it will be necessary, etc.?"

One thing we can state as an absolute fact, that at the present time this firm does not own or control a manufacturing plant at Barre, Vt.

Obituary.

Ernest C. Goodale, Treasurer of the Rawson & Morrison Manufacturing Co., Cambridge, Mass., died in Berlin, Germany, from an operation performed for peritonitis. Mr. Goodale left Boston on June 30, for a pleasure trip abroad, and word was received on August 3 that he was ill, and then came the news of his death. We have known Mr. Goodale for some time and we recall him as a young man—a hustler—and apparently in perfect health, and his death comes to us as a personal loss.

Jasper R. Rand, President of the Rand Drill Co., died July 18. He was born September 17, 1837, in Westfield, Mass., of a family dating its American ancestry from 1635 and including two colonial governors; and which was well represented in the Revolutionary War. He obtained his education in the public schools and academy of his native town and in Fairfax, Vermont.

His earliest business connection was with his father, who was a manufacturer of whips when Westfield was the headquarters of that industry. In 1865 his father retired from business, and Mr. Rand and his younger brother, Mr. Addison C. Rand, succeeded him.

In 1870 he removed to New York and was for a time associated with another brother, Albert T. Rand, President of the Laflin & Rand Powder Company. In 1872 Addison C. Rand began the manufacture of the Rand Rock Drills and other mining machinery, and the two brothers subsequently organized the Rand

A. C. RAND, DIED JULY 18.

Drill Company, with A. C. Rand as President and J. R. Rand as Treasurer, which arrangement continued until the death of A. C. Rand in March, which left the chief office vacant, when J. R. Rand was elected to the position. From small beginnings this business has developed into an important industry. When the Messrs. Rand became interested in Rock Drills, they were in the pioneer stage, with—at most—a small and uncertain future before them, but they have come to be an essential part of every mining outfit. Rock drills were among the first American machinery products to find recognition among foreign engineers, and there are today at work in nearly every country on the globe, where the mining industry has passed beyond the most primitive stage.

He was practically acquainted with every field of business life from that of traveling salesman up. He had a remarkable fund of wit and of pointed, but stingless repartee, which made him the most delightful of companions—qualities which naturally brought him friends without limit. These and other qualities also made him a presiding officer under whose gavel it was a delight to sit. He was interested in all public enterprises and contributed generously to their support.

Shipments of granite for the month of August from Quincy Adams were 3,618,699 pounds, West Quincy 7,871,730 pounds, Quarry Railroad 3,688,270 pounds, making a total of 15,178,669 pounds as compared with 17,277,117 pounds for the month of July.

George Ruxton, formerly a member of the firm of McIver & Ruxton, Barre, Vt., has arrived and has assumed his duties as Superintendent of the McDonnell & Sons' plant. Many additions and changes will be made to the plant. Mr. Ruxton is showing his watch, recently presented to him by his Barre friends, with a great deal of pride, not only for its intrinsic value, but for what it represents as a token of esteem and good fellowship of his many acquaintances left behind. By the way, they have given him one year to stay in Quincy. Not that they think he will not make a success, but that he cannot stay away from his Barre friends longer.

The condition of the granite business in Quincy remains about the same as at my last writing. If anything, however, it is a little better. A canvass among the cutting firms at South and West Quincy, finds them all busy, although it must be said that there are but few of what might be called large jobs in the city. The number of orders received in the city will compare favorably with the number received last year, notwithstanding the fact that there were several weeks' suspension of business during the early part of the season. While all the firms seem busy it is a noticeable fact that none of the firms are employing as many men as last fall. This, however, is not surprising. At that time it was a foregone conclusion that there would be a strike in the spring of 1900, and every firm put on all the men they could get so as to clean up all their orders before the first of March. However, if the firms are not employing large gangs of men, the business has a healthy tone, and unless all signs fail, business will be good next year.

McGillvary & Jones are among the most busy firms in the city, and they are also cutting some of the largest work in the city. Among their large work are several tombs which have already been noticed in detail in these columns. Some of the smaller of these jobs are of Quincy granite, but the largest work is being cut in foreign granite. They also have their share of medium sized memorials.

McIntosh & Sons continue to have plenty to do, and work is going on without interruption. This firm by its recent additions of pneumatic tools, etc., is in a better position than ever to handle all kinds of work with despatch, and a good job is assured all customers.

The annual outing of the Granite Manufacturers' Association was held at Nantasket, August 4. A more extended account of the outing will be found elsewhere.

Mr. Robideau, who has been freight agent at the West Quincy station for some time, has resigned his position as such and has entered the employ of the Granite Railway Co., as traveling salesman.

One hundred and twenty-five of the Cuban teachers who were attending the Harvard summer school, visited Quincy, August 8, and made a tour of inspection of the plants along the line of the Quincy Quarry railroad upon the invitation of Luther S. Anderson, Manager of the Granite Railway Co., and were very much interested in what was shown them.

The New York, New Haven & Hartford railroad has been having more trouble with its freight agent at the Quincy Adams station. Ernest W. Temple, who one morning last month, packed his little trunk, and, like the Arabs of old, folded his tent and quietly stole away. It is reported that his accounts are in a rather mixed up way and that the railroad officials would like to interview him in relation to certain money transactions. A petition has been signed by the granite men asking that George K. Carter, a former agent, be again placed in charge.

Fuller, Foley & Co. report that while they are quite busy they could do more. They see no reason, however, for complaint. They, like most of the other Quincy firms, have quite a lot of work on hand, but nothing they care to particularize as being better or more elaborate than their general run of work.

Hot weather this month has again compelled the yards to shut down for a few days. With the thermometer running way up into the nineties, it was almost impossible for the men to work.

Alexander Marnock, President of the Granite Manufacturers' Association, has the sympathy of the granite men throughout New England in the loss of his seventeen-year-old daughter, who died August 6, after a brief illness. Everything possible was done for the young lady, but her disease was beyond the power of all human aid. Mr. and Mrs. Marnock were almost prostrated with grief, and after her burial they found it impossible to reconcile themselves, and were obliged to go away for a few days

Patrick Maguire, the surviving member of Maguire & O'Hern, of East Milton, is getting ready to do a rushing business. He has long been cramped for room in his present location, and to overcome this he is building a new plant near his present location. In his new plant everything will be modern and up-to-date, covered sheds, pneumatic tools and power derrick. He has a large number of orders on hand and is employing his full complement of men.

The Merrymount Granite Co. continues to be as busy as at any time since the settlement of the strike. Previous to the strike they had a very large force of men employed, which has been somewhat reduced now. The most of their work is of the medium size kind, and is largely of Quincy stock. At their quarry they report that they have more than they can attend to, and that they have to work over time in order to keep up with their orders for rough stock.

Joss Bros. Co. are as busy now as at any time this year. They are running their full complement of men and have enough orders on hand to keep them going as long as it is possible for them to work. Much of their work is of the medium size kind, although they have several jobs that are larger than the average run. There are none that they care to particularize, however. Their plant is thoroughly equipped in all its branches, and as much care is taken with a small job as the largest.

Joseph Walker of the Aberdeen Granite Works, has a good lot of work on hand, but says that he is having considerable trouble in getting the rough stock. He can readily obtain all the medium and light stock he desires, but when it comes to getting extra dark it seems next to an impossibility. This is partly due to the condition many of the quarries were left in when they were turned over to the syndicate. Other than this he has no complaint to make. One of the recent jobs shipped by him was a handsome medium dark sarcophagus.

W. T. Spargo has a good number of orders on hand for medium sized work as well as a few orders for work that are larger than the ordinary run. He, therefore, has no fault to find with the condition of business. Among their work that might be mentioned is a sarcophagus with an all polished die and elaborately carved cap. He also has another sarcophagus with a polished die with raised carved wreaths on each end.

W. T. Spargo, Alex. Falconer, of Swingle & Falconer, and Andrew McIntosh, of McIntosh & Sons, have arrived home safe and sound from Europe. They report having had an enjoyable outing, and will, no doubt, have some interesting experiences to relate of their visit to gay Paris.

Herbert W. Beattie, the sculptor, continues to be busy. He has just completed the model of a life-size portrait, bas-relief, of Gov. Day of Buffalo, N. Y., which is to go on a rock face monument to be erected in Buffalo, September 30. He is also at work upon a number of small ornamental models which will be cast in bronze.

Books and Periodicals.

We have received a copy of the second edition of a book of prices, estimates and rules by James F. Brennan, Peterboro, N. H., for assistance in arriving at the cost of cutting, hammering, polishing and lettering plain surfaces, mouldings, draperies, statues, urns, etc., in different kinds of granite, also for determining the cost of granite in the rough. The book contains 64 pages with illustrations and should prove an invaluable assistant to the retail dealer. It is a revision of the first edition, made necessary by the changes in the bill of prices. The illustrations are a new feature. The book can be had by sending one dollar to the publishers of GRANITE.

We have received Vol. 1, No. 3, of the Granite Trade Notes published by the Alex. McDonald Co., Trenton, N. J. May it still continue to prosper.

Twenty-first Annual Dinner and Outing of the Quincy Granite Manufacturers' Association.

The twenty-first annual dinner and outing of the Quincy Granite Manufacturers' Association was held at the Pacific House, Nantasket Beach, August 4. A part of the entertainment provided by the committee was a ball game. The nines were made up from the members of the Association. The two nines were captained by William Spargo and Richard Prout. Our illustrations give some incidents of the game. Four innings were played, no errors were made (?) except by the losing team, which was that one held in control by William Spargo and this team made the error of not providing runs enough to beat the other team, hence their mistake. The game lasted two hours and provided considerable entertainment for those looking on, and brought into play muscles long out of active service by those who handeled the bat and did the running. At two o'clock, after having played four innings, everyone adjourned to the hotel where seating capacity was provided for one hundred and twenty-five, and the following menu was thoroughly enjoyed.

MENU.

Clam Chowder.   Fish Chowder.
Steamed Duxbury Clams, Drawn Butter.
___
Fried Native Perch, Tartar Sauce.
Broiled Fresh Bluefish, Maitre d'Hotel.
Julienne Potatoes.
Sliced Tomatoes.   Fresh Radishes.
___
Clam Fritters, Country Style.
Salmon Cutlets with Green Peas.
Sliced Cucumbers. Lettuce. Queen Olives.
___
PUNCH.
___
Turkey, Cranberry Sauce. Sucking Pig, Cider Jelly.
Chicken Salad.   Lobster Salad.
New Peas.   Green Corn.
___
Chocolate and Vanilla Ice Cream.
Assorted Fruit.   Assorted Cake.
___
Chilled Watermelon.
___
Toasted Crackers and Cheese.
___
Tea.   Coffee.   Hot Rolls.

One of the active members of the Association, William T. Spargo, who has for the last two years served upon the committee was unavoidably detained by an engagement in Paris, France, and other European points. His genial countenance was missed by many members of the Association. The William Spargo mentioned as captain of the ball team is the son and heir of William T. Mr. Spargo has for company on his European trip A. McIntosh who has always attended the Association outing, but this time it was necessary for him to be away as the companion of Mr. Spargo in order to show him the sights of gay Paris and other points, or Mr. Spargo showed him the sights; we cannot say which, as the two gentlemen mentioned have just returned. There are many rumors that some of the members present did not reach home until the small hours of the morning. Of this we cannot state definitely, but suffice to say everyone present enjoyed themselves and many thanks are due the committee for its excellent work.

INCIDENTS AT THE TWENTY-FIRST ANNUAL OUTING

OF THE

MEMBERS OF THE QUINCY GRANITE MANUFACTURERS' ASSOCIATION,

AT NANTASKET BEACH, AUGUST 4.

1. A star player, William Spargo by name, captain of one team, in the foreground. In the background is the umpire and Mr. Diack, of Birnie & Diack, one of the players.

2. Another star player, the best in the bunch, Richard Prout, of Prout Bros., called by his friends "Dick," captain of the cigar winners.

3. One of the Entertainment Committee, also a ball player, Harry Nichols, of the Nichols Granite Works.

4. Thomas Burke of Burke Bros., in the foreground, also one of the entertainment committee; immediately back of him is Alex. Marnock, of A. Marnock & Co., president of the Quincy Granite Manufacturers Association.

5. The first home run by the gentleman with the hat in his hand. The man behind him is the third baseman, something of a sprinter himself, but not a circumstance compared with the man with the hat, who is C. Theodore Hardwick, of C. H. Hardwick & Co.

6. Manufacturers incapacitated from playing the game by old age or that tired feeling, viewing and criticising.

AFTER THE GAME.

7. Showing one section of the table, just before the banquet, set on the piazza; there are one hundred other members around the corner and inside the hotel.

8. After the game was over; Captain "Dick" Prout, the man with the cigars, resting from his labors and explaining how it was done, and incidentally taking a glass of ice water (?).

Monthly Trade Record.

This department is compiled and edited by the United Mercantile Agency. Subscribers, in accordance with the terms of their contracts, are entitled to receive further information relative to the parties hereafter mentioned, upon application to the main office. As the names of many business men who are good will appear herein, subscribers can readily see the importance of making inquiries if interested, previous to taking any action.

COLORADO.
Denver, *M—Ollinger & Ives, 50.

GEORGIA.
Brunswick, *M—LaMance, Reed E., 20 $588.

ILLINOIS.
Beardstown, *M—Van Fossen, S. L., 50.
Chicago, *M—Sammis, F. H. Co., 20 $556.
Decatur, *M—Grindol, W. H. & Son, 43.
Edwardsville, *M—Illinois Marble Co., 39 cap $15M.
Galesburg, *M—King, Alex & Co., 76.
Lovington, *M—Carmichæl, W. A., 76.
Monticello, *M—Woolington & Bloyer succeed A. V. Woolington.
Mount Vernon, *M—Smith, Graham G., warranty deed to R. E. $2,400.
Quincy, *M—Daugherty & Co., 43.
Sparta, *M—Finnell, A R., 76.
Toulon, *M—Morris, J. M., 50.

INDIANA.
Bloomfield, *M—Chambers, Joseph, 80.
Bluffton, *M—Harsh, J. W., 80.
Marion, *M—Buchanan, A. & Son, 32 $4,000.
Veedersburg, *M—Drollinger, S. L., succeeds Drollinger & Virgin.

IOWA.
Council Bluffs, *M—Bloom, J. F. & Co., succeed J. F. Bloom.
Emmetsburg, *M—Godden & Ballard, 99 $700.
Fonda, *M—Smith & Boggs, 80.
Lansing, *M—Roggensack, Ed. J., 14 $500.
Le Mars, *M—Bogen Bros., succeed J. H. Smith.
Marshalltown, *M—Woods, W. W. & Son, 20 $89
Red Oak, *M—Seefeldt & Hobson, A. Z. Seefeldt 93 $1,250.

KANSAS.
Blue Rapids, *M—Munch & Holtzman, 80.
Jewell, *M—Whitney, C. W., 80.
Olathe, *M—Bradshaw, Harry, 80.
Wamega, *M—Anderson & Barge, 80.

KENTUCKY.
Bardwell, *M—Willis, L. L., 80.
Henderson, *M—Gensler, Eugene, 80.
Hillsboro, *M—Harrison & Garnett, 80.
Hopkinsville, *M—Brown, R. H., 86 to W. H. Shankin.
Lexington, *M—Pruden, M. J., 74 $95.

MARYLAND.
Baltimore, *M—Coyle, J. & Bro., 20 $594 vs. Richard J. Coyle.

MASSACHUSETTS.
Adams, *M—Adams Marble Co., 30 $5,000.
Quincy, GZ—Fuller, F. Wesley, 106.

MICHIGAN.
Lansing, *M—Marker, James, 14 $300.

MINNESOTA.
Hamel, *M—Birchen, Peter, 50.
Perham, *M—Muehler, Fred A., 76.

MISSOURI.
Pierce City, *M—Crumley, D. O., 76.
St. Louis, *M—Schrader & Conradi, 64.

NEW JERSEY.
Hoboken, *M—Couch, Thomas, 14 $1,000.

NEW YORK.
Fort Plain, *M—Selwood, Frank J., succeeds Selwood Marble & Granite Works.
Le Roy, *M—McGuire, James, 86.
Syracuse, *M—Linehan, C. & Sons, Cornelius Linehan, 78.

OHIO.
Bluffton, *M—Lehman, John, 50.
Findlay, *M—Smith, A. M., 74 $2,500.
Hamilton, *M—Menchen, Henry, 99 $2,000.
Urbana, *M—Bunnell, D. M., 99 $2,100.
Van Wert, *M—Rice, Samuel, 93 $650.

PENNSYLVANIA.
Scranton, *M—Lehr, Fred, 20 $200.

RHODE ISLAND
Woonsocket, MZ—Green, William George, 14 $600.

TENNESSEE.
Chattanooga, *M—Majors, R. E. L., 14 $300.

VERMONT.
East Barre, GZ—Raycroft, Hugh, 106.
West Dansville, GZ—Willcox & Armstrong, 106.

WASHINGTON.
Spokane, *M—United States Marble Co., 20 $5,000.

WISCONSIN.
Footville, *M—Davies, B. F., 50.
Praire du Chien, *M—Fagan & Stuart, 64, John Fagan, 58.

Wells, Lamson & Co. are pushing work on the Ehert mausoleum and will begin to ship some of it about the first of September. This job still holds the record as the biggest contract that has come to Barre this season, and with the addition of several other large jobs, it has kept business lively with this firm. They began on the mausoleum before the first of June and it will not be finished before the first of December. They estimate that it will require from 60 to 70 cars to transport the job.

Much interest just now centers at W. A. Lane's shop where the first automobile ever built in Vermont is now being constructed. The carriage which is approaching completion is to be propelled by a steam engine with gasolene for fuel. The general plan of

the carriage is not greatly different from the locomobile now in general use, though the minor variations are many.

The machinery for Burk Brothers' new shed has arrived and is being placed in position. The firm hopes to be able to occupy its new home not much later than September 1. The plant complete will be one of the best in the city.

James Milne has decided to take the advice offered him by GRANITE and will not make his home permanently in Scotland, but will return to Barre within a few weeks.

Pellegatti, Rizzi & Co. have just cut a double headstone that is something of a curiosity. It is for a man and his wife, the latter deceased and the former evidently expecting soon to be. The inscription on the half devoted to the wife ends with the invitation, "Come to see me." The husband's half contains the usual data with a blank space left for the time of his final departure from this life, and just underneath it his answer to his wife's summons, "By the grace of God I will."

James Mackay is not the only granite manufacturer running for office this year in Barre, for on the last day on which nominations could be made for the September election, the name of Eugene Sullivan was filed as an independent candidate for a seat in the legislature from Barre. Just what party or section Mr. Sullivan represents, he himself says is not clear, and he admits with his customary ingeniousness that the other candidates are likely to hinder his chances of election.

Geo. D. Bailey, granite manufacturer, Hardwick, Vt., has filed a petition in insolvency.

Public announcement was not made until shortly before noon August 11. That was the last day of grace for paying the cutters, and as their checks were not forthcoming explanations were in order. Mr. Bailey had some twenty odd men on his payroll.

Mr. Bailey's liabilities are filed at $23,875.09, of which $14,379.86 is secured; his assets are figured at $23,664.66, of which $1,055 is claimed exempt.

Mr. Bailey has our sympathy in his trouble. He has labored night and day to build up a business, starting from the bottom round of the ladder and working his way by strict attention to business. We have no doubt that he will come out of his present trouble successfully and go to work with new courage.

An immense block of dark granite was recently taken from the quarry of Wells, Lamson & Co., in Williamstown. It measured 100 x 25 x 12 feet and is estimated to have weighed 6,000,000 pounds. This is the block of granite mentioned in the August issue of GRANITE and credited to the Vermont Granite Co. by mistake.

One of the largest and most enjoyable picnics ever held on Millstone Hill occurred Saturday afternoon at the Wetmore & Morse grove. Those present were the employes of the Wetmore & Morse and Langdon quarries and their families and friends.

The afternoon was spent in games and sports and in enjoying the plentitude of refreshments furnished. The chief event of the day was the tug of war between the men of the two quarries. They were evenly matched and the result was a draw with the advantage slightly on the side of Boutwell's men. In the final tug the two sides struggled for 3 minutes and 15 seconds without either yielding.

A vote of thanks was extended to J. M. Boutwell, manager of the two quarries, for his liberality in giving the men their time for the afternoon and three rousing cheers were also given in Mr. Boutwell's honor.—Times.

Barre, Vt., Aug. 20.—The climax of the Vermont political campaign is now fast approaching, for election day in the Green Mountain State comes the first Tuesday in September, and consequently the warm time of the campaign is during the last two weeks of dog days, every other year.

As a usual thing the granite men of Barre and vicinity do not take any active part in state or local politics, but this year it is different for the reason that the Republicans have named as candidate for the general assembly from the city of Barre Mr. James Mackay, a member of the firm of Imlah & Co., and a vice-president of the New England Granite Manufacturers' Association.

Barre is a very close city politically, and when the Democrats early last week settled upon Ex-Postmaster Frank McWhorter to stand as their candidate for the legislature the Republican leaders at once saw that it would be necessary to put forward their strongest man if they expected to win. Several conferences developed the opinion that the choice lay between Mr. Mackay and Prof. O. K. Hollister, principal of Goddard seminary. The selection between the two was left to the Republican voters of the city last Saturday evening, and the decision was, by a decisive majority, in favor of Mr. Mackay. He is already president of the board of aldermen and it has been confidently predicted for some time that he would be the next mayor of the city, though if he is elected to the legislature it may side-track him for the municipal office.

The granite business has held up well all summer and most of the firms now have all that they can do and several would work more men if the men were obtainable. There has been a slight increase of cutters here owing to the recent outbreak of small-pox at Hardwick, which scared many cutters from that town, and a good share of them came to Barre.

Dayton E. Jones, of the firm of Jones Bros., is still detained from business by illness.

Continued on page 27.

"Granite," September, 1900.

Bottom Base . . . . T—V×P—R×V—CV
Second Base . . . . P—N×A—CC×V—N¾
Die . . . . P—V×A—R×A—P

Bottom Base	1 — P x P — T x C — C
Second Base	E — C C x R — C x V — C C
Die	E — V x A — R x A — P
Cap	P — C C x A — C x C — C

"GRANITE," SEPTEMBER, 1900.

BOTTOM BASE	I — G⅝ x P E⅛ x C — P	
SECOND BASE	T — N½ x R — R¼ x C — Y	
DIE	E — N x A — P x R — T	

General prosperity is evinced by the number of new sheds and other buildings connected with the granite business that have been erected this summer or are now in process of construction. Most of them have been already mentioned in these columns. One of the more recent is a new polishing mill which is being built by James Ingram. The mill is to be 95 x 40 feet, and will be leased to a new firm just starting in business. McDonald & Buchan are making a small addition to their shed and so also Milne, Carihew & Gray.

Emslie & McLeod some days ago shipped the Eckel monument to Syracuse, N. Y., where it was unveiled August 22. The monument is of Barre granite, a mixture of light and dark, 28 feet in height and surmounted by a granite statue of Philip Eckel, formerly Chief of the Syracuse Fire Department in whose honor the monument is erected. The statue is of Westerly granite, and is one of the best recently cut in Barre.

QUARRY ITEMS

ST. CLOUD, MINN.—The Arnold Granite Company has secured the contract to furnish all the granite to be used in the addition to be built to the Omaha public building. The contract will approximate $30,000. The original building is built of St. Cloud granite.

HUNTINGTON, MASS.—A change in the management of the Bowe Granite Company has been effected whereby the Flint Granite Company of Albany, N. Y., leases the mill and sheds in the village and will commence operating. The quarries remain in the control of the Bowe Company and it is understood that they have some contracts for paving and rough stone that will be finished, after which the future is uncertain. These quarries were opened up two years ago.

DENVER, COL.—The substitution of New England granite and the rejection of the home product on the mint has aroused a storm of indignation from stonemen throughout the state. The following reasons are given by the contractor:

"I will give any man $1,000 who can produce two stones from any other than the Arkins quarry of Colorado, that will be received by the government inspector for the coping of the mint building," said Contractor John A. McIntyre. The two granite stones for which this reward is offered must be eight feet square, two feet thick, without a blemish, and must match the Arkins granite used in the rest of the building.

When asked whether Colorado could not furnish all the granite instead of importing from Maine the last 5,000 cubic feet, Mr. McIntyre responded:

"We have plenty of granite good enough to adorn any building, but the rigid test to which what has been

introduced into the mint has been submitted would have forced any other contractor to resign the job long ago. You must remember there has never been any real granite used in any previous building constructed in this state. The Platte canon stuff that goes by that name is only decomposed stone. It will disintegrate in a few years. The Arkins stone is the only high one in Colorado that will stand a high polish."

"Why was it not used to finish the mint building?"

"The department decided to use Eastern granite for the coping of the top and we will save three months time thereby, as no stone in Colorado is ready. Some of the Colorado stone, which was submitted and rejected, would have made the building look like a checker board.

"No, I had no decision in the matter of selecting Eastern granite in preference to our home production. It all rested with the department."—News.

WASHINGTON, D. C.—The strike of the Washington granite cutters for eight hours a day is over. The men get an hour off the working day and an increase from 16 to 20 per cent. in wages.

ELKTON, MD.—The opening up of immense quarries on the lands in the Fifth, Sixth, Seventh and Eighth districts of this country, which were recently purchased by the Consolidated Granite Company, of which Thomas F. Degan is president, is now a certainty. The company will be the largest of the kind ever organized in America, with a capital of $5,000,000. The stock of the company is now being sold by brokers in New York city. Already there has been nearly $350,000 worth of the stock sold. As soon as $500,000 worth of the stock is disposed of operations will be opened at the quarries, which will be opened up in several different places. Mr. Deegan states that the company has submitted plans and estimates for the construction of concrete and granite piers and wharves for the North German Lloyd Steamship Company, to replace those recently destroyed at Hoboken, N. J. It is claimed that the granite in sight at present is estimated at about 300,000,000 tons, and that it is of a superior quality. When in operation nearly six hundred men will be given employment.—Exchange.

The long pending trouble over the granite cutting work on the new Chicago postoffice building has been practically settled, as, according to advices from New York, an agreement was entered into a few days ago in that city between John Pierce, contractor for the granite work on the building, and the International Granite Cutters' union by which the Pierce quarry at Mount Waldo, Me., is to be unionized as well as the quarry in New York state. In addition, eight hours are to constitute a day's work and all granite cutting on the postoffice is to be done by the day whereof it may be performed. In Chicago $3.60 is to be the minimum rate of wages, $4 for outside work, and $4.50 for carvers. On contracts other than the Chicago postoffice, eight hours shall constitute a day's work and 35 cents an hour the minimum rate of wages. Piece work will be based on that. This agreement was indorsed by the Chicago union.

CLAYTON, N. Y.—The Delancy granite quarries at the foot of Grindstone Island have been leased to the Powell Granite Co. of Toronto, for a term of 20 years. The general manager of the company is arranging for derricks, wharves and shops to be built on the site of quarries. The granite will be used for monumental work, building and a variety of uses for which the stone is peculiarly adapted. A polishing shed and possibly crushers are to be erected for the purpose of finishing the product. Already a small force is engaged in getting the quarries in shape for operation. The company own a large plant in Toronto and their own line of boats for the transportation of their product.—Exchange.

Proposed Monuments and Monumental News.

SULLIVAN, IND.—A movement has been inaugurated to erect monuments in this country over the graves of Captain Fairbanks and eight of his followers, and Lieutenant Morrison and five of his men who are buried in this country. Fairbanks was massacred by the Indians in 1812, while en route with provisions from Fort Knox to Fort Harrison, just north of Terre Haute.

OMAHA, NEB.—It is proposed to erect a monument to the memory of the soldiers of the Civil and Spanish-American Wars.

CHAMPAIGN, ILL.—A movement has been started here looking to the erection of a monument to the late Dr. John Milton Gregory, the first president of the University of Illinois. Interested citizens and alumni of the university have taken the matter in hand, and the purpose is to raise $12,500 by way of gifts, and then ask the legislature to appropriate a like sum at the session next winter.

LEOMINSTER, MASS.—A. M. Pollard proposes to erect a granite mausoleum in the local cemetery.

ROME, GA.—The Xavier Chapter of the Daughters of the Revolution are making ever effort to raise funds for the erection of a monument to mark the spot where the last battle between Xavier's men and the Indians was fought.

TOPEKA, KAS.—The Halliday Monument Association has been formed for the purpose of erecting a monument to the memory of Colonel Halliday. C. J. Drew is chairman.

CLEVELAND, OHIO.—The Ohio Shiloh Battlefield Commission is sending out to all organizations of veterans who are engaged in that great battle an interesting circular concerning the proposed monuments to be erected on the field where the battle was fought. The circular explains that the Ohio legislature appropriated $47,500 for the erection of monuments on the Shiloh battlefield at Pittsburg Landing, Tenn., and at Crump's Landing.

Proposals for the erection of the monuments have been invited and they are to be opened the middle of September at Columbus. The designs submitted are to be placed on exhibition in the State House at Columbus from August 20 until September 22, for the inspection of committees representing the veteran organizations interested. These committees will be invited to file statements as to their choice of monuments.

ALTOONA, PA.—John Broadwell has been appointed president of an organization formed for the purpose of collecting the necessary money for the erection of a monument to the memory of Editor James W. Kilduff of the Gallitzin Vindicator.

Port Chester. N. Y. has had a soldiers' monument for two years, and again an effort is being made to have it dedicated.

It is a granite pedestal on which is the figure of an officer in bronze. Two wealthy residents of Rye erected it at a cost of $10,000.

Charles Lawrence Post, G. A. R., originated the idea of a monument. Wealthy men, without consulting them, selected the design, built the monument, and gave it to the village. The Grand Army men objected to the figure of the officer, saying it should be that of a private.

The village spent several thousand dollars in building a park about the monument, but last Memorial Day the veterans ignored it and decorated a pile of stones in Rye cemetery instead.

PITTSBURG, PA.—An effort will be made to raise the necessary funds with which to erect a soldiers monument.

Among the Retail Dealers.

BANGOR, ME.—The granite cutters employed by Ambrose Fogg, the monumental worker, struck Aug. 1 for more pay and fewer hours They belong to the union and were working ten hours a day for $2 50. Appeals for an eight hour day and $2.80 were unheeded and the employes decided to quit.

PITTSBURG, PA.—The heirs and beneficiaries under the will of the late Charles L. Davis, better known as "Alvin Joslin," have completed arrangements to erect a fine monument to his memory. It will be of granite and will cost several thousand dollars. The contract for the monument has been given to P. C. Renier's Sons. A portrait of the actor will be carved in relief on the center of the shaft. Under this will be simply graven the name and dates of birth and death.

FORT PLAIN, N. Y.—The marble and granite works on the Selwood estate, which was established by the late Richard Selwood in 1855, has been purchased by Frank J. Selwood, son of the late owner, who will be the sole proprietor.

EVANSVILLE, IND.—T. J. Scholz & Son have contract for the building of the C. W. Pardridge mausleum in Chicago costing $17,500. Same is to be completed in December.

George S. Walker, West Newton, Pa., and Geo. C. Richards, Middleboro, Mass., were among our recent visitors. Mr. Walker is an old time granite cutter, having served his time during the palmy days on Clark's Island, Me.

MACON, GA.—One of the finest specimens of monumental work turned out by Artope & Whitt is to be seen at their yards in the shape of a monument for the Ladies' Memorial Society of Barnwell County, S. C.

The first and the second bases are of Georgia Quincy granite. The shaft is of Knox marble. At the four corners of the first base are four drums, carved from marble, mounted on pedestal. The die is carved with the coat of arms of the State of South Carolina, a majestic palmetto tree, and it is here that the witchery of the carver's chisel is displayed to the best advantage. It is a piece of art, and represents many days of slow and tedious toil. On each of the four sides of the plinth a raised figure representing the four branches of the service, artillery, infantry, cavalry and naval. The middle section of the shaft contains a Confederate battle flag on each of the four sides.

When put in place the shaft will be about 30 feet high.

Within the past few years Messrs. Artope & Whitt have had all they could do, and give regular employment to twenty cutters and carvers daily. They have their own designer and are in a position to compete with the largest concerns of the kind in the country. They have under construction now a massive granite monument for the Hildebrand family, which will be erected at Jacksonville, Fla.—Exchange.

FLEETWOOD, PA.—C. F. Hill is building a boiler house at his granite works and will receive an engine. Mr Hill used a gasolene engine at his works, but on account of heavy work he will put up a steam engine.

PATTERSON, N. J.—The special committee on the Pythian monument have examined eight designs submitted to them and decided to accept the plan of the Alexander McDonald Company, Trenton, after a few suggested changes have been made. This monument is to be of Barre granite, fifteen feet high, the general character of it being triangular. The base consists of three steps representing the three ranks of the order. The first step is twelve feet long, the second ten feet six inches and the third nine feet. From these spring three columns triangularly arranged. They support a triangular arch, under which is a granite block, representing the Pythian altar, upon which rests an open Bible and sword, emblems of the order. This is surmounted by another triangle, with a helmet of marble at the apex. On one side of the upper triangle is a shield with the letter F, on another shield with the letter C, and on the third a shield with the letter B. These letters are also emblematic of the order and mean friendship, charity and benevolence. On the front of the altar there will be an inscription which will give the name of the donor.

CARTHAGE, N. Y.—Both members of the firm of Crooks & McLean have recently returned from a business trip to the Vermont granite quarries, where they have been to purchase their fall stock of monumental

MIDDLETOWN, CT.—An order has been placed with Fox & Becker for a large and handsome monument. The monument is sarcophagus design, of Quincy granite and all polished. The contract includes the taking down of a monument erected some time ago in Farm Hill cemetery, and recutting and polishing the botton base.

FORT PLAIN, N. Y.—The granite and marble works established by the late Richard Selwood in 1855, have been purchased by Frank J. Selwood, son of the late owner, who will be the sole proprietor.

SPRINGFIELD, ILL.—The design presented by Thompson Stickle for a monument to be erected over the grave of Abraham Lincoln's mother—in Spencer County, Ind.—has been accepted by the Nancy Hanks Lincoln Monument Association.

.The Association accepted the offer of Col. J. C. Culver of Springfield, to build the monument by the use of as much granite as possible from the national Lincoln monument in this city, and stone from the temporary receiving vault where the body of Lincoln rests.

According to the design of Mr. Stickle the base will rest on a solid foundation, on which will be constructed a massive stone-faced pedestal, the brackets to form the support for the monument to be cut from the solid rock. On the face of the die block is to be carved a scroll, revealing the name "Nancy Hanks Lincoln" underneath.

Ivy, the emblem of affection, and a branch of oak, typifying nobility, are grouped in bas relief around the names Granite and Bronze with harmonious effect.

Granite and Bronze.

SPRINGFIELD, MO.—Final arrangements for the erection of the Confederate monument have been made, and the contract for building the pedestal has been prepared. The model for the statue, submitted by Sculptor Trentanore, has been accepted, and he has been ordered to proceed with his work. It is expected that the monument will be unveiled within a year.

The statue is to be of bronze, heroic in proportions and representing a private Confederate soldier with proper accouterments. The pedestal is to be of Vermont granite and will be eighteen feet above the ground level. One of the front panels will be a bas relief portrait of General Sterling Price.

LOUISVILLE, KY.—If there is a proper response from the people of the city, a magnificent bronze bust of Abraham Lincoln will soon grace some conspicuous site.

*

Saracenic Ornaments.

BY HERBERT W. BEATTIE, SC.

The Arabs had no art or artists of their own; they came from the desert, with no more taste or knowledge of such matters than a mere love of finery could give them; they could not but be struck by the gorgeous display of such cities as Damascus, which fell into their hands; new ambitions arose with their new power, and the Byzantine artists were pressed into the service of the Arabian caliphs and generals, and ordered to raise rich mosques and palaces. Damascus, Cairo and Cordova show the admirable ingenuity with which they accommodated themselves to their new circumstances.

The conditions of the new Mohammedan law were stringent; in the endless designs in mosaic, marquetry, or in stucco, there was to be no image of a living thing, vegetable or animal.

Such conditions led to a very individual style of decoration: vegetable forms were now excluded for the first time. However, by the seventh century, when the works of the Saracens commenced, the Byzantine Greeks were already sufficiently skillful to make light of such exclusions, and the exertion of ingenuity which they impelled gave rise to a more beautiful, simply ornamental style, than perhaps any that had preceded it, for there was no division of the artistic mind now between meaning and effect; and although the religious cycles and other symbolic figures which had hitherto taken so much of the artists' attention were excluded, the mere conventional symbolism, the ordinary borrowed forms and geometric symmetry, left an abundant field behind, which was further enriched by the peculiarly Saracenic custom of elaborating inscriptions in their designs.

Mere curves and angles or interlacings were now to bear the chief burden of design, but distinguished by variety of color; the curves, however, very naturally fell into the standard forms and floral shapes, and the lines and angles were soon developed into a very characteristic species of tracery or interlaced strapwork, very agreeably diversified by the ornamental introduction of the inscription. And although flowers were not palpably admitted, the great mass of the minor details of Saracenic designs are composed of flower forms disguised; the very inscriptions are sometimes thus grouped as flowers: this is especially the case in the later works of the Alhambra; still no actual flower ever occurs, as the exclusion of all natural images is the fundamental of the style in its purity.

The omission of the crescent in Saracenic or Mohammedan work generally is worth notice. It now crowns the great mosques of Constantinople, but it is not to be found in any early work, and it appears to be itself simply the trophy of the conquest of the Greek capital of Constantinople, the ancient Byzantium, of which it was the symbol, the town on one occasion having, according to an old tradition, been preserved from a night ambuscade by the timely appearance of the new moon; it occurs on old Byzantine coins; Constantinople was captured by the Turks about 1453.

One of the greatest works produced under these circumstances was the magnificent mosque of Touloun at Cairo, a monument of the ninth century, and the recorded work of a Greek. The ornaments are in stucco, and altogether offer the most characteristic example of the combination of Byzantine and Saracenic elements. With the Saracenic tracery and inscriptions, and other peculiar forms, have been combined several of the most popular ancient ornaments in their Byzantine garb, but somewhat more than ordinarily modified, as the fret, anthemion, the guilloche, the forms of pleanty and the fleur-de-lis. The more characteristic detail, that is, of original Saracenic elements, the disguised conventional foliage spoken of, is very beautifully elaborated in some of the accessory works of this mosque. They became standards in after ages, for the details of the diaper-tiles of the Alhambra, executed some five hundred years afterwards, are in many respects nearly identical with these details of the mosque of Touloun at Cairo.

In all these early Arabian buildings of Cairo, we have the pointed arch, which first appears in the great mosque of Amrow, a work of the seventh century; but the ogee, the crescent, and the scalloped arches, are more characteristic, perhaps of the Saracenic architecture generally, as the pointed arch has been made familiar by a later style; but the simple, round Romanesque arch also occurs in the Moorish works of Spain. This style became gradually richer as it advanced westwards from Egypt to Sicily, and especially in Spain, where the Alhambra, a work of the fourteenth century, still remains to bear witness to its unparalleled richness of detail.

The Saracenic was a period of gorgeous diapers, for their habit of decorating the entire surfaces of their apartments was peculiarly favorable to the development of this class of design: the Alhambra displays almost endless specimens, and all are in relief and enriched with gold and color, chiefly blue and red. Some give the idea of being more endurable imitations of the rich woolens or cashmere, which the Arabs always made great store of.

The Genoa damasks, Arras tapestries, and many modern wall papers, are taken from Saracenic wall diapers. The very word "Damask" means Damascus work. Damascus, however, was famous for such fabrics before the conquest by the Arabs. It was called Damask, and was a place of repute even in the time of Abraham. Damascus is still famous for its textile fabrics in a pure Saracenic taste, and it produces a great variety of patterns in silk and cotton, the designs of which are chiefly stripes and inscriptions, good wishes or pious sentences.

The Siculo-Norman, from which our round zig-zag,

and the pointed Norman, are derived, is as as much a variety of the Saracenic as of the Byzantine; it is indeed a free combination of the two styles; for the reserved mixture of the two hitherto practiced had its Christian character restored to it by the Normans, through the introducing of sacred figures, and a prominence which they gave to all the most palpable Christian symbols, more especially the cross, which never occurs in genuine Saracenic work. This renders the Siculo-Norman a very complete style, and it is displayed in great magnificence in the Cathedral of Messina.

The Alhambra does not exhibit that Byzantine character in its details which we find in Sicily or in the Mosques of Cairo; all the peculiar Arabian features are preserved, but the scroll and anthemion, which are so often in very rich developments on the monuments of Cairo, can with difficulty be traced in the Alhambra. We can discover the scroll in some of the interlacings, and there is a fan-shape which recalls the anthemion. The artists of the Alhambra were probably exclusively Saracenic. The beauty of this place is in its general richness of effect, in its endless combinations of columns, arches and gorgeous surfaces; its gold and silver flowers, and its intricate tracery, which all combine to give the impression of extraordinary splendor as a whole, though no particular part commands any special admiration. After a few words upon the Gothic style we will look over the modern work, taking up last of all some remarks upon the proportion of the human figure, illustrated.

*

Westerly, R. I.

A recent visit to this point shows more activity in the granite industry than for a number of years. The Westerly Granite Works are very busy in their shed and quarry, and are employing about forty men. The quarry which produces white granite is in very fair condition; several good sheets of granite in sight and in one from which they are quarrying some good sized pieces of stock. They have secured contract for a mausoleum job, to be cut from red granite, 14 x 14 in size, and they are proceeding to open a new quarry for the purpose of securing the stock. Taking it all together, this six months of the year have been very busy ones, fully up to—if not more than—previous years.

John Cotto, who has previously been located in the granite business at this point, has again started, and is opening up what, from every indication, will be a first class quarry. He has secured the contract from the Philadelphia Granite & Blue Stone Co., of Philadelphia, Pa., for a mausoleum to be erected for William J. Burns, at Pittsburg, Pa.

The ground measurements will be 18 ft. 8 in. x 22 ft. Roof stones will be 22 ft. long. Contract also calls for four columns 9½ ft. high, and the plan shows some elaborate carving. It will contain 32 catacombs and will keep this plant busy through the winter.

A new firm by the name of Joseph Dusa & Co. have recently started and are fully capable of handling the best class of carved work in granite.

The Smith & Newall trouble has not been settled as yet, although it is expected that a decision will be reached before this paper goes to press.

The Sweeney Granite Works succeeds Dixon Granite Company, the quarry property and plant having been bought at auction by Joseph W. Sweeney, attorney for the Dixon estate. Contrary to all expectations, he has succeeded in opening two good sized sheets of granite, and has every prospect of a good quarry. Pink is the predominating color of the granite produced.

*

The Granites of Norway and Sweden.

A recent issue of "The Stonemason" contains an interesting article on the granites of Norway and Sweden. The writer says:

"Although the stone industry, as one of the more important means of livelihood, is of comparatively recent origin in Norway and Sweden, the use of stone in these countries for constructive and decorative purposes dates back to a very early period. During the mediæval age, when Church architecture was flourishing, the soft rocks such as limestones and sandstones were used very extensively in the Cathedrals of Upsala, Linköping, Skara, Lund, and other places, as well as the country Churches of Gotland built before 1350, proving that the builders of that period possessed a sound judgment as to quality of stone and methods of use as well as of skill in masonry, which has not been surpassed in later times.

"During the following centuries at various periods the stone industry has shown high development, especially in the seventeenth century and early in the eighteenth, when Swedish architecture reached its most flourishing condition, and fine buildings, such as the Royal Castle in Stockholm and others were erected. This period was followed by one of decadence, characterized by a tendency to substitute for natural stone the cheaper artificial stone and plaster. In large and sparsely populated countries like Norway and Sweden this was quite natural so long as means of transportation were undeveloped.

"But later, as the country became traversed by numerous railways and canals, the stone industry again become more prominent, thus benefiting national architecture as well as constituting an important item of the many industries of the nation, and still more recently the building of light railways in Norway and Sweden has enormously increased the stone industry. In 1870 the total length of the railways in Sweden was 1,708 kilometers, in 1895 the total length had increased to 9,775 kilometers, so that during the interval of 25 years the total mileage was increased more than fivefold. The large development which has taken place in the stone industry in Norway and Sweden is due, however, not only to facilities of transport, but to a more general recognition of the beauty of the material, which is raised in those countries. Thirty years ago little was known of the granites which now find such a ready market in the United States, Germany, Denmark, and in this country, but since that period year by year the exports have increased until last year, which was a record on all preceding ones.

"The colors are many and vary from nearly white to gray, red and black, with all shades of these colors But the varieties most known in this country are principally celebrated for the bright bluish iridescence which arises from the reflection of felspar crystals seen on a dark ground. A very beautiful variety, medium grained, and containing blue quartz and generally known as Red Swede, has been very extensively used in Germany. Another which has met with great favor in the United States, contains dark red felspar and deep blue quartz, and has been sold under the name of Swedish Rose. In this country the Scandinavian granites most sought after are of comparatively recent introduction: they are known as Laurvik, Fuglevik, and Carnation.

"Of these Laurvik and Fuglevik are both gray in color, the one being somewhat darker than the other, but both shine with that peculiar opalescent gleam or pearl-like lustre which has been previously alluded to. Carnation is a deep rich red, and one of the most beautiful ornamental granites known. The future of the trade is a very promising one, perhaps no countries in the world possess better conditions for an extensive stone industry than Norway and Sweden, there is a long sea-coast and the fiords form numerous good harbors, while the influence of the Gulf Stream makes the climate much warmer than might be expected. Perhaps the day is not far off when these countries will become the leading stone states in Europe."—Stone.

Interesting Story of the Legal Battle for the Quarries at Mt. Heagan's Heights, Maine.

The famous Sargent Granite Co. case has at last reached a settling point. The litigation has been before the New York courts for nearly eight years. There have been trials, hearings and re-hearings, suits and counter-suits. Eminent legal lights on both sides have resorted to every resource and tactic known, as, indeed, the amount involved, rising $200,000, was game worthy of the struggle.

Now comes a decision which it is thought will be the finis of the case, although many other such have been looked upon in the same light, but always proved to have a loop hole and the case continued to drag its weary length along.

The history of this remarkable case in full would make a good sized and not wholly uninteresting book. The principal facts are practically as follows:

In 1889 a stock company was organized in New York to engage in the general business of manufacturing and quarrying stone.

Francis T. Sargent was the principal promoter and held half the stock, the balance being taken up by New York parties. A piece of land in the Frankfort, Me., granite region on what is known as Mt. Heagan, was leased for ten years from the owners.

The land was entirely unimproved, simply an expanse of ledge and scrub, a brambly wilderness, in fact. Mr. Sargent, as superintendent of the new company, soon caused the wilderness to blossom, as it were, and established a fine quarrying plant, erecting buildings, constructing a tramway, wharves, derricks, sheds and creating a plant employing 200 to 300 men.

The business was prosperous and money-making, so much so that one Mr. Baird, a New York contractor, was attracted by the glitter of gold in the paving stones and concocted a scheme to capture the business.

The organization of the company, which was known as the Sargent Granite Co., was as follows: president, F. T. Sargent, New York; treasurer, Matthew Baird, New York; directors, W. O. Sargent, Belfast; W. J. Clark, Matthew Baird, F. T. Sargent and H. S .Luce, New York.

Baird gradually bought up all the stock except that of Sargent, so that the property was owned equally by the two.

In 1892 Baird set in operation a scheme to get control of the plant and business at one fell swoop. He called a meeting of the Sargent Granite Co. in New York in October.

Mr. Sargent obtained counsel and being advised that the meeting was illegal, did not attend.

Mr. Baird conducted the meeting to suit himself. He elected himself president; his bookkeeper, W. J. Clarke, treasurer, and placed upon the board of directors, G. S. Harrington, his boss hostler, and W. H. Keyes, a foreman of a paving gang.

This gave the new president a good working majority in the directory. After the regular meeting, a meeting of the directors was called, and Mr. Baird, his bookkeeper, his boss hostler and his paving boss convened to deliberate. They voted to give Matthew Baird a bill of sale of all the property on Mt. Heagan, which was accordingly done.

The next thing was to oust Mr. Sargent, who held the mountain site. In order to do this the owners of the quarry site were induced to cancel the lease made to the Sargent Granite Co., and to make a new lease to Matthew Baird. Mr. Sargent, by advice of counsel, withdrew, but succeeded in having a receiver appointed, Hon. Peter B. Olney of New York, a brother of the ex-secretary of state, and with a reputation as the prosecuting attorney in the great Tweed ring cases.

Suit was brought by Receiver Olney against Baird to recover the property. The case was bitterly fought, and it was not until December, 1895, that a decision was finally received from Judge Beekman.

The decision was a complete defeat for Baird. It made the second lease of the quarry site null and void. It annulled all transfers of property by Baird and ordered him to make good all damage and all property shipped from the quarry since October, 1892, and to account for same to Peter B. Olney, receiver.

Baird continued business at the quarry, and it was

estimated that the stock on hand when he took possession, shipped by him and on hand would aggregate some $150,000.

Five hundred thousand paving blocks have been piled up at the quarry all this time waiting for the law to settle the matter of their ownership.

A referee was appointed to award damages and wind up the affairs of the company. The "end" of the case was five years ago. But Baird's counsel have kept the case alive by appeals and re-appeals.

The latest decision just received sustains the previous decision of Judge Beekman; that the original Sargent lease of the site holds good; that the receiver is entitled to possession of the quarry and all property thereon, including the 500,000 paving blocks and that Baird must replace all machinery removed and make good all damages.

As the damages assessed against Baird will pay all claims, Sargent will be entitled to property clear from incumbrance to the amount of some $150,000. It is considered that the case will now be settled as the numerous decisions and rescripts have been almost all to one effect, that of sustaining the original.—Exchange.

Public Service of Railways.

The number of passengers carried during the year ending June 30, 1899, as shown in the annual reports of railways, was 523,176,508, showing an increase for the year of 22,109,827. The number of passengers carried one mile—that is, passenger mileage—during the year was 14,591,327,613, there being an increase in this item of 1,211,397,609. There was an increase in the density of passenger traffic, as the number of passengers carried one mile per mile of line in 1899 was 77,821, and in 1898, 72,462.

The number of tons of freight carried during the year was 959,763,583, an increase of 80,757,276 being shown. The number of tons of freight carried one mile—that is, ton mileage—was 123,667,257,153. The increase in the number of tons carried one mile was 9,589,680,848. The number of tons carried one mile per mile of line was 659,565. These figures show an increase in the density of freight traffic of 41,755 tons carried one mile per mile of line.

In the report is inserted a summary of freight traffic analyzed on the basis of a commodity classification, and also a summary indicating in some degree the localization of the origin of railway freight by groups or commodities.

The average revenue per passenger per mile for the year ending June 30, 1899, was 1.925 cents; for the preceding year it was 1.973 cents. The revenue per ton of freight per mile was .724 cent, while for 1898 it was .753 cent. An increase of mileage earnings is shown for both passenger and freight trains. The average cost of running a train one mile increased nearly 3 cents as compared with 1898. The percentage of operating expenses to earnings show a slight decrease as compared with the previous year.

For the year ending June 30, 1899, the gross earnings from the operations of the railways in the United States, covering an operated mileage of 187,534.68 miles, were $1,313,610,118, being $66,284,497 more than for the preceding fiscal year. The operating expenses were $856,968,999, the increase in this item being $38,995,723. The details of gross earnings were as follows: Passenger revenue, $291,112,993—increase as compared with the preceding year, $24,142,503; mail, $35,999,011—increase, $1,390,659; express, $26,-756,054—increase, $847,979; other earnings from passenger service, $7,687,363—increase, $463,363; freight revenue, $913,737,155—increase, $37,009,436; other earnings from freight service, $4,261,804—decrease, $421,401; other earnings from operation, including unclassified items, $34,055,738—increase, $2,851,958. Gross earnings from operation per mile of line were $250 more than for the year ending June 30, 1898, being $7,005.

The operating expenses of the railways for the year under consideration were assigned as follows: maintenance of way and structures, $180,410,806; increase, $7,095,848. Maintenance of equipment, $150,919,249; increase, $8,294,387. Conducting transportation, $486,159,607; increase, $21,485,331. General expenses, $38,676,883; increase, $2,200,197; undistributed, $802,454. The operating expenses for the year in question were $4,570 per mile of line, or $140 more than for the previous year. An analysis of operating expenses for the year ending June 30, 1899, according to the fifty-three accounts embraced in the official classification, appears in the report, with a statement of the percentage of each item in the classified operating expenses for the years 1895 to 1899, inclusive.

*

A Peculiar Case.

A peculiar case is now on trial, that of C. M. Jenkins, administratrix, vs. Townsend & Townsend. The case is to settle the question of ownership of a large monument that was to have been erected in Hollenback cemetery to the memory of the late Steuben Jenkins. Townsend & Townsend were the plaintiffs, and W. H. Chapin, a marble dealer of Forty Fort, was the defendant in a certain suit, a debt, and the plaintiffs had the sheriff issue an execution on the defendant's property for the debt. The granite monument stood in Mr. Chapin's yard and was levied upon, when the Jenkins heirs claimed title to it and brought suit to obtain possession.

It seems that the widow of Steuben Jenkins purchased the stone for $350, and had the family name cut in the base. Other members of the family objected to the stone, and it was not placed in the cemetery. While it was standing in Chapin's yard execution was secured against the latter and the stone levied upon.—Wilkesbarre, Pa., Record.

Beacon of Progress.— Continued.

Professor Despradelle is now one of the heads of the architectural department of the Massachusetts Institute of Technology, where he has achieved wonderful success. Every year the designs of students in this department of the institute are submitted in competition with designs of students of other colleges and professional schools before the beaux-arts jury at Philadelphia, and the regularity with which first and second prizes and "first mentions" come to Technology is well known.

Last year Professor Despradelle entered in the world-wide competition for plans for the new building for the University of California at Berkeley, which was established by Mrs. Phoebe Hearst. He was one of the ten architects who qualified for the final trials, and made the trip to California with the others to look over the ground. In the final competition he was accorded a prize of $3,000.

This last design is the culmination of deep thought and patient labor, extending over a period of six years. Trips through the United States, taking in every portion of them from the Pacific to the Atlantic coast, awakened a realization of the vast resources of the country and of the energy of the people, and a desire to commemorate in a lasting memoriam the spirit of the people led to his undertaking this work.

That this beautiful creation is the result of the zeal of an enthusiast, who determines to solve a difficult problem for his own satisfaction rather than the desire or expectation of financial reward, is a true criterion of the man's character. His love of art, for itself alone, is the reason for his great success.

Professor Despradelle has not yet made known his selection for a site for this monument, but its erection is said to be assured. Shortly after the award of the first medal by the Salon, the French government cabled an offer for the plans to be put in the gallery at Luxembourg.

The price was not made public, but the fact of the offer itself is a very great honor, as it is the first original architectural composition ever purchased by the government.

Professor Despradelle sailed for Europe in the early part of June and went directly to Paris to superintend the finishing of the details by his force of draughtsmen there. Upon his arrival he was given a public ovation by the leading architects and men of affairs in honor of his success.

*

Milford Granite Manufacturers Association

The regular meeting of the Milford Granite Manufacturers' Association was held at the office of the D. L. Daniels Granite Company on July 11, which was quite fully attended. The meeting was under the direction of President D. L. Daniels. Various items of the main objects of the Association, which are in the nature of the protection to its interests of manufacturers were discussed. The Association voted to have a series of by-laws published. The Association is in a flourishing condition and includes in its membership nearly every manufacturer in Milford.

The Ingersoll-Sergeant Improved Stone Channeling Machine.

Used in Stone Quarries for producing dimension stone in marketable shape.

Thirty-five Ingersoll-Sergeant Track Channelers used on the Chicago Drainage Canal; also used successfully at the following quarries: Maxwell Blue Stone Co., Cleveland, Ohio; Romona Oolitic Stone Co., Romona, Ind.; Bedford Quarries Co., Bedford, Ind. (4); South Dover Marble Co., South Dover, N. Y.; Piedmont Marble Co., Tate, Ga.; Perry Matthews, Buskirk Co., Bedford, Ind., and many others.

QUARRYING MACHINERY.

ROCK DRILLS
STONE CHANNELERS
AIR COMPRESSORS
COAL CUTTERS
THE AIR LIFT PUMP

Machinery for the Quarry, Stone Yard, or for Excavations.

LITERATURE ON ALL TOPICS INCIDENT TO THE ABOVE.

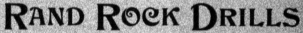

THE INGERSOLL-SERGEANT DRILL CO.

HAVEMEYER BUILDING, NEW YORK.

77 Oliver Street, - - Boston.

Rough Stock
or
Finished Monumental Work
in
Quincy or Concord
Granites.
*
Send for
Estimates.

J. ALBERT SIMPSON,
Treasurer.

L. S. ANDERSON.
Manager.

1826 - 1900.
Seventy-Four Years in the Granite Business.

QUARRIES:
West Quincy, Mass.,   Concord, N. H.

RANITE RAILWAY
COMPANY.

PRINCIPAL OFFICE: - WEST QUINCY, MASS.

DETAIL OF ILLUSTRATION BELOW:

No. 1. Looking West from Quarry No. 1.
No. 2. A corner in Quarry No. 2.   No. 3. A Bird's-eye View of Quarry No. 1.
No. 4. A Block of Extra Dark Blue Quincy Granite measuring 19 x 16 x 9½ feet,
weighing about 200 tons.
No. 5. Road from Yard to Quarries operated by an endless chain.

October, 1900

THE N YORK

Vol. X. No. 10

Granite

A. M. HUNT & CO.

PUBLISHERS

131 Devonshire Street

BOSTON, MASS., U.S.A.

Subscription Price, $1.00 Year

Wedging out a Spire, Upper Quarry,

Established 1848.

E. L. SMITH & CO.,
QUARRY OWNERS, MANUFACTURERS AND
WHOLESALE DEALERS IN

Barre Granite,
BARRE, VT.

Dark, Medium and Light Rough Stock

of any dimension to the limit of transportation.

Modern Equipped Cutting Plant especially designed for

handling Large Work.

☞ SEND FOR PRICE LISTS AND ESTIMATES. ☜

ADVERTISERS' DIRECTORY.

For Quick Working

TRAVELING CRANES

Up to Forty Tons Capacity, suitable

FOR GRANITE SHEDS,

WESTERLY GRANITE WORKS,

WESTERLY, R. I.

MONUMENTS, STATUARY, HEADSTONES and MARKERS.

FINE CARVING AND LETTERING IN WHITE, PINK, BLUE, AND RED WESTERLY GRANITES

ESTABLISHED 1873.

MARR & GORDON, BARRE, VT.

Western Office: 153 La Salle Street, Chicago, Ill., WILLIAM DUNBAR, Manager.

QUARRY
OWNERS
and
MANUFAC-
TURERS.

PNEUMATIC
TOOLS AND
ALL MODERN
APPLIANCES FOR
HANDLING,
POLISHING,
AND CUTTING
GRANITE.

This monument cut by us during the past year for Joseph Pajeau & Son, Chicago, and erected in
Oakwood Cemetery. Bottom Base, 14-6 x 9-8. Total height, 12 feet.

SIZES: Base. . . . 4-2 x 2-5 x 1-6
Die. . . . . 3-0 x 1-6 x 2-15

Send for Price.

EMSLIE AND BROWN
BARRE VT.

Hammered and Carved Work
a Specialty.

*Dealers in want of first-class work would do well to write
us. If you like the design of the monument illustrated in this
advertisement, send for prices. If not, send for prices on the
work you need. We can please you.*

ARE YOU

WEDDED TO ANY PARTICULAR CONCERN?

If not give **US** a share of your patronage.

We can name you prices on

Polished Work

that will fairly daze you. All our work guaranteed.

Hopkins, Huntington & Co.,

Quarry Owners and Manufacturers.   BARRE, VERMONT.

Attention, Dealers!

Why not deal with a quarry owner, manufacturer, and polisher direct and save the middleman's profit?

We are here to do business in all grades of **QUINCY** granite, from dark medium to extra dark.

All orders filled promptly and in first-class shape. Requests for estimates get our immediate attention. Try us, and we will get your trade.

McDONNELL & SONS,

QUINCY,   ▪   ▪   ▪   ▪   ▪   **MASS.**

P. O. Box 105.

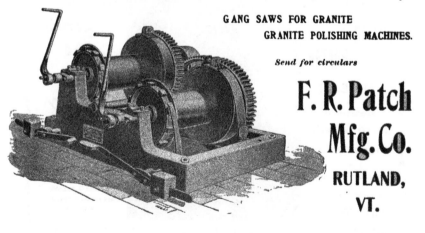

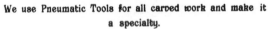

GRANITE

ENTERED AT THE BOSTON POST OFFICE AS SECOND-CLASS MAIL MATTER.

| Vol. X. | BOSTON, MASS. OCTOBER 1, 1900. | No. 10 |

A. M. HUNT, Editor.

Published Monthly in the interests of the Producer.
Manufacturer, and Retailer of Granite as used
for Monumental or Building Purposes.

Terms of Subscription

To Any Part of the United States or Canada:

One copy, one year - - - - - $1.00, in advance.
One copy, six months - - - - 75 cents, in advance.

ADVERTISING RATES FURNISHED UPON APPLICATION.

A. M. HUNT & CO., Publishers,

131 DEVONSHIRE STREET. - - BOSTON, MASS.

Editorials

HE quarry owners at St. George, N. B., who control the output of red granite known to the trade as the Bay of Fundy Red Granite, have given options on their quarries and plants to a syndicate said to be composed of the same individuals who recently acquired the sardine factories located at Lubec, Eastport and Robertson, Me. Whether this is guess work or a fact is an open question; any way, the promoter of the proposed syndicate was the promoter of the sardine syndicate.

As we think of it, the connection is rather an odd one, and we are of the impression that if the plans to form a trust of the granite industry are carried through, the managers will find a wide difference between the granite and sardine industry. Owing to the prohibitive duty, the sale of finished Bay of Fundy granite is confined to the Province of Ontario, and a very small amount is sold in the States; again, Scotch granite shipped from Aberdeen is a strong competitor, therefore the sale is restricted, and as the options given were not given with an idea of losing money, we believe that the future would not be a brilliant one. Possibly the promoter has other ideas regarding the water power, which is an excellent one, and had it been located at or near any of the granite producing centres in the States, it would be invaluable, as only a small part of the power is used. The options given expire on November 1, 1900, and it is the general opinion that the offers will not be taken up, as the sardine business this year has been a failure. Odd, the connection between the two, isn't it?

NDER another heading we publish the career of one Charles F. Baxter, as salesman, wherein it is alleged that by reported sales to individuals who never existed, or parties who never purchased, the said Baxter secured from the firm that he represented about $3,000 in commissions. It is also reported that the same Baxter secured from another firm, previous to his last engagement, more money in a similar manner. It does seem strange that this should be possible. A simple method would have avoided this loss, as follows: When an order is received from a salesman, acknowledge receipt of same to the purchaser, asking him to verify the original order in every particular. In other words, send him a copy of the order, and do not under any circumstances commence work upon the job until you receive an acknowledgement from the purchaser. It seems to us that the firm who neglects to do this is placing a premium upon dishonesty and deserves to lose, as they are bound to.

T this season of the year, when county fairs are in progress and other fairs in the cities are about to commence, the question enters the mind of the pushing retail dealer and granite manufacturer, Do exhibitions of granite monumental work pay? One of the largest exhibitions ever held in this line was at the World's Fair in Chicago. This exhibition consisted solely of the different styles of monumental work, polished and unpolished, rock faced and hammered, and we understand that the entire exhibit was disposed of with a few exceptions and it resulted in further orders. Of course this would be the natural result from the thousands of persons who viewed the exhibit. But the question as to whether or not an exhibition of monumental work leaves any lasting impression upon the average mind, those who attend fairs do it as an outing, and the sight of a monument or monuments to the average mind is grewsome and to be avoided rather than sought. There have been many exhibits by retail dealers at the various county fairs, but they have been entirely confined to simply the monument itself; in other words, to the completed article. Never to our knowledge has there been an exhibit which would show the methods of working stone. It is our opinion that one of the first questions asked is how this work is done, if a polished monument, how is it polished; if a carved monument, how is the carving completed. This is all to be explained by word of mouth with nothing to illustrate the methods of doing the work. It is our opinion that a working plant consisting of a polishing wheel and pneumatic tools and a man or men at work would attract and hold the crowd, for it would be a novel exhibit to the average individual who only has one occasion usually in a life-time to look up the question of monumental work, and it would be a liberal education for those who at some future time find it necessary to purchase a monument and give an idea as to the cost and labor required in doing the work. And aside from this, it would be an excellent advertisement for the firm or association who would take up this matter and illustrate the making of a monument starting from the rough stock as it comes from the quarries.

*

E have been requested by the trade, upon numerous occasions, to publish a cheaper class of designs. Although we are anxious to please our subscribers, yet we have no desire to publish that which we do not like ourselves and take no pleasure in seeing erected in the cemeteries. In other words, we draw a line upon the "Cheap John" article which is turned out by the dozen and sold regardless of anything except cheapness in price. We recall one firm of manufacturers who in the past made a specialty of cheap, rock-faced work, which they sold by the carload, and as a consequence they never sold the same firm twice, and were always looking for new trade. This firm, at the present time is doing one-half of the business which they have done in the past, but it is all together in a different line of work, and a member of the firm stated to us recently that the present business is much more satisfactory. And so with our publication, we do not hope to secure for subscribers, firms, or individuals who have no desires beyond the cheap grade work; we mean by this, the poorly cut, any-old-price kind, but we do hope to secure and are securing for subscribers, those who desire to sell a class of monuments that can be pointed out to with pride and serve as an entering wedge for another sale. The designs which we publish may at

times seem elaborate, but they can be simplified and still retain their artistic appearance.

Maguire & O'Heron, East Milton, have the foundation completed for their new shed, or rather his new shed, as the firm is composed of P. T. Maguire alone. The plant when completed will be 60x132, and will be equipped with a ten-ton travelling derrick made by the Lane Manufacturing Co., Montpelier, Vt. The plant will also be equipped with two gasolene engines furnishing 40 horse power, air compressor and pneumatic tools. Smith, Whitcomb & Cook, Barre, Vt., furnish the polishing wheels. A boom derrick will also be provided to handle the rough stock outside of the shed. When completed the plant will not be surpassed from the standpoint of completeness by any plant in New England.

The condition of business in Quincy remains about the same as last month, although, if anything, it has fallen off a little. As a whole, however, business can be said to be good. There is but little large work in the city and it is not expected that there will be much this fall. The principal reason for this is the approach of the presidential election. Business of all kinds is quiet just previous to a national battle of ballots, and as the granite business is a little different from most kinds of business it is not surprising that this should be one of the first to feel the effects. Once this is out of the way, and the country has settled down for another four years, manufacturers believe there will be a revival in the granite business, and as the possibilities of labor trouble have been reduced to a minimum, there is no reason why things in this line should not boom for the next four years.

The large plant of McDonnell & Sons, which has been somewhat quiet for a few months, is once again assuming its air of business activity. Mr. Ruxton, the new superintendent, has arrived upon the scene, taken off his coat and is fast getting things moving again. At present nearly three gangs of cutters are employed, and he reports that he has work enough to keep them busy all winter if the weather will permit of their working. Mr. Ruxton does not spend much of his time in the office, but is about the works looking after the minor details. The office of the firm has been connected by telephone, and anyone who desires to communicate with him telephonically, should call up "Quincy 131-5."

The Merry Mount Granite Co. continues to be busy and report that they have not much complaint to make. At their quarry they are extremely busy and have all the orders that they can fill.

W. T. Spargo reports that he is quite busy, although work as a whole is a little quiet. Some new orders are being booked, but there is nothing among them out of the ordinary run of work. He has finished and shipped three good-sized jobs this month. All were of Quincy granite and of sarcophagus design. One was all polished, another with an elaborately carved second base and cap, and the third was a fine hammered job.

Joss Bros. Co. find business exceptionally good and have found it necessary to put on another gang of cutters. They have a large number of orders upon their books, among which are several good sized jobs Of these the following might be mentioned: An elaborately carved top and second base of a Westerly granite job. Three Quincy granite sarcophagi jobs. The latter are to be of fine hammered work with polished sides on the die.

McGillvray & Jones find business a little quiet just at present. This does not mean that they have nothing on hand, because they have quite a lot of orders upon their books. They also say that they are in condition now to handle any large job and hope to land one. They have completed and shipped this month a large vault job with coping. The outside dimensions of the vault were 16x9-9. The stones comprising the job weighed over 150 tons.

Joseph Walker, of the Aberdeen Granite Works, says that he has not much reason to complain, only that he would like to see business a little better than it is at present. He has considerable work on hand, however, of the medium sized kind. This year's business as a whole has been the best he has ever experienced. He has been busy all of the year and has turned out some good sized jobs. The only complaint he has to make is the close prices and his inability to secure extra dark stock as readily as he would like.

Fuller, Foley & Co. have considerable work upon their books, mostly of the medium size kind. New orders, they report, are coming a little slow just at present. They, however, look for a good season's work next year and hope for better prices.

Following are the newly elected officers of the Quincy Granite Manufacturers' Association: President, Alexander Marnock; vice-president, Harry S. Nicol; treasurer, Walter R. Fagan; secretary, Thomas J. Dumphy; executive committee, president, vice-president and treasurer, ex-officio, William Deacon, John Q. A. Field, Tobias H. Burke, William T. Spargo, George McFarlane, Patrick T. Fitzgerald; figuring committee, Thomas F. Burke, James McGillvray, John C. Murray; membership committee, Thomas W. Smith, John A. McDonnell, Patrick W. Driscoll, Fred Barnicoat.

Granite shipments for the month of August show a marked increase over the previous month, the exact increase being 4,328,134 pounds. Each of the three terminals showed an increase, the largest being at West Quincy, where it was over two million pounds, Quincy Adams over one million pounds, and the Quarry railroad 244,000 pounds. The August shipments were: West Quincy, 10,605,708 pounds; Quincy Adams, 4,968,755 pounds; Quarry railroad, 3,933,340 pounds; total, 19,507,803 pounds.

HARDWICK, VT.—The Woodbury Granite Company is making preparations for a heavy winter's work. Among other improvements they are getting ready to erect a sixty-ton derrick. Any one in search of work, laborers or quarrymen, can obtain it by applying at the office of the quarry. One tenement can be obtained near the quarry.

WATERBURY, VT.—Drew Daniels will move from his present location at Morrisville to Waterbury, Vt. A new modern shed will be constructed with ample facilities for shipping his finished work. The location is a particularly good one, being much nearer the Barre quarries than before, and on the main line of the Central Vermont Railway. The distance from Montpelier is ten miles, and from Barre sixteen miles.

The granite business in Barre continues to break all records, and all the sheds are still full of work, with enough in sight to last until well into cold weather. Of course there may be some manufacturers anxiously waiting for orders—there always will be, but they are the exception and not the rule. Nearly all the manufacturers are looking for more good men. It is generally believed by the employers that with the present system of apprenticeship there will always be a shortage of good cutters wherever business is good. It is certainly true that the demands of the present are for a better class, or at least a more skilful class, of cutters than ever before, and in this respect the future is likely to prove even more exacting.

Novelli & Corti have just completed what is perhaps the finest specimen of the granite cutters' art ever set in a local cemetery. Until within a short time the cemeteries of Barre and vicinity were unpleasantly conspicuous for not containing anything in their line to which the granite men could "point with pride," but this is now gradually changing, and the monument just referred to would be a matter of pride anywhere. It is of rustic boulder form, with the back and two sides finished in the rough. On the front side is a beautifully carved and absolutely perfect scroll, polished and with every detail brought out as though it were parchment. On top is a carved bouquet of callas, carnations, roses and other flowers, which must be seen to be appreciated.

Since the September issue of GRANITE, Burke Brothers have moved into their new shed, where they now have as complete a granite cutting plant as there is to be found in Barre. The main shed is 170 feet in length and 60 feet wide, and a traveling derrick of almost unlimited lifting capacity will run at the rate of 240 feet per minute to any part of the shed. The polishing mill contains two of the largest machines made by Smith, Whitcomb & Cook. There are four beds. The blacksmith shop is on one side of the main shed and the boxing room on the other. An electric motor furnishes power, and there is an air compressor that is capable of keeping 19 pneumatic tools going. The motor, air compressor and derrick were all manufactured by the Lane Manufacturing Company of Montpelier.

Wells, Lamson & Co. are still busily engaged on the Ehret mausoleum and are shipping more or less every week. They also have plenty of other work in hand and are figuring on another large mausoleum.

George C. Mackie, formerly the head of the well known firm of Mackie, Hussey & Co., is ill. He has a serious pulmonary complaint, and is advised by his physicians to seek a milder climate than that of Vermont for the winter.

A. Anderson & Son are erecting a new shed at North Barre, and while it is not yet completed they have begun to cut stone in it. It is in the same circle as the shed they previously occupied.

Hopkins, Huntington & Co. have just booked an order for a fine sarcophagus monument to be cut of the best dark Barre stock. It is to go to Cincinnati when completed.

George Walker & Sons are among the Barre firms that will soon be housed in new sheds of their own. They are erecting a 50-foot shed, with all modern conveniences, at North Barre.

Smith, Whitcomb & Cook are unusually busy this fall and have work enough ahead to keep up the gait for some time to come. Like many other users of water they are seriously inconvenienced by low water.

*

Gothic Ornaments.

ARRANGED BY HERBERT W. BEATTIE.

The third and last great Middle Age style is the Gothic; it grew from the Byzantine and flourished chiefly on the Rhine, in the north of France and in England. Salisbury Cathedral is the first great work of the kind in England. The Gothic was developed in the thirteenth century, and was perfected in the fourteenth; its most characteristic monument perhaps, is Cologne Cathedral; in the fifteenth century it rapidly declined and became almost extinct in the sixteenth.

Of the numerous subdivisions three only can be strictly termed Gothic, viz., the early English Gothic, the decorated Gothic, and the perpendicular Gothic. Ornamentally, the Gothic is the geometrical and pointed element elaborated to its utmost; its only peculiarities are its combinations, or details; at first the conventional and the geometrical prevailing, and afterwards these combined with the elaboration or natural objects in its decoration. The most striking feature of all Gothic work is the wonderful elaboration of its geometric tracery,—vesicas, trefoils, quatrefoils, cinquefoils and an infinity of geometric varieties besides. The tracery is so paramount a characteristic that the three English varieties, the early English, the decorated, and

the perpendicular, are distinguished almost exclusively by this feature; it is the same with the French flamboyant or flame style, from the waving lines of its tracery. The tracery establishes the fact of a style's being Gothic or not.

The early English has an extensive application of foliage, with the trefoil leaf, commonly called the early English leaf, as the most characteristic ornament. It is sometimes as formal as a clover leaf, at other times very irregularly formed, but always with a fulness or roundness of the parts, as contrasted with the somewhat similar, but flat or even hollow norman foliage, of which it is a variation.

The so-called tooth, or dog's-tooth, occurs comparatively rarely in the early English, and in the early specimens only, and considerably varied in detail. This ornament was probably in its original form a simple vesica cross, but being contracted to fill hollows, was developed into its ordinary character, so common in the Transition work.

Early English ornament is the most perfect, both in principle and in execution, of the Gothic period. There is as much elegance and refinement in modulations of form as there is in the ornament of the Greeks. It is always in perfect harmony with the structural features and always grows naturally from them. It fulfils every one of the conditions which we desire to find in a perfect style of art. But it remained perfect only so long as the style remained conventional. As this style became less idealized and more direct imitation, its peculiar beauties disappeared and it ceased to be an ornamentation on structural features, but became ornament applied.

In the capitals in early English architecture the ornament arises directly from the shaft, which above the necking splits up into a series of stems, each stem terminating in a flower.

In the decorated style, on the contrary, where a much nearer approach to nature was attempted, it was no longer possible to treat a natural leaf as part of the shaft; and, therefore, the shaft is terminated by a bell shape, round which the leaves are twined. The same thing occurs in the bosses which cover the intersection of ribs. On the vaulting in the Early English bosses the stems of the flowers forming the bosses are continuations of the mouldings of the ribs, whilst in subsequent periods the intersection of the ribs were concealed by the overlaying of the boss, which was here as much an application as was the acanthus leaf to the bell of the Corinthian capital.

In the spandrils of the arches, so long as the conventional style was retained, one vigorous main stem was distributed over the spandril, from which sprang the leaves and flowers; but when the natural was attempted, the stem ceased to be the guiding form of the ornament, and lost all grace in the endeavor to represent in stone the softness of nature. The main stem as a leading feature gradually disappears, and the spandrils are often filled with three immense leaves springing from a twisted stem in the centre.

The "Decorated" period succeeded the early English, and was chiefly characterized by a more magnificent development of the leading elements of the early English, more especially the tracery; but it has its own features, such as the ogee arch, etc., but the so-called ball flower, and the common serpentine vine scroll, are the most characteristic details of the period. There is also much natural foliage or imitation in the decorative details than in any of the other Gothic varieties. The running ornament known as the Tudor flower, so much used in the very latest of the Gothic period, is a remnant of the Byzantine. Its name of Tudor flower, or Tudor rose, is appropriate only in the sense that it is almost the only mediæval ornament preserved in that style: the original type of this ornament is the old Byzantine alteration of the lily and the cross, common as the decoration of a crown, and for edges or borders of many other kinds. In ornamental art as in architecture, it is geometrical tracery which will stamp a design with a Gothic character; decorate it with natural flowers only, it would still be Gothic; it would be made more characteristic by the introduction of some of the historic ornaments of the period,—as the Tudor flower, fleur-de-lis, crocket leaf, trefoil or English leaf, vine scroll, or any other of the more familiar ornaments of the style. As the Gothic is a style which has flourished exclusively in cold countries, its ornaments of a natural class to be characteristic, should be from such plants as are native to Gothic latitudes; tropical plants would be inconsistent. All plants that are not symbols, should be excluded.

With the exception of the tooth ornament, Norman ornaments are not admissible in the Gothic.

Classical ornaments, likewise, are of course excluded; even the scroll occurs only in the Gothic as a serpentine. Gothic ornaments independent of the tracery are nearly exclusively fruit, flowers, or leaves, and as a general rule, their execution is extremely rude.

We have now been over a rough outline of the course of ornamental art among the most prominent people of mediæval history, for a period of more than a thousand years. We have seen that all varieties, however individual in character, are intimately connected with those which preceded them; an advantage once gained was not allowed to be lost, and the remarkable transition from the Byzantine to the Saracenic, so totally different in spirit and in detail, yet both developed by the same artists, shows that it is not from a persevering manual routine that variety and beauty are to be derived, but from the active intelligence of the controlling mind.

Next month we will begin the Renaissance styles, which will complete this short review of the ornamental styles of many centuries. The term Renaissance is used in a double sense: in a general sense implying the revival of art, and specially signifying a peculiar style of ornament, that is, implying both an epoch and a style. The Renaissance styles are only those which were associated with the gradual revival of the ancient art of Greece and Rome.

Correspondence.

Can you give us any information about the preparation that is being used in New York City on public monuments to preserve the granite? It was used on the "Cleopatra Needle," Central Park. We have an inquiry from one of our customers in regard to this material and do not know who it is handled by in New York City. Any information you can give us will be appreciated.—Kavanagh Bros., 170 Columbus avenue, Boston.

Can any of our readers supply the information?

DOYLESTOWN, PA.—The granite quarries in Warwick township, Chester county, have suspended operations.

NIANTIC, R. I.—An attachment on certain property of J. B. Reinhalter, in a suit for alleged debt was brought by George T. Hutchings of the same village. The property attached included rough stock on flat cars on a siding, and tools, derricks, and stock at the quarry. Mr. Hutchings places his damages at $2,000.

CONCORD, N. H.—The Westinghouse company has come off victor in a legal battle of some importance, having been granted an injunction and an order for accounting in a suit against the New England Granite Company. The suit was brought to restrain the latter company from using the famous invention of Tesla for utilizing all the force of a dynamo and preventwaste, which had never been accomplished till after Tesla's invention, the rights to which were afterward purchased by the Westinghouse Company.

GROTON, VT.—Work is being rapidly pushed on Pine Mountain quarry. Four carloads of granite have recently been drawn to the station. They have the order to furnish all the stock for a large monument to be erected in the cemetery in Manchester, N. H.—Times.

CHESTER, VT.—The manufacturers are having trouble finding granite cutters.

FITCHBURG, MASS.—Jeremiah Shea, stone contractor, signed September 6, what is said to be the largest single contract for granite ever made in this city. The stone is to be used in the construction of the eight great piers of the new bridge which will connect Boston with Cambridge. The contract calls for some 7,000 cubic yards, or 20,000 tons of cut stone, and the contract price is $80,000.

WEST SULLIVAN, ME.—The co-operative scheme of quarrying, which was begun by some of the granite cutters at West Sullivan, has fallen through because the owners of the Stimpson quarries refused to give a lease of the property for a longer period than one year. The cutters would just get fairly started and be in condition to handle contracts when, in case the lease could not be renewed, they would have to quit. The reason for refusal for a longer lease, it is said, is because the property is in the market for sale, and recent inquiries give owners reason to hope that a sale may be effected within a year.

SPARTANBURG, S. C.—Three hundred stone cutters will be at work in the near future grinding out the granite for the completion of the state house building in Columbia. The Pacolet quarry secured the contract for supplying the granite for this work. The contract amounts to over $300,000.

Among the Retail Dealers.

JOHNSTOWN, PA.—C. Keim, proprietor of the marble and granite works here, has just completed a splendid memorial scene, representing the trunk of a tree, broken in its parts as to limbs, thus delineating parted dear ones; ferns clinging, the "Rock of Ages" ingrown; and most beautiful of all, gracefully placed in a shelter of the trunk, a bird's nest as natural as life, with four little bird's eggs in it. The carving of this beautiful memorial is most exquisite. The bark of the tree is up to nature, even to the growths of punk and moss that only need coloring to make them absolutely true. Surmounting this masterpiece is a splendidly carved cross, of exact proportions, appealing at once to the artistic age and the religious feeling. This design is Mr. Keim's original idea. It is the admiration of everybody and beautiful beyond comparison, speaking volumes for Mr. Keim as a master workman.—Exchange.

TOLEDO, OHIO.—The Lloyd Bros. Co. are the successful bidders on the new soldiers' monument for Woodlawn cemetery and have been given the contract at $4,000. The memorial will consist of a Vermont granite shaft, 44 feet high, with an 11-foot base It will be completed in time to be unveiled next Memorial day. George B. Eckhardt, who was one of the bidders, has taken exception to the award on the ground that favoritism was shown. Mr. Eckhardt says: "A request had been made of the monument committee to tabulate all the sizes, giving height, size, square of each piece, with cubic contents, and attach same to the several designs, and expose all in the room without any indications whose designs they were, so that an impartial decision could be made, but the designs were exhibited with no details placed thereon; one dealer's card was placed on each of his designs, and when it was pointed out that the design which was finally selected contained less cubic feet, was less in height and plain, the remark was made, 'We know of whom we want to buy; we are choosing the man, not the monument,' or something to that effect. One dealer was permitted to go in the room where the designs were exhibited, talking to various ones of the committee, thus giving him privileges not accorded to any other dealer. I am satisfied there were quite a number of the committee that did not fully understand the dimensions of any of the monuments in competition"- Exchange.

CHAMBERSBURG, PA.- D. J. Shull & Son have just placed a $5,000 sarcophagus on the McGovran lot in Cedar Grove cemetery. The material is of light Barre granite and the structure weighs twenty-six tons. It is a very artistic piece of work.

BLOOMINGTON, IND.—The contract for the erection of the Monroe County Soldiers' monument in Rose Hill cemetery has been let to Curry & Sons of this city for $1,047.65.

PITTSFIELD, MASS.—A sarcophagus monument, made by McGregory & Casman, has been set in the local cemetery in memory of the late Solomon N. Russell. There is to be a new lake in the Pittsfield cemetery, in the east section of the grounds.

HARTFORD, CT.—The soldiers' monument in Moodus, which was designed and made by Stephen Maslen, was accepted by the committee. The monument is of granite and is surmounted by a granite figure of a soldier of the Civil War. The statue is regarded as one of the finest designs in granite erected in the State.

WATERTOWN, N. Y.—Crooks & McLean have purchased a building known as the iron block and the adjoining lot. They will repair the present structure so that it can be used during the winter and in the spring will begin the erection of a handsome two-story brick block, 75 by 40 feet.—Exchange.

WHEELING, W. VA.—The use of compresseid air in cutting and carving granite has been recently put in operation in the Monumental Works of J. F. Burley & Co., of this city. This firm is one of the very few enterprising monumental dealers who have introduced modern machinery and methods into their work.—Exchange.

MANNINGTON, W. VA.— The Stewart Granite Works have been awarded the contract for a monument to be erected by the John B. McCoy family, which, it is said, will be one of the finest in West Virginia. It will be cut from Barre granite. The design calls for a monument of the Obelisk order. Height, about 30 feet; weight, 25 tons; the cost approximating $3,000.

Proposed Monuments and Monumental News.

INDIANAPOLIS, IND.—The monument association for the national home for disabled volunteers soldiers of Grant county will erect a monument at the military home at Marion. The estimated cost is $10,000.

RALEIGH, N. C.—Camp H. T. Walker, United Confederate Veterans, is sending out a letter for the purpose of raising funds to build a monument to General Walker, who fell in the battle of Atlanta.

AUGUSTA, GA.—There is a movement for the erection of a monument to Sylvester B. Price, formerly mayor of Macon, Ga.

SCRANTON, PA.—The Harrison Granite Company, the contractors erecting the soldiers' monument, have been afflicted with a streak of bad luck for some time, which culminated August 29 in the smashing of the huge derrick, although without any loss of life or injury to limb. The derrick comprised two sticks 96 feet high and about 2 o'clock in the afternoon the workmen were making a slight change in its position in order that it might be easier to handle some of the large blocks of granite. The derrick was held in place by large wire guy ropes, one of which was attached to some blocks and tackle. A smaller wire was connected between the stationary engine and tackle and this was being paid out when the derrick was moved. For some reason, which cannot be explained satisfactorily, the guy rope attached to the engine broke and the derrick fell with a terrific crash, the two heavy pieces of timber snapping as if kindling wood. The

engineer had a marvelous escape. He was standing in line with one of the falling logs and jumped quickly out of danger. He was struck on the shoulder by the rope, but his injury was slight. Quite a number of people were standing near by, interested in the work of moving the derrick and with the sway of the guy rope quickly run away. The portion of the rope that snapped seemed as if it had been "spliced" at some time and the work imperfectly done.

CHICAGO, ILL.—At a meeting of the directors of the Leif Erikson Monument Association, held September 14' it was decided to raise enough money to build the monument as quickly as possible. Several thousand dollars for the statue are in hand, and the association intends to get the remainder of the desired amount in several months. Subscription lists will be opened and much of the money will be got in that way.

SIOUX CITY, IA.—Knights of Pythias in Sioux City soon will issue an address to the Pythian lodges of Iowa asking them to join in the erection of a suitable monument in the memory of Knight Andrew G. Anderson.

CHATTANOOGA, TENN.—The New York monument commission some time ago began the work of excavating for an $80,000 peace memorial to be erected on Point Lookout to the memory of the soldiers of both armies. The only railroad running up Lookout mountain, on which freight could be hauled, has been torn up and the only dirt road running up the mountain is dangerous and almost impassable, having a grade of 15 per cent. The question now confronting the commissioners is how to get the material to the top of the mountain, 1,500 feet above this city. A New York firm, to whom the contract was let some time ago, after viewing the ground, threw up the job as an impossible one. The New York commissioners now propose to erect the monument, if a new road with a 6 per cent grade, at a cost of $14,000, has to be built over which to haul the material to the top.

ATLANTA, GA.—Application was made to the superior court September 13 for a charter for the Brumby Monument Association. It is set forth in the petition filed that the petitioners desire to be incorporated for a term of twenty years. The object of the association looks to the erection of a monument to the memory of Flag Lieutenant Thomas Brumby, of Georgia, who was with Dewey at the storming of Manila and later died in Washington of fever contracted in the Philippines. He was buried some months ago in Oakland cemetery.

DENVER, COL.—Great indignation has been aroused among the local owners of granite quarries on account of the order received from Washington recently substituting New England granite for Colorado stone in the new coinage mint being built here. The quarrymen held a meeting July 8 to devise a plan of action, but came to no conclusion after the receipt of a telegram from Senator Wolcott saying that the matter was out of his hands. The amount of stone needed will keep a hundred men employed several weeks in quarrying as well as cutting, which will be done in the East to save freight as well as to avoid the employment of Colorado stonecutters, who struck for higher wages several weeks ago.

A Well Carried Out Swindle.

George H. Baxter, formerly agent of the Flint Granite Company of Albany, N. Y., is a fugitive from justice upon a charge of swindling the company. Baxter was well known among local club men, having the entree to all the fashionable and exclusive clubs in town. He was a good dresser, a liberal spender and a man of pleasing address. As the agent of the Flint Granite Company he made large contracts, but they have since been discovered to have been bogus. He was a slick salesman, however, and his employers say of him:

"I doubt if there was a man in the country better acquainted with the monument business. He knew all about monuments and vaults and of the grades of granite."

Baxter came to the end of his tether on August 30th when he was called to Albany from his home at White Plains, N. Y., to explain certain inaccuracies in his accounts. Taken before Attorney James W. Eaton he confessed to having forged $60,000 worth of contracts. His commission was but ten per cent, but he had collected little more than $3,000 from the firm. Baxter was engaged by the Flint Granite Company last February. Before that time he had worked for the New England Monument Company of New York City. He was dismissed on account of irregularities in his transactions. The company proceeded to institute a case against him, but the pleadings of his wife had their effect. The affair was hushed up and Baxter started anew. To President Flint he stated he owned a house at White Plains free from debt and worth from $4,000 to $5,000. To insure the company against loss, he offered to convey to them "his property." This was acceptable and a deed of transfer was duly drawn and acknowledged. Baxter then asserted that he owned fifty shares of stock in the Kinsico cemetery, New York. He seemed anxious to give Mr. Flint this stock in lieu of the deed. He said his wife was sick and he didn't want her to know he had committed forgery. By agreement Messrs. Flint and Baxter went to New York. Shortly after their arrival, Baxter stopped short and said he forgot his keys to the safe deposit vault of the bank where the securities were kept.

"I'll go up to White Plains and get them and will meet you at the Grand Central at 11.25."

Mr. Flint waited and watched for hours but Baxter came not. His employer became suspicious and went to White Plains to investigate. Arriving in that village he discovered that Baxter and his wife had disappeared. A search in the county clerk's office revealed the fact that the Baxter's "property" was still owned by J. W. Carpenter, of whom the former claimed he had purchased it. Baxter was simply a tenant. Mr. Flint swore out a warrant for Baxter's arrest, but the police are unable to find him. Baxter's modus operandi was novel and daring, to say the least. He turned in several legitimate contracts, of course, but it is believed that his bogus orders will amount to $100,000. Mr. Flint estimates the company's loss at about $3,000, and perhaps less. There is $40,000 in contracts yet to be investigated. One of the fraudulent contracts was signed by H. L. Horton, of 66 Broadway, New York City. This called for a $10,500 monument. But a let-

Continued on page 27.

"GRANITE," OCTOBER, 1900.

BOTTOM BASE . . . I — T x E — Y x C — V   PRICE:
SECOND BASE . . . T — C x R — I x C — C   Westerly Granite, C C G V
DIE . . . . E — R x A — G x C — N   Barre Granite, N G E
CAP . . . . E — N x R — A x C — T

"GRANITE," OCTOBER, 1900.

BOTTOM BASE . . . : T — V x R — V x C — A
SECOND BASE . . . : E — A x A — A x V — C C
DIE . . . . . : P — T x C — T x R — Y

PRICE:
Wes'erly Granite, T R Y
Bar're Granite, P I R
Quincy Granite, E Y Y

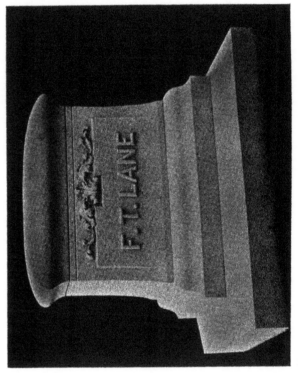

BOTTOM BASE . . . . T—VxP—VxC—P'
SECOND BASE . . . . P—TxA—NxC—V
DIE . . . . . . R—GxC—CCxA—R
CAP . . . . . . R—CCxA—CxC—V

PRICE:
Westerly Granite, E A R
Barre Granite, R 1 E
Quincy Granite, P A R

"GRANITE," OCTOBER, 1900.

BOTTOM BASE	. . .	T — V x R — T x C — A
SECOND BASE	. . .	P — C C x A — E x C — C
DIE	. . . . . .	P — A x C — R x A — R
CAP	. . . . . .	P — P x C — C V x C — G

PRICE:
Westerly Granite, I V V
Barre Granite, E Y V
Quincy Granite, F A E

ter to Mr. Horton, asking him if he desired to make any change in the design, brought the reply that he had never ordered the work. Another contract called for a $1,400 monument to be placed in a lot in the Holleywood cemetery of Richmond, Va., owned by Dr. James Vedder of Whitesboro, N. Y. The monument was built and shipped. Baxter said Dr. Vedder would be in Richmond in a few days to oversee the erection of it. The firm sent a letter to the address given as Dr. Vedder's Richmond residence. It went to the dead-letter office and came back promptly to the granite company. Baxter was in Albany at the time and Mr. Flint showed him the undelivered letter.

"Why," explained Baxter, "it has been misdirected. I'll go down to Richmond right away and see that the monument is put up."

There was no bluff about it. Baxter went to Richmond. "And," related Mr. Flint, "he sent us a telegram from there saying that the foundation had been laid and everything was ready for the monument, which would be set up the first of the following week. He said he would get returns in 30 days."

At this point in Baxter's game, suspicions of irregularity took hold of Mr. Flint's mind. He dispatched his bookkeeper to Richmond to investigate, who couldn't get the slightest trace of Dr. Vedder. He learned, however, that no foundation for the monument had been laid. He came back and imparted his facts and suspicions to his employer. Then came the expose and subsequent confession. The wily agent had played a daring game but was caught at it too soon. Only a day or two before the expose he had asked for a large check. but already suspicion pointed to fraud and the check was held.—Exchange.

*

Monthly Trade Record.

This department is compiled and edited by the United Mercantile Agency. Subscribers, in accordance with the terms of their contracts, are entitled to receive further information relative to the parties here. after mentioned, upon application to the main office As the names of many business men who are good will appear herein, subscribers can readily see the importance of making inquiries if interested, previous to taking any action.

ARKANSAS.
Little Rock, G—Arkansas Granite Co,, Fred Hanger 78.
ARIZONA.
Tucson, *M—Jones, M. W., 86 to L. T. King.
CALIFORNIA.
Santa Anna, *M—Lee & Garner succeed H. L. Talbott.
CONNECTICUT.
Hartford, *M— Beij, Karl J., 14 $500.
New Haven, *M—Phillips, Thomas & Sons, John H. Phillips 78.
ILLINOIS.
Alton, *M—Thompson, F. S., 76.
Aurora, BQ—Riddle, H., 20 $1476.
Casey, *M—Sedgwick, W. D., succeeds Hollis & Sedgwick.
Chicago, *M—Bagley, F. P., 74.
Chicago, *M—Gall, John, succeeds De Camp & Bowen.
Chicago, *M—Hirshovich. Isaiah, 106.
Blue Island, *M—Heimburger, J. & Co., 86.
Decatur, *M—Brown & Son, 20 $291 released
Galena, *M—Homrisch & Lehner. 64.
Rock Island, *M—Ehmer, A. E., 14 $1.200.

INDIANA.
Indianapolis, *M—Miller, J. Willis Co., 74 and 89.
Spencer, *H—Viquesney, E. M., 84.
IOWA.
Marshalltown, *M—Woods, W. W. & Son, suit in foreclosure, $2,500.
Ottuma, *M—McCreery & Marts succeed L. C. McCreery.
Sheldon, *M—Haag & Bumgardner, 76.
Spencer, *M—Shafer, W. T., 74 $182.
Woodbine, *M—Greenizen, Mrs. R. W., 93 $1,000.
KANSAS.
Topeka, *M—Guild & Lewis succeed C. W. Guild.
Wichita, *M—Peniwell Monument Works, 14 $999.
KENTUCKY.
South Carrollton, *M—Hocker, A. C., 88 to Central City.
LOUISIANA.
New Orleans, *M—Kursheedt, Edwin I., 74 $150.
MARYLAND.
Baltimore, *M—O'Meara, James, 20 $50.
MASSACHUSETTS.
Boston, *M—Linscott, G. A., 14 $13,000.
Lowell, *M—Goodrich, A. F., 104.
MICHIGAN.
Ann Arbor, *M,—Harvey & Lane, 14 $700.
Coldwater, *M—Beard & Son, 64.
MISSOURI.
Hermitage, *M—Hewitt, Daniel, 76.
NEW HAMPSHIRE.
Manchester, *M—Manchester Granite Co., George F. Bond 14 $100.
Union, *M—Johnson, Myron L., succeeds C. W. Lowe.
NEW JERSEY.
White House Station, *M—Bonnell & Melick 64, R. A. Bonnell 58.
NEW MEXICO.
Albuquerque, *M—Jones, M. W., 76.
NEW YORK.
Dormansville, *M—Powell & Wood, 88 to Altamont.
Boonville, *M—Grosjeau, Stephen, 78.
Syracuse, *M—Francis & Co., 64.
Troy, *M—Kester, George J., 106.
Woodlawn, *M—King, T. J. & Co., 86 to Joseph Havender.
Ohio Circleville, *M—Price & Co., W. T. Price 93 $800 and 99 $1,600.
Fremont, *M—Jeffers, William, 14 $100.
Piqua, *M—Hirt, Jacob, 99 $500.
Rockford, *M—Dull, J. B., 93 $1,500.
Troy, *M—Kesler, George J., 106.
West Union, *M—Richards, J. L. & Son, W. L. Richards 93 $500.
PENNSYLVANIA.
New Castle, *M—Beer & Goodyear, 64, F. G. Beer 58.
South Bethlehem, *M—Harwich, Monroe B.. execution $720.
SOUTH DAKOTA.
Sioux Falls, *M—Smith, J. H., 76.
TEXAS.
Jacksonville, *M—Norton, J. H., 76.
VERMONT.
Barre, GZ—Bilodeau & Lanciault. 64.
WISCONSIN.
Lake Mills, *M—Biehle. O. H., 76.

An Unfortunate Break.

While workmen were engaged in placing in position the monster granite Doric column which was designed to occupy the central position in the front entrance to the St. Louis Trust Company's new building, the huge monolith suddenly broke in two pieces.

An examination by workmen showed them that the break in the column was such as to render the stone valueless for the purposes for which it was designed, and of comparatively little value for any other purpose.

There was a ragged, oblique break in it midway between the capital and base, which represents a loss of a' least $5,000 to the contractor who is doing the stone work on the building.

The St. Louis Trust Company's new building is classic in design. The outer walls are constructed of rough-dressed gray granite. The material is being furnished from a quarry in Amberg, Wis. The plans call for a granite column for the centre of the front entrance on Fourth street 32 feet in height, 3 feet 6 inches in diameter at the base and 3 feet in diameter at the

top. A block of granite sufficiently large to furnish a column of these dimensions is not to be had every day, and the work of securing this block was a task of great magnitude. It required six months' work to turn out the finished product. As it was laid down on the cars here, the cost of this column was close on to $6,000. The task of transferring it from the car to the building was another undertaking requiring ingenuity and the expenditure of much labor, but it was finally placed in a horizontal position, close to the foundation upon which it was to stand. Preparations were made to raise it to its erect position.

A derrick had been erected, equipped with a powerful set of tackle blocks for this purpose. A steel wire rope was attached to the column near the capital, the idea being to hoist the shaft by the crown and swing the base into position on the foundation without the aid of rollers. After everything was made ready, the engineer in charge of the hoisting apparatus started his engine, the wire rope creaked and shivered as the immense strain was brought to bear upon it, the top of the monster column was lifted a few inches from its supports and then there was a sharp, sudden crack as the column snapped in two, almost in the middle. The engineer, warned by the sound, immediately shut down his power, and then, realizing what had occurred, lowered away until the upper portion of the broken column again rested upon its supports.

As soon as the full nature of the catastrophe became known, word was sent to Contractor Hinsdale, who hurried over to the scene. When the stone had settled down again upon its supports, there was a space of three inches separating the severed parts sufficient to allow of an examination of the break. Mr. Hinsdale made a close inspection, and, he says, found a flaw which explained the break to his satisfaction.

"Such instances are very rare, and we have no way of providing against such a contingency," said Mr. Hinsdale. "To all appearances the stone was perfect, and we accepted it as such. The break was due to the stone itself, and was no fault of the men engaged in the work of erecting it. Had the stone been thoroughly sound, the accident could not have occurred. It represents a loss of nearly $6,000 to us, as the stone is now practically valueless for any other purpose. We had no insurance on it. The accident may retard the completion of the building somewhat, as the work of securing a perfect stone of the dimensions required will take considerable time."

Take Pleasure in Their Graves.

READING, PA.—Samuel Reinert, who is digging his own grave in the Union Church cemetery near Shoemakersville, is only one of many people about here who are making similar preparations for death. Reinert made up his mind to superintend his future earthly home, so he lined out his grave with granite slabs and arranged the bottom just as he wanted it. He wants the flooring well drained and secure, then concreted and then laid with a stone slab.

In a nearby cemetery are twin marble tombstones. On one is an inscription showing the death of a farmer's wife. On the other is simply the name of the woman's husband. He is still alive and in good health.

When he dies he will be buried there, and the tombstone maker will cut out the date of his death and his age. In life the farmer has the satisfaction of seeing exactly how his grave will be marked.

In another nearby cemetery are three twin stones, for husbands and wives, where the husbands are dead and the widows living. A widow with her gravestone in place at the churchyard has never been known to marry a second time. Twin gravestones therefore seem to have the effect of keeping widows in their weeds and of making them content to live without marrying again. Some time ago a country gravestone cutter was asked by a friend what he would charge to remove a twin gravestone and what he would allow the widow for the marble. He peremptorily refused to have anything to do with such a job, and told his visitor to tell the widow to get married if she wished to, and that when she died he would see that she was buried by the side of her first husband. The widow remained unmarried. The gravestone cutter said that to remove such a stone would mean the worst luck for him as long as he lived.

In some neighborhoods, where the surviving husband or wife does not put up a twin stone, it is taken for granted that he or she will soon be in the field for a second marriage. Where a widower puts up a twin stone the marriageable women folks don't bother him. It is taken for granted that he will never marry again. It is the same with a widow; she is expected to remain a widow.

Plenty of men in Eastern Pennsylvania have their graves dug and walled up all ready for occupancy. They visit their graves once a week and take good care of the turf and the flowers. They have the satisfaction of knowing that when death does come the burial lot won't be disfigured by earth thrown on the grass, from the newly dug grave. The earth to fill these ready made graves is brought in wagons. Some men want such earth brought from a particular spot near their home.

Elderly women also have their graves prepared in advance in accordance with their ideas. One old lady has her grave walled up with stones taken from an ancient bake-oven in which her grandmother baked the best custards she ever ate in her life. She says she knows it is only a notion, but she wants it that way.

An old sexton of Lehigh county has charged the young minister of the church with one sacred duty, as he calls it. The preacher must see to it personally that he is buried without a coffin. He wants his body wrapped in a sheet and lowered into a grave eight feet deep and then covered with yellow sand from a nearby hill where he played when a boy. The floor of the grave is to be of the same sand a foot thick. He says the brave soldier boys were buried in their blankets, and a sheet is enough for him.

Many girls and young men choose their graves; but if they marry, then the conditions change and their funeral arrangements are reconsidered. In the lower part of Berks county a hermit in the Oley hills owns a far-away corner in an obscure cemetery, where he wishes to be buried, entirely separated from any other grave. The hermit's plot will not be encroached upon in a hundred years. He says he wants no company even in death, and his gravestone is to be inscribed "Here lies nobody." An aged church organist died last year. His last request was that he should be

buried on a hill in a certain cemetery and that an æolian harp should be erected over his grave. He left $300 to the graveyard trustees to pay the expense of keeping such a wind instrument always in good repair, so that he would have music whenever there was a breeze. Near the borders of Schuylkill county a well-to-do farmer has his grave dug and in the side near the bottom is an opening four feet long and two feet wide, a sort of crypt. At his death, his favorite bulldog is to be killed and buried in the crypt, and his own coffin is then to be lowered by the side of his dog. He never had a wife and says his dog is his best friend. He is so well off and has so much influence that the church trustees will not refuse a cemetery burial to the dog.

An eccentric old stage driver has his grave dug and the bottom of it is so bricked that the head of the coffin will be two feet higher than the foot. The old man suffers from asthma and cannot lie down to sleep, but has to be reclining. He wants to have his head elevated even in death.—New York Sun.

Rifting and Grain in Granite.

(Written for the Engineering and Mining Journal by C. L. Whittle.)

A study of a large part of the earth's surface shows that the rocks composing its crust, while traversed by joints often very diverse in direction are nevertheless frequently cut by two or more prominent sets of planes making essentially, rectangular intersections. The cause of this jointing was early attributed to shrinkage of the rocks during cooling (in the case of igneous rocks) and the drying out or compacting of the sedimentary rocks. This theory does not explain all the phenomena, and it has given place to the hypothesis of torsion, as illustrated by Laubree's experiments, or the earthquake wave hypothesis, or these two processes in combination. Daubree has shown that a thick, homogeneous glass plate, fixed at one end with a twisting force applied at the other end will, at the moment of rupture, break into two sets of plane surfaces having angles of nearly 90°, which angle is bisected by the axis of torsion. It has also been shown experimentally by Professor Crosby that a jar applied to rocks undergoing a torsion of this kind, precipitates and hastens the process of breaking. The artificial jar applied in the laboratory is likened to the propagated earthquake shock traversing the earth's superficial rocks.

It is a matter of observation that the planes of weakness in many rocks (notably in the granites and allied eruptives) also intersect at right angles, and it is by taking advantage of these planes of weakness that quarrymen are able to split rocks along definite directions with powder or by means of plugs and shims. It is further noticed that the direction of the prominent joints in a given quarry is often in close agreement with the course of the "rift" and "grain," and it is a fair conclusion that the processes which produced the former also gave rise to the latter. Professor Tarr, from a study of joints and rifting in the granite at Rockport, Mass., advances this view, and he was able to trace rift planes passing into joints. In addition he showed by a microscopic study of rock sections cut at right angles to the rift, that the rocks were traversed

by minute cracks and strains, and that these were the prime factors on which the regular breaking depends.

While fissuring is very evident under the microscope, it is not prominently visible to the naked eye in most granites. I have studied the polished surfaces of a large number of granites and other rocks, and, while the planes of potential rifting are seldom plainly visible, yet in certain granites, the phenomena are distinctly discernible.

I have received information from the Maine & New Hampshire Granite Company, that the rift in the granite quarried at Redstone, N. H., is exceptionally well developed, and that while the grain is excellent, it is inferior to the rift. The unusual perfection of these two planes of fracture is shown by a remarkable monolith recently quarried from this stone, having a length of 145 ft., a thickness of 28 ft., and a width of 32 ft., weighing 10,826 tons. Crushing tests of this stone made by the United States Government at Watertown, Mass., give a strength of 22,370 lbs. per square inch, and from this it appears that the strain which produced the incipient and visible cracks to which the rift and grain are due, has had no serious effect in weakening the stone as compared with the normal resistance to pressure of other granites.

The Proposed Cadillac Memorial at Detroit, Michigan.

The president of the chapter of architects presented the report of the committee and the plans for the monument, and two other members of the committee were present who explained the plans at a recent meeting.

The plans include two sections. The first one, or the nearest to Jefferson avenue, is to be occupied by the monument. A large platform, reached by one or two steps on the upper side and seven or eight on the lower side, surrounds the base of the monument. A low coping with high corner posas surrounds the platform.

The shaft itself is of renaissance style. With its pedestal it is to be six feet in height, and is a massive piece of stone. On each side of it is a smaller pedestal, the one on the lower side to be surmounted by a bronze statue of Cadillac, eight feet in height.

For the present no plans are prepared for figures for the other three pedestals, although in time they could be filled with appropriate figures. The monument will still present a finished appearance without them, however. At the upper corners of the heavy shaft, which is practically the same size all the way up to the cap, which has four convex sides, bronze eagles are to be placed.

The platform, pedestals and shaft are to be erected of light granite, according to the plans, while the figure of Cadillac and other figures, if they are added, are to be of bronze, with the descriptive tablets on the sides of the pedestal of the same metal. The distance from the pavement to the top of the shaft is 36 feet.

This upper section will be about seventy feet long. Below it is a space of ten feet, and then comes the second section, the same size, in which is to be placed a handsome fountain with a cascade and basin, surrounded by a stone railing. This structure will conform to the grade of the street, so that it will serve as a setting for the shaft and statue of Cadillac as seen from the river and lower Woodward avenue.

The committee estimated the cost of the shaft with its pedestal and the platform surrounding it at $30,000. The bronze figure of Cadillac and the other bronze work is figured to cost $9,000, while the second section complete is figured to cost $10,000, making a total cost of $49,000 for the whole memorial.

There was some discussion as to the style and cost of the memorial and it was finally decided to have the architects prepare another plan, more simple, so that both may be presented to the public at once, and the one the people seem most willing to subscribe to will be erected. Steps were taken to get the movement on foot at once.

A Large Contract.

Before we go to press the bids will have been opened for the new Wachusett dam at Clinton, Mass.

The description says the dam is to be built across the south branch of the Nashua river in Clinton, with its water face about 275 feet below the centre line of a temporary earth dam already built across the river. The dam is to be constructed of masonry, built upon the solid rock, the main dam to be 850 feet long, with a maximum height of 200 feet. At its northwesterly terminal, to be known as the bastion, the dam turns up stream and continues with its top at a low level, as a waste weir, 450 feet, to a small abutment at the shore.

Each bid made was accompanied by a certified check for $15,000, to be forfeited if the contract is not accepted when awarded, and a bond in $200,000 will be required for the faithful performance of the contract, no individual or company to become surety for a sum exceeding $100,000. There were 55 items in the specifications and they include 267,000 yards of earth excavation, 98,000 yards of rock excavation, an overhaul equivalent to 600,000 cubic yards hauled 100 feet, 265,000 cubic yards of rubble stone masonry, 50,000 cubic yards of same laid on an incline, 18,000 square feet of rough pointed work, and 30,000 square feet of fine pointed work and many smaller items.

A Supposed Granite Cutter.

Almost complete loss of memory as the result of a lightning stroke prevents a patient in the hospital at White Plains, N. Y., from being sent home to his family, probably residents of Chicago.

On July 6 the man was brought into the hospital unconscious. The physicians said he had been struck by lightning. Consciousness slowly returned, but with it came forgetfulness of his past life, his name, his friends, and the locality of his home. His memory for events after the shock is clear, but all things before July 6 seem beyond his power of recollection.

He is able, however, to recall a few facts which may serve to identify him. He says his father's name was Thomas, his mother's name Margaret. He has a sister named Millie, who is a milliner, and a brother whose name is James. He remembers having lived near Chicago.

The patient, while he can think of these few things, is utterly incapable of saying what is his own name. In a vague way he talks of having worked in a granite quarry in New England and of superintending the labor of a gang of men there.

The Ingersoll-Sergeant Drill Company Exhibit at Paris.

One of the most extensive exhibits of the United States is that of the Ingersoll-Sergeant Drill Co., of New York City, which company has exhibits of its air compressing, mining, tunneling and quarrying machinery in three places. On the Champ de Mars, in the Palace of Machinery and Electricity, it has established its headquarters in the midst of the United States Machinery Section. Here, one of the company's Class "H" Compressors is in operation, supplying air for all the pneumatic tool companies' exhibits and the tubular despatch of the Batcheller Pneumatic Tube Co. This compressor has duplex steam and compound air cylinders. The former are 12 inches by 12 inch stroke, and the latter 18 inches diameter for low pressure, 12 inches diameter for high pressure and 12 inch stroke.

The engine is of the well known Tangye frame type, mounted on a solid base which contains a special cooler through which the air passes on its way from the low to the high pressure cylinder. In this way, its temperature is reduced to about that of running water, and the work required to compress a given volume of air is considerably reduced.

Adjustable cut-offs are used for the steam cylinders, with a range of from 1-8 to 3-4 cut-off, while an automatic regulator, which is attached to the air receiver or reservoir, maintains a constant air pressure, cutting off the steam supply or opening up to a greater or less extent, as the air pressure runs up or drops below the set pressure. In this case, the compressor regulates to within 1 to 1 1-2 lbs., when set for 100 lbs.

In Group IV, Civil Engineering & Transportation, are found a small motor-driven compressor and some interesting models, all exhibited by the same company. This compressor has a single air cylinder, 6 by 6 inches. It has, on its base, a 5 H. P. direct current motor, to which it is geared with a single reduction. When running at full speed, about 150 revolutions per minute, it has a capacity of 28 cubic feet per minute to a pressure of 50 lbs. per square inch. This machine was installed by the U. S. Commission to furnish air for operating models of the machinery used in the excavation of the Great Chicago Drainage Canal.

Among these machines are found four little working models, made to 1-8 scale and illustrating in a most pleasing way the construction of a bar channeler, a track channeler, both being machines for cutting out work in quarries, canals or railway cuts, and also showing a Standard Rock Drill and one of the company's Class A Compressors.

There is, in addition, a full sized pneumatic or compressed air Coal Cutter, such as is coming into extensive use in the United States, and an interesting series of photographs showing other apparatus manufactured by this concern.

It is, however, at Vincennes, where they have their main exhibit that the most interest centres. Occupying a space 41 by 34 1-2 ft., or about 1400 sq. ft., in a prominent position, it has two compressors and all of its mining and quarrying apparatus in the form of rock drills, coal cutters, and channeling apparatus.

The largest compressor, occupying one side, is a horizontal Cross Compound Corliss type, with steam cylinder 12 by 22 inches and a 30-inch stroke. The low pressure air cylinder is 16 1-4 by 30 inches, and the high pressure 10 1-4 by 30 inches. Between them is placed a Sergeant Vertical Intercooler. This device effectually removes the heat resulting from compression in the first cylinder. and at the same time acts as a receiver or reservoir from which the high pressure cylinder draws.

The low pressure cylinder has an exceedingly novel and satisfactory form of inlet and discharge valve devised by Mr. H. S. Sergeant, the engineer of the company. This is a type of mechanical valve which avoids the difficulties inherent with air compressor valves which have rigid rod connections, and it depends upon compressed air for its operation. In this way, a perfect adjustment can be obtained. and cards taken from the cylinder are as regular as those obtained from a well adjusted Corliss Steam Cylinder.

The high pressure cylinder is provided with the well known Sergeant system of piston inlet valve. In this type, which has a higher volumetric efficiency than any other form of compressor cylinder, owing to the remarkably small clearance volume necessary, the large valve openings and the rapid opening and closing of valves resulting from the peculiar construction of the valves themselves.

The piston is hollow and has a hollow extension at the back end which passes out through a suitable stuffing box in the head of the cylinder. The piston, it will be seen, has in either face a circular slot, concentric with the piston rod. These slots are closed by a ring which, in a cross section, resembles a letter "T." No springs are needed to open or close these valves, as the inertia resulting from the movement of the piston throws them open or closed at the proper moment. It will be seen that this form of valve admits of a remarkably small clearance. In addition. the constant inrush of cold air passing in one direction helps to prevent excessive heating of the piston, while the water jacketed cylinder and heads hold their temperature down to a low point.

Both compressors discharge into a receiver which resembles the inter-cooler already described. This again reduces the temperature of the air to that of running water and, as a result, precipitates nearly all of the moisture contained in the air.

From this reservoir, a 4-inch pipe line is run straight away for over 900 feet to the Palace of Civil Engineering & Transportation. The air supplied by this line runs two Baldwin locomotives, the New York Air Brake Company's exhibit. that of the Westinghouse Brake Co., Westinghouse Signal System, the Standard Signal System and other exhibits.

A second and smaller line runs the entire length of the Machinery Annex Building. which taps off to the O. & C. Pneumatic Tool Co.. the Standard Pneumatic Tool Co.. the Chicago Pneumatic Tool Co.. the Jeffrys Manufacturing Co.. the Rall Engine Co.. and the Bullock Diamond Drill Co.

Both compressors take steam at from 100 to 120 lbs., and furnish air at from 100 to 105 lbs., the two ma-

chines having a volume of about 1,000 cubic feet of free air per minute.

It is interesting to note that the compressors of this company were the first apparatus in the entire American Machinery Section to operate on "Opening Day," April 14th, excepting the boilers installed by the Commission. They were also among the very first steam engines in the entire Paris Exposition to run with steam from the Administration mains.

Coming now to the mining machinery exhibited by this company, we first notice a large machine which they term a track channeler, in other words, a machine running on a track, and intended for cutting a long, narrow, vertical slot in rock of any sort. Thirty-five of these were used on the Great Chicago Drainage Canal, where for miles they cut vertically through hard or uncertain rock to a depth of from 24 to 36 ft. deep in three steps of 12 ft. each. This machine consists of a fair sized vertical tubular boiler mounted on a heavy frame, in turn supported by four flanged wheels which run on a track made in sections. At one side, and supported on a substantial bracket frame are the cylinder guide, valves and controlling mechanism. Steam passes over from the boiler through flexible connections to the cylinder and causes the piston to reciprocate, rapidly raising and driving down the cutting bars, which are clamped to the guide chuck on the end of the piston rod.

The cutting points are under absolute control of the operator, who can strike hard, rapid blows or light, slow ones, or he can cause the cutting to occur at the upper or lower part of the stroke. The single lever which shifts the machine along the track is also within easy reach, as are all the lubricators, adjustments, etc. Machines of this type and make have cut as much as 475 square feet in 10 hours, although the average on large work is from 160 to 175 square feet for the same time.

Another interesting machine intended for quarries and places where the output would not warrant the expense of the large machine just described is called the Bar Channeler. Briefly, it consists of a frame mounted on four adjustable legs. This frame has two long cylindrical slides, on which are mounted a carriage holding a powerful air or steam drill, and a small engine which feeds the carriage back and forth along the frame. In operation, the machine is set up. the frame given the desired inclination, which may be varied from vertical through all angles to horizontal. and the drill and shifting mechanism is started. This combination of rapid and powerful blows from the cutting points, and the side movement of the feed result in a narrow slot the length of the frame and 7 1-2 feet deep, which is so smooth that stone cut this way needs only facing to be ready for use in buildings or for other purposes.

The Standard Rock Drills of which the company has several of its small and medium sizes set up for operation, must not be neglected. Described in a general way, these drills have a cylinder mounted in a guide frame and provided with a screw, which is used in operation to advance the cylinder as the drill cuts the rock. In the cylinder is a piston which forms part of the piston rod and chuck or device for holding the bit or cutting tool. There is also a special cylindrical slide valve which admits air to one or the other ends of the cylinder at the proper instant, and this causes

the piston rod and chucks holding the drill bit to rapidly reciprocate. The drills are mounted on the Sergeant Universal Tripod, which permits a rapid adjustment in any direction and which, while exceedingly light in weight, is unusually rigid owing to the method of construction, and clamping of the parts. Other forms of mountings, for shafts and tunnels are also shown. This company yearly produces over 2500 of these drills of different sizes, and it has already sold over 30,000 drills of all sorts.

Correspondence.

We publish below letters showing the renewals of subscriptions to GRANITE for one day; this does not include the new subscriptions taken—they are continually coming in. We publish the letters to show that retail dealers find their money's worth in taking GRANITE and if they do, why not you? GRANITE is the only publication published strictly in the interest of the granite industry.

We thank you for continuing subscription to GRANITE and enclose bill in payment for the same.

We intended to forward renewal before, but in the hurry of arranging for a short vacation, it passed from our memory. We take all the trade journals we know of and find it a great advantage to keep posted on what is going on in the monumental world.
Wishing you great success, we remain—Edward J. Kisling, Jr. & Co., Newark, N. J.

Please find check for $1.00 for the continuance of my subscription—A. W. Rudy, Baltimore, Md.

Enclosed please find One dollar ($1.00) in payment for my subscription to GRANITE for one year ending Aug., 1901.—H. Froehlich, Toledo, Ohio.

Enclosed you will please find check for one dollar ($1.00) in payment of subscription for GRANITE for 1 year.—Busch & Russell, Muncie, Ind.

We enclose you herewith one dollar for subscription of GRANITE for the year ending Aug. 1901.—F. J. Scholz & Son, Evansville, Ind.

When to Stop Advertising.

An English journal requested a number of its largest advertisers to give their opinions concerning the best time to stop advertising, and the following replies were received:

When the population ceases to multiply, and the generations that crowd on after you and never heard of you stop coming on.

When you have convinced everybody whose life will touch yours that you have better goods and lower prices than they can get anywhere else.

When you stop making fortunes right in your sight solely through the direct use of the mighty agent.

When you can forget the works of the shrewdest and most successful men concerning the main cause of their prosperity.

When younger and fresher houses in your line cease starting up and using the trade journals in telling the people how much better they can do for them than you can.

When you would rather have your own way and fail than take advice and win.

Monument for an Indian.

Monuments to celebrate the virtues or achievements of Indians are naturally of rather modern origin in a country where the popular conception of the red man for many years did not adorn his character with much of grace or beauty. The latest project in this line is for a commemorative statue of Sequoyah, the Cherokee Indian, who in the earlier part of the present century invented a written language for his people. An association has been formed, with headquarters at Tahlequah, I. T., called the Sequoyah Monument Society, with E. M. Landrum for its president, and a board of trustees including such well-known Cherokees as ex-Chief Harris, Chief Mayes and ex-Treasurer Ross among others. The society wishes to raise $20,000 toward which it has already made a fair start, and proposes to set up the monument in Capital square, Tahlequah. Times being dull in Indian Territory, it is calling upon friends outside to aid in its work.

It is scarcely strange, in view of the fact that the Cherokees had no written language till Sequoyah gave them one, that the origin of his work should be shrouded in at least a thin veil of mystery. There are traditions which vary considerably among the Cherokees of Indian Territory, and still others survive in Georgia, where Sequoyah lived at the time of his invention, he being one of the Cherokees who did not migrate to the Territory. From this mixture, romantic and practical, a few entirely probable inferences may be drawn.

Sequoyah had an English name, George Guess, supposed to be a corruption of the name of a Virginia military man named Gist, who lived for a time among the Cherokees in the latter part of the last century. While other young Indians interested themselves in war or the chase, Sequoyah is said to have spent most of his time by himself, wandering alone for days in the forests, immersed in meditation. It presently appeared that he recognized as the most important difference between the red race and the white, to the latter's advantage, the fact that one white man could send a silent message to another at a distance by writing it, and that any generation of white men could transmit all their knowledge to their children, and their children's children forever, by the same means. He induced a white man to explain to him the principle of a spelling-book, and soon set about devising a visible sign for every syllabic sound in the Cherokee tongue. There being eighty-six of these, the task was a pretty serious one. He persevered, however, building up his alphabet letter by letter. The last part of it came slower than the beginning, because after he supposed that he had provided for all the syllables possible, he would occasionally detect a new one while in conversation with other Indians, and for that he would have to make an additional symbol. For writing materials he used sand and a stick, or bark and home-made paints.

Wherever his efforts were observed by other Indians, they met with utter derision. His time for triumph came, however, when his young daughter, having learned his alphabet from him, was able to prove its practicability by staying in one place while her father went to another at a long distance, and writing on a piece of bark any message given her by an unbeliever, who would then carry it himself to her father and hear it read aloud word for word as he had dictated it. Then Sequoyah would take a dictation at his end of the line, the incredulous experimenter would carry it to his daughter, and the daughter would decipher it orally in the same way. As it gradually dawned upon the Cherokees that Sequoyah had really given them a great boon, derision changed to admiration, and his position in the tribe became as high, in its way, as a chief's. Then the white missionaries and settlers in the neighborhood learned Sequoyah's alphabet, the settlers using it in written business transactions with the Indians, and the missionaries translating passages from the Bible and other literature with which they wished to familiarize the Indians. Sequoyah set up a newspaper in the Cherokee language, but in this enterprise he was a trifle ahead of his time, and it died for lack of support. Several periodical publications are now, however, printed in Cherokee.

One of the most interesting things in connection with Sequoyah's work is its demonstrations of the advantage of a syllabary over an alphabet such as we use. Sequoyah at first thought of inventing a separate symbol for each word; but the Cherokee vocabulary, although not so large as that of some civilized Caucasian peoples, is large enough to make the memorizing of a whole dictionary of word symbols impracticable. At the other extreme, an alphabet like that in use for most written languages is clumsy because it requires a vast amount of study of combinations of letters before it can be effectively used. Sequoyah's syllabary struck the golden mean. It required the memorizing of more than three times as many symbols as are in our alphabet, but, these once mastered, it was necessary only to know the sound of a word to put it together on paper. It is said that anyone with a correct ear and a reasonably quick intelligence can take dictation in Cherokee language, even without understanding its meaning, after from one week's to four weeks' study.

If we were the only people of our race with a distinct written language of our own, and the inventor of that language had been so lately with us that his identity and his right to the credit could not be called in question, we should probably feel liking paying some handsome tribute to his memory. Sequoyah's best monument will always be the Cherokee literature, but it will do no harm to supplement this with something which will preserve for posterity the image of his face and form.—LINCOLN, in Boston Transcript.

WALTER W. FIELD,

117 Main Street, Cambridgeport, Mass.

...TELEPHONE 73 CAMBRIDGE...

NEW ENGLAND AGENT FOR

THE LAMBERT
HOISTING ENGINE CO.

**500 Styles and Sizes.
Built to Gauges and Templates.**

For Mining, Quarrying, Coal Handling, Pile Driving, Builders' use, Logging and General Contracting.

**Electric Hoists, Single and Double Drums,
with Improved Automatic Brake.
Suspension Cableways.**

—— *SEND FOR NEW CATALOGUE B.* ——

Horizontal, Locomotive and Upright

BOILERS.

Engine in Stock for Quick Delivery.

**Standard Double Cylinder Double Patent Friction Drum Double Winch
Hoisting Engine, with Boiler and Fixtures Complete.**

FOUNTAIN AIR BRUSH.

SEND FOR CATALOGUE.

THAYER & CHANDLER, 146 WABASH AVENUE, CHICAGO.

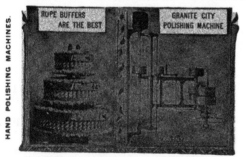

60 Designs for $4 00 including
a Subscription to Granite
for One Year.

We shall publish 500 Sets, containing Sixty different designs of Monuments. They will be reprints of those which we have already issued in this publication, and will be printed upon heavy paper without reading matter. Sizes and prices will be given upon a separate sheet. Prices of Monuments will run from $200 upwards.

November, 1900   Vol. X. No. 11

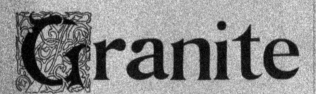

Granite

A. M. HUNT & CO.
PUBLISHERS
131 Devonshire Street
BOSTON, MASS., U.S.A.

Subscription Price, $1.00 Year

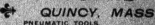

Established 1868.

E. L. SMITH & CO.

QUARRY OWNERS, MANUFACTURERS AND
WHOLESALE DEALERS IN

Barre Granite,
BARRE, VT.

Dark, Medium and Light Rough Stock

of any dimension to the limit of transportation.
Modern Equipped Cutting Plant especially designed for
handling Large Work.

☛ SEND FOR PRICE LISTS AND ESTIMATES. ☚

Wedging out a Spire, Upper Quarry.

ADVERTISERS' DIRECTORY.

ARE YOU

⌐WEDDED TO ANY PARTICULAR CONCERN?

If not give **US** a share of your patronage.

We can name you prices on

❀ *Polished Work*

that will fairly daze you. All our work guaranteed.

opkins, Huntington & Co.,

Quarry Owners and Manufacturers. ⌐ BARRE, VERMONT.

GRANITE

INTERIOR VIEW OF

Novelli & Corti Works,

BOX 57. ——————— BARRE, VERMONT.

BELT AND STEAM POWER HOISTERS

Traveling Cranes operated by electricity, steam or manila rope

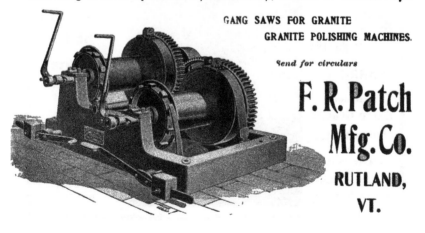

GANG SAWS FOR GRANITE
GRANITE POLISHING MACHINES.

Send for circulars

F. R. Patch
Mfg. Co.
RUTLAND,
VT.

McDONALD & BUCHAN,

BARRE, VT.

Jockey Hollow Granite Works.

OPERATED BY WATER POWER.

THIS is the reason why they can always give the best work at the right price. We have all kinds of machinery. Anything that can be done in granite we can do. ROUND WORK, SQUARE WORK, SARCOPHAGUS WORK, CHOCOLATE GRINDING ROLLS, Etc. Samples flat or in spheres. It will be a pleasure to answer correspondence.

ROGERS & ARKLEY,

BARRE, VT.

Barre Granite Monuments

And General Cemetery Work.

We use Pneumatic Tools for all carved work and make it a specialty.

All Correspondence Answered Promptly.

SEND FOR PRICES ON OUR
No. 18,
ILLUSTRATED ABOVE.

McIVER & MATHESON,

SUCCESSORS TO

McIVER & RUXTON

BARRE, VT.

Manufacturers of

Barre Granite Monuments.

QUARRY OWNERS
of
Fine Light and Medium
Barre Granite.

 Artistic Carving and Granite Statuary.

A SPECIALTY.

Monument in accompanying illustration cut by McIVER & RUXTON, and erected in Cemetery, BARRE, VT.

ENTERED AT THE BOSTON POST OFFICE AS SECOND-CLASS MAIL MATTER.

Vol. X. BOSTON, MASS., NOVEMBER 1, 1900. **No. 11**

A. M. HUNT, EDITOR.

Published Monthly in the interests of the Producer,
Manufacturer, and Retailer of Granite as used
for Monumental or Building Purposes.

Terms of Subscription

To ANY PART OF THE UNITED STATES OR CANADA:

One copy, one year - - - - $1.00, in advance.
One copy, six months . - - 75 cents, in advance.

ADVERTISING RATES FURNISHED UPON APPLICATION.

A. M. HUNT & CO., Publishers,

181 DEVONSHIRE STREET, - - BOSTON, MASS.

Editorials

HE following letter was received by
one of the Barre granite manufacturers :—

"It has been a long time since
you have heard from us with an order and will say that
my work has been largely from Quincy granite this
season, the trade in Barre granite being very light.
This has been due to a great extent on account of an
agent selling white bronze monuments, and he states
that there are erected in the cemetery at Barre, Vt.,
forty white bronze monuments. I have contradicted
this, and write to you for information as to the truth
of this statement.

"Yours,
"MYRON H. CHAPMAN,
"Franklinville, N. Y."

The manufacturer to whom this letter was addressed
made an investigation and found that there were ten
bronze monuments erected in the cemeteries of Barre,
the last one having been erected about seventeen
years ago. In other words, it dates back previous
to the time of cutting of monumental work from granite quarried at Barre, and therefore those who purchased the white bronze article have no apologies to
offer or excuses to make for going away from home.

We publish this for the benefit of any retail dealers
who may run up against the same experience as Mr.
Chapman. We have nothing to say regarding the
present condition of the bronze monuments, but any
dealer who would like to become thoroughly posted
upon the matter, and who will visit Barre, can see for
himself.

N conversation with a granite manufacturer
who makes a point of keeping his books so
that he can determine at the end of each
month the profit or loss of the preceding
month or months, he complained that although the
firm had done more business the past year than previous year or years, their profits were less. When asked
how to account for it, he said, "We have figured too
low."

He further adds that in figuring the advance due to
the increase of wages of the cutters on March 1st, he
had added 20 per cent. Yet, his monthly reports
showed that they were making too small a profit and
that they must figure higher, at least 15 per cent.
more, or go out of business, as we are now working
night and day and only making half a living.

We believe that there is a way to solve the problem
of higher prices. Let each firm so keep their books
that at the end of each month they will show the
amount of money made or lost. Perhaps our reader
will say it takes too much time to do this. Possibly
so, but we think it would be better to give a little
money and time in this direction than to be continually
accusing our neighbors of selling below cost when
you may be in the same boat yourself and not know it.

E publish below a letter which may prove interesting.

"I notice in this month's issue of GRANITE that you have been requested by the trade upon many occasions to publish a cheaper class of designs. I agree with you in your efforts to publish a nice class of designs. We have a number of journals who publish designs, and if each would publish one cheap, or rather simple, design once a month, that would fill the desired requests of the different dealers. The trouble has been that many designs have been too expensive for some sections, but the different trade journals have of late published here and there some cheaper designs. Of course, there is room for improvement, and great improvement, too, for great skill and taste can be expressed in simplicity. In the line of headstones there is room for simple designs, as the market is flooded with designs too expensive. The same is true of crosses. There are beautiful and elaborate cross designs in the market, but what the trade desires most are designs not too elaborate, but showing some carving and a moderate price.

"I am much pleased with your designs. The sizes given in writing I think are a little inconvenient when asked questions, and no man can answer them readily. I do not own GRANITE and your way of giving sizes may suit others, so I will not growl on the subject, but as regards designs there is room for improvement in monuments, headstones and crosses, so that here and there one among the different trade journals would in time make a fine collection.

"Yours cordially and sincerely,
"LEONARD DONSBACH,
"Utica, N. Y.
"Agent, E. L. Smith & Co."

We fully agree with the ideas expressed above, and are doing our best to follow up our belief. Regarding the prices and sizes appearing in letters instead of figures, we have stated before that we do not desire those who receive sample copies to have the same privileges which a subscriber is entitled to, who pays the subscription price.

The condition of the granite business in Barre and vicinity for this month is, on the whole, satisfactory, though the volume of work being done is smaller than for several months past. There has been nothing of the nature of a slump, but several of the larger firms have gotten over their rush and, in some instances, a few men have been let go. Most of the sheds are now busy enough, but it is easier to get good men than at any time since last spring, which indicates a somewhat lessened demand for labor.

The flush condition of business the past summer has resulted in one serious mistake—carelessness in the matter of credits. In their eagerness to book work at good prices while it was being placed, several firms did not give sufficient attention to the essential detail of finding out the reliability of their customer and, according to the natural order of things, these firms are now busy trying to collect claims more or less doubtful in value. Of course, bad debts are accumulated every year in every line of business, and granite manufacturing is no exception, but with the conveniences now available it is, in two cases out of three, the dealer's own fault when he gets taken in by a man who never was and probably never will be entitled to credit. One dealer, who frankly states that he is ashamed of himself, has requested the correspondent of GRANITE to call attention to this little matter.

It is easy to trace the effect of a good job in bringing new work to town. Some weeks ago John P. Corskie & Son set a splendid drinking fountain of handsome Barre granite in one of the public squares of the city of Portland, Ore. The fountain was given by one of the leading and wealthy citizens of the city, and is one that would attract attention anywhere. The result has been that orders for Barre granite from Portland and vicinity have been more numerous than ever before, and the end is not yet.

Another creditable job that has also had something to do with building up business for Barre dealers at Portland, Ore., was the Goodnough monument cut by the Vermont Granite Company. This monument was erected over the grave of the late Charles Goodnough, by Alfred Goodnough, his brother. Mr. Alfred Goodnough has been spending a few days in Barre and Montpelier during the past month, and while here purchased two carloads of rough granite stock for a friend in Portland in the retail granite business.

E. L. Smith & Co. have just completed and shipped two large vault roof stones and a large die of medium stock, on which they have been engaged for some time.

Novelli & Corti, as usual, are engaged on some as fine granite work as is often seen. One job is now nearly ready for shipment. One job on which they have been at work for upwards of four months is expected to be completed by the first of November. It is the life-size figure of an angel with outspread wings set into the concave face of an immense block of rough granite. The block as it will stand has a height of eleven feet and a breadth of seven feet four inches. The block at each end is four feet thick, and the labor of concaving it and carving the figure from the solid block to stand out in bold relief made the work one of exceptional magnitude. The figure is well to the right of the concave face, while to the left is the name "McKelvy." The monument is to go to a retail dealer at Petersburg. Va. Two of Novelli & Corti's expert carvers are busily engaged on the Boucek monument, which is also to go to Petersburg when completed. The design shows an angel with outspread wings on an upright cross, and this design is rapidly taking form in enduring granite from one of the well known quarries on Millstone hill.

Wells, Lamson & Co. are still giving employment to the same large force which they have worked all summer. Mr. Lamson states that they are still busy with the Ehret monument, which they are hurrying along as much as possible, while in the meantime they have enough other small work on hand and coming in, to fill out the corners.

The biggest job on the books at Jones Brothers just now is a 50-foot shaft that is to be set in a cemetery in New York state when completed. The bottom base is to be seven feet two, and the second base four feet two.

Smith, Whitcomb & Cook have just booked an order for a 40-ton derrick to be shipped to Chester, Mass., for the Hudson & Chester Granite Company. Smith, Whitcomb & Cook have been doing a splendid business of late if the amount of goods shipped from their plant is any criterion.

Barclay Brothers recently shipped a large sarcophagus monument to Concord, N. H., where it was set on the cemetery lot of George M. Kimball, an eminent physician of that city. The monument is of light medium Barre granite and is one of the few important specimens of Barre stone to be found in or around the granite city of Concord.

Greatson & Beckett Co., of Williamstown, have secured plans and will shortly begin work on an entirely new plant which will, when completed, be the best in that village. The new shed will be 160 by 71 feet, and will be equipped with a new 20-ton traveling derrick, made by the Lane Manufacturing Company, of Montpelier, one of their new style fast ones.

The E. L. Smith Co. are pushed by many orders at their quarries to a degree not usually known at this season of the year. They have several large spires to get out before cold weather, and numerous smaller contracts.

James Ingram, of the firm of Forsyth & Ingram, has presented the Barre Civic Federation with enough granite curbing to surround the small park opposite the Presbyterian church. Mr. Ingram's new polishing mill on Center street is completed and has been leased.

Judging from appearances at Marr & Gordon's, they will soon find it necessary to enlarge their quarters. There is not a shed in Barre containing more large work than theirs. To specify any one job would be to omit several others equally as deserving of mention. They are working every available man, and could use more if they had room for them.

Beck & Beck are shipping some creditable work this month. Sometime next week they will ship a handsome mausoleum, which is to go to Minneapolis. It is not large, but is beautifully cut and of striking pattern.

Innes & Cruickshank have added several men to their force within a few days, in view of orders recently booked.

Alderman James Mackay, of Imlah & Co., since his defeat for a seat in the General Assembly of Vermont, has eschewed politics, though his duties as president of the city council keep him before the public, and his friends say they will surely run him for mayor next spring.

The dull season is in full control of Quincy just at present. This does not mean that Quincy manufacturers have nothing to do, for as a rule all of the manufacturers are busy, and none of them have found it necessary, up to the present time, to reduce their force of help. All of the firms seen this month reported that they had considerable work on hand of small and medium-sized work, but there was a scarcity of what might be called large work. To be sure, there is some large work being cut in Quincy, the most of which has been mentioned in previous issues of GRANITE. Where the dullness comes in, therefore, is in new orders. A certain amount of uncertainty always prevails during the heat of a national campaign, and many who will eventually place orders for granite memorials are very apt to put off ordering until the election is over. Not that the election will make any material difference in prices whichever of the two great parties is successful, but they have an idea that it will. Of course, should the Democratic candidate be successful, it might mean a change in the tariff laws, which would raise the price of granite, but at best it would not be until late next year before any change would be made. Some few new orders are being booked by the Quincy firms, but as a rule they are for medium-sized memorials. In fact, in looking back over the past season it can not be said that work cut in Quincy, as a rule, has been of unusual size. Some large work has been cut, but recently all large memorials of late have been cut of some other granite than Quincy. Quincy manufacturers claim there is nothing so durable or that will stand the hydraulic pressure that Quincy granite will, but the ordinary customer does not give this quality much consideration. On the other hand, they are looking for the party that will give them the most for the money. That is to say, they can not see why a memorial of some granite other than Quincy that would cost $100 is not just as good to all intents and purposes as though, built of Quincy granite, which would cost considerable more. Were they able to live long enough, however, they would see in the end that for durability no granite yet used can stand the test of time as Quincy granite.

To look ahead, however, there is a general feeling of confidence among Quincy manufacturers that an era of prosperity is before them, and that next year will see business much better than it has been for years. Many inquiries are already being received for estimates, and they feel that as soon as the excitement incident to the national election is over, that there will be a general revival of business. Meanwhile the firms have enough orders to keep them busy until the severe winter prevents much work in this line being done. Fuller, Foley & Co. have considerable work upon hand just at present, some of which is above the ordinary size. Among their work which might be mentioned is a dark Quincy sarcophagus. On the die rests a neck piece and cap, both of which are to be elaborately carved.

W. T. Spargo, Alexander Marnock, McGillvary & Jones, the Merry Mount Granite Co., and other firms at Quincy Adams report that while new orders are a little slow at present, they have quite a lot of work on hand and are busy finishing up some of their large work, of which mention has already been made, so as to get it shipped before cold weather sets in.

Herbert W. Beattie, the sculptor, is busy making models of ornamental work which is to be cast in bronze. Much of his ornamental work is original and is copyrighted.

McIntosh & Sons report that they are quite busy, and anticipate that they will be able to keep their full gang of men at work all winter. If work gets quiet he keeps his men at work on stock jobs.

A call at the sheds of Joss Bros. Co., and Joseph Walker of the Aberdeen Granite Works, found these two firms busy with fall orders. Both firms report that they have considerable work on hand which they are rushing to get off before the cold weather. They are booking some new orders, but do not expect any great influx of work until the middle of November.

There have been a large number of Barre and Montpelier granite men in town this month, advantage having been taken of the excursions from these places to Boston.

McDonnell & Sons are very busy. They have a gang of thirty cutters at work, and have enough work on hand to keep them going until late in the winter. This work, as a rule, is larger than the ordinary run, although they have some small work. Of their new work that might be mentioned are two draped urn sarcophagus jobs. One has a 7 x 4-8 base and the other a 5-8 x 3-8 base. The dies are polished and the caps are carved. They also have a scroll cap job with a 7 x 4-2 base. All are to be cut in Quincy stock.

Kavanagh Bros. & Co. and A. Malnati, who deal almost exclusively in Westerly granite, continue to be almost as busy as at any time this year. They have many orders on hand, and as a rule it is fairly good sized work they are cutting. The most of their work calls for considerable carving, which shows up well on this fine grained stock. They use pneumatic tools exclusively in this kind of work, as it gives much better results than the old method of hand-cutting, as well as saving considerable time.

The total amount of shipments of granite for the month of September was 14,850,450 pounds, or nearly five million pounds less than the previous month. The returns from West Quincy show a loss of 5,081,648 pounds, and the Quincy railroad a loss of 18,740 pounds. Quincy Adams, however, shows a gain of 443,035 pounds. The September figures were: Quarry railroad, 3,914,600 pounds; West Quincy, 5,524,060 pounds; Quincy Adams, 5,411,790 pounds.

Among The Retail Dealers.

TAUNTON, MASS.—Carpenters are now at work on the interior wood work finish of J. F. Reagan's new ware rooms. In the front of the building is the office and leading from it a toilet room. To the rear is the show room and back of that the work rooms. On the second floor over the office is the draughting department.

LYNN, MASS.—The firm of Blothen & Curry has been awarded the contract to furnish the granite work for the Barnard factory, the material to be of Concord, N. H. granite.

JERSEY CITY, N. J.—Agents of the North German Lloyd Steamship Company have given a contract to Michael Regan, the local monument builder, to erect a monument on the acre plot in Flower Hill cemetery, North Bergen, where the bodies of the victims of the big Hoboken water front fire are buried. The monument will be of rough granite. A suitable inscription referring to the catastrophe will be placed upon it, and an iron fence will be built around the plot.

MACON, GA.—The local paper speaks of the firm of Artope & White as having filled many large contracts in the South for monumental work. Twenty cutters are employed in their yards.

PITTSBURG, PA.—The plans for the magnificent statue that Andrew Carnegie purposes to erect to the memory of Capt. James Anderson, the founder of the first public free library, have about been completed, and it is expected that work will be begun on the erection of the memorial shortly after the arrival of the donor in this country. Several suggestive drawings for the proposed tribute have been prepared by Daniel C. French, of New York, the well-known American sculptor. These will be submitted to Mr. Carnegie when he comes to Pittsburg. It will cost about $30,000.

The equestrian statue of General Hancock at Gettysburg, by F. E. Elwell, was struck by lightning several years ago. No damage was done to the statue, but the pedestal, constructed of large blocks of granite set on strips of lead two inches wide, was considerably injured, the lead being fused and the stone badly splintered. In all the later statues erected outdoors it is now customary to connect the bronze with a large copper wire leading into the ground. It is said that the huge statue of Penn on top of the Philadelphia City Hall has been struck more than once, but there has been no damage, owing to its having direct communication with the earth.

THOU ART A PRIEST
FOREVER.

The New Jersey Sons and the New Jersey Daughters of the Revolution are reviving the movement for the erection of a fitting monument to the memory of the gallant 400 who defeated the 2000 Hessians at Red Bank on Oct. 22, 1777. The historic and surpassing beautiful spot, now known as National Park, on the Delaware, and which is exactly opposite League Island Navy Yard, is marked by a simple shaft of dark marble. Through years of neglect and the heartless work of vandals it is almost a complete wreck, and two years ago, when the Sons of the Revolution visited the park, they were amazed to discover its condition. Since then the movement for a new monument has assumed definite shape, and it is likely that a regularly organized plan for securing funds will be started at a meeting to be held on the anniversary of the battle.

NEW YORK, N. Y.—On behalf of a movement among some Armenians of this country, a meeting was held recently for the purpose of securing funds for placing a monument over the grave of Dr. Cyrus Hamlin, a pioneer missionary and founder of Robert College, Constantinople. The grave is at Lexington, Mass., and the monument is to be erected as a token of gratitude of the Armenian people for the lifelong services of Dr. Hamlin in their behalf, paid for by contributions from Armenians only. A committee was appointed to take charge of the affair, consisting of S. M. Minasian, chairman; Dr. M. G. Dadirrian, vice chairman and treasurer; and the Rev. H. H. Khazoyan, of the Armenian Evangelical church, secretary.

SYRACUSE, N. Y.—At a meeting of the White Memorial Committee Sept. 27, the committee were empowered to close a contract for a monument. All designs received so far have been rejected and it will be the work of the committee to look for new ones, make a selection and arrange the contract.

LOCK HAVEN, PA.—A unique soldiers' monument was unveiled at McElhattan. It was formerly one of the round stone pillars which stood in front of the burned capitol building at Harrisburg, and is over forty feet high. On the monument are carved the names of all soldiers who served in the Revolutionary and Civil wars from the vicinity.

ELMORE, OHIO.—The citizens propose to erect a monument to the memory of soldiers of the Civil and Spanish wars.

A monument is about to be erected on a mountain in Switzerland to Barry, the most famous of St. Bernard dogs. Barry in ten years, saved forty lives. His most creditable achievement was when he found a child of ten years in the snow, succumbing to the fatal slumber which preceded death. The dog first warmed the child with its breath, and licked it till it woke. Then, by lying on its side, gave the child an obvious invitation to ride. The child mounted on his back, and Barry carried it to the convent. The dog's death was due to the timidity of an unknown man, who fancied that his open mouth looked threatening, and .... g on the head killing him.

ELMIRA, N. Y.—A fund has been started to be used in erecting a memorial monument to the late Rev. T. K. Beecher, pastor of Park church.

JACKSONVILLE, FLA.—The Democratic organization of Florida will erect a monument to Ex-Governor Drew. Governor Drew was the first Democratic executive of Florida after the war. He was a native of New Hampshire.

WEST CHESTER, PA.—A monument of granite will be erected to commemorate the centennial celebration. It will cost $2,000.

RICHMOND, VA.—The Central Committee of the Daughters of the Confederacy, who have charge of raising the funds for the Davis monument, have published a souvenir Confederate calendar for 1901, which is to be sold for the benefit of the monument fund. The calendar, which was compiled by Mrs. William Robert Vawter, is an artistic piece of work. It is also valuable in that it contains in brief form many of the most important events in southern history. The Confederate flags, in colors, are printed on the white cover. The illustrations are handsome, and each appropriate to the state in connection with which it is used. There is a page for each of the Southern states.—Exchange.

HUNTINGTON, MASS.—The removal of the Flint Granite Company back to Albany does not mean the abandonment of the Bowe plant. There has been a good deal of money laid out there and there are shrewd men behind the investment. Then the location and other considerations are in favor of a resumption of business. Another spring will probably see it.

MILFORD, N. H.—The Daniels Granite Company of Milford have elected officers as follows: President, R. M. Wallace; treasurer, C. B. Dodge; manager, D. L. Daniels; directors, A. E. Pillsbury, R. M. Wallace. C. H. V. Smith, D. L. Daniels, C. B. Dodge.

The Conway Granite Co. has been organized under the laws of the state of Maine, for the purpose of carrying on a general quarrying business with $100,000 capital stock of which $700 is paid in. The officers are: President, Alessandro Morton of Quincy, Mass.; treasurer, J. P. Sears of Quincy, Mass. Certificates approved Oct. 8, 1900.

ST. PAUL, MINN.—The East and West crews in the immense bore under the Cascade mountains have met. Now that the tremendous task of boring out over two miles of granite has been accomplished, the work of laying the tracks is comparatively insignificant. It is estimated that the tunnel when completed will cost $5,000,000. The average progress was from 18 to 20 feet per day.

PORTLAND, ME.—The American Stone Company, recently organized in Maine, of which Washington Hull of New York, is president and treasurer, has leased Deake's wharf, and will build granite sheds, which they propose to shortly have in operation. The company has granite quarries in North Jay, from which the stone is to be shipped to Portland for manufacture and then distributed by water from this port. They will employ 150 men.

NIANTIC, R. I.—J. B. Rienhalter has brought suit against George T. Hutchins, alleging breach of covenant, and setting the damages at $7,000. Attachments have been placed on real estate and personal property to cover the claim.

YARMOUTH, ME.—One of the busiest places on the Yarmouth Foreside is the Casco Bay White Granite Co.'s quarries. Between 50 and 60 stone cutters are employed there. The new boarding house, 20 x 30, which is nearly completed, furnishes accommodations for about 70. A new tramway is being put in over which the paving will be hauled to the landing. A steam derrick has been installed and is in operation. An artesian well, 100 feet deep, and situated not far from the wharf, furnishes a supply of excellent water.

WORCESTER, MASS.—James H. Phillips, of the firm of J. H. Phillips & Son, marble and granite dealers, has just returned from St. Lawrence County, N. Y., where he went to view a granite deposit owned by M. W. Spaulding of Rennsalaer Falls, N. Y., and Chester Buck of Harrisburg, Pa. Mr. Phillips is much pleased with his examination of the deposit, which consists almost entirely of pure granite of a dark pink color, closely resembling a fine Scotch granite. He quarried two blocks, which he will have finished and set up in his salesrooms for inspection.—Exchange.

ROCKLAND, ME.—The Clark Island Granite Co.'s plant is running along smoothly. There are something over three gangs of cutters at work there. The company have recently set up a large compressor, running most of their works by compressed air, by which blocks of granite are sawed to any required thickness. Pneumatic tools are also used. The company have done considerable since they started, the first of the summer. They employ over one hundred men on their works.

MILFORD, MASS.—Fully 150 men are at work at the Bay State granite quarry and it seems probable that they will be employed all winter, the firm having several large jobs. At the Pink Granite quarries two gangs of cutters are at work and the chances are said to be excellent for straight winter's work for that number and probably more.

Granite Business Dull in Hancock County, Maine.

While the granite business in Hancock County is not at a standstill by any means, there is very little as compared with that of last year. The reason for this is traced to the formation of stone cutters' unions in this vicinity, which includes in members the greater number of fine cutters. Thus it is that little but rough work is being done and few hands are employed. At Sullivan and Franklin, the latest towns to suffer from the strike, one finds some 125 men employed, working on edge stone, blocks and paving. Franklin has about a similar number, on the same work. This means that the larger portion of working men are unemployed and are likely to remain so as there are no better prospects of an adjustment of this strike than when begun in April. Then as will be remembered, a bill was presented to the employers demanding increased wages to conform with the National Union rules and regulations. A conference of the contractors was held at North Sullivan when representatives of the firms employing stone cutters in Franklin and Sullivan were present and it was agreed not to accede to the demands. The unionists were so notified, and after working the required number of days, quit. It was thought that long before this a settlement would have been reached and business flourishing as of yore, but according to all appearances the breach has widened rather than otherwise. There has been talk of the Stimson quarry being re-opened by out of town parties, when a portion of a contract held by the Mount Waldo men would be filled for which union prices would be paid. But of late nothing has been heard of it. Some of the cutters have left town and found employment elsewhere, while others are looking forward to the time when they will have work at home. In the opinion of those most interested men who understand the situation, stone cutting will not be brisk nor flourishing until this trouble is settled.

At East Bluehill, one quarry, that of the Chase Granite Co., is in operation with a small force of some 75 men. Here the number at work is not to be compared with what has been, for East Bluehill was once filled with stone cutters and employment was furnished for many, men even coming from other states to assist.

At Hall's quarry, the Standard Granite Co. have some 75 men at work on a cutting job, quarrying rough stone and random work. The number found here last year was somewhere in the neighborhood of 500 filling a large government contract. Strikes have affected this place as well, and both business and men are suffering from it. It is probable that the Standard Granite have sufficient orders to keep the men now at work employed during the winter. The firm of Campbell & Macomber at Quarryville, are operating on a small scale and shipping cargoes each month to Philadelphia. Their shipments are chiefly of rough stone.

South Brooksville also has not been entirely idle this summer and small crews have been at work on two quarries, getting out stone for shipment to Massachusetts. What effect the strikes will have on stone cutting for the year 1901 no one can foretell, but all are hoping for an adjustment satisfactory alike to unionists and employers, when the business will again be booming as of yore.—Bangor News.

"GRANITE," NOVEMBER, 1900.

BASE . . . . A — A x C — Y x C — V
DIE . . . . C — G x Y — N½ x A — R

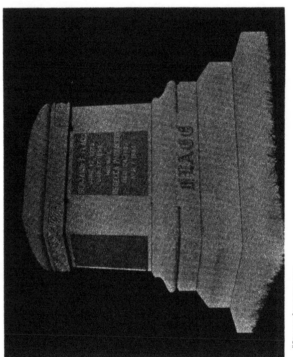

"GRANITE," NOVEMBER, 1900.

BOTTOM BASE . . . . T — Y x P — T x V — C Y
SECOND BASE . . . . E — Y x R — E⅜ x Y — C C
THIRD BASE . . . . P — P x A — C Y x C — A
DIE . . . . R — T x R — A x A — V⅞
PANEL . . . . C — C Y ½ WIDE
PANEL RELIEF . . . . C ⅛ RELIEF

"GRANITE," NOVEMBER, 1900

BOTTOM BASE	. . . .	E — N x R — C V x C — A
SECOND BASE	. . . .	P — P x A — T x C — Y
DIE	. . . .	R — N x C — C V x R — A
PRICE	. . . .	$A 1 V

"GRANITE," NOVEMBER, 1900.

BOTTOM BASE . .	R — P x R — P x C — Y
SECOND BASE	A — E½ x A — E½ x Y — C C
DIE TOP	C — T x C — T x A — A½
DIE BOTTOM	A — Y x A — Y x A — A½
CAP	A — C x A — C x C — R
DIAMETER OF BASE . . .	A — O

Joseph Newall & Co. Win Their Case Against The Smith Granite Co.

Once more the long spun out and much variegated case of the Smith Granite Company against Joseph Newall & Co., et al., comes to public attention, this time in consequence of an opinion delivered in the appellate division Sept. 22.
The case involves a fight over quarries at or near Westerly, R. I. The Smith Granite Company some time ago took in the quarry of Joseph Newall & Co., which was a leading competitor, forming a combination known as the Smith-Newall Company. A partial payment was made and a trust mortgage deed of the Smith Granite Company's property was executed to the Industrial Trust Company to secure bonds to the amount of $200,000. The bonds were placed to be sold. The bonds were considered as security for $90,000 due Newall & Co., and the broker was to pay Newall & Co. the first $90,000 realized from the sale of the bonds. The broker was not successful in finding purchasers for the bonds at par, and so the Smith Company offered to return the Newall Company the quarry and restore everything as near its condition before the absorption as possible.
But Newall & Co. were not agreeable to this proposition. They claimed that they ought to have a lien on the $200,000 worth of bonds secured by the mortgage. The Smith Company held that the agreement for the purchase of the property of Newall & Co. should be rescinded, as it was impracticable to dispose of the bonds at par. It also held that the bonds should be retired and the mortgage discharged.
The Newalls argued that they were not responsible for the failure to place the bonds at par, and that they were entitled to a lien for what was due them under the agreement. The court said:
"We find that said Joseph Newall & Co. have fully complied with the terms of their agreement, except that they have withheld a sum of money that was to have been transferred to the complainants, but as under the agreement the complainants are indebted to them in an amount greatly in excess of the sum so retained, that amount may well be treated as a partial payment made by said complainants in order to avoid the idle ceremony of handling the same over and back again, and in no event would it constitute a ground for rescinding the agreement. * * *
The complainants have not paid the purchase price as they agreed, and their excuse is that they have been unable to sell their bonds at par, that said bonds can not be sold, and that they are powerless to procure the amount necessary to enable them to perform their part of the agreement, and therefore that the performance is impossible. * * *
We see no reason for rescinding the agreement that has been executed on the part of Joseph Newall & Co., and therefore refuse to cause such recision to be made or to cause a reconveyance of said property to be made by said complainants to said Joseph Newall & Co. But, on the contrary we find that said agreement has been executed by said Joseph Newall & Co., and that they are entitled to recover from said complainants the balance due them under said agreement, with interest; and are also entitled to have and maintain a vendor's lien upon the real estate by them sold to said complainants for the unpaid portion of said purchase money.
We find that the mode of payment agreed upon by said parties has become impossible, that said bonds can not be sold at par, even by virtue of a decree that they be sold at part for the benefit of the respondents, Newall & Co., under said pledge. The parties should be relieved from the consequences of having them and the mortgage securing them, outstanding, one of which is the present priority of said mortgage over said vendor's lien.
Therefore, we determine that said bonds shall be delivered up to be cancelled, and that said mortgage shall be discharged.

A Large Turning Lathe.

For the cathedral of St. John the Divine, in New York City, thirty-two magnificent granite columns will be supplied each as high as a four-story house, and to shape them a remarkable piece of machinery has recently been constructed in Philadelphia and sent to the quarries in Vinalhaven, Maine. It is nothing less than a turning lathe of unparalleled strength and proportions.
The finished columns of the Episcopal cathedral will be 54 feet long and have a diameter of 6 feet. When finished each will weigh 160 tons. But to begin with, a block is quarried out that is 67 feet long, measures 8 1-2 by 7 feet in cross sections and weighs about 310 tons. This burden must be sustained by the two rotating ends of the machine recently sent to Vinalhaven. Before the lathe is put in operation it is intended that a little rectangular edge shall be taken from each block by hand.
Eight cutting tools will be adjusted close to each other, one going a little deeper than its predecessor. Each is designed to cut off three inches of stone, so that together they would be capable of making a cut 24 inches in depth. By suitable mechanism these cutters are slowly shifted from one end of the lathe to the other, so as to traverse the whole length of the column. But they are set in such a manner that they cannot make the diameter less than six feet.
When a column has thus been brought down to the proper size, it still has rather a rough surface. The stone must now be polished. This second operation is conducted with the lathe also, but the rotation is effected at a somewhat higher rate of speed. There are two polishing processes. The first or "rough" polishing is done in a cup-shaped device that has a lot of hardened steel shot in contact with the moving surface. In the final operation, sand and emery are employed. A period of about six weeks is required for each column. It will take nearly four years, therefore, to get out the whole 32 columns.
This machine is 86 feet long and weighs 135 tons. It is much larger than any other stone-cutting lathe ever before constructed. It is driven by a 50 horsepower engine. When engaged in cutting, its speed is one and three-quarters revolutions a minute. The change of speed is effected by gearing. The work of constructing the lathe was begun in December last.

and it was delivered to the granite company in May. But it was not put into operation until a few days ago. —Exchange.

Lives in His Wife's Tomb.

In the tomb of his dead wife Jonathan Reed of Brooklin, N. Y., has lived for five years.

Beside the coffin of his departed spouse Reed has placed a receptacle for his own remains when he shall lay down the burden of life. Over his wife's coffin he has placed a pall of bright colors. By lifting its corner he may see through the glass the features of the woman whom he loved in the life.

Faithful to the vows which he made his wife as she breathed her last, he has never left her alone one day in the tomb since she died in 1895.

Beside his strange home in Evergreen cemetery a reporter found the old man. He was painting a vase which stood beside the open door to the vault

"A few minutes before she lost the power of speech we spoke of the world she was going to. I told her that I did not think it would be long before I would follow, and then I made a solemn promise.

" 'So long as I am alive in this world,' I said, 'I shall never leave your body alone. It shall be decked with the freshest flowers of spring. In the tomb I shall make a house of memory. All your little keepsakes and treasures I shall place beside you so that I shall be reminded of you, even should I forget for a moment that your body lies in its coffin.'

"She seemed pleased with this promise, though she could only answer with a smile.

"As I had saved money from my business, I resolved to build a tomb myself. Consulting with a mason, I decided to build the tomb you see. It was not the finest in the world, but it answered my purpose.

"Death may divide, it cannot divorce. Though my wife lies in her coffin, I know that she is waiting for me. I don't believe that death should divide our loved ones from us. If I spend all my time at my wife's grave, why should I not do so? Who shall gainsay me?

"When I die I shall be placed in the coffin beside my wife. There will be no great difference between that and the life I lead. I shall rest more.

"If you look into the tomb you will see little souvenirs which once belonged to her. I treasure them because they were hers. She painted the picture you see on the left; she embroidered the fancy work just over her coffin; she loved that little crayon picture there in the dark corner. Why should I not treasure these things?"—New York World.

Bids for Clinton, Mass. Big Dam of Granite.

Bids for building the Wachusett dam were opened Sept. 25.

The names of the bidders are as follows: McArthur Brothers, Chicago, Ill., $1,603,635; Beckwith & Quackenbush, Boston, $1,680,870; The National Contracting Company, New York City, $1,748,950; Shanahan, Casparis, Langhorne & Co., Covington, Va., Columbus, O., Louisville, Ky., $1,817,875; Jesse Moulton, Clinton, $1,875,525; Norcross Brothers, Boston, $1,889,748; Grattan & Jennings, Buffalo, N. Y., $1,918.552; Nawn & Brock, Boston, $1,966,210; C. E. Loss & Company, Inc., Chicago, Ill., $1,970,051; Jones & Meehan, Boston, $2,002,450; J. J. McCarthy, M. F. Mcarthy, C. H. Wellington, Franklin, Walpole and North Oxford, Mass., $2,715,255.

After the reading of the bids the board announced that there would be no award for a few days, the commissioners taking the various estimates under consideration.

The dam is to be built of rubble masonry, faced with coursed ashlar and dimension stone masonry, and founded upon the solid rock. The distance across the valley at the level of the crest is about 1250 feet, and the total length of the dam, including the waste-wier, which is placed at an angle with the dam, will be about 1400 feet. In the deepest part of the valley the top of the dam will be 145 feet above the bed of the river, and about 200 feet above the rock. Where the dam is highest it will have a thickness of about 175 feet at the base, and at the top the thickness will be about 23 feet. The depth of earth excavation in the bottom of the valley will be about 60 feet. Temporary dams and a flume for protecting the excavations from the water in the river have been constructed already. The board owns an undeveloped quarry within one and one-half miles of the site of the dam, from which the contractor will be allowed to take granite. The construction of the dam and its appurtenances will require about 260,-000 cubic yards of earth excavation, 100,000 cubic yards of rock excavation, and 280,000 cubic yards of masonry.

Some idea of the magnitude of the undertaking may be obtained from the fact that all bids were accompanied by a certified check for $15,000 and a bond for $200,000 must be given by the successful bidder, no individual or company, however, being received as surety for more than $100,000. According to the terms of the contract, the work must be completed on or before Nov. 15, 1904.

Monumental Inscriptions.

When a great deed has been done, or a life of heroism finished, we usually begin to think about a monument, and when the money for a monument has been subscribed and the architect or sculptor selected, then comes the question of what words the stone shall bear to express what we think of the deed or of the man. The study of epitaphs has furnished grim amusement to many generations, and the study of inscriptions on monuments, on bells, on gateways and on college buildings is no less interesting.

There is a grim suggestiveness, for instance, in the inscription upon a stone seat built by the class of 1892 at Cornell.

To those who shall sit here rejoicing,
To those who shall sit here mourning,
Sympathy and greeting,
So have we done in our time.

The inference is, I suppose, that some of the 1892 students passed their examinations and others "flunked," and this information was considered by the class as worthy of record, containing as it does the consolation of companionship in misery for those of their successors who have to take re-examinations and come up before the faculty.

Excellent advice, though a trifle "hifalutin," as the author of "Bigelow Papers" might put it, is found upon the Cascadilla gateway in Ithaca.

So enter
That daily thou mayest become more learned and thoughtful.
So depart
That daily thou mayest become more
Useful to thy country and to mankind.

The monument in the Soldiers Feld at Harvard bears an inspiring quotation:

Though love repine and reason chafe
There came a voice without reply,
'Tis man's perdition to be safe
When for the truth he ought to die.
The cynical young man in the story of "The Peda-

gogues" compares this inscription to a brass band. He says that with this in mind and a band behind him playing martial airs he thinks he could die a glorious death charging up the rock of Gibraltar. There might well have been some sincerity behind the jest.

I found two remarkable Civil War monuments in a day's trip in Northern Pennsylvania last week. One, located in a town whose citizens would prefer, perhaps, not to have the name of the place published in this connection, is a monument to the unknown dead who gave up their lives in the Civil War. A worthy aim was behind the movement to erect this monument, but there seems to have been more haste than judgment in the act, for they built the monument out of pine boards, and the decent coat of drab colored paint is now mostly worn off, together with the inscription. A prominent citizen told me that the thing is to be pulled down and hauled away in a few weeks, and that will be, on the whole, a more patriotic act than the raising of the monument was. It would be better to live only in the memory of a few veteran survivors than to be commemorated by a decayed pine box standing on end.

The other monument is a simple shaft of stone. It stands in the center of the village of East Smithfield a community of perhaps 300 inhabitants and the only village of any size in the township. Yet that township has the splendid record of fifty-four East Smithfield men who lost their lives in the service during the war of secession. The inscription reads thus:

This monument
Is erected by citizens of this township
To perpetuate the memory of fifty-four of
its soldiers
Whose names are hereon inscribed
And who, with patriotic zeal,
Left their homes at the call of their country
And lost their lives in its service.
"Honor to the brave."

I do not remember to have read anywhere a more simple, dignified and moving inscription, or a better example of saying the right thing in the best way. The young men of East Smithfield, brought up in such an atmosphere, ought to be an honor to Pennsylvania; and I believe they are. It may be noted, incidently, that no Aguinaldo mass meetings are held in Smithfield township.

Nothing has been said, so far as I know, about an inscription for the White memorial. If there is to be any inscription beyond the brief recital of the facts of Hamilton White's career, it is a matter which will demand some thought. Words that are to be carved in bronze and granite need to be carefully chosen.
P. M. P., in Syracuse Post.

Making a Statue.

"Doesn't a sculptor take a mallet and chisel and carve a figure from a block of marble?"
"No. He first has to make a clay model."
"I always imagined that Michael Angelo, Phidias

and others simply hammered away on a marble block and created their masterpieces."

"You are not the only one who has this wrong impression."

"What is first needed in modelling?"

"Clay."

"What else?"

"Talent and more clay."

"You mean that if one had these he would become a great sculptor?"

"No. To be that you need genius beside the clay."

"How do you start a figure or bust?"

"First, build a skeleton or framework to hold the clay in place. This is made of iron and lead pipe; crosses of small pieces of wood are tied to the iron and the pipe to give the clay a better hold. In the case of a bust a simple iron bar, fastened to a square piece of wood, with a cross bar to hold the shoulders and a few cross pieces of wood, called butterflies, is all that is necessary. When the framework is finished put on the clay. If the figure is life size or larger make a small sketch model first. After the clay is on the framework the modelling commences.

"After the bust is finished it is ready for casting in plaster. The moulder comes and places thin strips of tin around the bust, thus making a dividing line between front and back. This accomplished, he proceeds to mix the plaster for the first coat. He adds a little color to it, either blue, yellow or red."

"Why?"

"To enable him to distinguish the plaster model, which later on will be cast in the mould from the latter. The model is white plaster, while the mould is colored—ergo, he can see which is which.

"The moulder has covered half the bust with the thin layer of colored plaster. In about ten minutes the plaster has hardened, or 'set.' This colored layer is about one-quarter of an inch thick; now he covers the surface with a wash of clay water."

"Why?"

"He does this that the next coat of white plaster shall not adhere too much to the colored layer.

"After application of the clay water, the moulder proceeds to cover the colored layer with a coat of white plaster about one and one-half inches thick. He then removes the tin strips, cleans the joint, oils it, and goes through the same performance on the second half of the bust as he did on the first. After he has accomplished his task, the mould is ready to be taken apart. First, the mould is opened slightly with a chisel. In the opening about two or three wooden wedges are inserted. Water is slowly poured in the open joint The water, assisted by a little pressure, will drive the mould apart. Following this the patches of clay are removed from the mould, the same cleaned with soap and water, and also thoroughly soaked in the latter element. This is done that the plaster which afterwards is poured into this mould shall not stick to it. This part of the work executed, the mould is put together, bound with rope, and the plaster cast into it."

"What does the moulder do next?"

"Lights his pipe, cleans his tools, gets his chisel and mallet ready, waits for the plaster to set, and then cuts off the mould."

"Does he get it off in the original halfs?"

"No; he cuts it off in little pieces; first, the white coat, and then, very carefully, the colored stratum. This is the most delicate part of the operation, lest the surface of the plaster model be fractured and disfigured."

"But, according to your description, the mould is now broken up, and cannot be used again?"

"So it is; therefore, this process is called 'waste moulding.' After the moulder has finished his task, he passes the model to the sculptor, who retouches it; that is, removes the line of the joint and other defects which might have occurred during the process of moulding. Then he gets a pointer."

"A pointer on what?"

"A pointer is an artisan who, with the aid of a pointing machine, an instrument of intricate mathematical construction, is able to reproduce by a number of points, a perfect fac-simile of the model."

"Why does not the sculptor point the bust himself?"

"In the first place, the sculptor would trust his eye too much. The pointer is a workman who does not know anything about modelling or drawing, and, therefore, is obliged to depend entirely on the instrument. The pointing machine has three points which fit on the model, two on the base and one on top of the head. The pointer marks those points; he then takes his machine and finds three corresponding points on the of marble.

"After he has found them, he takes the instrument back to the plaster mould, inserts it to the points, moves the pointing needle, for instance, to the point of the nose; marks that point with a pencil, simply a dot. Then he moves his machine with the pointing needle in the same position to the block of marble and puts it in position on the three points, takes his mallet and chisel and carves enough marble away till the needle shows him the point of the nose. He marks this point with a pencil dot. He repeats this manoeuvre till he has the whole plaster model and also the marble covered with points, several hundred in number. When he has finished his task he turns the bust over to the sculptor, who puts on the finishing touches. The price to point and cut a bust in marble—that is, the money the pointer gets—is generally $350."

"How much does the sculptor get?"

"All he can. You have seen that he is not without considerable expense in the prosecution of his work A good sculptor in this country gets all the way from $1000 to $3000 for a bust."

"When does a bust or figure look best, in clay, plaster or in marble?"

"There is an old saying, 'Clay is life, plaster death and marble the resurrection.'"

"But if the sculptor has to make the bust in bronze?"

"In that case he gives the plaster mould to the bronze founder. There are two processes of casting in bronze—or, rather, there are three. The third is bogus bronze, called white bronze, colored with metallic paint to resemble the real article. It is nothing more than zinc."

"What is standard bronze?"

"About 90 per cent. copper and 10 per cent. zinc. There is, in the first place, the process of casting in sand moulds. This is a very delicate and intricate work, and unless extreme caution is observed, the mould, costing hundreds of dollars, is frequently destroyed. It is not the cost of the metal that makes a bronze cast so expensive. The metal costs only about 22 cents a pound. It is the making of the mould and the chasing afterward.

"Another process of bronze casting is the 'cire perdue,' or lost wax method.

"It has been used in this country about three years, and it is a great blessing to the sculptor, for it enables him to have a casting which requires no chasing. First, he gives the founder his model; second, the moulder in the foundry makes a mould over it; third, he casts that colored wax in the mould the thickness the bronze afterward should be; fourth, the sculptor retouches this wax cast, then gives it to the moulder, who makes a mould over it; fifth, the moulder heats the mould thoroughly for about two days, till the wax is entirely melted out. Then he pours bronze into the space which once contained the wax, removes the mould, and the cast is finished, barring some cleaning. The result is by far superior to the process of sand casting."

"Is there any other way to perpetuate a model?"

"Yes; in terra cotta In this case you give the model to a moulder in some terra cotta works; he makes a piece mould over it—that is, a mould which is made of a number of pieces held together in a case of plaster. After finishing this mould he gives it to the 'presser,' who presses terra cotta clay into it; lets it dry for a couple of hours, until the mould absorbs some of the water in the clay, then removes the mould —that is, one piece after another. This done, the sculptor retouches the clay model and sends it to the drying room; here it dries slowly, till not a particle of water is left in the clay. Then it is put in a kiln for 10 or 12 days, and when it comes out is as hard as stone."

Granite is also used for the purpose of reproducing models, both busts and ideal figures. The process of reproducing them in granite being the same as used in marble, only the finer qualities of granite being used.

Some New Subscriptions and Renewals.

We publish below a few letters received with new subscriptions and renewals. Some of them are old friends who have been with us from the start. Others are new ones who subscribe because the paper helps them in their business. If it helps them, why will it not help you? Try it one year; it will cost you $1.00, and if you do not like it cross it off your list at the end of the year and charge it to experience.

Enclosed please find $1.00 for subscription for GRANITE for one year.—John J. Kitteridge, Worcester, Mass.

Enclosed you will find check for $1.50, for which please send me "Imperial Design Book" and GRANITE for one year beginning July, 1900.—T. Sullivan, Marlboro, Mass.

I received your card today. It is an oversight that I have not attended to this before. Hoping everything is all O. K.—J. M. Brewer, Adams, N. Y.

Your card of 10th to hand. Enclosed find express money order for $1.00, payment for subscription for GRANITE one year.—W. W. Babcock, Hornellsville, N. Y.

Enclosed find check for one dollar, for renewal of my subscription to your valuable paper, GRANITE. Kindly change address as indicated at top of this letter-head and much oblige.—Osbert J. Copeland, New York City.

I enclose $1.00 for my subscription to your valuable paper. Business is just picking up with us, owing to the leather tanning business having gone to the dogs, and the trust which has taken control—the population here being mostly poor people. I enjoy your paper very much.—John J. Hern, Woburn, Mass.

As a premium for an original monument design, writer is receiving another publication in the interests of the trade, and intended allowing yours to drop at expiration of subscription. It having continued to come, notwithstanding my failure to remit the usual fee, is such a mark of confidence, that I take pleasure in enclosing draft for amount to pay for current year, and no doubt will look expectantly for its regular visits. Its appearance is up to date, and exhaustive in detail. If it continues to improve in the future, in the same ratio as in the past, no firm can afford to be without it.—A. E. Weeks, Lockport, N. Y.

The year of 1900 has been without exception the best year we have ever had. We have booked upwards of five hundred orders, which is certainly good for the very small town we are located in, which proves that by fair dealing and furnishing the very best of work will build up a business. We hope to increase our business next year, for we certainly will be in the best point in Michigan, and will not be barred with the disadvantage of poor shippinig facilities.

We hope you will give us a call the first time you are in our part of the state.—A. Black & Son.

We thank you for your kind invitation, and will accept, hoping that in the near future we may be able to call.—ED.

The firm of A. Black & Son, who have been located for more than a quarter of a century at Hastings, Mich., will move their plant to No. 4 Pearl street, Grand Rapids, Mich., Dec. 1st, where they are fitting up one of the best plants in the state. They will have a show room 25 x 100 feet, also a work room the same size, located in the heart of the business portion of the city. We understand they expect to put in a number of pneumatic tools and other necessary machinery at once.

This firm has built up a very large business, and are to make the change to secure better shipping facilities, Grand Rapids being the best railroad point in the state, and very centrally located for their field.

Messrs. A. Black & Son would like to correspond with air compressor and pneumatic tool manufacturers.

also with any one having any good random monuments or tablets on hand in Barre, Quincy, Westerly, or Milford worth $150.00 and less ; please send tracings with prices to them at Hastings, Mich.

❀

Monthly Trade Record.

This department is compiled and edited by the United Mercantile Agency. Subscribers, in accordance with the terms of their contracts, are entitled to receive further information relative to the parties hereafter mentioned, upon application to the main office. As the names of many business men who are good will appear herein, subscribers can readily see the importance of making inquiries if interested, previous to taking any action.

CONNECTICUT.
Bridgeport, *M—Smith, Daniel, 93 $1,700.

FLORIDA.
Ocala, *M—Leavengood & McMullen, 89.

INDIANA.
Monticello, *M—Hoffman, W. H., 86.
Sullivan, *M—Cummins & Drake succeed Bailey & Hawkins.
Terre Haute, *M—Hollis & Clancy succeed James Clancy.

IOWA.
Des Moines, *M—Messett & Lynn 64. Harry Messett, 58.
Des Moines, *M—New England Marble & Granite Co., succeed Western Granite & Marble Co.

KENTUCKY.
Louisville, *M—Myers & Kehoe, 50.

MAINE.
Dixfield, *M—Churchill & Taylor succeed George Holt & Son.
North Jay, *M—Bryant & Saunders, 86.

MASSACHUSETTS.
Taunton, *M—Reagan, J. F., sold R. E. $1,900.

MICHIGAN.
Hastings, *M—Black, A. & Sons, 88 to Grand Rapids.
Marine City, *M—Thatcher, Emerson, 106.
Port Huron, *M—Truesdell, Philo, 78.

MISSISSIPPI.
Jackson, *M—Carson, T. B., 106.

MISSOURI.
St. Louis, *M—Schrader & Conradi, 64.

MONTANA.
Billings, *M—Hazelton, H., 80.
Billings, *M—Mooney Bros., 76.
Butte, *M—Ketchin, R. A., 14 $1,908.
Butte, *M—Tuite, J. E., 86.

NEBRASKA.
Omaha, *M—Baumeister, Anton, 20 $415.
Omaha, *M—Bloom, J. F. & Co., certificate of partnership.

NEW HAMPSHIRE.
Concord, GZ—Gannon, M. G. & Son, 14 $110.

NEW YORK.
Syracuse, *M—Deland & Soule succeed Francis & Co.

OHIO.
Bluffton, *M—Lehman, John, 106.
Canal Dover, *M—Tuscarawas Valley Monument Co., 76.
Forest, *M—Steinman, J. F., 76.
Toledo, *M—Eckhardt Monumental Co., 93 $4,000 and 99 $3,000.

PENNSYLVANIA.
Allegheny, *M—Beggs, Alex & Son Co., William D. Beggs, 78.

RHODE ISLAND.
Niantic, *M—Hutchins, George T., 30.

VERMONT.
Barre, GZ—Dundas, A., 106.

WISCONSIN.
Manitowoc, *M—Kittenhofen, M., warranty deed $2.500.

❀

Causes of Death of Stonecutters in the Past five Years as Compiled by The Stonecutters Journal.

1—militis.
1—pluritis.
65—consumption.
8—drowned.
11—typhoid fever.
1—exposure.
1—mental derangement.
2—nephritis.
2—apoplexy.
1—cdriahestis liver.
15—heart disease.
28—phthisis pulmonalis.
15—tuberculosis
3—pulminium.
2—tutereoclus.
8—killed by train.
1—phthisis fever.
28—pneumonia.
16—pulmonary tuberculosis.
6—lung trouble.
1—astes sarcoma.
1—auleo sarcoma.
3—Bright's disease.
1—chr. phthisis.
3—dropsy.
1—asthma.
4—accidental fall.
3—cancer.
2—tubercular disease.
1—strangulation of bowels.
1—asthmatic attacks.
1—carceuma of stomach.
1—surgical pneumonia.
1—abscess of liver.

1—locomoter ataxia.
1—inflammation of bowels.
1—shot (suicide).
1—killed in mine.
2—ulceration of bowels.
1—killed by horse.
5—hemorrhage.
1—chills and fever.
1—acute phthisis.
2—dysentery.
1—cancer of stomach.
1—paralysis.
1—intestinal catarrh.
1—chronic bronchitis.
1—chronic diarrhea.
1—catarrhal fever.
1—diabetes.
1—intestinal dyspepsia.
1—the grippe.
1—sun stroke.
1—overcome with heat.
1—congestion of brain.
1—old age.
1—angina pectoris.
1—sytic embolism.
2—pleurisy.
1—overdose morphine.

1—appendicitis.
1—chronic gastritis.
2—fractured skull.
1—cancer of tongue.
1—tibriod phthisis.
2—aoatis opetic.
1—chronic myocarditis.
1—typhoid-malaria.
1—yellow jaundice.
1—epilepsy.
1—throat trouble.
1—burned.
1—cushois of lungs.
1—mitral stenosis.
19—phthisis.
1—frozen to death.
1—Cerebral hemorrhage.
1—hypertrophy of heart.
1—tubercular meningitis.
1—pyo-thorax.
5—bronchitis.
1—carcamone of liver.
80—not given.
1—suicide.
1—shot by soldier.
Total, 401.

40　·GRANITE·

QUINCY AND ALL OTHER NEW ENGLAND GRANITES.

McGILLVRAY & JONES, QUINCY, MASS.

Estimates furnished on Vaults, Tombs, and all classes of Monumental Work.

EQUIPPED FOR HANDLING LARGE WORK.

WHY DON'T YOU

have A. ANDERSON & SONS quote you prices on that work you are about to place? They have all the latest machinery for turning out first-class work, and can guarantee you A1 stock and workmanship. Give them a trial.

PNEUMATIC TOOLS. DIES, CAPS AND BASES SQUARED AND POLISHED.

A. ANDERSON & SONS, - BARRE, VT.

ROBINS BROTHERS,

Manufacturers of

Barre Granite Monuments,
BARRE, VT.

Pneumatic Tools.

A. MALNATI,
QUINCY, MASS.

OWNERS OF THE QUARRIES AT EAST LYME, CONN., PRODUCING THE CELEBRATED

Golden Pink Granite

Rough Stock Furnished to the Trade at the Lowest Prices.
Send for Sample.
Address all communications to Quincy, Mass.

ARTISTIC MONUMENTS AND STATUARY,

Portrait Busts and Ideal Figures
From My Own Models.

WESTERLY AND QUINCY GRANITE.

Power furnished by my own steam plant recently erected for operating pneumatic tools, derrick, etc.

IMLAH & CO., -:- BARRE, VT.

———DEALERS IN———

BARRE GRANITE MONUMENTS,
VAULTS AND ARTISTIC MEMORIALS.

First-Class Work Guaranteed and prices as low as can be quoted for honest work. Carved Work, Squaring and Polishing for the trade a Specialty.

WANTED, FOR SALE, ETC.

Advertisements inserted in this column, 15 cents a line each insertion; six words to a line. No advertisement to cost less than 50 cents.

Draughtsman wants situation. Has air brush.　E. H. GIBSON, 45 Milk St., Boston.

FOR SALE.

MAINE GRANITE QUARRIES ON EASY TERMS.

Located within 500 yards from Maine Central Ry. and 1000 yards from tide water; developed and supplied with necessary equipment for a large out-put, also cutting sheds and polishing mill for finished stock. Well established reputation for quality. A rare opportunity for a practical granite man. Address "INVESTMENT," care GRANITE.

WANTED.

Position by man experienced in all branches of both wholesale and retail granite work — expert draughtsman; detail and air brush, and fine salesman on high class trade — now holding position as manager of wholesale manufacturing plant. Address A. B. C., care of this paper.

Wanted by a retail firm, a first-class designer, most be familiar with Mausoleum work, use the air brush, and capable of making good wash sketches.
Address S. B. & Co., care "GRANITE."

Partner Wanted; or For Sale. Steam Granite Works, sales amounted to over $20,000 in past year, could be doubled. Situated in town of 16,000. Sickness reason for selling.
Address Charles Poole, Waverly, N. Y.

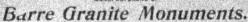

60 Designs for $4.00 including a Subscription to Granite for One Year.

We shall publish 500 Sets, containing Sixty different designs of Monuments. They will be reprints of those which we have already issued in this publication, and will be printed upon heavy paper without reading matter. Sizes and prices will be given upon a separate sheet. Prices of Monuments will run from $200 upwards.

December, 1900   Vol. X. No. 12

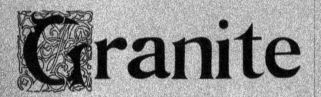

Granite

A. M. HUNT & CO.

PUBLISHERS

131 Devonshire Street

BOSTON, MASS., U.S.A.

Subscription Price, $1.00 Year

ADVERTISERS' DIRECTORY.

2

TROY GRANITE CO.,

Worcester, Mass.

Monuments, Mausoleums and Tombs.

Write us for Prices in Rough Stock or Finished Work. We make a Specialty of Troy White.

QUARRIES ARE AT TROY, N. H.

NEW RED BEACH GRANITE

Is a Fine Grained <u>DARK RED GRANITE.</u> The Quarries produce perfect stone of any size. Over <u>125,000</u> feet have been taken from the Quarries the past year.

IT IS THE BEST RED GRANITE ON THE MARKET FOR MONUMENTAL STONE.

<u>LOW PRICES</u> quoted on any kind of Monumental, Building, or Machine Work Also, Rough Stock. We have one of the <u>Best Water Powers</u> in the country, and an <u>Up-to-date Mill.</u> <u>WRITE US.</u>

MAINE RED GRANITE CO.,

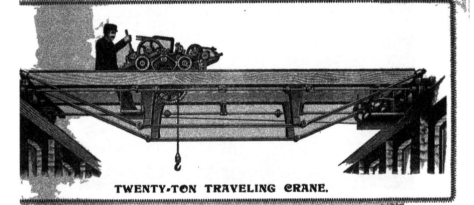

INTERIOR VIEW OF

Novelli & Corti Works,

BOX 57. —————————BARRE, VERMONT.

BELT AND STEAM POWER HOISTERS

Traveling Cranes operated by electricity, steam or manila rope

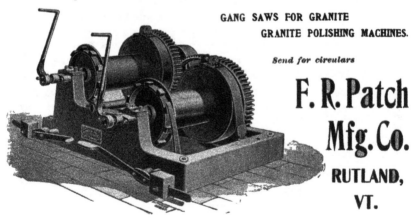

GANG SAWS FOR GRANITE

GRANITE POLISHING MACHINES.

Send for circulars

F. R. Patch
Mfg. Co.
RUTLAND,
VT.

GRANITE

ENTERED AT THE BOSTON POST OFFICE AS SECOND-CLASS MAIL MATTER.

Vol. X. BOSTON, MASS., DECEMBER 1, 1900. No. 12

A. M. HUNT, EDITOR.

Published Monthly in the interests of the Producer.
Manufacturer, and Retailer of Granite as used
for Monumental or Building Purposes.

Terms of Subscription

To ANY PART OF THE UNITED STATES OR CANADA:

One copy, one year   -   -   -   - $1.00, in advance.
One copy, six months   -   -   -   75 cents, in advance.

ADVERTISING RATES FURNISHED UPON APPLICATION.

A. M. HUNT & CO., Publishers,

131 DEVONSHIRE STREET, - - BOSTON, MASS.

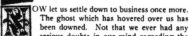

E take the following from the Stone Trade Journal: — "It is somewhat surprising that so little use is made of what are known as the waste materials of our quarries. These are generally dumped down in unsightly heaps, a source of expense to the quarry-owner and an eyesore in the landscape. Experience, however, has shown that much of this refuse can be profitably used in the manufacture of artificial stone, and quarry-owners would do well to give more consideration to this branch of the stone trades than they have done in the past. For years the "granites" of Leicestershire, Westmoreland, and other counties have been largely utilised for making artificial paving, and more recently one of the York stone firms near Halifax has commenced the manufacture of artificial flags from cement and stone scraps with, we believe, profitable results. And now we learn that Mr. Evan Reese has succeeded in producing an excellent paving material by utilising refuse of slate quarries. There can be no doubt that artificial paving for footways and other purposes has certain advantages over natural stone. The surface presents a better appearance than the ordinary qualities of natural stone, and as the blocks are of regular sizes and properly squared, they require less labor in laying. A further advantage is that the joints are true throughout the thickness of the material, and are consequently better adapted for making a vermin-proof floor. Some artificial paving, however, wears to a smooth and slippery surface, and this is one of the defects which the manufacturer must try to avoid.

"As far as our experience goes, nothing has been done with the refuse from the various granite quarries in the United States, except by the railroads in filling in a deep cut where it did not cost too much to transport it. There awaits for a man who will invent some process whereby large quantities of grout can be used, an independent fortune and the thanks of a long-suffering public in the quarrying districts."

OW let us settle down to business once more. The ghost which has hovered over us has been downed. Not that we ever had any serious doubts in our mind regarding the outcome of the presidential election, yet the matter was before us and it had not been settled, and therefore there remained a doubt which we are pleased to say has been set at rest forever. We can say that from our personal standpoint that we did not help to bring about the result, for we were ten miles back in the woods and did not hear of it until one week after the election, and what may seem stranger still, thought of it only in a general way. Whether or not this was on account of our confidence in our fellow citizens, or possibly the influence of the wilderness with its snow-covered mountains and solitude was upon us and lulled us into forgetfulness of the past and extreme indifference of the future. It was only upon our return to civilization that we were made acquainted with the fact that there had been an election, and we again took up the burden of life with its many cares with a feeling that we had lost something, but were sincerely glad of it. We do not believe that presidential elections have the disturbing influence upon business that they have had in the past. During a business trip which extended over a period of six weeks just previous to election, it was seldom that the prospective election was mentioned, and then only in a general way. We believe the modern way of doing away with torch light processions, and to a large extent the mud-slinging of the past has some bearing upon this; anyway there certainly has been a change for the better for which we should be duly grateful.

WE were asked a short time since if we believed in a future of the granite industry and we answered the question Yankee-like by asking another, Do you? We have recently visited all the granite manufacturing centres and we have seen on every side evidences of prosperity in the way of new cutting plants just erected, in course of erection, or contemplated, all with modern equipments. The quarries are adding from time to time heavier derricks, engines and other machinery to keep pace with the growing demand for large work. It is not now an uncommon thing for a quarry to have orders for two or three shafts, varying in size from twenty-five to forty feet in length. During a visit to one of the large quarries we noted three shafts, one twenty feet long on the cars ready for shipment, one thirty feet long laying in the quarry near the bed from which it had been taken, and one forty feet long about half quarried; also the base, about twenty-five feet square. In fact the quarrymen of today take orders for any size to the limit of transportation. It is not an uncommon thing for a manufacturer to report orders for two or three mausoleums on hand, from that up to fourteen, which is the extreme limit reached by any one firm. Do we believe in the future of the American granite industry? We believe in it as thoroughly as anything that we are certain of, and we further believe that it has but just commenced. New machinery will be invented in the future for the quarrying and cutting of granite, made necessary by the increasing demand. There is a field yet to be entered, namely, the furnishing of granite veneers for building-fronts. This is an industry which is carried extensively in Scotland, but has not been touched on this side of the water as yet. Every source from which we gather information regarding future contracts show many large ones to be placed. From our own standpoint we do not see a cloud in the horizon of the business world, but this does not mean if you sit still by the wayside that the plums will drop into your lap. No; it will be a case of hustle in the future as in the past, and he who hustles will have results to show for it.

More About the Smith Granite Co. vs. Joseph Newhall Co. Case.

The litigation between the Smith Granite Co. and the Joseph Newall Co. refuses to down. In spite of the opinion of the Supreme Court, handed down recently, and which was favorable to the respondents, the case came up again before the full bench in Appellate Division on the complainant's motion to amend the bill. This amendment is of an important nature. It and at the time of the execution

of the contract of October 12, 1898, Orlando R. Smith was at the Presbyterian Hospital, Philadelphia, suffering greatly, and had been great physical and mental weakness, and that he was therefore incapacitated and incompetent to transact business.

It is claimed that while he was in this condition he was approached by representatives of the Newall interests and persuaded to sign an agreement to purchase from Joseph Newall & Co. a quarry for a very much larger sum than it was actually worth. It is set forth that the paper was then presented to Julia E. Smith, and that she, seeing her brother's signature and relying upon her brother's business judgment, affixed her name to the document.

At first objection was made on the part of counsel for the respondents to the entering of this motion. They asserted that the case came up for a final decree and that if any motion like this was to have been brought they should have had notice of it. They finally agreed, however, to allow the motion to be presented to the court without further delay.

After the motion had been read one of the counsel for the respondents asserted that all this had been covered in the testimony. He said that if the complainants had thought that Mr. Smith was incapable of transacting business they would not have waited until it was time for the final decree to be entered before presenting such a claim. All the circumstances had been gone into in the testimony. He affirmed, too, that the last prayer of the motion for amendment was in entire disregard of the opinion of the court.

The counsel for the complainant, affirmed that these facts were not known when the bill was filed. He said it was only a question of whether they would be allowed to present an amendment to the bill or whether they would be compelled to file an entirely new bill. He intimated that if the amendments were not accepted, then an entirely new bill would be filed. The complainants had always seemed to be in a hurry prior to this time, and he thought it would facilitate matters to allow the respondents to simply amend their bill without delaying to prepare a new bill entirely.

The counsel for the respondents said we are in a hurry and had reason to be. He said that they had done a good business, but that for two years they had been robbed, not only of their property, but of their money. He thought that it was time that they had relief, the court having decided that the contract was valid. He thought it strange that during all the time the case had been in litigation the complainants had not discovered the facts alleged in the proposed amendment. He said that Mr. Smith had made a will subsequent to the time that the contract was made, and that the will had been admitted to probate, and no quesion of unsound mind had been raised in connection with that instrument. It was on the statement of the doctor in charge of Mr. Smith at the hospital, to the effect that Mr. Smith was fully capable of attending to business, that he had been approached on this matter.

The counsel for the complainant objected to the statement that the respondents had been robbed. He said that the complainants offered to retransfer the property to the Newalls, but that the latter were anxious to hold everything under the guise of having a lien on a certain issue of bond, and that it was their own fault if they had lost money.

The amendment was taken under consideration by

the court. One of the counsel for the respondents then started upon the presentation of the final decree perpared in the case. He reached a point where, in the opinion of the court, he had provided for something contrary to the opinion of the court, in relation to the issuance of the bonds and the possession of a lien upon them, when he was interrupted. When informed that the proposed decree was in this point contrary to the opinion handed down, he said that counsel for the respondents would like to have a reargument of this phase of the case, and accordingly counsel was given until October 27 to file briefs.

The Largest Granite Turning Lathe ever Constructed.

The product of Philadelphia's workshops and skilled labor has for many years been going out into the world to revolutionize various fields of labor and enterprise, but there are few machines sent out from any locality which will have such a wonderful influence in some departments of building and architecture as the mammoth lathe built by the Philadelphia Roll and Machine Company for the Bodwell Granite Company, of Vinalhaven, Me. To a certain extent it was the plans for a great New York church, the Cathedral of St. John the Divine, that led to the construction of this wonderful lathe.

The cathedral will have many columns of granite These columns will be of various dimensions, but the largest of them will be 54 feet long and 6 feet in diameter. In all, there will be 32 of these mammoth columns, and each one of them will weigh about 160 tons. There will also be columns of smaller dimensions, and all are to be made by this lathe that has been manufactured in Philadelphia.

The lathe is the idea of two Boston men, H. A. Spiller and E. R. Cheney, who have patented it. It was begun nearly a year ago, and it was delivered in the quarries in Maine in May last, but it was not until August that it was placed in operation. Since it has been installed it has been doing wonderful work, and has commanded much attention.

The blocks of granite from which the largest columns are turned are like the one portrayed in the illustration. This one weighs 310 tons. It is 67 feet long, 8 1-2 feet high and 7 feet wide.

The lathe itself is 86 feet long. It weighs 135 tons and swings 6 1-2 feet by 60 feet. It is fitted with eight tools or cutters, and as each cutter will reduce the column three inches, the entire eight reduce it 24 inches in passing over its length. The knife or tool used in cutting is a circular disk of steel 7-8 inch in thickness and 10 inches in diameter. It has a V-shaped cutting edge, and when in operation is set at an angle to the axis of the stone being dressed. It is the huge stone that revolves, and as it does so it imparts a rotary motion to the cutting disks, and they are pulled into the stone by means of the feed screw. The nature of the cut made by the tools is in the form of splintering, as stated, about three inches deep. The lathe is operated by a 50-horse power engine. When running at cutting speed it makes 1 3-4 revolutions per minute, and at polishing speed the revolutions per minute number three. The adjustment of the machine is so perfect that after the belt has been cast off the lathe will run freely for about a quarter of a minute.

At a meeting of the creditors of A. Dundas, it was brought out that they had no visible assets, no books. Three men and the principal have worked about two years. Liabilities, $2.000; assets, $1,000; 350 exempt chattel mortgages, $230; book accounts $350, all disputed; machinery and tools over estimated, $150.

The Leland & Hall Company have leased the shed formerly occupied by Barclay Bros. before their acquiring the plant formerly owned by Mackie, Hussey & Co. The cutting sheds which they have leased are two of the largest circular sheds in Barre and the derricks are fully capable of handling sixty tons. The polishing mill attached to the plant is fully equipped and places the Leland & Hall Company in a position to handle any reasonable sized contracts. James Sector, formerly of the firm of James Sector & Company, who will have charge of the plant, is one of the oldest manufacturers in Barre, and fully capable in every way, having thorough knowledge of the business from experience, and aside from this a reputation for doing the best quality of work.

The condition of the granite business in Barre and vicinity is not quite as good as the manufacturers and men would like to see it, but nevertheless it is much better than anybody would have predicted a few months ago that it could possibly be at this time. More than that, it seems to be improving a little and the prospects for the winter are of the best.

In years of national elections preceding this year there has always been a stagnation of business beginning anywhere from two months to four months preceding election, and lasting for from one month to six months afterward. The dull spell came as usual this year, but it did not begin until within two weeks of election and already it appears to be giving way to improved business conditions in the near future.

During the past summer there has been an unusual number of new sheds built and enlargements made, while there has not been a year in seven or eight during which there has been so much money invested in Barre and vicinity in new and improved machinery as for the year now just drawing to a close. There is not one first-class granite manufacturing establishment in Barre that has not materially improved its equipment during the past twelve months. There is more call for Barre granite than ever before in history, and the Barre granite men are prepared to take all the advantage possible of their expanding market.

Fowlie Brothers plant on the Batchelder meadow was damaged to an extent of fully $4,000 by fire on the night of November 12. Some repairs were being made in the engine house and a lamp in use there exploded, starting a fire that would have destroyed the entire plant but for the prompt work of the Barre fire department, which made a good record and confined the flames almost wholly to the engine house, which was destroyed. A new engine has been ordered by the firm and it will be put in position as soon as possible, but in the meantime the plant is practically shut down, as is also that of James Adie, who got his power from Fowlie Brothers' engine. The loss was fully covered by insurance, which was promptly adjusted.

A representative of the firm of Hyde, Grace & Co. of New York is now in town to place an order for a mausoleum to cost $20,000 and be set in Cypress Hill cemetery. The name of the family for whom the mausoleum is to be erected in Guggenheim and it will bear that name across the front. Several of the larger firms are figuring on the job and it will be let doubtless within a few days.

Another prospective job that will probably help to make business good in Barre this winter is reported by Imlah & Co., who have recently had correspondence with New York parties, who state that they have practically closed a hundred-thousand-dollar contract to be filled with Barre granite. Imlah & Co. are informed that the work will be demanded in a rush, and on that account several firms are likely to get a chance at it.

Pellegatti, Rizzi & Co. are at work on a sarcophagus monument to be surmounted by the carved figure of an angel that will be a most attractive specimen of granite work. It is to be set in Detroit, and will stand sixteen feet in height when completed. The bottom base is ten feet five by seven feet seven and one foot and four inches thick.

An almost exact duplicate to the above is being cut at Novelli & Corti's sheds. The elegant and expensive job at Novelli & Corti's described in GRANITE last month has been completed and shipped to Pittsburg, Pa., where it is now being set.

McDonald & Cutler have just started up again after being shut down for two weeks while repairs were being made on the shed and machinery.

Work on Walker & Son's new straight shed at North Barre, which was delayed for a long time to await the arrival of the lumber, is now in process of building. The outfit of the new shed will include a first-class travelling derrick from the works of the Lane Manufacturing Company at Montpelier.

Littlejohn & Milne will build a 50-foot addition to their shed in Jockey Hollow, and during its construction are trying to take care of their steadily increasing business in their old quarters. They find this impossible, but when the addition is completed they will show their customers what's what.

The firm of Rogers & Arkley dissolved partnership on November 15. Joseph L. Arkley has sold his share of the business to Chauncey Whiteford, and the firm of Rogers & Whiteford from now on will be found at the old quarters of Rogers & Arkley and always ready for business. Mr. Whiteford, the new member of the firm, is an experienced and progressive young granite man and the firm should prosper.

One of the progressive and pushing firms that is doing a good business this fall is Mortimer & Camp-

bell. They have a good run of work, and while the representative of GRANITE did not find either of the proprietors present when he made his monthly call recently, the appearance of the shed indicated that they were not preparing to shut down for lack of work.

Wells, Lamson & Co. find that in spite of all their efforts they will not complete the Ehret mausoleum job before the first of January and still keep up with their other orders.

The firm of McDonnell & Sons state that their business has been the best that they have had for a number of years and are receiving complimentary reports from a great many of the dealers to whom they have shipped work, many of them old customers of the firm who have dealt with them this summer for the first time for a number of years. They also stated that they were more than pleased with the way their orders were executed and prompt shipments.

Business in Quincy is upon the whole a little quiet this month. By that, we mean that business is quiet as far as new orders are concerned. Other than that, business remains fully as good as it has been for the past two or three months. A canvass among the manufacturers, and the query: "How is business?" brought the same general answer,—"It is not as good as I would like to see it." There have been some calls for estimates for spring work, but as yet spring orders have not begun to come in so fast that they cannot be handled easily. There is, however, a general feeling of confidence among the manufacturers and one and all look to see business better next month. They argue that it takes some few weeks after the excitement of a national election for business to become settled again, and there is not much doubt but what the volume of new business next month will come up to the expectations. Should this winter prove to be as open as a year ago there will be few idle days in the yard, and with no labor trouble staring them in the face, next year should show a good increase in the volume of trade. Meanwhile the several Quincy firms continue busy finishing up work that is to be shipped before snow flies and in no case did your correspondent find that help had been reduced. All the firms seen reported that they were temporarily busy and were still giving employment to their full complement of men, and if their wishes are carried out there will be no material reduction in help this winter. This, considering what Quincy has to contend with in the way of competition speaks well for her granite industry and the enterprising men that are engaged in it.

McDonnell & Sons have encouraging reports to make. They say that they have a large amount of work on hand, enough to keep them busy for some weeks yet, and as they are receiving some calls for estimates they do not anticipate any suspension in

Dayton, Ohio October 15, 1900.

DREW DANIELS,
        Morrisville, Vt.

Dear Sir:

        We are pleased to inform you that the cross monument which you made for us is as good a cut job as we have ever received and the stock is as good as we have ever seen. Our customer is more than pleased with this monument, especially with the carving.

        Thanking you for sending us such a good cut job, we are,

                        Yours very truly,

                        (Signed), F. C. MERKLE, SON & CO.

work. They are making some extensive repairs to their cutting sheds, so that the workmen may be protected during the cold weather and be able to work comfortably, no matter how severe the winter storms are. This is a modern idea and one to which thoughtful manufacturers are giving their attention.

W. T. Spargo says that he is as busy now as at any time since the early summer rush. They have a good lot of large work on hand which they are finishing up and shipping. As nearly all of their large work has been mentioned in previous issues of GRANITE, much of their work is of Quincy stock, although they have a few jobs that call for other than Quincy stock. They have booked a few orders for spring delivery.

Joss Bros. & Co. have one of the smoothest working travelling power derricks of any firm in the city. With this piece of simple, yet powerful machinery, the largest blocks are hoisted and transferred to any part of the sheds desired with the utmost ease. With this the old-fashioned back-breaking crank has passed into history. When seen this month and asked as to the condition of business, Mr. Joss replied that he did not have much grounds for complaint. They were fortunate enough during the summer months to secure a lot of work upon which they were now at work, and his only desire was that the weather conditions would remain favorable that he might experience no difficulty in clearing his books so as to be able to tackle spring orders in good season.

Alexander Marnock & Co. did not have much in the way of news to impart this month. Of course they are busy and had a lot of work on hand, but were not getting as much new work as desired. However, they had no fears but what another month would see business start up, and the calls for estimates already received led them to believe that next season would be one of the best ever experienced by Quincy manufacturers.

Joseph Walker of the Aberdeen Granite Works did not have as much work on hand as he would like, yet he says on the whole he has not much reason for complaint. He is busy finishing up several large jobs so as to ship them early in December. The columns and die are polished and the cap is polished and moulded. He also has several other jobs of about the same size that he is finishing up. He still has some difficulty in getting the kind of stock he desires, for he is very particular to use nothing but the best.

Fuller, Foley & Co. report that business is a little quiet with them just at present. They have considerable work on hand, however, but as a rule it is of the small and medium. Their plant is situated in an excellent position as far as transportation facilities are concerned, which in a measure accounts for the promptness with which they ship all work.

The Quincy Granite Quarry Co. has about completed a handsome job which will forever stand as a lasting monument to the quality of work that can be and is constantly being executed in Quincy. It is a base for a bronze statue of Thomas Jefferson, which is to be set up in Louisville, Ky. The status, which is feet high, stands on a die of Quincy granite.

The dimensions of this pedestal are as follows: Bottom base, 19x19x0-10; second base, 16x16x0-10; third base, 13x13x0-10; die, 10x10x5. The stock used is from the famous Hitchcock quarries, and the total weight is something like 38 tons. Each base was quarried in two pieces, each of which in the rough weighed nineteen tons. The land upon which the Hitchcock quarry is located was formerly owned by President John Adams, the predecessor of Jefferson.

McGillvary & Jones are busy finishing up several large jobs, of which previous mention has been made in GRANITE, and are ready to receive and have the facilities for handling any job, no matter how large or how small, with dispatch. A trial order will convince the customer that this is no fairy tale.

The Merrymount Granite Co. had nothing new to report this month other than that they were holding their own and were quite busy, especially at their quarry, where they were more than rushed.

Granite shipments for the month of October were somewhat larger than during the previous month. This was probably due to the fact that manufacturers are hurrying to get off their orders before snow flies. The largest increase was from West Quincy, the amount being 2,609,980 pounds. The Quarry Railroad came next with an increase of 2,549,780 pounds, and Quincy Adams with 284,280 pounds. The total for the month was 20,294,490 pounds, divided as follows: West Quincy, 8,134,040 pounds; Quincy Railroad, 6,464,380 pounds; Quincy Adams, 5,696,070 pounds.

Herbert W. Beattie, the sculptor, has just completed several portrait, bas-relief models and he is at work upon several ornamental designs which will be cast in bronze. He has recently issued a very fine set of photographs of carving, large in size and suitable to carve from, or to be used as suggestions to show customers. They are original corner ornaments, mouldings, panels, etc.

James Craig is building some new sheds on Water street, on the site formerly occupied by McDonnell & Cook. They are of the more modern design and can be heated in winter.

McIntosh & Co. are fully as busy as any of the firms in the city. Their plant is now equipped with every facility for getting out first-class work, and no matter how large or how small, every detail is considered and a first-class job necessarily follows. They have quite a lot of work on hand, some of which is above the ordinary size. Like other Quincy firms at present, however, the majority of their work is of medium size.

A Business Monument.

At George S. Gibson's Marble Works, Clinton, Mass., is in process of completion something out of the ordinary run in cemetery work. It is a combination of monumental work and advertising, for it will show when done not only the name of the owner of the lot in the cemetery where it is to be placed, but will give carved designs of the various branches of mercantile life in which he figures during his life.

George A. Flagg of Boylston is the man for whom the work is being done. He drew the designs himself and everything is being done under his immediate supervision. He will have, when the work is done and set up, a monument of marble and four markers of the same stone. The monument will be five feet and six inches high, which is just his own height.

The four markers are 14 inches square and 18 inches high. The tops are beveled down and on the sloping face of one of them is a house, cut in the marble. This is illustrative of the real estate business which Mr. Flagg does. Another has a cow, which typifies the live stock business which he is engaged in.

The third of the markers has a representation of a pile of wood cut in the stone, and this speaks for itself in the illustration of another line of business which Mr. Flagg carries on. The fourth marker has a barrel, and this reminds the observer of the cider mills, which are in Boylston near the line of the Worcester & Clinton street railway, and which are an important branch of Mr. Flagg's property.

Mr. Flagg explains his action in having these symbolic stones made for him by saying there are a lot of people bearing his name, and when he is dead there will be nothing in the ordinary epitaph or inscription to tell which one of them he was when he was alive. But with the emblematic stones and the inscription on the monument to the effect that the markers illustrate his life work and business, there will be no difficulty on the part of succeeding generations when discriminating between him and the others of the family.

The specifications for the work were drawn up by Mr. Flagg, and he was particular to see he got just what he called for.

An Interesting Decision to All Granite Manufacturers.

An important decision was rendered in the superior court at Dedham November 1, which is of interest to all the granite manufacturers. It was in the case of Fred Martel of Quincy vs. the Quincy Granite Manufacturers' Association, the damages being placed at $10,000. The plaintiff alleged that said association was an unlawful conspiracy, as it assessed its members and imposed a fine upon those who purchased granite of manufacturers not members of the association.

During the trial of the case, which lasted several days, the plaintiff alleged that before the organization of the association he had a large and lucrative business, but because of the requirements of the association his business had suffered, and he claimed damages to the extent of $10,000.

The judge in his review of the case decides the association is a lawful association, and that it had a right to assess its own members. It was proper co-operation not coercion. He therefore found for the association. The case will be taken to the supreme court.

The Progress of Granite Quarrying in Aberdeenshire.

As fifty years ago the work of granite quarrying in the county of Aberdeen was carried on by very primitive methods. Although the output was very limited, it was equal to the requirements of the time, as the days of granite monuments, polished fronts for large buildings, and other artistic work in granite had not dawned, kerbing and setts being then the almost exclusive product for export trade. At that period the principal grey granite quarries included Rubislaw, Persley, and the Dancing Cairns, while red granites were obtainable in the vicinity of Blackburn and Peterhead, the former place being about eight miles from the city, and the latter nearly forty. Owing to the absence of suitable machinery it was almost impossible to operate a quarry unless it was situated on rising ground where there were good facilities for the disposal of quarry waste, and where a cart road could be made right into the quarry. It may be mentioned, however, that in the case of the Rubislaw quarries they managed to sink to a considerable depth by means of a winding road which lessened the gradient, and thus enabled the carts to reach the bottom of the quarries. It was only in the larger quarries that horses were employed to remove the rubbish, while barrows were made to do duty in the smaller workings, or what might be termed the guerilla system of quarrying.

At the time of which we are writing the work of the quarryman was hard compared with what it is now, and the results less satisfactory. All the rock drilling for blasts had to be done by the hand, while the stones were cut into the required dimensions by oblong holes made with heavy picks, into which were inserted huge wedges, which were driven until the stone was broken by equally heavy and clumsy-looking hammers; but a large amount of rock drilling is now done by steam, and neat little hand drills have superseded the unseemly-looking "picks," which have now been relegated to the limbo of oblivion. Had there been no improvement on the old and obsolete method of quarrying, the quarries in Aberdeenshire would have been practically closed many years ago as a result of the accumulation of rubbish and the lack of appliances for sinking operations. But the advent of the steam crane some forty years ago, which was followed by the introduction of cableways about ten years later, has revolutionised the whole system, and marked an era in the history of the quarrying industry. Previous to this, horizontal quarrying was the only method employed, but now this system has almost entirely disappeared with all its antiquated forms of operation, and perpendicular quarrying is recognised as the most suitable method. Many new quarries have been opened since the inauguration of the present system, and in many cases old workings which it would have been impossible to operate before have been deepened so as to render them both workable and remunerative. The introduction of those steam appliances made it possible to raise stones from almost any depth, and to build up the rubbish heaps to a height which could never have been done with the old hand crane, now looked upon by many of the present generation as one of the curiosities of a bygone age.

Before the introduction of steam power the quarries presented a rather dull appearance, there being in many cases only a few men employed here and there in small openings. What a contrast to the scenes of activity which are to be witnessed now at the quarries, where steam cranes are moving about the gigantic blocks with the greatest ease and rapidity, and cableways are raising the stones from the bottom of quarries

THOMAS ROCHE
BORN JULY 5, 1875 — DIED MAY 7, 1891
ALICE ROCHE
BORN APRIL 14, 1875 — DIED FEB. 16, 1897

THOMAS ROCHE

"GRANITE," DECEMBER, 1900.

"GRANITE," DECEMBER, 1900.

BOTTOM BASE . . . R — E ½ x C — C Y x C — A
SECOND BASE . . . A — C Y x C — P x Y — Z ½
DIE TOP . . . . . A — C Y x C — A
BOTTOM . . . . . R — R ½ x C — I ½ x A — N

"GRANITE," DECEMBER, 1900.

BASE . . . P — C x C — 1¼ x C — F
DIE. . . . R — P½ x V — C V½ x A — V

"GRANITE," DECEMBER, 1900.

Sizes and Price will be given in January issue.

300 feet deep, after which they are placed on bogies, run out on rails, and deposited in their respective places. Steam cranes also move about on rails performing gracefully their various functions, while the rapid action of the steam drill is to be seen at work on the rock, and the water being pumped from a depth of about 400 feet by steam power. All this is done with the utmost regularity which makes the scene at once interesting and instructive.

Blasting operations were only occasionally brought into requisition in the olden times, and that on a very small scale, too. Seldom did the drill holes exceed 7 feet deep for blasting purposes, while 4 or 5 feet deep would have been about the general rule. A considerable quantity of the rock was dislodged by placing iron wedges into the joints and driving them home until stone after stone was dislodged from its position. This was indeed a very slow and equally laborious process of displacing the rock, which would not be tolerated at the present day, unless any special occasion demanded the careful preservation of a large and valuable block from the danger of being fractured by powder. Like all the other departments of the granite quarrying industry, the methods of dislodging the rock have greatly improved. Holes are now bored to a depth of 20 feet, and when suitable opportunities present themselves, two, three, or four of these holes may be drilled into the rock in line with each other to any depth that might be considered necessary. Then after being charged the whole is exploded simultaneously by means of electricity, the effect being in many cases the dislodgment of huge masses of valuable rock. No other granite quarries in the United Kingdom, and perhaps not in the whole world, are so well equipped with the most advanced appliances for expeditiously carrying on the work as those situated in Aberdeenshire. The writer, who has a practical knowledge of the different departments of quarry work, has visited Scotland, England, and Ireland, as well as some of the granite quarries in Russia and the United States of America, but has never seen quarries so scientifically operated as those in Aberdeen. It must be borne in mind, however, that great progress is being made with the introduction of the most modern appliances in some of the English granite quarries, and the time may not be far distant when they will rival the Scotch in point of efficient equipment.

The progress of the granite quarrying industry in Aberdeenshire may be best illustrated by the number of new quarries that have been opened during the last five years, or rather the reopening of old workings that had been formerly tried but found unremunerative. During the year 1896 seven new granite quarries were opened in different parts of the country, four in 1897, two in '98, one in '99, and three since the advent of the present year, making a total of seventeen within that short period. Three of these quarries have, however, been closed since then because of their unremunerativeness, but some of the others have been largely developed since they were opened, and now add considerably to the total tonnage produced. All these quarries were of grey granite, with the exception of two, which are of a rich red color, and are chiefly worked for monumental purposes. One of the causes of this remarkable progress in the granite quarrying industry is the abnormal demand that has sprung up in recent years for granite setts. Hitherto the quantity called for was small compared with what is now re-

quired both for local and export trade. The quantity of granite paving blocks exported from the Aberdeen harbors for the years 1892-'93 was 17,436 tons, while in 1898-'99 the quantity had risen to 38,984 tons, which shows that during the last six years the exportation of granite setts has been more than doubled. A great improvement has taken place in the manufacture of granite setts within the last decade ; they are no longer the large, rough, and irregular sized stones that were formerly used, and which made a rough carriageway with the maximum of noise, but they are now neatly cut into small blocks, which minimises the noise, while at the same time they are regularly sized and well dressed on the face, making a fine, smooth carriageway compared with the streets that were formed of the antiquated paving setts. No doubt the exceptional demand for granite setts is due in some measure to the improvement that has taken place in the article produced. There is another feature in connection with the quarrying industry which has contributed in no small degree to its successful progress. Hitherto granite monuments formed a very small portion of the orders, while embellished facades for the chief buildings in our large cities and other ornate work in granite were practically unknown ; but now nearly one-half of the quarries in Aberdeenshire are chiefly worked for the production of granite for polishing purposes. As showing the expansion that has taken place in this branch of the granite trade, it may be mentioned that the quantity of fine dressed and polished granite exported in 1893 was only 5,915 tons, while last year the tonnage was 9,590, an increase of about 80 per cent for the last six years. This article would be incomplete were no reference made to the increase that has taken place in the number of men employed at the granite industry in Aberdeenshire. In the early history of the trade the aggregate number of hands employed at the different branches would probably not have exceeded 800, but now it is estimated that there are between 8,000 and 9,000, while the number of those dependent on the trade would not fall far short of 40,-000. Enough has been said to show that the granite trade forms one of the most important industries in the East of Scotland, and its rapid progress is due largely to the enterprise and inventive genius of those connected with it.—Stone Trades' Journal.

St. Cloud, (Minn.) Strike.

The Arnold Granite Company has two small strikes on its hands, and as a result some sixty men, divided about equally between cutters and quarrymen, are out. Some time ago the union permitted a cutter, who was not considered skilled, according to the schedule of the union, to work for the Arnold Company at $2.50 per day, whereas, the full wages paid skilled cutters is $3 for eight hours' work. Some few days ago, it is claimed, the union held a meeting and decided that the wages to this man must be $3 per day from the start, but as the Arnold people had not been notified that full-cutters' wages was to be paid, they stoutly refused to pay the extra 50 cents for the time worked, with the result that the men went out. The local company is willing to pay $3 to this man from now on, but stand out on the back-pay proposition.

The quarrymen are out for the reason that there were two men employed at the quarry, former members of the union, but who had allowed their memberships to lapse. The men were notified to attend the meeting of the Quarrymen's Union, pay $5 and take out membership and get a receipt for back dues. They did not appear, but were given a couple of days to make good, and, having failed to come to the scratch, the union men refused to work with them further.

Granite Combine.

The Bay State Granite Company, which controlled the Darling Bros. and Shea granite quarries, has secured the Milford Pink Granite Co. properties from the proprietors, Woodbury & Leighton of Boston, who in turn take an interest in the new Bay State Company. This consolidation makes it one of the largest companies in New England.

Fully 1,000 acres of fine pink granite property is thus added to the excellent quarries already held by the purchasing company.

The whole property is to be greatly improved early next spring, work now being in progress. An electrical stone saw and a monster power derrick run by electricity, and an underground railway from the quarries to the cutting sheds, that will be greatly increased in capacity—75 feet in length and width being added.

The electric power will be furnished by a new and powerful plant being placed there, including three 300-horse power boilers, with dynamos and adequate engines, so that the entire plant of all the quarries will be lighted and the sheds and offices heated and power furnished for the railway, saw, derrick and other uses.

The officers of the Bay State Company are: George Otis Draper of Hopedale, president; Lewis Brittan of Milford, treasurer; D. W. Darling of Worcester, general manager; Albert E. Crafts of Worcester, figuring agent; George B. Gibson, superintendent.

The American Stone Company.

The story that United States Senator William A. Clark of Montana, the great mining king of the northwest, is to establish granite quarries at North Jay, Me., is followed by a report to the effect that Portland has been determined upon as the shipping port of this plant.

In October a corporation was formed in Portland. This corporation is called the American Stone Company, and Hon. George E. Bird, one of the partners of the firm, is clerk. The president is Washington Hull of New York, and the treasurer is Mr. Atwater of New York. The capital of the company is not large. Senator Clark is not named in the company, but it is authoritatively stated that he owns a large share of its stock. Mr. Hull is a member of a well known firm of architects in New York and is a gentleman who stands very close to Senator Clark. When the senator decided to build his palatial residence in New York, of which so much has been written and said during the past year or more, he engaged Mr. Hull as the architect for the structure. The granite for this residence was to have been furnished by a granite com-of this State. Then a difference arose over the · paid, whereupon Senator Clark turned

about and determined to buy a quarry for himself so that he might furnish his own granite. This resulted in the buying of quarries at North Jay.

The Portland end of the enterprise is to be located on Deake's wharf. Soon after the American Stone Company was formed one of the first steps that was taken was to look about for wharf and pier privileges in that city. After a thorough examination of the field the agent of Senator Clark made an offer to lease a wharf formerly occupied by John L. Dalot. The offer was accepted. The lease is taken for a term of years and a clause in the lease stipulates that at the expiration of this term the lease may be renewed for another term of years.

Renaissance Ornament.

FROM NOTES ARRANGED BY H. W. BEATTIE, SC.

The course of ancient and modern art has been much the same; both commenced in the symbolic, and ended in the sensuous. The essence of all middle-age art was symbolism, and the transition from the symbolism to the principles of beauty is the great feature of the revival; art was wholly separated from religion in the Renaissance, but this transition was only gradually developed.

It was in Italy that these new styles were developed. Two distinct schools were flourishing there in the twelfth century, the pure Byzantine at Venice, and the Siculo-Norman in the south, containing all the Saracenic elements, not excluding even the inscriptions. From these and the introduction of natural forms wholly irrespective of symbolism arose a new style, composed almost exclusively of foliage and tracery.

This change was due to the gradually growing influence of the Saracenic, not as an absolute style, but as affording new elements of beauty, especially its varied and intricate interlacings, which were so very prominent for a while as to constitute the chief characteristic of a new style. The first step of the transition from middle-age to modern art was the Trecento.

The Trecento may be considered a negative style, as its peculiarity consists in its exclusion of certain hitherto common ornamental elements.

The great features of this style are its intricate tracery or interlacings, and delicate scroll work of conventional foliage, the style being but a slight removal from a combination of the Byzantine and Saracenic, the symbolism of both being equally excluded; the foliage is not, however, exclusively conventional, and it comprises a fair amount of the classical orders.

In the Quattrocento, the next style, we have a far more positive revival. Lorenzo Ghiberti may, perhaps, be instanced as its great exponent or representative in ornamental art. The bronze gates of the Baptistery of San Giovanni, by Ghiberti, exhibit one feature of this style in perfection—the prominence of simple natural imitations which now nearly entirely supersede the conventional representatives of previous times. Nature no longer supplied mere suggestions, but afforded directly exact models of imitations, fruit, flowers, birds or animals, all disposed simply with to the picturesque or ornamental. The selection of the details might still have some typical signification, but this had no influence in the manner of their execution, which was as purely imitative as their arrangement was ornamental. In this style, also, we have the first appearance of cartouches or scrolled shield work, which became so very prominent in the 16th and 17th centuries. One of the oldest examples we can refer to is the shield containing the Lion of St. Mark, on the water gate of the Ducal Palace at Venice.

This kind of decoration certainly seems in some way connected with heraldry—many of its forms are surely armorial shields, which became very common in architectural decoration of a later period; and the fact of such forms being afterwards used as mere elements of ornament does not in any way invalidate such an origin.

There are none of these forms on the gates of Ghiberti, but it abounds with medallions containing portraits, which perform a similar service in the design as the shields in other examples.

Another feature of this style is the introduction, for the first time, of the grotesque arabesque after the ancient models of Rome and Pompeii; although in the Quattrocento the religious symbolism was generally excluded from the ornamental details, the religious sentiment was by no means absent from Quattrocento art itself; on the contrary, the Quattrocento was essentially a religious style, but the religious sentiment was transferred from a secondary to a primary object in the design; we have the actual representation instead of the mere symbol. As, for instance, in the second pair of Ghiberti gates—the history of Moses is the principal subject of illustration of these gates—the ornaments are but the decorations to several panels; so it is in all other great schemes, of which the Certosa of Pavia offers many examples.

There is little decoration but what is merely auxiliary to some religious design.

We speak of the Renaissance as an epoch and as a style, but the only true or literal revival is in the style called the Cinquecento; in this the figures and subjects themselves are a mere part and often secondary to the ornamental scheme, and the religious element comparatively disappears.

We must not omit a few words in regard to the Elizabethan; this variation exhibits a very striking preponderance of strap and shield work. These two features are sufficient to date a building; the tracing and strap work, without shield-work, will indicate the time of Elizabeth; the predominance of shield work the time of James 1st. We have now been over a number of varieties of the revival, distinct from its perfect form the Cinquecento.

A design containing all the elements of this period is properly called the Renaissance.

If a design contain only tracery and foliage of the period it would be more properly called Trecento; if it contain besides these, elaborate natural imitations, festoons, scroll work, and occasional symmetrical arabesques, it is of the Quattrocento, the Italian Renaissance of the 15th century; and if it display a decided prominence of strap-work and shield-work it is Elizabethan. In all these styles the evidence of their Byzantine and Saracenic origin is constantly preserved, in the tracery, in the scroll work and foliage and in the rendering of classical ornaments.

The Renaissance is, therefore, something more approximate to a combination of previous styles than a revival of any in particular.

It is the first example of selection that we find, and it is a style that was developed solely on æsthetic principles from a love of forms and harmonies themselves, as varieties of effect or arrangements of beauty, not because they had any particular signification, or from any superstitious attachment to them as ancestral heirlooms. The decorators of the Renaissance were, in fact, the first artists in ornamental art since the classic periods; they suffered no limits or restrictions but those of harmony or beauty.

THE CINQUECENTO.

We may now proceed to the consideration of the Cinquecento, which as an art development is the most perfect of all the modern styles. The term Cinquecento does not imply simply sixteenth-century art, but the most prominent style of the sixteenth century; and it is the real goal of the Renaissance, to which all the efforts of the fifteenth century tended. The varieties we have just gone over are but the wanderings by the way, for it was only after a great accumulation of materials that it was possible to appreciate thoroughly the spirit of the ancient arabesques.

The true spirit of ancient art was only now thoroughly comprehended, and with such capacities as those of Raphael, Romano, Lombardi, Michael Angelo and others, no wonder that it started suddenly into new life, and grew into a more splendid development than it had ever known, perhaps, in the most gorgeous Roman period.

In establishing a style from examples made with only a general regard to its prominent characteristics, there is, of course, much to reject before we have a characteristic illustration of the style; and the Christian symbols and other arbitrary forms which we occasionally find in Raphael's arabesque, must be scrupulously excluded, or the Cinquecento becomes merged into the mixed Renaissance, which led to it, and the distinction of style is lost.

(To be continued.)

*

Among The Retail Dealers.

MOBILE, ALA.—During the past week an important contract in monuments was given out by the Workingmen's Timber and Cotton Benevolent Association, which exhibited that this organization is one of the wealthiest in the South, and that a local firm dealing in stone, marble and sculpture, Messrs. McDonald, March & Co., can successfully bid on the highest class work against firms from three Southern states. The awarding of the contract, which called for an expenditure of $1,500, is another tribute to the solidity of Mobile employes and Mobile employers. The Timbermen require the highest class of work in the monuments to their dead, and they have gone to the firm which can give it to them. The specifications contemplate the entire renovation of the 40x50 lot which the Timbermen own in Magnolia cemetery. The monument in the centre of the lot will be applicable to the craft represented by the members of the organization, the central figure being a timberman in stone, on a monolith twenty-two feet high surrounded by the well known emblems of the stevedores, and on all sides the granite column will be tablets for the reception

the names of deceased members of the association. This shaft will also depict the loading of a steamer and sailing vessel. Taken in all, the monument which the Workingmen's Timber and Cotton Association will erect in Magnolia cemetery will not alone be the finest in that necropolis, but will be one of the most striking in the state.

TAUNTON, MASS.—The firm of John B. Sullivan & Son report a very prosperous season in the monumental business. They have erected many handsome memorials during the past year and are now engaged in cutting several large jobs; among them being a memorial for the Lawrence family, to be erected at New Bedford, Mass. It is to be cut from blue Westerly granite. The monument is about twenty feet in height, six feet square at the base and will be surmounted by a figure of Hope carved in Westerly granite. They also report orders for several handsome monuments to be erected in the local cemeteries and have secured the contract for seven large and costly monuments which will be set out of town.—Exchange.

Obituary.

WILLIAM DAVID BEGGS.

William David Beggs, prominent in Allegheny, Pa., business circles, died September 22. Mr. Beggs was stricken with typhoid fever. He was president of the firm of Alexander Beggs & Son, stonecontractors and monumental dealers. The business was established a number of years ago by his father, Alexander Beggs. who died ten years ago, since when the son has conducted the affairs of the concern.

Proposed Monuments and Monumental News.

NEW YORK.—Bartholdi's statue of liberty is in a deplorable condition, and an expenditure of from $75,-000 to $100,000 will be required to put it in proper repair. It is fourteen years since the pedestal was declared to be finished and the goddess was placed in position. But today the right arm of the goddess holding the torch supposed to enlighten the world, is fully twenty degrees out of plum, so that visitors are cautioned against climbing to its dizzy height; the iron work inside the statue and pedestal is heavily coated with rust, showing a lack of paint, and the work of vandals is everywhere visible, simply because the one solitary watchman cannot be at every point at the same time. Several efforts have in past years been made to have Congress appropriate sufficient money to complete the pedestal and grounds, but the bills were always defeated. Meanwhile everything is permitted to go to wreck and ruin.

FLEETWOOD, PA.—C. F. Hill's marble and granite works made numerous changes to his plant, and he has built an annex to his works 18 by 56 feet and erected a large steam engine of 50 horse power, removing a 10 horse power gasoline engine. He also put a 20 horse power air compressor to run automatic tools and rock drills, etc. Mr. Hill's plant is compelled to work 16 to 18 hours a day to get the work out he has on hand and daily orders coming in.

NEWBURYPORT, MASS.—The fund for the soldiers' and sailors' monument is assuming large proportions, it having received the substantial addition of $10,000 by the will of the late Mary A. Roaf, to be available at the death of her brother and nephew.

SWARTHMORE, PA.—The citizens have decided to erect a suitable memorial to the memory of Benjamin West, the painter, who was born here, and who was buried in St. Paul's Cathedral, London. It is proposed to erect a monument to him here, and with this purpose in view a committee has been named.

SAN FRANCISCO, CAL.—Designs for the monument to be erected to the memory of the soldiers and sailors of California who died in the late war with Spain were unveiled November 1 at the Hopkins Art Institute. A score of models were submitted, and the committee having the matter in charge began their inspection. It has been decided to prepare the entire display for public view at the fall exhibition of the art association. The cost of the monument will be defrayed by the fund of $25,000, which is the balance remaining from the reception fund of the California Volunteers, and no piece exhibited will exceed that amount in cost. The designs, as a whole, make a noble and grand display, but at the present time only the artists who are interested will be permitted to view the models. These are greatly varied in style, there being plain and ornamental shafts,and sculptured groups mounted on heavy bases and with theatrical settings. There are figures of men defending the flag, California as the mother with her children dying at her feet, swords, laurel wreaths, eagles, cannon, dogs of war and victory. Competitors hail from every section of the United States.—Exchange.

PEORIA, ILL.—The soldiers' and sailors' monument, one of the finest granite shafts in the country, erected somewhat more than a year ago at a cost of almost $50,000, may be sold because of the inability of the committee in charge to raise $13,000 still due on it. A proposition to pay the balance on the monument out of the county fund was submitted to the voters at the election, and the vote was a negative one. The county has already given $10,000 to the monument fund, and the city has given a like amount. Now the managers have an offer of $20,000 more than the shaft cost, and the understanding is that it will be sold unless something is done by the citizens of Peoria to raise the balance.

SEWICKLEY, PA.—The will of Robert Dickson, late of Sewickley, directs that a monument costing not more than $1,000 be erected on his burial lot in the Sewickley cemetery and that headstones costing not more than $200 be erected over the graves of his deceased wife, Eliza, and his sons, James M. and John S. Dickson. He gives his silver watch to his grandson, Robert Dickson. How thankful the grandson must be for the watch.

PENN YAN, N. Y.—Yates county citizens have vo' ' to erect a soldiers' monument.

82 · GRANITE

WAKEFIELD, MASS.—At a town meeting some months ago a committee was appointed to take under consideration the matter of a monument for Wakefield soldiers in the civil war. The committee, in conjunction with a like committee of the H. M. Warren post 12, G. A. R., held a meeting November 10. Some twenty designs for a monument were shown by Boston firms. It was voted, however, to call for designs and bids from other concerns, and to select one suitable and report at the annual town meeting in March.

SAN FRANCISCO, CAL.—A monument to commemorate the victory of Admiral Dewey at Manila is to be erected in this city. The committee to which the designs offered in competition were submitted have accepted that sent in by George T. Brewster of New York. It is a classical Doric column, surmounted by a winged figure of victory. About the square base will be reliefs illustrating the naval battle which gave the Philippines to this country.

DRAVOSBURG, PA.—A monumental association has been organized to erect a memorial in Richland cemetery to the soldier dead in the burying ground.

NEW YORK, N. Y.—The committee on site and design of the monument to the sailors who perished in the Maine disaster and the soldiers who died in the Spanish-American war, after examining forty-three submitted designs, has selected as the best three in the first competition the designs of the following: Austin Hays, sculptor, and Donn Barber, architect; O. Piccirilli, sculptor, and H. Van Buren Magonigle, architect, and George Julian Zolnay, sculptor, and Joseph Henry Freedlander, architect. The fund for this monument, which amounts to about $100,000 cash in hand, was raised by "The New York Journal."

SAVANNAH, GA.—A fund has been started for the purpose of erecting a monument to the memory of Oglethorpe, the founder of the city.

SAN FRANCISCO, CAL.—The design submitted by George T. Brewster of New York has been selected by the committee appointed to select one for a monument to commemorate the Manila Bay victory. The design shows a fluted column on a square base, surmounted by a figure representing victory. On the four sides of the base are to be figures typical of battle. The fund to be expended in erecting the monument amounts to $32,000.

AUSTIN, TEX.—The money for the construction of the Terry Ranger monument has now reached the sum of $8,500. The monument will be erected across the capitol walk from the Alamo monument and promises to be one of the handsomest monuments ever erected in Texas.

United States Engineer Betts, of Chickamauga Park commission, has received the new plans of the New York state peace monument to be erected on Lookout Mountain. The principal change over the original design is that the main shaft will be in nine pieces, instead of five, ...der to facilitate transportation to the top of the .. The New York commission has notified ...ner that plans for the transportation have

been decided upon and that there is no doubt that the monument will be erected. It will cost $100,000, and from its elevation will be one of the most imposing in the United States.

PHILADELPHIA, PA.—A movement is on foot to build a monument to William B. Curtis, the "Father of American Athletics," who died in a blizzard on Mount Washington last June. The plan is to organize a fund in such a manner that all the amateur athletes in the country will receive an opportunity to unite in the testimonial to the memory of their late leader.

BOONVILLE, N. Y.—The committee in charge of the soldiers' monument has secured subscriptions near enough to the amount required to warrant placing the order, and the contract has been awarded to Howard Grosjean to prepare the stone.

Monthly Trade Record.

This department is compiled and edited by the United Mercantile Agency. Subscribers, in accordance with the terms of their contracts, are entitled to receive further information relative to the parties hereafter mentioned, upon application to the main office. As the names of many business men who are good will appear herein, subscribers can readily see the importance of making inquiries if interested, previous to taking any action.

FLORIDA.
Jacksonville, *M—Clark, George W. Co., 93 $1,050.

ILLINOIS.
Freeport, *M—Schadle & Franz, John F. Franz, 93 $5,000.
Galva, *M—Bates & Ladd, 64, W. H. Bates, 58.
Springfield, *M—Richter, C. S., 86 to Springfield Monument Co.

INDIANA.
Madison, *M—Lemen, Charles, 14 $800.
North Manchester, *M—Noftzger & Heeter, J. P. Noftzger 74 $600.
Peru, *M—Clevell & Son, 14 $133.

IOWA.
Council Bluffs, *M—Lewis, W. E., 106.
Council Bluffs, *M—Bloom, J. F. & Co., 88 to Omaha, Neb.
Harlan, *M—Deen & Welch, succeed D. M. Deen.
Ottumwa, *M—Naugle, Noah, succeeds John Naugle & Son.

KANSAS.
Belleville, *M—Baldwin Bros., succeed A. O. Baldwin.
Cottonwood Falls, *M—Graham, A., 76.
Cottonwood Falls, *M—Hunt, W. H., 86.
Eldorado, *M—Sinclair, Hector, 14 $405.

KENTUCKY.
Irvington, *M—Tebow, J. M. & Co., 76.
Maysville, *M—Murray & Thomas, W. F. Thomas, 93 $500.

MAINE.
Alfred, *M—Hodgson & Linscott, 64, George L. Hodgson, 58.
Bangor, *M—Fogg, Ambrose, 104.
Dixfield, *M—Chandler & Taylor, succeed George

Holt & Son.
North Jay, *M—Bryant & Sanders, 14 $1.
Portland, *M—Thompson, Enoch M., sold R. E., $1.
Stonington, *M—Grant, Charles S., 86.

MASSACHUSETTS.

Lynn, *M—McHugh, Frank, 104.
Taunton, *M—Cullen, Patrick, 93 $800.
Taunton, *M—Reagan, J. F., 93 $1,900.
Woburn, *M—Hern, John J., 93 $4,700.

MICHIGAN.

Allegan, *M—Fish & Bensley, succeed F. H. Knapp.
Detroit, *M—Cardoni, Frank A., 87 $2,500 renewed, 74 $433.
Reading, *M—Clark & Peck, succeeded by Powers & Peck.

MISSOURI.

Carthage, *M—Griffith, W. A., 14 $175.

MONTANA.

Butte, *M—Ketchin, R. A., 14 $1,908.
Butte, *M—Tuite, James E., 86 to R. A. Ketchin.

NEW JERSEY.

Passaic, *M—Maybury Granite Co., inc. cap. $50m.

NEW YORK.

Cuba, *M—O'Malley, Edward, 93 $1,200.
Elmira, *M—Cartledge, Joseph, succeeds A. W. Ayers & Son.
Middletown, *M—Koch, Emil B., 106.
Rochester, *M—Sayre & McGee, E. M. Sayre 93 $8,000.

NORTH DAKOTA.

Wahpeton, *M—Hutchinson Marble Works, 76.

OHIO.

Bluffton, *M—Lehman, John, 86.
Washington, C. H., *M—Burke, P. J., 93 $1,466.

PENNSYLVANIA.

Erie, *M—Stohlman, E. T., 80.
Harrisburg, *M—Compton, Samuel F., execution $530.
Scranton, *M—Henry, Michael W., execution $200.

SOUTH DAKOTA.

Tyndall, *M—Rapalee, D. W., 88 to Sioux City, Ia.

TENNESSEE.

Paris, *M—Townley, J. M., 80.

TEXAS.

San Antonio, *M—McGrath, J. & Co., 70.

VERMONT.

Barre, GZ—Fowlie Bros., 70.

WISCONSIN.

Madison, *M—Kelly & Oates, 76.
Oconomowoc, *M—Olson & Handford 64, Thomas Handford 58.

ONTARIO.

Hagersville, *M—Theyer, H. A., 76.
Sarnia, *M—Elder & Paul 64, George M. Paul 58.

QUARRY ITEMS

CHESTER, MASS.—The Flint Granite Company of Albany, N. Y., who have been running the Bowe Granite Company's sheds for the past three months, have closed down for the winter. They have employed about 30 stonecutters at the works.

ELLICOTT CITY, MD.—There has not been for many years past such activity in the granite quarrying business in this vicinity as at the present time, and the operators of quarries near this place have recently been forced to employ double the usual number of hands in order to fill the contracts already taken. In some instances it was necessary to fit up shanties to accommodate the hands. Among the important contracts of Albert Weber include the supplying of a large quantity of stone to be used in the construction of the tunnels along the main line of the Baltimore and Ohio Railroad.

ROCKLAND, ME.—The Clark Island Granite Company's plant, at St. George, is running along smoothly. There is something over three gangs of cutters at work there, and more are wanted. The company has recently set up a large compressor, running most of their works by compressed air, by which blocks of granite are sawed to any required thickness. Pneumatic tools are also used.

WESTERLY, R. I.—A Westerly granite firm has an order for a granite memorial to the late head of the Sessions foundry at Bristol, Conn. It is to comprise a big slab of granite, on pillars, standing on an elevated site in the cemetery. This piece of granite, which is 11 feet square, was quarried at the company's Niantic quarry and was carted to the Niantic station. The Consolidated Railroad refused to take it, alleging that it was too big to go under its three bridges near the Westerly station. It will be cut, either at Niantic, or at the company's redstone quarry, on the railroad between Westerly and Niantic.—Exchange.

STONY CREEK, CONN.—The granite cutting business is very dull in this place. At the Norcross Bros.' works only thirteen cutters are at work at present with the prospect looking gloomy for livelier times. This firm has been turning out some fine polished work lately, a soldiers' monument to be shipped to New York being a splendid specimen of machine polishing.
The Stony Creek Red Granite Co. have just commenced cutting stone for New York parties. About thirty cutters are now employed.
Beattie Bros., at Leets Island, are doing nothing at present, but are always on the lookout for contracts.

PORTLAND, ME.—The work of rebuilding Deske's wharf is progressing rapidly. A large number of new piles are being driven and other work is being done to fit the wharf for the use of the American Granite Co., which has leased it. The understanding is that

INGRAM BROS.

Milford, - - N. H.

—MANUFACTURERS OF—

MONUMENTAL WORK FROM NEW WESTERLY GRANITE

DARK BLUE NEW WESTERLY GRANITE
Rough Dimension Stock for Statuary and Carved Work

HENRY W. HAYDEN,
Milford, ✗ ✗ ✗ N. H.

Joss Brothers Company,

— PAY FOR THIS SPACE —

To Keep Themselves in the Public Eye.

WE ARE PREPARED TO PROVE ALL STATEMENTS MADE IN OUR ADVERTISEMENTS
IN PREVIOUS ISSUES OF THIS AND OTHER TRADE JOURNALS.

☞ REMEMBER US WHEN YOU HAVE GRANITE WORK TO BUY. ☜

JOSS BROTHERS COMPANY,

Granite Merchants.

Office and Mills: 10 and 12 Garfield Street. QUINCY, MASS., U. S. A.

Pittsburg, Pa., Office, 908 Publication Building,
W. A. LINDSEY.

New Cutting Plant Showing Travelling Power Derrick.

Interior View Showing Shipping Facilities.

Box-Car in back ground.

New Shed Furnished With All Modern Stone-Working Machinery.

W. S. LITTLEJOHN. A. MILNE.

LITTLEJOHN & MILNE,

BARRE, VT.

Manufacturers and Dealers in

BARRE GRANITE MONUMENTS.

Rough Granite from Our Own Quarries.
SQUARING AND POLISHING FOR THE TRADE.

Price ($1.50) includes subscription to the paper for one year. ৶৶৶৶৶

Ask for——————➤

Imperial Design Book

No. 1.,

Containing twenty-four half-tone cuts of artistic Granite Monuments. ৶

The cuts are the same size as the ones contained in the center pages of this edition of GRANITE. We believe that there is a growing demand for the better class of monumental work with carving; and therefore it is our intention to publish only this class of designs. You will find that the *Imperial Design Book* illustrates the best.

A. M. Hunt & Co.,

Publishers,

131 Devonshire St.,
Boston, Mass.

Lightning Source UK Ltd.
Milton Keynes UK
UKHW010600051218
333419UK00009B/732/P